MW00954421

1

LETTERS OF FRANZ LISZT

Volume I, "From Paris to Rome; Years of travel as a Virtuoso"

Collected by LA MARA

translated by

Constance Bache in 1894

Reedited by Philippe Ballin

In February 2017

CONTENTS

BRIEF BIOGRAPHICAL SKETCH

The Austrian composer Franz Liszt (1811-1886) was a pianistic miracle. He could play anything on site and composed over 400 works centered around "his" instrument. Among his key works are his Hungarian Rhapsodies, his Transcendental Etudes, his Concert Etudes, his Etudes based on variations of Paganinini's Violin Caprices and his Sonata, one of the most important of the nineteenth century. He also wrote thousands of letters, of which 260 are translated into English in this first of a 2-volume set of letters.

Those who knew him were also struck by his extremely sophisticated personality. He was surely one of the most civilized people of the nineteeth century, internalizing within himself a complex conception of human civility, and attempting to project it in his music and his communications with people. His life was centered around people; he knew them, worked with them, remembered them, thought about them, and wrote about them using an almost poetic language, while pushing them to reflect the high ideals he believed in. His personality was the embodiment of a refined, idealized form of human civility. He was the consummate musical artist, always looking for ways to communicate a new civilized idea through music, and to work with other musicians in organizing concerts and gatherings to perform the music publicly. He also did as much as he could to promote and compliment those whose music he believed in.

He was also a superlative musical critic, knowing, with few mistakes, what music of his day was "artistic" and what was not. But, although he was clearly a musical genius, he insisted on projecting a tonal, romantic "beauty" in his music, confining his music to a narrow range of moral values and ideals. He would have rejected 20th-century music that entertained cynical notions of any kind, or notions that obviated the concept of beauty in any way. There is no Prokofiev, Stravinsky, Shostakovich, Cage, Adams and certainly no Schoenberg in Liszt's music. His music has an ideological "ceiling," and that ceiling is "beauty." It never goes beyond that. And perhaps it was never as "beautiful" as the music of Mozart, Bach or Beethoven, nor quite as rational (Are all the emotions in Liszt's music truly "controlled?"). But it certainly was original and instructive, and it certainly will linger.

DEDICATION

To the Memory of
MY BROTHER WALTER,
AND TO OUR
DEAR AND HONORED FRIEND
A.J. HIPKINS, ESQ.,
I DEDICATE THIS TRANSLATION.
—C.B.

PREFACE TO THE ENGLISH EDITION, BY CONSTANCE BACHE

In writing a few words of Preface I wish to express, first and foremost, my appreciation of the extreme care and conscientiousness with which La Mara has prepared these volumes. In a spirit of no less reverence I have endeavored, in the English translation, to adhere as closely as possible to all the minute characteristics that add expression to Liszt's letters: punctuation has, of necessity, undergone alteration, but italics, inverted commas, dashes and other marks have been strictly observed. It may be objected that unnecessary particularity has been shown in the translation of various titles, names of Societies or newspapers, quotations, etc.; but there are many people who, while understanding French, do not read German, and vice versa, and therefore it has seemed better to translate everything. Where anything has been omitted in the printed letters I have adhered to the sign .——. employed by La Mara to indicate the hiatus. It has seemed best to preserve the spelling of all proper names as written by Liszt, and not to Anglicise any, as it is impossible to do all; and therefore, even at the risk of a seeming affectation, the original form of the name has been preserved. In the same spirit I have adhered to the correct form of the name of our adopted composer

Handel, and trust I may be pardoned for so doing on the strength of a little joke of Liszt's own "The English," he said, "always talk about Gluck and Handel!"

La Mara says in her Preface that this collection can by no means be considered a complete one, as there must exist other letters— to Liszt's mother, to Berlioz, Tausig, etc.—which it is hoped may yet be some day forthcoming. In like manner might there not also be letters to his daughter Madame Ollivier (not to mention his still-living daughter Madame Wagner)? [Another volume of Liszt's letters, of a still more intimate character, addressed to a lady friend, will be published later on.]

The English edition is increased by four letters one to Peter Cornelius, No. 256A in Vol. I., which is interesting in its reference to the "Barbier"; and, in Vol. II., a kind letter of introduction which the Master gave me for Madame Tardieu, in Brussels; one letter to Walter Bache, and one to the London Philharmonic Society (Nos. 370A and 370B); one of these, it is true, is partially quoted in a footnote by La Mara, but at this distance of time there is no reason why these letters should not be inserted entire, and they will prove of rather particular interest, both to my brother's friends, and also as having reference to that never-to-be-forgotten episode—Liszt's last visit to England.

This visit, which took place in 1886, a few months before the Master's death, was for the purpose of his being present at the performance of his Oratorio of St. Elizabeth (see Letter 370 and subsequent letters).

More than forty years had elapsed since Liszt's previous visit to our shores; times had changed, and the almost unknown, and wholly unappreciated, had become the acknowledged King in a realm where many were Princes. Some lines embodying in words England's welcome to this king—headed by a design in which the Hungarian and the English coats-of-arms unite above two clasped hands, and a few bars of a leading theme from the St. Elizabeth—were written by me and presented to Liszt with a basket of roses (emblematic of the rose miracle in the Oratorio) tied with the Hungarian colors, on his entrance into St. James's Hall on April 6th, 1886.

As a memento of that occasion it has been chosen as frontispiece to the Second Volume.

Constance Bache
London, December 1893

TABLE OF LETTER CONTENTS (LETTER NUMBER, FOLLOWED BY ADDRESSEE):

Leipzig. May, 1838 14. The Gesellschaft der Musikfreunde in Vienna. June 1st, 1815 15. Simon Lowy in Vienna. September 22nd, 1838 16. Pacini in Paris. September 30th, 1838 17. Breitkopf and Hartel. January 3rd, 1839 18. Princess Christine Belgiojoso in Paris. June 4th, 1839 19. Robert Schumann. June 5th, 1820 20. Breitkopf and Hartel. June, 1839 21. The Beethoven Committee at Bonn. October 3rd, 1839 22. Count Leo Festetics in Pest. November 24th, 1839 23. Clara Wieck. December 25th, 1839 24. Robert Schumann. March 27th, 1841 25. Franz von Schober in Vienna. April 3rd, 1840 26. Maurice Schlesinger in Paris. May 14th, 1840 27. Franz von Schober. May or June, 1840 28. the same. August 29th, 1840 29. Buloz in Paris. October 26th, 1840 30. Franz von Schober. December 5th, 1840 31. Breitkopf and Hartel. May 7th, 1841 32. Simon Lowy. May 20th, 1841 33. Franz von Schober. March 3rd, 1842 34. The Faculty of Philosophy at the University of Konigsberg. March 18th, 1842 35. Freiherr von Spiegel in Weimar. September 12th, 1842 36. Carl Filitsch2 or 1843 37. Franz von Schober. March 4th, 1844 38. Franz Kroll. June 11th, 1844 39. Freund. June 11th, 1844 40. Franz von Schober. March 3rd, 1845 41. Franz Kroll in Glogau. March 26th, 1845 42. Abbe de Lamennais. April 28th, 1845 43. Frederic Chopin. May 21st, 1845 44. George Sand. May 21st, 1845 45. Abbe de Lamennais. June 1st, 1845 46. Gaetano Belloni in Paris. July 23rd, 1845 47. Mme. Rondonneau in Sedan. February 11th, 1846 48. Grillparzer 1846 (?) 49. Franz von Schober in Weimar. April 11th, 1846 50. the same. May 28th, 1846 51. Alexander Seroff.

September 14th, 1847 52. Carl Haslinger in Vienna. December 19th, 1847 53. Baron von Dornis in Jena. March 6th, 1848 54. Franz von Schober. April 22nd, 1848 55. Bernhard Cossmann in Baden-Baden. September 18th, 1848 56. Carl Reinecke. March 25th, 1849 57. Count Sandor Teleky(?) May 5th, 1849 58. Belloni(?). May 14th, 1849 59. Carl Reinecke. May 30th, 1849 60. Robert Schumann. June 5th, 1849 61. the same. July 27th, 1849 62. the same. August 1st, 1849 63. Carl Reinecke. September 7th, 1849 64. Breitkopf and Hartel. January 14th, 1850 65. the same. February 24th, 1850 66. J. C. Lobe in Leipzig. July 10th, 1850 67. Friedrich Wieck in Dresden. August 4th, 1850 68. Simon Lowy. August 5th, 1850 69. Mathilde Graumann. October 11th, 1850 70. Carl Reinecke. January 1st, 1851 71. Leon Escudier in Paris. February 4th, 1851 72. Carl Reinecke. March 19th, 1851 73. Dr. Eduard Liszt in Vienna1 74. Count Casimir Esterhazy. June 6th, 1851 75. Theodor Uhlig in Dresden. June 25th, 1851 76. Rosalie Spohr in Brunswick. July 3rd, 1851 77. the same. July 22nd, 1851 78. Breitkopf and Hartel. December 1st, 1851 79. Louis Kohler in Konigsberg. April 16th, 1852 80. Carl Reinecke. April 16th, 1852 81. Carl Czerny. April 19th, 1852 82. Gustav Schmidt in Frankfort-on-the-Maine. May 18th, 1852 83. Robert Schumann. June 8th, 1852 84.the same. June 26th, 1852 85. Peter Cornelius. September 4th, 1852 86. Clara Schumann. September 11th, 1852 87. Carl Czerny. September or October, 1852 88. Breitkopf and Hartel. October 30th, 1852 89. the same. November 10th, 1852 90. Julius Stern in Berlin.

November 24th, 1852 91. Wilhelm von Lenz in St. Petersburg. December 2nd, 1852 92. Robert Radecke in Leipzig. December 9th, 1852 93. Bernhard Cossmann. December, 1852 94. Wilhelm Fischer in Dresden. January 13th, 1853 95. Edmund Singer. January 15th, 1853 96. To Frau Dr. Lidy Steche in Leipzig. February 14th, 1853 97. Gustav Schmidt. February 27th, 1853 98. Heinrich Brockhaus in Leipzig. March 22nd, 1853 99. Dr. Franz Brendel in Leipzig. April 3rd, 1853 100. the same. April 30th, 1853 101. Louis Kohler. May 6th, 1853 102. the same. May 24th, 1853 103. the same. August 1st, 1853 104. Richard Pohl in Dresden. November 5th, 1853 105. Wilhelm Fischer. January 4th, 1854 106. Escudier in Paris. January 21st, 1854 107. the same. January 28th, 1854 108. Dr. Franz Brendel. February 20th, 1854 109. Louis Kohler. March 2nd, 1854 110. Dr. Franz Brendel. March 18th, 1854 111. Louis Kohler. April or May, 1854 112. Dr. Franz Brendel. April 26th, 1854 113. Louis Kohler. June 8th, 1854 114. Dr. Franz Brendel. June 12th, 1854 115. Carl Klindworth in London. July 2nd, 1854 116. Dr. Franz Brendel. July 7th, 1854 117. Anton Rubinstein. July 31st, 1854 118. Dr. Franz Brendel. August 12th, 1854 119. Anton Rubinstein. August, 1854 120. Alexander Ritter in Dresden. September 6th, 1854 121. Bernhard Cossmann. September 8th, 1854 122. Gaetano Belloni. September 9th, 1854 123. Dr. Eduard Liszt October 10th, 1854 124. Anton Rubinstein. October 19th, 1854 125. Dr. Franz Brendel. Beginning of November, 1854 126. Anton Rubinstein. November 19th, 1854 215 127. Dr. Franz Brendel. December 1st, 1854 128. J. W.

von Wasielecvski in Bonn. December 14th, 1854 129. William Mason in New York. December 14th, 1854 130. Rosalie Spohr. January 4th, 1855 131. To Alfred Dorffel in Leipzig. January 17th, 1855 132. Anton Rubinstein. February 1st, 1855 133. Louis Kohler. March 16th, 1855 134. Dr. Franz Brendel. March 18th, 1855 135. the same. April 1st, 1855 136. Anton Rubinstein. April 3rd, 1855 137. Freiherr Beaulieu-Marconnay. May 21st, 1855 138. Anton Rubinstein. June 3rd, 1855 139. Dr. Franz Brendel. June, 1855 140. the same. June 16th, 1855 141. Edmund Singer. August 1st, 1855 142. Bernhard Cossmann. August 15th, 1855 143. August Kiel in Detmold. September 8th, 1855 144. Moritz Hauptmann. September 28th, 1855 145. Dr. Eduard Liszt December 3rd, 1855 146. Frau Meyerbeer in Berlin. December 14th, 1855 147. Dr. Ritter von Seiler in Vienna. December 26th, 1855 148. Dr. Eduard Liszt February 9th, 1856 149. Dr. von Seiler. February loth, 1856 150. Dr. Franz Brendel. February 19th, 1856 151. Dionys Pruckner in Vienna. March 17th, 1856 152. Breitkopf and Hartel. May 15th, 1856 153. Louis Kohler. May 24th, 1856 154. the same. July 9th, 1856 155. Hoffmann von Fallersleben. July 14th, 1856 156. Wilhelm Wieprecht. July 18th, 1856 157. Edmund Singer. July 28th, 1856 158. Joachim Raff. July 31st, 1856 159. Anton Rubinstein. August 6th, 1856 160. Joachim Raff. August 7th, 1856 161. Anton Rubinstein. August 21st, 1856 162. Dr. Eduard Liszt September 5th, 1856 163. Louis Kohler. October 8th, 1856 164. Dr. Gille in Jena. November 14th, 1856 165. Dr. Adolf Stern in Dresden. November

14th, 18293 166. Louis Kohler. November 21st, 1856 167. Dr. Eduard Liszt November 24th, 1856 168. Alexander Ritter in Stettin. December 4th, 1856 169. L. A. Zellner in Vienna. January 2nd, 1857 299 170. Von Turanyi in Aix-la-Chapelle. January 3rd, 1830 171. J. W. von Wasielewski. January 9th, 1857 172. Alexis von Lwoff in St. Petersburg. January 10th, 1857 173. Johann von Herbeck in Vienna. January 12th, 1857 174. Franz Gotze in Leipzig. February 1st, 1857 175. Dionys Pruckner. February 11th, 1857 176. Joachim Raff. February, 1857 177. Ferdinand David. February 26th, 1857 178. Wladimir Stassoff in St. Petersburg. March 17th, 1857 179. Wilhelm von Lenz in St. Petersburg. March 24th, 1857 180. Dr. Eduard Liszt March 26th, 1857 181. Georg Schariezer in Pressburg. April 25th, 1857 182. Dr. Eduard Liszt April 27th, 1857 183. Frau von Kaulbach. May 1st, 1857 184. Fedor von Milde in Weimar. June 3rd, 1857 185. Johann von Herbeck. June 12th, 1857 186. Countess Rosalie Sauerma. June 22nd, 1857 187. Ludmilla Schestakoff in St. Petersburg. October 7th, 1857 188. Carl Haslinger. December 5th, 1857 189. Stein in Sondershausen. December 6th, 1857 190. Alexander Ritter. December 7th, 1857 191. Max Seifriz in Lowenberg. December 24th, 1857 192. Alexander Seroff. January 8th, 1858 193. Basil von Engelhardt. January 8th, 1858 194. Felix Draseke. January Loth, 1858 195. Louis Kohler. February 1st, 1858 196. L.A. Zellner. February 8th, 1858 197. Peter Cornelius. February 19th, 1858 198. Dionys Pruckner. March 9th, 1858 199. Dr. Eduard Liszt March Loth, 1858 200. Fran Dr. Steche. March 20th,

1858 201. L. A. Zellner. April 6th, 1858 202. Dr. Eduard Liszt April 7th, 1858 203. Adolf Reubke in Hausneinsdorf. June 10th, 1858 204. Prince Constantin von Hohenzollern-Hechingen. August 18th, 1858 205. Frau Rosa von Milde. August 25th, 1858 206. Dr. Franz Brendel. November 2nd, 1858 207. Johann von Herbeck. November 22nd, 1858 208. Felix Draseke. January 12th, 1859 209. Heinrich Porges. March loth, 18379 210. Max Seifriz. March 22nd, 1859 211. Dr. Eduard Liszt April 5th, 1859 212. Music-Director N. N. April 17th, 1859 213. Peter Cornelius. May 23rd, 1859 214. Dr. Franz Brendel. May 23rd, 1859 215. Felix Draseke. July 19th, 1859 216. Peter Cornelius. August 23rd, 1859 217. Dr. Franz Brendel. September 2nd, 1859 218. Louis Kohler. September 3rd, 1859 219. Dr. Franz Brendel. September 8th, 1859 220. Johann von Herbeck. October 11th, 1859 221. Felix Draseke. October 20th, 1859 222. Heinrich Porges. October 30th, 1859 223. Ingeborg Stark. November 2nd, 1859 224. Johann von Herbeck. November 18th, 1859 225. Dr. Franz Brendel. December 1st, 1859 226. Anton Rubinstein. December 3rd, 1859 227. Dr. Franz Brendel. December 6th, 1859 228. Dr. Eduard Liszt December 28th, 1859 229. Josef Dessauer. December 30th, 1859 230. Wilkoszewski in Munich. January 15th, 1860 231. Johann von Herbeck. January 26th, 1860 232. Dr. Franz Brendel. January 25th, 1860 233. Friedrich Hebbel. February 5th, 1860 234. Dr. Franz Brendel. February, 1860 235. the same March or April, 1860 236. Louis Kohler. July 5th, 1860 237. Dr. Eduard Liszt July 9th, 1860

THE LETTERS OF FRANZ LISZT, VOL. 1

1. To Carl Czerny in Vienna.

[Autograph in the possession of M. Alfred Bovet at Valentigney.— The addressee was Liszt's former teacher, the celebrated Viennese teacher of music and composer of innumerable instructive works (1791-1857).]

My very dear Master,

When I think of all the immense obligations

under which I am placed towards you, and at the same time consider how long I have left you without a sign of remembrance, I am perfectly ashamed and miserable, and in despair of ever being forgiven by you! "Yes," I said to myself with a deep feeling of bitterness, "I am an ungrateful fellow; I have forgotten my benefactor, I have forgotten that good master to whom I owe both my talent and my success."…At these words a tear starts to my eyes, and I assure you that no repentant tear was ever more sincere! Receive it as an expiation, and pardon me, for I cannot any longer bear the idea that you have any ill-feeling towards me. You will pardon me, my dear Master, won't you? Embrace me then… good! Now my heart is light.

You have doubtless heard that I have been playing your admirable works here with the greatest success, and all the glory ought to be given to you. I intended to have played your variations on the "Pirate" the day after tomorrow at a very brilliant concert that I was to have given at the theater of H.R.H. Madame, who was to have been present as well as the Duchess of Orleans; but man proposes and God disposes. I have suddenly caught the measles, and have been obliged to say farewell to the concert; but it is not given up because it is put off, and I hope, as soon as ever I am well again, to have the pleasure of making these beautiful variations known to a large public.

Pixis [a notable pianist (1788-1874)—lived a long time in Paris] and several other people have spoken much to me of four concertos that you have lately finished, and the reputation of which is already making a stir in Paris. I should be very much pleased, my dear Master, if you would commission me to get them sold. This would be quite easy for me to do, and I should also have the pleasure of playing them FROM FIRST HAND, either at the opera or at some big concerts. If my proposition pleases you, send them to me by the Austrian Embassy, marking the price that you would like to have for them. As regards any passages to be altered, if there are any, you need only mark them with a red pencil, according to your plan which I know so well, and I will point them out to the editor with the utmost care. Give me at the same time some news about music and pianists in Vienna; and finally tell me, dear Master, which of your compositions you think would make the best effect in society.

I close by sending you my heartfelt greetings, and begging you once more to pardon the shameful silence I have kept towards you: be assured that it has given me as much pain as yourself!

Your very affectionate and grateful pupil,

F. Liszt

December 23rd, 1828

P.S.—Please answer me as soon as possible, for I am longing for a letter from you; and please embrace your excellent parents from me. I add my address (Rue Montholon, No. 7bis).

2. To De Mancy in Paris

[Autograph in the possession of M. Etienne Charavay in Paris.]

December 23rd, 1829

My Dear M. de Mancy,

I am so full of lessons that each day, from half-past eight in the morning till 10 at night, I have scarcely breathing time. Please excuse me therefore for not coming, as I should have liked to do, to lunch with Madame de Mancy, but it is quite impossible. The only thing I could do would be to come about 10 o'clock, if that would not be too late for a wedding day, and in that case I will beg M. Ebner [Carl Ebner, a Hungarian, a talented violinist (1812-1836)] to come with me. I don't write you a longer letter, for there is a pupil who has been waiting for me for an hour. Besides, we are not standing on ceremony. Ever yours,

F. Liszt

3. To Carl Czerny

[Autograph in the Musical Society's Archives in Vienna. Printed in a German translation: "La Mara, Letters of Musicians extending over Five Centuries." II. Leipzig, B. and H. 1887.]

My dear and beloved Master,

It would be impossible to explain to you the why and wherefore of my leaving you so long without news of me. Moreover, I have now only five minutes in which to write to you, for Mr. Luden, a pianist from Copenhagen, is starting shortly, and for fear of delaying his journey I must be brief; but what is postponed is not lost, so cheer up, for very soon you will get a great thick letter from me, which I will take care to prepay, as I should not like to ruin you.

Among all the circles of artists where I go in this country I plead your cause tremendously: we all want you to come and stay some time in Paris; it would certainly do you a great deal of good, and you are so widely esteemed that you will doubtless be well satisfied with the reception you will meet with here. If you ever entertain this idea, write to me, I entreat you, for I will do for you what I would do for my father. I have been making a special study of your admirable sonata (Op. 7), and have since played it at several reunions of connoisseurs (or would-be connoisseurs): you cannot imagine what an effect it made; I was quite overcome by it. It was in a burst of enthusiasm caused by the Prestissimo, that Mr. Luden begged for a few words of introduction to you; I know your kindness, indeed I could never forget it. I therefore commend him in all confidence of your goodness, until the time when I am so happy as to embrace you myself and to show you (however feebly) all the gratitude and admiration which fill me.

F. Liszt

Paris, August 26th, 1830

4. To Alphonse Brot in Paris

[Autograph in the possession of M. Etienne Charavay in Paris.]

(Paris, Beginning of the 30th year.)

It would give us great pleasure, my dear M. Brot, if you would come and dine with us without ceremony tomorrow, Monday, about 6 o'clock; I do not promise you a good dinner,—that is not the business of us poor artists; but the good company you will meet will, I trust, make up for that. Monsieur Hugo [the poet] and Edgard Quinet [French writer and philosopher] have promised to come. So do try not to disappoint us, for we should miss you much. My good mother told me to press you to come, for she is very fond of you. Till tomorrow then! Kind regards and thanks.

F. Liszt

I have been at least six times to you without having the pleasure of seeing you.

61, Rue de Provence.

5. Monsieur Pierre Wolff (Junior), Rue de la Tertasse, Geneva, Switzerland

[Autograph in the possession of M. Gaston Calmann-Levy in Paris.]

Nous disons: "Il est temps. Executons, c'est l'heure." Alors nous retournons les yeux—La Mort est la! Ainsi de mes projets.—Quand vous verrai-je, Espagne, Et Venise et son golfe, et Rome et sa campagne,

Toi, Sicile, que ronge un volcan souterrain, Grece qu'on connait trop, Sardaigne qu'on ignore, Cites de l'Aquilon, du Couchant, de l'Aurore, Pyramides du Nil, Cathedrales du Rhin! Qui sait?— jamais peut-etre!

[We say: "Now it is time. Let's act, for 'tis the hour." Then turn we but our eyes—lo! death is there! Thus with my plans. When shall I see thee, Espagna, And Venice with her gulf, and Rome with her Campagna; Thou, Sicily, whom volcanoes undermine; Greece, whom we know too well, Sardinia, unknown one, Lands of the north, the west, the rising sun, Pyramids of the Nile, Cathedrals of the Rhine! Who knows? Never perchance!]

Earthly life is but a malady of the soul, an excitement which is kept up by the passions. The natural state of the soul is rest!

Paris, May 2nd [1832]

Here is a whole fortnight that my mind and

fingers have been working like two lost spirits, Homer, the Bible, Plato, Locke, Byron, Hugo, Lamartine, Chateaubriand, Beethoven, Bach, Hummel, Mozart, Weber, are all around me. I study them, meditate on them, devour them with fury; besides this I practice four to five hours of exercises (3rds, 6ths, 8ths, tremolos, repetition of notes, cadences, etc., etc.). Ah! provided I don't go mad, you will find an artist in me! Yes, an artist such as you desire, such as is required nowadays!

"And I too am a painter!" cried Michael Angelo the first time he beheld a chef d'oeuvre... Though insignificant and poor, your friend cannot leave off repeating those words of the great man ever since Paganini's last performance. Rene, what a man, what a violin, what an artist! Heavens! what sufferings, what misery, what tortures in those four strings!

Here are a few of his characteristics:——

[Figure: Liszt here writes down several tiny excerpts from musical scores of Paganini's violin music, such as his famous "Caprices"]

As to his expression, his manner of phrasing, his very soul in fact!——

May 8th [1832]

My good friend, it was in a paroxysm of madness that I wrote you the above lines; a strain of work, wakefulness, and those violent desires (for which you know me) had set my poor head aflame; I went from right to left, then from left to right (like a sentinel in the winter, freezing), singing, declaiming, gesticulating, crying out; in a word, I was delirious. Today the spiritual and the animal (to use the witty language of M. de Maistre) are a little more evenly balanced; for the volcano of the heart is not extinguished, but is working silently.—Until when?—

Address your letters to Monsieur Reidet, the receiver-general at the port of Rouen.

A thousand kind messages to the ladies Boissier. I will tell you some day the reasons which prevented me from starting for Geneva. On this subject I shall call you in evidence.

Bertini is in London; Madame Malibran is making her round of Germany; Messemaecker (how is he getting on?) is resting on his laurels at Brussels; Aguado has the illustrious maestro Rossini in tow.— Ah—Hi—Oh—Hu!!!

6. To Ferdinand Hiller

[This letter, published by F. Niecks ("F. Chopin, Man and Musician," Vol. 1. German by Langhans. Leipzig, Leuckart, 1890), was written by Liszt and Chopin jointly, and was also signed by Chopin's friend Franchomme, the violoncellist. The part written by Chopin is indicated here by parentheses ().—Addressed to the well-known composer and author, afterwards Director of the Conservatorium and Concert Society at Cologne (1811-1885).]

This is the twentieth time, at least, that we have tried to meet, first at my house, then here, with the intention of writing to you, and always some visit, or some other unforeseen hindrance, has occurred. I don't know whether Chopin will be strong enough to make excuses to you; for my part, it seems to me that we have been so unmannerly and impertinent that no excuses are now permissible or possible.

We sympathized most deeply in your bereavement, and more deeply did we wish that we could be with you in order to soften, as far as possible, the grief of your heart. [Hiller had lost his father.]

(He has said it all so well that I have nothing to add to excuse me specially for my negligence or idleness, or whim or distraction, or—or—or—You know that I can explain myself better in person, and, this autumn, when I take you home late by the boulevards to your mother, I shall try to obtain your pardon. I am writing to you without knowing what my pen is scribbling, as Liszt is at this moment playing my Studies, and transporting me away from all suitable ideas. I wish I could steal his manner of rendering my own works. With regard to your friends who are staying in Paris, I have often seen, during this winter and spring, the Leo family [August Leo, banker in Paris], and all that follows. There have been evenings at certain ambassadresses' houses, and there was not a single one at which somebody living at Frankfort was not mentioned. Madame Eichthal sends you many kind messages— Plater [Count Plater, Chopin's countryman, and a friend also of Liszt], the whole family were very sorry for your departure, and begged me to give you their condolences.) Madame d'Apponyi [Apponyi, the Austrian ambassador in Paris] was very much vexed with me for not having taken you there before your departure; she hopes that when you come back you will be sure to remember the promise you made me. I will say as much of a certain lady who is not an ambassadress.

Do you know Chopin's wonderful Studies?— (They are admirable! and moreover they will last only until yours appear) = an author's little piece of modesty!!! (A little piece of rudeness on the part of the regent, for—to explain the matter fully—he is correcting my spelling) according to the method of Monsieur Marlet.

You will come back in the month of (September, isn't it? tr)y [Tach]ez] to let us know the day; we have determined to give you a serenade or charivari [mock serenade]. The company of the most distinguished artists of the capital = M. Franchomme (present), Madame Petzold, and the Abbc Bardin [passionate lover of music, who had a great many artists to see him], the leaders of the Rue d'Amboise (and my neighbors), Maurice Schlesinger [music publisher], uncles, aunts, nephews, nieces, brothers-in-law, sisters-in-law, and—and ("en plan du troisienae," etc.). ["in the third row—i.e. less important people]. The responsible editors,

F. Liszt

(F. Chopin) (Aug. Franchomme.)

(By-the-bye, I met Heine yesterday, who begged me to grussen you herzlich and herzlich.) [to send you his warmest and most heartfelt greetings]

(By-the-bye, also, please excuse all the "you's" [Instead of the more familiar "thee" and "thou."]—I do beg you to excuse them. If you have a moment to spare, give us news of yourself, which would be most welcome. Paris, Rue de la Chaussee d'Antin, No. 5. At present I am occupying Franck's lodging

[Dr. Hermann Franck, author, friend of Chopin and of many other celebrities; editor also for a short time, in the forties, of Brockhaus's "Deutsche Allgemeine Zeitung"]—he is gone to London and Berlin. I am most happy in the rooms which were so often our meeting-place. Berlioz sends greetings.

As to pere Baillot, he is in Switzerland, at Geneva. So now you can guess that I can't send you the Bach concerto.

June 20th, 1833)

7. To Abbe F. de Lamennais

[Autograph in the possession of M. Alfred Bovet at Valentigney.— Addressed to the celebrated French author (1782-1854), who followed his brilliant apology of Catholicism, "Essai sur l'Indifference en Matiere de Religion" (Essay on Indifference in Matters of Religion, 1817-1823), by the "Paroles d'un Croyant" (Words of a Believer, 1834), a veritable "Ode to revolution in the sublimest biblical style," and sought to bring religious and political liberty into accord with true religiousness. The latter work made an unheard-of sensation, but brought upon him the anathema of the Church. He obtained a great influence over Liszt, who was on intimate terms with him.]

Four months have actually passed, dear Father, since we parted, and I feel very sad at not getting a word from you!—at the same time I do not wish to complain, for it seems to me that you can never doubt my deep and filial affection…Much more, I even know that you have been willing to accept it, and, however humble it may be, to count it for something…What more then can I desire?…

Eugene, whose brotherly friendship becomes dearer to me day by day, has often given me good tidings of you. The last time I saw him he told me confidentially that you were working at a sort of Introduction, or developed Preface to your works.— Although I know perfectly well that my interest counts for nothing in this matter, I may be permitted nevertheless to tell you how glad I am to know that you are occupied with this work. To yourself, first of all, I think you owe it—your name and glory will shine out all the more powerfully for it. And, secondly, for the public it will be a work of art the more (and this commodity becomes rather rare as time goes on), and which will besides have the double advantage of aiding and fixing them in the understanding of your past works, whilst at the same time preparing them for, and initiating them into, your future thoughts.

And, lastly, for us who love you, and who would glory and be proud to be one day called your disciples, we rejoice in it because the world will learn to know you better by this means, and because it will probably be another opportunity for us to show our sympathetic admiration as well as our unalterable devotion for you.

Unless something very unforeseen occurs, I shall come again and beg you to receive me for a few days towards the middle of July; I trust sufficiently to your sincerity to tell me that you would rather not have me if my individuality would trouble or bother you too much.—Before that, I shall have the honor of sending you a little work, to which I have had the audacity to tack a great name—yours.

—It is an instrumental De profundis. The plain-song that you like so much is preserved in it with the Faburden. Perhaps this may give you a little pleasure, at any rate, I have done it in remembrance of some hours passed (I should say "lived") at La Chenaie.

Farewell, dear Father. I don't give you any news of Paris,—you know all that. You know that Ballanche wants to be an Academician, and accepts Salvandy and Dupaty as competitors,—you know the little check of January,—the miserable petty intrigues of court and newspaper and vestry;—in a word, you know how men are wanting in noble and generous sentiments, and how they make the most of their own ignoble ends and interests, to which their words and actions yet give the lie.

Farewell once more, dear Father. Think as often as possible of all the good you have done, and of that which men have a right to expect of you. Think sometimes also of the help and the wealth of affection that you have showered on me in particular, and may the remembrance of this be sweet to you!…

Yours ever, for life—from heart and soul,

F. Liszt

January 14th, 1835

Tomorrow morning I have to leave for two months. If you should be so good as to write to me before my return, please address always, 61, Rue de Provence. My mother will take care that I have your kind letter.

8. To his Mother

[From a copy, by Mr. Vladimir Stassoff of St. Petersburg, the original of which is in Russia. The letter in itself is unimportant, but it is the only one to Liszt's mother which the editor could get, and gives a fresh proof of the devotion of the artist to his mother.]

Dear Mother,

Please send me at once, without any delay, the Pianist's

Glossary, which you will get at Lemonier's, Rue de l'Echelle.

Simply put it in a cover, and put it in the post (General

Office), and I shall get it, at latest, by Monday or Tuesday.—

Address to Mr. Hermann Cohen, Grande Rue, No. 8.

[Cohen was a frequently mentioned pupil and favorite of Liszt's who was born at Hamburg in 1820, much thought of as a pianist in Paris, and immortalised as "Puzzi" by George Sand ("Lettres d'un Voyageur"); he followed Liszt to Geneva, and gave lessons there. In 1850 he entered the order of Carmelites, and, under the name of Pater Augustin, died in Berlin in January 1871, whither he had gone with French prisoners.]

I have an immense deal to do this morning, so that I have barely time to tell you that I love you with all my heart, and that I rejoice above everything at the prospect of seeing you again soon—that is to say, in six or eight months.

F. Liszt

You will hear of me from Mr. Pinondel, who

passed a day with us.

9. To the Abbe F. de Lamennais, La Chenaie

[Autograph in the possession of Mr. Marshall in London.]

[Paris, May 28th, 1836—according to the stamp of the post office]

Dear and venerable Father,

I shall expect you. Whatever sorrow there is in the depth of my soul, it will be sweet and consoling to me to see you again.

You are so wonderfully good to me! and I should suffer so much by being so long away from you!—

Au revoir then, once more—in eight days at latest it will be, will it not? I do nothing else than keep expecting you.

Yours, with the deepest respect and most sincere devotion,

F. Liszt

10. To Mademoiselle Lydie Pavy, of La Glaciere, Lyons

[Autograph in the possession of M. Etienne Charavay in Paris.]

St. Gervais, August 22nd [1836].

Your postscript deserves a punishment, and here it comes dated from St. Gervais. I do not know whether your charming sister-in- law, Madame Pavy, will consider this stamp of St. Gervais worthy to appear in her collection; be that as it may, it gives me no less a pleasure to converse a little with you who are always so charming, so versatile, so excellent, and, permit me to say, so kind to me.

Mademoiselle Merienne, whom I saw only

quite lately (for you must know that during the whole month of July, of glorious memory, I have barely condescended to go down once or twice to Geneva; I was living in a little bit of a house on the mountain, whence, let me say parenthetically, it would have been quite easy for me to hurl sermons and letters at you); Mademoiselle Merienne (what shall I say to you after such an enormous parenthesis?), somewhat like (by way of a new parenthesis) those declaimed discourses of Plantade or Lhuillier, which put a stop to music whilst nevertheless admitting that there is such a thing, whether at the beginning or at the end— Mademoiselle Merienne—au diable Mademoiselle Merienne! You guess by this time that she gave me tidings of you, that she is a delightful and enchanting person, that she makes admirable portraits, and that mine, amongst others, has been a wonderful success. Etc., etc., and always etc…

And yet I do wish to talk to you about this good Mademoiselle Merienne, for she said a heap of charming things to me for your sake, which will certainly not astonish you. But how to set about it after all this preamble of parentheses? Ah, I have it! —In three or four weeks I shall come and knock at your door.—And then? Well, then we will chatter away at our ease. So much the worse for you if you are not satisfied with my cunning stratagem. Now let us talk business; yes, seriously, let us talk business!

Has your brother returned from his journey? And is he well? And has no accident happened to him on the way? You are surprised, perhaps, at my anxiety; but by-and-bye you will understand it without difficulty, when I have explained to you how terribly interested I am in the fact of his journey being safely accomplished.

Just imagine that at this moment I have only 200 fr. in my purse (a ridiculously small sum for a traveler), and that it is M. Pavy who is to be my financial Providence, considering that it is to him that my mother has confided my little quarterly income of a thousand francs. Now at this point I must entrust you with a little secret, which at present is only known to two individuals, Messrs. Paccard and Roger (charming names for confidants, are not they?), and which I beg you to make known as quickly as possible to your brother. It concerns a little scrap of paper (which these rogues of bankers call a draft, I believe), for a thousand francs, by which Messrs. Paccard and Roger are authorized by my signature, which is at the bottom, to demand the above sum of a thousand francs (which my mother entrusted to M. Pavy in Paris) from M. Pavy, junior, living at La Glaciere at Lyons, after the 22nd of August, 1836.

A thousand pardons for troubling you with these details, but I should never have had the courage to write direct to your brother, on account of my profound ignorance in money matters.

You tell me that you passed part of the fine season in the country—why did not you arrange so as to tour for a little among the mountains of Switzerland? I should have had such pleasure in doing the honors, and Mademoiselle Merienne also...but don't let us speak any more of Mademoiselle Merienne (who, be it observed in parenthesis, must have already appeared a dozen times in this letter), for fear of again falling into inextricable parentheses.

Au revoir then; in five weeks at latest I shall come and warm myself at your "glacier."

F. Liszt

11. To Abbe de Lamennais

[Autograph in the possession of M. Alfred Bovet at Valentigney.]

My friend Louis de Ronchaud writes me word that he has had the honor of seeing you, dear Father, and that you were kind enough to give him a message of affectionate remembrance for me. I am very happy to know that you continue to keep this precious and friendly feeling for me, of which you have already given me so many proofs, and which I shall endeavour always to deserve as far as is in my power.

I am still not very far advanced in my Italian journey. The beauty of these parts, the necessity of writing with some little continuance, and also, if all be said, some altogether unexpected successes, have kept me in Milan and the neighborhood (Como and the delicious shores of the lake) much longer than I had foreseen. As regards musical matters, the presence of Rossini, whom I frequently see, gives a certain impetus to this country. I have been singularly well received here, so I shall probably pass the greater part of the winter here, and shall not start for Venice till towards the beginning of March. Thence I shall go to Florence and Rome, where I expect I shall stay a good long time.

D. has no doubt talked to you of our stay at

Nohant last summer. I think that he got rid there of a good many old prejudices about me. It was a sweet satisfaction to me to learn through him how good and indulgent you have been towards me on several occasions, even so far as to contradict and defend me warmly against him and against others who knew me still less. I had charged our secret friend to defend me in his turn from a slight wrong which I had, only apparently, committed, but even "apparently" is too much, and I think I have entirely justified myself with regard to it. I don't know whether in his noble carelessness he will have thought of it. However that may be, I shall always count on your paternal affection more than all the rest.

What can I say to you of Italy that you do not know, and that you have not said in such manner as to cause despair for ever to the makers of observations!—It is always the same status quo, the excellent and perfectly happy government that you know.—I am hoping and longing ardently for your next book [probably "Le Livre du Peuple": Paris, 1837], which I shall read with my whole heart and soul, as I have read all that you have written for four years. I shall owe you just so many more good and noble emotions. Will they remain for ever sterile? Will my life be for ever tainted with this idle uselessness which weighs upon me? Will the hour of devotion and of manly action never come? Am I condemned without respite to this trade of a Merry Andrew and to amuse in drawing-rooms?

Whatever may be my poor and humble destiny, do not ever doubt my heart. Do not ever doubt the deep respect and unalterable devotion with which you have inspired me.

Yours for ever,

F. Liszt

Como, December 18th, 1837

12. To Breitkopf and Hartel in Leipzig

[Autograph in the possession of Herr Hermann Scholtz,

Kammervirtuoso   in   Dresden.]

I thank you much, gentlemen, for the obliging letter that you have written me. Up to the present time I have had none but the most pleasant business relations with Mr. Hofmeister, who has the kindness to publish the greater part of my works in Germany. As I do not know very much of the laws which regulate literary and musical proprietorship in Saxony, I had spoken to him about the Beethoven Symphonies, of which I have undertaken the arrangement, or, more correctly speaking, the pianoforte score. To tell the truth, this work has, nevertheless, cost me some trouble; whether I am right or wrong, I think it sufficiently different from, not to say superior to, those of the same kind which have hitherto appeared. The recent publication of the same Symphonies, arranged by Mr. Kalkbrenner, makes me anxious that mine should not remain any longer in a portfolio. I intend also to finger them carefully, which, in addition to the indication of the different instruments (which is important in this kind of work), will most certainly make this edition much more complete. If, then, as I imagine, it is impossible for Mr. Hofmeister to publish them, I shall be very grateful if you will undertake it. The reputation of your house is European, and I perfectly remember having had the pleasure of seeing Mr. Raymond Hartel in Paris. It will be a pleasure to me to conclude this little business with you, at the rate of eight francs a page. Up to the present time I have only finished three Symphonies (that in A major), but I could promise to let you have the others successively, according as you might wish, or I could limit my work to the four most important Symphonies (if I may express my opinion), namely, the Pastoral, C minor, A major, and the Eroica. I think those are the ones which are most effective on the piano.

I start tomorrow for Vienna, where I expect to remain till the end of April. Please address to me to the care of Mr. Tobias Haslinger till the 25th of April, and after that to Mr. Ricordi, Milan, who has undertaken to forward me all my letters while I am in Italy. My compliments and affectionate thanks.

F. Liszt

13. To Robert Schumann

[Addressed to the celebrated German Tone-poet (1810-1856). Liszt had spoken of Schumann's Op. 5, 11, and 14 in the Gazette Musicale, 1837, with equal enthusiasm and understanding, which soon brought the two together.]

[Without a date; received by R. S. May 5th, 1838.]

My dear Monsieur Schumann,

I shall not attempt to tell you how grateful and touched I am by your friendly letter. Mademoiselle Wieck, whom I have been so happy as to meet here, will express to you, better than I can, all the sympathy, all the admiring affection I have for you. I have been such a nomad latterly that the pieces you were kind enough to address to me at Milan only reached me on the eve of my departure from Venice about a fortnight ago; and since then we have been talking so much of you, day and night, that it hardly occurred to me to write to you. Today, however, to my great astonishment, I get a fresh token of your friendly remembrance, and I certainly will not delay thanking you many times for it, so I have just left a charming party of very pretty women in order to write these few lines to you. But the truth is you need hardly thank me for this little sacrifice, for it is a great pleasure to me to be able to have a little chat with you.

The "Carneval" and the "Fantasiestucke" have interested me excessively. I play them really with delight, and God knows that I can't say as much of many things. To speak frankly and freely, it is absolutely only Chopin's compositions and yours that have a powerful interest for me.

The rest do not deserve the honor of being mentioned…at least, with a few exceptions,—to be conciliatory, like Eusebius.

In six weeks to two months I shall send you my twelve Studies and a half-dozen of "Fantasiestucke" ("Impressions et Poemes")—I consider them less bad than others of my making. I shall be happy to think that they do not displease you.

May I confess to you that I was not very much struck with Henselt's Studies, and that I found them not up to their reputation? I don't know whether you share my opinion, but they appear to me, on the whole, very careless. They are pretty to listen to, they are very pretty to look at, the effect is excellent, the edition (thanks to our friend Hofmeister) is most carefully done; but, all counted, I question whether H. is anything but a distinguished mediocrity. [How highly Liszt thought, later on, of Henselt's Concerto and other of his compositions is well known, and is spoken of in a subsequent letter to Baroness Wrangel, in May, 1883.] For the rest, he is very young, and will doubtless develop. Let us, at least, hope so.

I am extremely sorry that I cannot come and pay you a little visit at Leipzig at present. It is one of my keenest desires to make your personal acquaintance and to pass some days with you. But as that is not possible now, let us, at least, try not to be entirely separated, and let us combat, as far as we can, the laziness about writing, which is, I think, equally in us both.

In a fortnight I am returning to Venice. I shall be back in Milan at the time of the coronation (towards the end of August). Next winter I expect to pass in Rome, if the cholera or some other plague does not stop it. I will not induce you to come to Italy. Your sympathies would be too deeply wounded there. If they have even heard that Beethoven and Weber ever existed, it is as much as they have done.

Will you not have what you have sent me printed? Haslinger would have it gladly, I think, and it would be a great pleasure to me to see my name associated with yours.

If I might make a request, I would ask you to

write some trios, or a quintet or septet. It seems to me that you would do that admirably, and for a long time nothing remarkable in that line has been published. If ever you determine to do so, let me know at once, as I should be anxious to have the honor of making them known to the public. Adieu, my dear Monsieur Schumann; keep me always in affectionate remembrance, and accept once more my warm sympathy and devotion.

F. Liszt

14. To the "Gesellschaft der Musikfreunde" in Vienna

[Society of Musical Dilettanti, or Amateur Musical   Society.
Autograph in the Archives of the Society in Vienna]

Gentlemen,

I am extremely grateful for the honor you have done me in admitting me among you as a member of the Vienna Musik-Verein [Musical Union]. I cannot, unfortunately, flatter myself that I have as yet deserved this distinction, but allow me to say that it will not be my fault if I do not become worthy of it.

If ever the occasion should offer in which I can be agreeable or useful to the Society of the Musik-Verein, be assured that I shall gladly avail myself of it, and that you will henceforth have a claim on my gratitude and devotion.

I have the honor to be, gentlemen,

Yours faithfully,

F. Liszt

Venice, June 1st, 1838

15. To Simon Lowy in Vienna

[Autograph in the possession of Herr O. A. Schulz, bookseller in
Leipzig.—Addressed to a Vienna banker, an intimate friend of
Liszt The "Soirees de Vienne," composed on Schubert Valses, are
dedicated to him.]

I am very sensible, my dear sir, of your friendly remembrance. Your kind letter found me in the midst of the official hurly- burly of the coronation fetes. What business on earth had I to do with such an affair? I have not the least idea. Thank Heaven we are now at the end of it all, safe and sound, rejoicing, and sated with amusement!

I found at Milan a certain number of my Vienna connections. One or two of the persons whom you will not mention to me (and whose anonymity I respect) were also there. I know that a great many of the people who approach me with a smile on their lips, and protestations of friendship on their tongues, have nothing better to do than to pull me to pieces as best they can as soon as they are outside my door. It is, moreover, the fate of all the world. I resign myself to it willingly, as I do to all the absurd and odious necessities of this lower world. There is, besides, just this much good in these sad experiences of various relations with men— which is, that one learns to relish and appreciate better the devotion of the few friends whom chance has thrown in your path.

In a few days from now I shall start for Bologna, Florence, and Rome. In spite of all my desire to return to Vienna, where people have been so kind and indulgent to me, I do not yet see when I shall be able to get there. However this journey may be put off, I hope, nevertheless, my dear sir, that you will continue till then the affectionate feelings you so kindly entertain towards me. Receive in return my assurances of consideration and affectionate devotion.

F. Liszt

Milan, September 22nd, 1838

Will you be so good as to give the enclosed note to the charming woman who is good enough to remember me so kindly?

16. To M. Pacini, Music Publisher in Paris

[Autograph in the possession of M. Alfred Bovet at Valentigney.]

My Dear Monsieur Pacini,

In two or three days at latest from now you will receive the manuscript for which you asked me for the book of the Hundred and One. [A collective work with contributions by celebrities of the day.] Mr. Hugot has kindly undertaken to bring it to you.

As the title implies, it is an Etude (di Bravura) after Paganini. [Bravura Studies on Paganini's Capricci, arranged for the pianoforte, brought out by Haslinger, Vienna, in 1839. A second, newly arranged edition, dedicated to Clara Schumann, "Grandes Etudes de Paganini," was brought out by Breitkopf and Hartel in 1851.] You will oblige me by recommending the engraver to engrave it very spaciously. In addition, you had better, I think, reprint directly afterwards this Etude facilitee, which I have also sent you. This second arrangement is by

M. Schumann, a young composer of very great merit. It is more within the reach of the general public, and also more exact than my paraphrase.

Many apologies for having kept you waiting so long for such a small thing, and kind remembrances to Emilien.

Yours affectionately,

F. Liszt

Please send the corrected proofs of this study to Haslinger, musical editor to the Court, at Graben, Vienna.

I must have at least two corrected proofs. Prego! Prego!! [I beg!] leave only such mistakes as are absolutely necessary in order that an edition may be supposed to be correct.

Padua, September 30th, 1838

17. To Breitkopf and Hartel.

[This is the first of the Liszt letters extant in the archives of the firm.]

I am really grieved, gentlemen, at the trouble you have been good enough to take about these unlucky Symphonies, and I hardly know how to express my acknowledgments. As I have already had the honor of telling you, Mr. Mori had been previously engaged to publish these Symphonies, and, as the steps you have taken have not been crowned with success, I will keep to this first publisher, with whom I have every reason to be satisfied up to now.

You can then publish this work in two or three months from now. [Pianoforte scores of the C minor and Pastoral Symphonies of Beethoven.] Only it is essential that I should correct the last proof, so that the edition may be absolutely correct. I also wish to add the fingering to several passages, to make them easier for amateurs. Be so good, therefore, as to send me, through the Embassy (or by any other opportunity which is not too expensive), two proofs to Rome, where I shall be in about twelve days, and where I expect to remain till the middle of March.

I hope, gentlemen, that you will not have cause to regret the obliging advances that you have made to me in this matter, and for which I am sincerely grateful to you. If you will be so good as to add to the proofs of the Beethoven Symphonies such of the songs of Beethoven (or Weber) as you would like me to transcribe for piano solo, I will then give you a positive answer as to that little work, which I shall be delighted to do for you, but to which I cannot assent beforehand, not knowing of which songs you are the proprietors. If "Leyer und Schwert" was published by you, I will do that with pleasure. I think that these songs, or at any rate four or five of them, would be rather satisfactory for the piano.

Accept, gentlemen, the expression of my high esteem.

F. Liszt

Florence, January 3rd, 1839

18. To Princess Christine Belgiojoso in Paris

[Autograph in the possession of M. Alfred Bovet at Valentigney.— Addressed to the celebrated writer and patriot. In 1837 a charity concert took place in her salons, at which Liszt and Thalberg both played.]

It would be self-conceit in me, Princess, to complain of your silence. Your letters have always been for me a favor, a charm. I am not meaning to say that I have the slightest right to them. Nevertheless, as you do not reply to me any more, I hope you will at least permit me to tell you how very much I feel the very slightest marks of your kindness, and what a price I set upon your remembrance.

Some numbers of the Gazette or Revue Musicale, which have accidentally fallen into my hands at the house of one of my Russian friends (for in this happy country of the Arts, and of music in particular, you can well imagine that no one is foolish enough to spend a thirty francs' subscription on the Revue Musicale), have informed me that you had decidedly raised altar for altar, and made your charming salon echo with magnificent harmonies. I confess that this is perhaps the one regret of my winter. I should so immensely have liked to be there to admire you, to applaud you. Several people who had the honor of being present at these choice evenings have spoken to me about them with enthusiasm.

What a contrast to the tiresome musical soliloquies (I do not know what other name to give to this invention of mine) with which I contrived to gratify the Romans, and which I am quite capable of importing to Paris, so unbounded does my impudence become! Imagine that, wearied with warfare, not being able to compose a programme which would have common sense, I have ventured to give a series of concerts all by myself, affecting the Louis XIV. style, and saying cavalierly to the public, "The concert is—myself." For the curiosity of the thing I copy one of the programmes of the soliloquies for you:—

1. Overture to William Tell, performed by M. L.

2. Reminiscences of the Puritani. Fantaisie composed and performed by the above-mentioned!

3. Etudes and fragments by the same to the same!

4. Improvisation on themes given—still by the same. And that was all; neither more nor less, except lively conversation during the intervals, and enthusiasm if there was room for it.

A propos of enthusiasm, I ought at least to talk to you of St. Peter's. That is the proper thing to do when one writes from Rome. But, in the first place, I am writing to you from Albano, whence I can only discern the dome, and, secondly, this poor St. Peter's has been so disguised, so embellished by papier-mache wreaths, horrid curtains at alcoves, etc., etc., all in honor of the five or six last saints whom His Holiness has canonised, that I try to put away the recollection of it. Happily there have not been any workers of miracles to glorify at the Coliseum and the Campo Vaccino, otherwise it would have been impossible to live in Rome.

If nothing occurs to prevent it, I expect to pass the end of next winter (March and April) in Paris. Will you permit me then to fill up all the gaps in my correspondence from the Rue d'Anjou? [Here the Princess lived.] I count always upon your friendly and indulgent kindness. But shall you extend this so far as to give me a sign of life before the close of my stay in Italy? I do not know. In any case, letters addressed poste restante, Florence, will reach me till the 1st of next September.

I beg you, Madame la Princesse, to accept the expression of my profound and most devoted respect.

F. Liszt

Albano, June 4th, 1839

Will you be good enough to remember me affectionately to (Madame) your sister and to Mr. d'Aragon?

19. To Robert Schumann

[From a copy from the Royal Library in Berlin.]

Albano, June 5th, 1839

My dear Monsieur Schumann,

At the risk of appearing very monotonous, I must again tell you that the last pieces you were so kind as to send me to Rome appear to me admirable both in inspiration and composition. The "Fantaisie" dedicated to me is a work of the highest kind—and I am really proud of the honor you have done me in dedicating to me so grand a composition.

Op. 17, C dur. With the motto:—

"Durch alle Tone tonet
Im bunten Erdentraum
Ein leiser Ton gezogen
Fur den, der heimlich lauschet."

("Through all the sounds of nature,
In earth's fair dream of joy,
An under-current soundeth
For him whose ears can hear."]

I mean, therefore, to work at it and penetrate it through and through, so as to make the utmost possible effect with it.

As to the "Kinderscenen," I owe to them one of the greatest pleasures of my life. You know, or you don't know, that I have a little girl of three years old, whom everybody agrees in considering angelic (did you ever hear such a commonplace?). Her name is Blandine-Rachel, and her surname Moucheron. [Pet name; literally, "little fly."] It goes without saying that she has a complexion of roses and milk, and that her fair golden hair reaches to her feet just like a savage. She is, however, the most silent child, the most sweetly grave, the most philosophically gay in the world. I have every reason to hope also that she will not be a musician, from which may Heaven preserve her!

Well, my dear Monsieur Schumann, two or three times a week (on fine and good days!) I play your "Kinderscenen" to her in the evening; this enchants her, and me still more, as you may imagine, so that often I go over the first repeat twenty times without going any further. Really I think you would be satisfied with this success if you could be a witness of it!

I think I have already expressed to you, in one of my former letters, the desire I felt to see you write some ensemble pieces, Trios, Quintets, or Septets. Will you pardon me for pressing this point again? It seems to me that you would be more capable of doing it than any one else nowadays. And I am convinced that success, even commercial success, would not be wanting.

If between now and next winter you could complete some ensemble work, it would be a real pleasure to me to make it known in Paris, where that sort of composition, when well played, has more chance of success than you perhaps think. I would even gladly undertake to find a publisher for it, if you liked, which would moreover in no wise prevent you from disposing of it for Germany.

In the interim I mean to play in public your "Carnaval," and some of the "Davidsbundlertanze" and of the "Kinderscenen." The "Kreisleriana," and the "Fantaisie" which is dedicated to me, are more difficult of digestion for the public. I shall reserve them till later.

Up to the present time I only know the
following works of yours:—
Impromptus on a theme by Clara Wieck.
Pianoforte Sonata, dedicated to Clara.
Concerto without orchestra.
"Etudes Symphoniques"
"Davidsbundlertanze"
"Kreisleriana."
"Carnaval."
"Kinderscenen" and my "Fantaisie."

If you would have the kindness to complete your works to me it would be a great pleasure to me; I should like to have them bound all together in three or four volumes. Haslinger, on his side, will send you my Etudes and my other publications as they come out.

What you tell me of your private life has interested and touched me deeply. If I could, I know not how, be in the least pleasant or useful to you in these circumstances, dispose of me as you will. Whatever happens, count on my absolute discretion and sincere devotion. If I am not asking too much, tell me if it is Clara of whom you speak. But if this question should seem to you misplaced, do not answer it.

Have you met at Leipzig Mr. Frank, [Dr. Hermann Frank edited Brockhaus' Allgemeine Zeitung for a year.] at the present moment editor of the Leipzig Allgemeine Zeitung? From the little I know of him (for he has been much more intimate with Chopin and Hiller than with me) I think he is capable of understanding you. He has left a charming impression behind him in Rome. If you see him, give him my affectionate regards.

My plans remain the same. I still intend to be in Vienna at the beginning of December, and in Paris at the end of February. I shall be capable of coming to look you up in Leipzig if you will let me make the journey from Paris with you. Try! Adieu, my dear Monsieur Schumann; write soon (address care of Ricordi, Florence: I shall be in the neighborhood of Lucca till the middle of September), and depend always on my sincere esteem and lively affection.

Yours in all friendship,

F. Liszt

20. To Breitkopf and Hartel

[Milan, June, 1839]

Gentleman,

About three weeks ago I gave to Mr. Ricordi (who was on his way to Rome) the proofs of the two Symphonies you addressed to me. I hope they have reached you by now. Forgive me for having kept them so long, and also for having corrected them with so much care. But, firstly, they did not reach me till about the 20th of February, and then I did not know how to send them to you direct, for the diligences in this happy country are so insecure. I am therefore of necessity (though very unwillingly) behindhand.

Allow me to ask you for a second proof (for it is of great consequence to me that the edition should be as correct as possible), and this time I will beg you to send me three proofs of each Symphony, so that I may forward one to Paris and the other to London. Probably there will not be any more corrections to make in this second proof, and in that case I will let you know in two words (without returning your proof), telling you at the same time the date of publication.

My intention being to visit Vienna, Munich, and perhaps Leipzig at the beginning of next year (before going to England in the month of April), I shall take advantage of this opportunity to let the Symphonies be heard at my concerts, so as to give them a certain publicity.

I have looked through the Lieder you have been good enough to send me. I shall certainly do the "Adelaide," however difficult it may seem to me to transcribe simply and elegantly. As regards the others, I am afraid I cannot find the necessary time. Moreover, that good Haslinger overwhelms me with Schubert. I have just sent him twenty-four more new songs ("Schwanengesang" and "Winterreise"), and for the moment I am rather tired with this work.

Would you be so kind as to send me, at the same time with the proofs of the Beethoven Symphonies, Mr. Mendelssohn's "Preludes and Fugues"? It is an extremely remarkable work, and it has been impossible to get it in Italy. I shall be greatly obliged if you will send it me.

When you see Mr. Schumann please remember me very kindly to him. I have received the "Fantaisie" which he has done me the honor to dedicate to me, and the "Kinderscenen." Don't you think you ought to publish a book of Studies by him? I should be extremely curious to make acquaintance with them. All his works interest me in a high degree. It would be difficult for me to say as much of many of the compositions of my respected colleagues, with some exceptions.

I beg to remain, Gentlemen,

Yours most sincerely,

F. Liszt

Address the Symphonies to Mr. Ricordi, Florence. From the 15th of
June till the 1st of September I shall be in the neighborhood of
Lucca. Ricordi's address is the safest.

21. To the Beethoven Committee at Bonn

[Printed in L. Ramann's Biography of Liszt, vol. 1]

Gentlemen,

As the subscription for Beethoven's monument is only getting on slowly, and as the carrying out of this undertaking seems to be rather far distant, I venture to make a proposal to you, the acceptance of which would make me very happy. [In Bonn, Beethoven's birthplace, a committee had been formed to erect a Beethoven monument. Yet, in spite of the assent which met the proposal, the contributions flowed in so meagrely—Paris, for example, contributed only 424 francs 90 centimes—that Liszt, on reading this in a paper, immediately formed the noble resolution mentioned in the above letter. "Such a niggardly almsgiving, got together with such trouble and sending round the hat, must not be allowed to help towards building our Beethoven's monument!" he wrote to Berlioz. Thus the German nation has in great measure to thank Franz Liszt for the monument erected to its greatest composer at Bonn.]

I offer myself to make up, from my own means, the sum still wanting for the erection of the monument, and ask no other privilege than that of naming the artist who shall execute the work. That artist is Bartolini of Florence, who is universally considered the first sculptor in Italy.

I have spoken to him about the matter provisionally, and he assures me that a monument in marble (which would cost about fifty to sixty thousand francs) could be finished in two years, and he is ready to begin the work at once. I have the honor to be, etc.,

Franz Liszt

Pisa, October 3rd, 1839

22. To Count Leo Festetics in Pest

[Printed in F. von Schober's "Letters about Liszt's Sojourn in Hungary."]

Dear Count,

Shall you like to have me again at Pest this year? I know not. In any case you are threatened with my presence from the 18th to the 22nd of next December. I shall come to you a little older, a little more matured, and, permit me to say, more finished an artist, than I was when you saw me last year, for since that time I have worked enormously in Italy. I hope you have kept me in remembrance, and that I may always count on your friendship, which is dear to me.

What joy, what an immense happiness it will be to be once more in my own country, to feel myself surrounded by such noble and vigorous sympathies, which, thank God, I have done nothing to forfeit in my distant and wandering life. What feelings, what emotions will then fill my breast! All this, dear Count, I will not attempt to express to you, for in truth I should not know how. Let it suffice you to know that the love of my country, of my chivalrous and grand country, has ever lived most deeply in my heart; and that, if unhappily it does not seem likely that I can ever show to my country what a love and devotion I feel for it, the sentiments will remain none the less unchanged in my heart.

But I will not tire you any longer with myself and my sentiments.

I forgot to tell you that for nearly a week I have been confined to my bed with a very severe fever, which might easily have become more serious still. My second concert was obliged to be put off on account of it. Today my doctor has given me permission to play on Wednesday. I don't really know whether I shall be able to do it, for my hand trembles fearfully. Excuse this horrible writing, but I did want to send you a few words. It is a sort of anticipation of Pest, which is sweet to me.

A revoir then very soon, dear Count; meanwhile believe me, as ever, yours most sincerely,

F. Liszt

November 24th, 1839, in bed

23. To Clara Wieck

[The great pianist, afterwards Schumann's wife.]

Pest, December 25th, 1839

How grateful I am, Mademoiselle, for the kind remembrance you keep of me! And how much I am already rejoicing at the thought of seeing you and hearing you again soon in Leipzig! I was so vexed not to be in Paris last winter when I knew you were going to spend some time there. Perhaps I should have been able to be of some little use to you there. You know that, at all times and in every country, I shall always be at your service. I should become too lengthy if I allowed myself to reply in detail to your kind questions about my new compositions. I worked immensely hard in Italy. Without exaggeration I think I have written four to five hundred pages of pianoforte music. If you have patience to hear half a quarter of them I shall be delighted to play them to you, so so.

The "Studies after Paganini," which are dedicated to you, will only appear in two months' time; but I will bring you the proofs, which have long been corrected, to Leipzig.

Once more many thanks, and many tender and respectful wishes for everything that can contribute to your happiness. And above all a bientot.

Yours in admiration and sympathy,

F. Liszt

24. To Robert Schumann in Leipzig

[Autograph in the Royal Library in Berlin.]

Dresden, March 27th, 1840

My dear Schumann,

It is all splendid. Only I should prefer to play the "Hexameron" last, so as to finish with orchestra. Please, therefore, have the "Etudes" and the "Carnaval" put after the Mendelssohn Concerto! [Refers to Liszt's third concert in Leipzig, on March 30th, 1840, for the benefit of the Orchestral Pension Fund.]

Best remembrances to Mendelssohn and Hiller; and believe me yours ever,

F. Liszt

I shall certainly return Monday morning, for on Sunday I am giving a concert for the poor here. But if it should de possible for me to come on Sunday...but I doubt it. [Together with this letter a friend, Carl K[ragen?], writes to Schumann: "He [Liszt] has played me the glorious Mendelssohn Concerto. It was divine! Tomorrow Tieck is to read Faust for Liszt at my mother's house, and Liszt is to play at our house with Lipinski!, Do come for it! Ah, if you could only induce Mendelssohn and his wife to come too!"]

25. To Franz von Schober in Vienna

[The autographs of all the letters in this collection to Schober are in the possession of Fran

Babette Wolf at Dresden.-Addressed to the poet and writer, an intimate and worthy friend of Franz Schubert. He became Councillor of Legation to Weimar, and died at Dresden in 1882.]

Metz, April 3rd, 1840

I did not get any news from you at Leipzig, dear Schober, as I expected. I am afraid I was very indiscreet in asking you to be so good as to undertake this work, which I should have valued so much, coming from you. [In answer to the distorted reports in various newspapers of Liszt's visit to Hungary (January, 1840), Schober, who had been an eyewitness, thought it right to clear up the misrepresentations, which he did in the form of "Letters about Liszt's Sojourn in Hungary"; these he published, but much later (Berlin, Schlesinger, 1843)] But I will not speak of it any more. If by any chance you have already done it I should be grateful to you to send it me—otherwise we will not speak of it any more.

Do you know that I have been pursued by one constant regret during my journey, the regret not to have induced you to accompany me? Your society has always been beneficial and strengthening to me: I do not know why, but I imagine that we should live smoothly together. Your qualities, your faults (if you have any), your character and temper, all please me and attach me to you. You know that I flatter myself I can understand and appreciate you…Should you see any great difficulty in joining me somewhere next autumn-at Venice, for example—and in making a European tour with me? Answer me frankly on this matter. And once more, the question of money need not be considered. As long as we are together (and I should like you to have at least three free years before you) my purse will be yours, on the sole condition that you consent to undertake the management of our expenses,—and that you are thoroughly convinced beforehand of the gratitude I shall feel towards you.

Excuse me, my dear good friend, for entering so plainly into matters, but we have talked together too openly, it seems to me, for it to be possible that your delicate feeling on certain points should be wounded by this.

I have sent back Kiss, of Dresden. He is a good fellow, but a little awkward, and wanting in a certain point of honor, without which a man is not a man as I understand the word. So I am alone now, and am not going to have any one tacked on to me. A former pupil of mine, Monsieur Hermann, has undertaken to arrange my concerts, which is a great relief to me. A propos of concerts, I gave six (in nine days!) at Prague, three at Dresden, and the same number at Leipzig (in twelve days)—so I am perfectly tired out, and feel great need of rest. That was good, wasn't it? Adieu, my dear good friend-let me hear from you soon (address 19, Rue Pigalle, Paris), and depend entirely upon me—nunc et semper.

Yours ever sincerely,

F. Liszt

Will you be so good as to go to Diabelli's [Music publisher in Vienna] when you pass by, and advise him again not to publish the third part of the Hungarian Melodies (which I sent him by Hartel) without first sending me a proof to Paris to correct. Adieu.

Best remembrances to Kriehuber [A well-known Vienna painter and lithographer, from whom a number of Liszt portraits have come.] and Lowy. Why does not the latter write to me?

26. To Maurice Schlesinger, Editor of the Gazette Musicale in Paris

[Given by L. Ramann, "Franz Liszt," vol. ii., i.]

Sir,

Allow me to protest against an inexact assertion in your last number but one:—

"Messieurs Liszt and Cramer have asked for the Legion of Honor," etc.

I do not know if M. Cramer (who has just been nominated) has obtained the cross.

In any case I think that you, like every one else, will approve of a nomination so perfectly legitimate.

As to myself, if it be true that my name has figured in the list of candidates, this can only have occurred entirely without my knowledge. It has always seemed to me that distinctions of this sort could only be accepted, but never "asked for."

I am, sir, etc.,

F. Liszt

London, May 14th, 1840

27. To Franz von Schober

[London, May or June, 1840]

My worthy friend,

A fortnight ago my mother wrote me word that she had given several letters, which had come for me from Germany, to a gentleman who was to bring them to me to London. I suppose there was one from you among the number, but up to now I have not received anything.

Allow me to repeat once more the request, which I have already made to you, to come for some time with me (a year or two, and more if you can); for I feel deeply that, the more we are separated by time and space, the more my thoughts and my heart go out to you. I have rarely felt this so strongly, and my wish to feel you settled with me grows daily stronger.

Moreover the persuasion that I feel that we should pass a happy and serious life together, makes me again press you further.

Try then to be at liberty as soon as possible, and once for all make a frank and friendly resolve. I assure you that it will not be difficult to ameliorate, by each other, our two lives, which in their different ways are sad and bad thus separated.

Let me have two words in reply on this point —which, to tell the truth, is the only important one for us both at this moment. Speak quite freely to me, and depend on me thoroughly.

Yours ever,

F. Liszt

Address care of Erard, 18, Great Marlborough Street.

Need I again assure you that any question will not be a question between us?

28. To Franz von Schober

Stonehenge, Salisbury, August 29th, 1840

It is with an unspeakable feeling of sadness

and vexation that I write to you today, my dear good friend! Your letter had done me so much good; I was so happy at the thought of our meeting at the end of the autumn at latest; I wanted so to feel that I could rest on your arm, and that your heart, so full of kindness and brotherly help, was near me,—and, lo and behold! I am obliged to give it up, or at least to put it off...

An unfortunate engagement which I have just renewed, and which will keep me in England till the end of January, makes it impossible for me to say to you the one word which I wish to say, "Come!"—

England is not like any other country; the expenses are enormous. I really dare not ask you to travel with me here, for it would almost ruin us. Moreover we should hardly be able to be together, for I have three or four compulsory companions, from whom it is impossible for me to separate. I hoped to have done with all that by the beginning of October, but now I have to begin again in the middle of November. If I have time to make my journey to Russia this year it will be the utmost I can do, but it is a journey that I am in a way obliged to make after the gracious invitation of Her Majesty the Empress at Ems. On the 15th of next May I return again to London, probably by the steamer coming direct from St. Petersburg.

Where shall I find you in a year—fifteen months? It is very possible that I shall come and look for you in Vienna, but then I shall assuredly not leave without taking you with me.

I have some thoughts of spending the following winter at Constantinople. I am tired of the

West; I want to breathe perfumes, to bask in the sun, to exchange the smoke of coal for the sweet smoke of the narghileh [Turkish pipe]. In short, I am pining for the East! O my morning land! O my Aborniko!—

My uncle writes that you have been very good and obliging to him. I thank you warmly.—Do you meet Castelli from time to time? When you see him beg him from me to translate the article I published in the Paris "Revue Musicale" (of August 23rd) on Paganini, and to get it put into the "Theater-Zeitung". I should be very glad also if it could be translated into Hungarian, for the Hirnok (excuse me if I make a mess of the word!), but I do not know who could do it.

A propos of Hungarian! I shall always value highly the work on my sojourn in Pest. Send it me as soon as you possibly can, and address it to Madame la Comtesse d'Agoult, 10, Rue Neuve des Mathurins, Paris. Most affectionate remembrances to Kriehuber. His two portraits of me have been copied in London. They are without doubt the best.

Adieu, my dear excellent Schober. In my next letter I shall ask you about a matter of some consequence. It is about a Cantata for Beethoven, which I should like to set to music and to have it given at the great Festival which we expect to organize in 1842 for the inauguration of the Statue at Bonn.

Yours ever most affectionately,

F. Liszt

29. To Buloz

[Published in Ramann's "Franz Liszt," vol. ii., I.]

Editor of the Revue des Deux Mondes.

Sir,

In your Revue Musicale for October last my name was mixed up with the outrageous pretensions and exaggerated success of some executant artists; I take the liberty to address a few remarks to you on this subject. [The enthusiastic demonstrations which had been made to him in Hungary, his native land, had been put into a category with the homage paid to singers and dancers, and the bestowal of the sabre had been turned into special ridicule. Liszt repelled this with justifiable pride.]

The wreaths thrown at the feet of Mesdemoiselles Elssler and Pixis by the amateurs of New York and Palermo are striking manifestations of the enthusiasm of a public; the sabre which was given to me at Pest is a reward given by a NATION in an entirely national form. In Hungary, sir, in that country of antique and chivalrous manners, the sabre has a patriotic signification. It is the special token of manhood; it is the weapon of every man who has a right to carry a weapon. When six of the chief men of note in my country presented me with it among the general acclamations of my compatriots, whilst at the same moment the towns of Pest and Oedenburg conferred upon me the freedom of the city, and the civic authorities of Pest asked His Majesty for letters of nobility for me, it was an act to acknowledge me afresh as a Hungarian, after an absence of fifteen years; it was a reward of some slight services rendered to Art in my country; it was especially, and so I felt it, to unite me gloriously to her by imposing on me serious duties, and obligations for life as man and as artist.

I agree with you, sir, that it was, without doubt, going far beyond my deserts up to the present time. Therefore I saw in that solemnity the expression of a hope far more than of a satisfaction. Hungary hailed in me the man from whom she expects artistic illustriousness, after all the illustrious soldiers and politicians she has so plentifully produced. As a child I received from my country precious tokens of interest, and the means of going abroad to develop my artistic vocation. When grown up, and after long years, the young man returns to bring her the fruits of his work and the future of his will, the enthusiasm of the hearts which open to receive him and the expression of a national joy must not be confounded with the frantic demonstrations of an audience of amateurs.

In placing these two things side by side it seems tome there is something which must wound a just national pride and sympathies by which I am honored.

Be so kind as to insert these few lines in your next issue, and believe me, sir,

Yours obediently,

Franz Liszt

Hamburg, October 26th, 1840

30. To Franz von Schober

I will write German to you, dear Schober, in order to tell you all the quicker how much your letter pleased me. I have to thank it for a really happy hour; and that comes so rarely in my intolerable, monotonous life! For a fortnight past I have again put my neck into the English yoke. Every day which

God gives—a concert, with a journey, previously, of thirty to fifty miles. And so it must continue at least till the end of January. What do you say to that?—

If I am not more than half-dead, I must still go at the end of February to Berlin and Petersburg,— and come back to London by the first steamer at the beginning of May. Then I think I shall take a rest. Where and how I do not yet know, and it depends entirely upon the Pecuniary results of my journeys. I should like to go to Switzerland, and thence to Venice, but I can't yet say anything definite.

.—. I have today written a long letter to Leo Festetics. I am hungering and thirsting to go back to Hungary. Every recollection of it has taken deep root in my soul…And yet I cannot go back!

I am grieved that you can tell me nothing better of Lannoy. I cannot understand how that is possible. The news of the Queen has given me great pleasure—if you hear anything more about her let me know. I have a kind of weakness for her.

About the Cantata I will write to you fully later.

Farewell, and be happy if possible, dear Schober; write again soon, and remain ever my friend.

F. L.

Excuse the spelling and writing of these lines! You know that I never write German; Tobias [Tobias Haslinger, the Vienna music publisher.] is, I think, the only one who gets German letters from me.

Manchester, December 5th, 1840

31. To Breitkopf and Hartel

London, May 7th, 1841

Schlesinger has just told me that Mendelssohn's Melodies which I sent you from London have come out. I can't tell you, my dear Mr. Hartel, how much I am put out by this precipitate publication. Independently of the material wrong it does me (for before sending them to you these Melodies were sold in London and Paris), I am thus unable to keep my word to Beale and Richault, who expected to publish them simultaneously with you.

The evil being irremediable I have only thought how to get a prompt vengeance out of it. You will tell me later on if you think it was really a Christian vengeance.

The matter is this: I have just added a tremendous cadenza, three pages long, in small notes, and anentire Coda, almost as long, to Beethoven's "Adelaide". I played it all without being hissed at the concert given at the Paris Conservatoire for the Beethoven Monument, and I intend to play it in London, and in Germany and Russia. Schlesinger has printed all this medley, such as it is. Will you do the same? In that case, as I care chiefly for your edition, I will beg you to have the last Coda printed in small notes as an Ossia, without taking away anything from the present edition, so that the purists can play the integral text only, if the commentary is displeasing to them.

It was certainly a very delicate matter to touch "Adelaide", and yet it seemed to me necessary to venture. Have I done it with propriety and taste?

Competent judges will decide.

In any case I beg you not to let any one but Mr. Schumann look over your edition.

In conclusion allow me to remind you that I was rather badly paid for "Adelaide" formerly, and if you should think proper to send me a draft on a London bank, fair towards you and myself, I shall always receive it with a "new pleasure"—to quote the favorite words of His Majesty the King of the French.

With kind regards, believe me, my dear sir, yours most sincerely,

F. Liszt

Be so kind as to remember me very affectionately to Mendelssohn.

As for Schumann, I shall write to him direct very shortly.

32. To Simon Lowy In Vienna

[Autograph in the possession of Madame Emilie Dore in Vienna.]

London, May 20th, 1841

I am still writing to you from England, my dear friend. Since my last letter (end of December, I think) I have completed my tour of the three kingdoms (by which I lose, by the way, 1000 pounds sterling net, on 1500 pounds which my engagement brought me!), have ploughed my way through Belgium, with which I have every reason to be satisfied, and have sauntered about in Paris for six weeks. This latter, I don't hide it from you, has been a real satisfaction to my self-love. On arriving there I compared myself (pretty reasonably, it seems to me) to a man playing ecarte for the fifth point. Well, I have had king and vole,—seven points rather than five! [The "fifth" is the highest in this game, so Liszt means that he won.]

My two concerts alone, and especially the third, at the Conservatoire, for the Beethoven Monument, are concerts out of the ordinary run, such as I only can give in Europe at the present moment.

The accounts in the papers can only have given you a very incomplete idea. Without self-conceit or any illusion, I think I may say that never has so striking an effect, so complete and so irresistible, been produced by an instrumentalist in Paris.

A propos of newspapers, I am sending you, following this, the article which Fetis (formerly my most redoubtable antagonist) has just published in the "Gazette Musicale". It is written very cleverly, and summarises the question well. If Fischhof [A musician, a Professor at the Vienna Conservatorium.] translated it for Bauerle [Editor of the Theater-Zeitung (Theatrical Times).] it would make a good effect, I fancy. However, do what you like with it.

I shall certainly be on the Rhine towards the end of July, and shall remain in that neighborhood till September. If Fischhof came there I should be delighted to see him and have a talk with him. Till then give him my most affectionate compliments, and tell him to write me a few lines before he starts.

In November I shall start for Berlin, and shall pass the whole of next winter in Russia.

Haslinger's behaviour to me is more than inexcusable. The dear man is doing a stupidity of which he will repent soon. Never mind; I will not forget how devoted he was to me during my first stay in Vienna.

Would you believe that he has not sent me a word in reply to four consecutive letters I have written to him? If you pass by Graben will you be so kind as to tell him that I shall not write to him any more, but that I expect from him, as an honest man of business, if not as a friend, a line to tell me the fate of two manuscripts ("Hongroises," and "Canzone Veneziane") which I sent him.

I have just discovered a new mine of "Fantaisies"—and I am working it hard. "Norma," "Don Juan," "Sonnambula," "Maometto," and "Moise" heaped one on the top of the other, and "Freischutz" and "Robert le Diable" are pieces of 96, and even of 200, like the old canons of the Republic of Geneva, I think. When I have positively finished my European tour I shall come and play them to you in Vienna, and however tired they may be there of having applauded me so much, I still feel the power to move this public, so intelligent and so thoroughly appreciative,—a public which I have always considered as the born judge of a pianist.

Adieu, my dear Lowy—write soon, and address, till June 15th, at 18, Great Marlborough Street, and after that Paris.

Yours most sincerely,

F. Liszt

Is the Ungher [Caroline Ungher, afterwards Ungher-Sabatier, a celebrated singer.] at Vienna?

Will you kindly give or send to her the letter which follows?

Have you, yes or no, sent off the two amber pieces which I gave you at the time of my departure? I have been to fetch them from the Embassy, but they were not there. Let me have two words in reply about this.

33. To Franz von Schober

Truly, dear friend, I should like pages, days, years, to answer your dear letter. Seldom has anything touched me so deeply. Take heart for heart, and soul for soul,—and let us be for ever friends.

You know how I am daily getting more concise; therefore nothing further about myself, nothing further about Berlin. Tomorrow, Thursday, at 2 o'clock, I start for Petersburg.

I have spoken to A. It is impossible on both sides. When we meet and you are perfectly calm, we will go into details. I still hope to meet you next autumn, either in Florence or on the Rhine.

Leo [Count Festetics] has written to me again. Write to me at once to Konigsberg, to tell me where to address my next letter to you. But write directly-simply your address.

I have sent all the proofs of your pamphlet to Brockhaus. Be so good as to give him direct your final orders in regard to this publication. I shall be so pleased to have some copies of it while I am in Petersburg. The subject is very congenial to me; I thank you once more most warmly for it.

One more shake of the hand in Germany, dearest friend, and in heartfelt love yours ever,

F. Liszt

Remember me kindly to Sabatier, [The husband of Caroline Ungher, the celebrated singer previously mentioned.] and don't quarrel with him about me. To Caroline always the same friendship and devotion.

Berlin, March 3rd, 1842.

34. To the faculty of philosophy at the university of Konigsberg.

[Printed in L. Ramann's "Franz Liszt," vol. ii., I.]

Much Esteemed and Learned Gentlemen,

It is in vain for me to attempt to express to you the deep and heartfelt emotion you have aroused in me by your rare mark of honor. The dignity of Doctor, granted by a Faculty in which, as in yours, men of European celebrity assemble, makes me happy, and would make me proud, were I not also convinced of the sense in which it is granted to me.

I repeat that, with the honorable name of Teacher of Music (and I refer to music in its grand, complete, and ancient signification), by which you, esteemed gentlemen, dignify me, I am well aware that I have undertaken the duty of unceasing learning and untiring labour.

In the constant fulfillment of this duty-to maintain the dignity of Doctor in a right and worthy manner, by propagating in word and deed the little portion of knowledge and technical skill which I can call my own, as a form of, and a means to, the True ["The beautiful is the glory of the true, Art is the radiancy of thought." (Author's note.)] and the Divine—

In the constant fulfillment of this duty, and in

any results which are granted to me, the remembrance of your good wishes, and of the touching manner in which a distinguished member of your Faculty [Professors Rosenkranz and Jacobi invested Liszt with the Doctor's Diploma.] has informed me of them, will be a living support to me.

Accept, gentlemen, the expression of my highest esteem and respect.

F. Liszt

Mittau, March 18th, 1842

35. To Court-Marshal Freiherr von Spiegel at Weimar

[Given by L. Ramann, "Franz Liszt," vol. ii., 1.]

Monsieur le Baron,

It is very difficult to reply to so gracefully flattering a letter as your Excellency has been good enough to write to me.

I must nevertheless say that I wish with all my heart and in all ways that I could answer it. I shall reach Weimar, bag and baggage, towards the middle of October, and if I succeed in communicating to others a little of the satisfaction I cannot fail to find there, thanks to the gracious kindness of their Highnesses and the friendly readiness of your Excellency, I shall be only too glad.

Meanwhile I beg to remain, Monsieur le Baron, with respectful compliments,

Yours obediently,

Cologne; September 12th, 1862. F. Liszt

36. To Carl Filitsch.

[Autograph in the possession of Count Albert Amadei in Vienna.— Addressed to the talented young pianist, born at Hermannstadt in the Siebenburgen in 1830, died at Venice 1845, studied with Chopin and Liszt in Paris in 1842-43, and created a sensation with his concerts both there and in London, Vienna, and Italy. According to Lenz, Liszt said of him, "When the youngster goes travelling I shall shut up shop!"]

Compiegne, Wednesday Morning [1842 or 1843].

Dearly beloved conjurer,

How sorry I am to disappoint [Literally. "to make a false skip," a play-of-words with the next sentence.] you of our usual lesson tomorrow! Your "false skips" would be a great deal pleasanter to me! but, unless we could manage to put you where we could hear you from the towers of Notre Dame to the Cathedral of Cologne, there is a material impossibility in continuing our sort of lessons, considering that by tomorrow evening I shall already be at Cologne.

If I return, or when I return—I really don't know. Whatever happens, keep a little corner of remembrance of me, and believe me ever yours affectionately,

F. Liszt

Affectionate remembrances to your brother Joseph. Farewell again.

I embrace you affectionately.

37. To Franz von Schober in Paris

Berlin, March 4th, 1844

You are a dear, faithful friend, and I thank you with all my heart for your kind letter. God reward you for your love to such a jaded, worn-out creature as I am! I can only assure you that I feel it deeply and gratefully, and that your words soothe many spasmodic annoyances.

At the end of this month we shall certainly see each other in Paris. Villers [Alexander von Villers, a friend of Liszt's, attache of the Saxon Embassy in Vienna.] is coming also. In case Seydlitz is still there make my excuses to him, and tell him that, owing to my delay at Dresden, I only got his letter yesterday. I will answer him immediately, and will address to Lefebre, as he tells me to do. I have had several conferences with the H[ereditary] G[rand] D[uke] and Eckermann. [The editor of Goethe's "Gesprachen"] Our business seems to me to stand on a firm footing. Next autumn the knots will be ready to tie. [Refers probably to Schober's subsequent appointment at Weimar.]

My room is too full. I have got a tremendous fit of Byron on. Be indulgent and kind as ever!

Remember me to the Sabatiers, and stick to me! Yours most affectionately,

F. Liszt

38. To Franz Kroll

[Pupil and friend of Liszt's (1820-1877); since 1849 settled in Berlin as a pianoforte teacher; rendered great service by his edition of Bach's "Das wohltemperirte Clavier."]

My dear good Kroll,

What a first-rate man you are to me, and what pleasure your letter has given me! Probably you already know that I also have been figuring as an invalid these last five weeks.—God be thanked and praised that I am already pretty fairly on my legs again, without rheumatism in the joints or gout! In a few days I shall begin my provincial tour (Lyons, Marseilles, Toulouse, Bordeaux), and then towards the end of August by steamer to Stockholm and Copenhagen. Weymar, our good, dear Weymar, will again be our Christmas Day! Oh what beautiful apples and trifles we will hang on our Christmas tree! and what talks and compositions, and projects and plans! Only don't you disappoint me, and mind you come fresh and well. Leave the bad looks to me, and see that you fill out your cheeks properly. This winter we must be industrious, and struggle through much work.

Your Mazurkas are most excellent and talented. You have put a great deal into them—and, if you will allow me to speak quite freely—perhaps too much into them, for much of it halts. Although the dedication to me is both pleasing and gratifying, I cannot help thinking that it would be to your interest not to publish anything before next spring. Take advantage of being as yet unknown, and give to the public from the beginning a proper opinion of your talent by a collective publication. Write a couple of pleasing, brilliant Studies—perhaps also a Notturno (or something of that sort), and an effective Fantasia on some conspicuous theme. Then let Schlesinger, Hartel, or Mechetti (to whom I will most gladly speak about your works beforehand) publish the six pieces—your Concerto and the C major Study, together with the later pieces—all together, so that publisher, critic, artist, and public all have to do with them at the same time. Instead of dishing up one little sweetmeat for the people, give them a proper dinner. I am very sorry I did not follow this plan myself; for, after much experience, I consider it far the best, especially for pianoforte works. In Weymar we will talk more fully and definitely about this. Conradi [Musician and friend in Berlin] is also to come. I don't require the Huguenot Fantasia at present. He will have time enough for it in Weymar. En attendant, [A German letter, so Liszt's own French expression is kept] Schlesinger will give him a modest payment for the work he has begun. Please kindly see about the enclosed letters for Freund as soon as possible.

With all good wishes, I am, dear Kroll,

Yours most sincerely,

F. Liszt

Port Marly, June 11th, 1844

39. To Freund

[Autograph in the possession of Professor Hermann Scholtz in
Dresden.]

I am shockingly behindhand with you, my dear Freund, but I won't make any excuses, although an illness of more than a month comes rather a propos to justify me fully and even more.

Herewith letters and cards for Baron Lannoy (Haslinger will give you the address), for Prince Fritz Schwarzenberg, and for Doctor Uwe, Kriehuber, and Simon Lowy, who will soon be back in Vienna. I shall be glad if you will give them in any case, whether now or later. If you want to give me a pleasure you will go and see my uncle Eduard

Liszt, and try to distract him a little.

I detest repeating myself in letters so much that I can't write over again to you my plans of travel up to the beginning of winter; these I have just told Kroll in full, and you already know them from Hanover.

Teleky, Bethlen (Friends of Liszt's), and Corracioni are here, and form a kind of colony which I call the Tribe of the Huns!

Probably Teleky will come and pick me up at Weymar towards the middle of February, and we shall go together to Vienna and Pest— not forgetting Temesvar, Debreczin, and Klausenburg!

I hope then to find you in Vienna, and shall perhaps be able to give you a good lift.

Meanwhile acknowledge the receipt of these lines: enjoy yourself, and remain to me always friend Freund. [A play on his name Freund, which means friend.]

Yours most sincerely and affectionately,

F. Liszt

Port Marly, June 11th, 1844.

40. To Franz Von Schober.

Gibraltar, March 3rd, 1845.

Your letter pleases me like a child, my dear good Schober! Everything comes to him who can wait. But I scarcely can wait to congratulate you and to see you again in Weymar [as Councillor of Legation there]. Unhappily it is not probable that I can get there before the end of next autumn. Keep me in your good books, therefore, until then, and accept my best thanks in advance for all you will have done for me and fought for me till then, both in

Weymar and in Hungary!

With regard to Vienna, Lowy writes me almost exactly the same as you. To tell the truth I am extremely thankful to the Vienna public, for it was they who, in a critically apathetic moment, roused and raised me [When he came from Venice to Vienna in the spring of 1838, to give a concert for the benefit of his Hungarian compatriots after the inundations, on which occasion, although Thalberg, Clara Wieck, and Henselt had been there before him, he aroused the utmost enthusiasm.]; but still I don't feel the slightest obligation to return there a year sooner or later. My Vienna journey will pretty much mark the end of my virtuoso career. I hope to go thence (in the month of August, 1846) to Constantinople, and on my return to Italy to pass my dramatic Rubicon or Fiasco.

So much for my settled plans.

What precisely is going to become of me this coming spring and summer I do not exactly know. In any case to Paris I will not go. You know why. My incredibly wretched connection with _____ has perhaps indirectly contributed more than anything to my Spanish- Portuguese tour. I have no reason to regret having come, although my best friends tried to dissuade me from it. Sometimes it seems to me that my thoughts ripen and that my troubles grow prematurely old under the bright and penetrating sun of Spain…

Many kind messages to Eckermann and Wolff. [Professor Wolff, editor of "Der poetische Hausschatz."] I will write to the latter from the Rhine, where I shall at any rate spend a month this summer (perhaps with my mother and Cosima). If he is still inclined to return to his and your countries (Denmark and Sweden), we can make a nice little trip there as a holiday treat.

Good-bye, my dear excellent friend. Allow me to give you as true a love as I feel is a necessity of my heart! Ever yours,

F. Liszt

What is Villers doing? If you see him tell him to write me a line to Marseilles, care of M. Boisselot, Pianoforte Maker.

41. To Franz Kroll at Glogau

Weymar, March 26th, 1845

My very dear Kroll,

The arrival of your letter and the packet which accompanied it decided a matter of warm contest between our friend Lupus [Presumably Liszt's friend, Professor Wolff (1791-1851).] and Farfa-Magne-quint-quatorze! [For whom this name was intended is not clear.] It consisted in making the latter see the difference between the two German verbs "verwundern" (to amaze) and "bewundern" (to admire), and to translate clearly, according to her wits, which are sometimes so ingeniously refractory, what progress there is from Verwundern (amazement) to Erstaunen (astonishment). Imagine, now, with what a wonderful solution of the difficulty your packet and letter furnished us, and how pleased I was at the following demonstration:—

"We must admire (bewundern) Kroll's fine feeling of friendship; we may be amazed (verwundern) at the proof he has given of his industry in copying out the Mass; should this

78

industry continue we shall first of all be astonished (erstaunen), and by degrees, through the results he will bring about, we again attain to admiration (Bewunderung)."

I don't know how you will judge, critically, of this example, but what is certain is that it appeared to be quite conclusive to our auditory.

Ernst [The celebrated violinist (1814-65)] has just been spending a week here, during which he has played some hundred rubbers of whist at the "Erbprinz." His is a noble, sweet, and delicate nature, and more than once during his stay I have caught myself regretting you for him, and regretting him for you. Last Monday he was good enough to play, in his usual and admirable manner, at the concert for the Orchestral Pension Fund. The pieces he had selected were his new "Concerto pathetique" (in F~ minor) and an extremely piquant and brilliant "Caprice on Hungarian Melodies." (This latter piece is dedicated to me.) The public was in a good humor, even really warm, which is usually one of its least faults.

Milde, who is, as you know, not much of a talker, has nevertheless the tact to say the right thing sometimes. Thus, when we went to see Ernst off at the railway, he expressed the feeling of us all —"What a pity that Kroll is not here!"

For the most part you have left here the impression which you will leave in every country— that of a man of heart, talent, tact, and intellect. One of these qualities alone is enough to distinguish a man from the vulgar herd; but when one is so well born as to possess a quartet of them it is absolutely necessary that the will, and an active will, should be added to them in order to make them bring out their best fruits,—and this I am sure you will not be slow to do.

Your brother came through here the day before yesterday, thinking he should still find you here. I have given him your address, and told him to inquire about you at Schlesinger's in Berlin, where he expects to be on the 8th of April; so do not fail to let Schlesinger know, in one way or another, when you get to Berlin. As M. de Zigesar [The Intendant at Weimar.] I was obliged to start in a great hurry for The Hague, in the suite of the Hereditary Grand Duchess, I will wait till his return to send you the letters for Mr. de Witzleben. I will address them to Schlesinger early in April.

We are studying hard at the Duke of Coburg's opera "Toni, oder die Vergellung," ["Toni, or the Requital"] which we shall give next Saturday. The score really contains some pretty things and which make a pleasing effect; unluckily I cannot say as much for the libretto.

Your castle in the air for May we will build up on a solid basis in Weymar; for I am quite calculating on seeing you then, together with our charming, good, worthy friend Conradi. Will you please, dear Kroll, tell Mr. Germershausen and his family how gratified I am with their kind remembrance? When I go to Sagan I shall certainly give myself the pleasure of calling on him.

Believe me ever your very sincere and affectionate friend,

F. Liszt

42. To Abbe de Lamennais

[Autograph in the possession of M. Alfred Bovet at Valentigney.]

Permit me, illustrious and venerable friend, to recall myself to your remembrance through M. Ciabatta, who has already had the honor of being introduced to you last year at my house. He has just been making a tour in Spain and Portugal with me, and can give you all particulars about it. I should have been glad also to get him to take back to you the score, now completed, of the chorus which you were so good as to entrust to me ("The iron is hard, let us strike!"), but unfortunately it is not with music as with painting and poetry: body and soul alone are not enough to make it comprehensible; it has to be performed, and very well performed too, to be understood and felt. Now the performance of a chorus of the size of that is not an easy matter in Paris, and I would not even risk it without myself conducting the preliminary rehearsals. While waiting till a favorable opportunity offers, allow me to tell you that I have been happy to do this work, and that I trust I have not altogether failed in it. Were it not for the fear of appearing to you very indiscreet, I should perhaps venture to trespass on your kindness for the complete series of these simple, and at the same time sublime, compositions, of which you alone know the secret. Three other choruses of the same kind as that of the Blacksmiths, which should sum up the most poetical methods of human activity, and which should be called (unless you advise otherwise) Labourers, Sailors, and Soldiers, would form a lyric epic of which the genius of Rossini or

Meyerbeer would be proud. I know I have no right to make any such claim, but your kindness to me has always been so great that I have a faint hope of obtaining this new and glorious favor. If, however, this work would give you even an hour's trouble, please consider my request as not having been made, and pardon me for the regret which I shall feel at this beautiful idea being unrealized.

As business matters do not necessarily call me to Paris, I prefer not to return there just now. I expect to go to Bonn in the month of July, for the inauguration of the Beethoven Monument, and to have a Cantata performed there which I have written for this occasion. The text, at any rate, is tolerably new; it is a sort of Magnificat of human Genius conquered by God in the eternal revelation through time and space,—a text which might apply equally well to Goethe or Raphael or Columbus, as to Beethoven. At the beginning of winter I shall resume my duties at the Court of Weymar, to which I attach more and more a serious importance.

If you were to be so very good as to write me a few lines, I should be most happy and grateful. If you would send them either to my mother's address, Rue Louis le Grand, 20; or to that of my secretary, Mr. Belloni, Rue Neuve St. George, No. 5, I should always get them in a very short time.

I have the honor to be, sir, yours very gratefully,

F. Liszt

Marseilles, April 28th, 1845

43. To Frederic Chopin

[Autograph in the possession of M. Alfred

Bovet at Valentigney.— The great Polish tone-poet (1809-49) was most intimate with Liszt in Paris. The latter, in his work "F. Chopin" 1851, second edition 1879, Breitkopf and Hartel; German translation by La Mara, 1880), raised an imperishable monument to him.]

Dear Chopin,

M. Benacci, a member of the Maison Troupenas, and in my opinion the most intelligent editor, and the most liberal in business matters, in France, asks me for a letter of introduction to you. I give it all the more willingly, as I am convinced that under all circumstances you will have every reason to be satisfied with his activity and with whatever he does. Mendelssohn, whom he met in Switzerland two years ago, has made him his exclusive editor for France, and I, for my part, am just going to do the same. It would be a real satisfaction to me if you would entrust some of your manuscripts to him, and if these lines should help in making you do so I know he will be grateful to me.

Yours ever, in true and lively friendship,
F. Liszt
Lyons, May 21st, 1845
44. To George Sand.

[Autograph in the possession of M. Alfred Bovet at Valentigney.— A friendship of long years subsisted between Liszt and France's greatest female writer, George Sand. At her home of Nohant he was a frequent guest, together with the Comtesse d'Agoult. Three letters which he wrote (in 1835 and 1837) for the Gazette Musicale—clever talks about Art, Nature, Religion, Freedom, etc.—bear George

Sand's address.]

Without wishing to add to your other inevitable troubles that of a correspondence for which you care little, allow me, dear George, to claim for myself your old indulgence for people who write to you without requiring an answer, and let me recall myself to you by these few lines through M. Benacci. Their ostensible object is to recommend the above-mentioned Benacci, so that you, in your turn, may recommend him more particularly to Chopin (and I may add in parenthesis that I should abstain from this negotiation were I not firmly persuaded that Chopin will never regret entering into business relations with Benacci, who, in his capacity of member of the firm of Troupenas, is one of the most important and most intelligent men of his kind); but the real fact of the matter is that I am writing to you above all— and why should I not confess it openly? —for the pleasure of conversing with you for a few moments. Therefore don't expect anything interesting from me, and if my handwriting bothers you, throw my letter into the fire without going any further.

Do you know with whom I have just had endless conversations about you, in sight of Lisbon and Gibraltar? With that kind, excellent, and original Blavoyer, the Ahasuerus of commerce, whom I had already met several times without recognising him, until at last I remembered our dinners at the "Ecu" (Crown) at Geneva, and the famous Pipe!

During the month's voyage from Lisbon to Barcelona we emptied I cannot tell you how many bottles of sherry in your honor and glory; and one fine evening he confided to me in so simple and charming a manner his vexation at being unable to find several letters that you had written to him in Russia, I think, and which have been stolen from him, that I took a liking to him, and he did the same to me. The fact is that there could not possibly be two Blavoyers under the sun, and his own person is the only pattern of which he cannot furnish goods wholesale, for there is no sort of thing that he does not supply to all parts of the globe.

A propos of Lisbon and supplies, have you a taste for camellias? It would be a great pleasure to me to send you a small cargo of them from Oporto, but I did not venture to do it without knowing, in case you might perhaps have a decided antipathy to them.

In spite of the disinterestedness with which I began this letter, I come round, almost without knowing how, to beg you to write to me. Don't do more than you like; but in any case forgive me for growing old and arriving at the point when noble recollections grow in proportion as the narrowing meannesses of daily life find their true level. Yes, even if you thought me more of a fool than formerly, it would be impossible for me to hold your friendship cheap, or not to prize highly the fact that, somehow or other, it has not come to be at variance nor entirely at an end.

As the exigencies of my profession will not allow me leisure to return so soon to Paris, I shall probably not have the opportunity of seeing you for two years. Towards the middle of July I go to Bonn for the inauguration of the Beethoven Monument.

Were it not that a journey to the Rhine is so commonplace, I should beg you to let me do the honors of the left and of the right bank to you, as well as to Chopin (a little less badly than I was able to do the honors of Geneva!). My mother and my children are to join me at Cologne in five or six weeks, but I cannot hope for such good luck as that we might meet in those parts, although after your winters of work and fatigue a journey of this kind would be a refreshing distraction for you both.

At the close of the autumn I shall resume my duties at Weymar; later on I shall go to Vienna and Hungary, and proceed thence to Italy by way of Constantinople, Athens, and Malta.

If, therefore, one of these fine days you should happen to be in the humor, send me a word in reply about the camellias; if you will send your letter to my mother (20, Rue Louis le Grand) I shall get it immediately. In every way, count upon my profound friendship and most respectful devotion always and everywhere.

Lyons, May 21st, 1845

F. Liszt

45. T Abbe De Lamennais

[Autograph in the possession of M. Alfred Bovet at Valentigney.]

Oh no, there is not, and there never could be, any indiscretion from you towards me. Believe me that I do not deceive myself as to the motive which determined you to write to me with such great kindness, and if it happened that I replied too sanguinely and at too great length I beg you to excuse me. Above all do not punish me by withdrawing from me the smallest particle of your sacred friendship.

M. de Lamartine, with whom I have been spending two or three days at Montceau, told me that you had read to him "Les Forgerons," so I played him the music. Permit me still to hope that some day you may be willing to complete the series, and that I, on my side, may not be unworthy of this task.

Yours most heartily,

Dijon, June 1st, 1845

F. Liszt

46. To Gaetano Belloni in Paris

[Autograph in the possession of M. Etienne Charavay in Paris.—
Addressed to Liszt's valued secretary during his concert tours in
Europe from 1841-1847.]

Dear and Most Excellent Belloni,

Everything is moving on, and shall not stop either. Bonn is in a flutter since I arrived and I shall easily put an end to the paltry, under-hand opposition which had been formed against me. By the time you arrive I shall have well and duly conquered my true position.

[This refers to the Festival in Bonn, of several days' duration, for the unveiling of the Beethoven Monument (by Hahnel), in which Liszt, the generous joint-founder of the monument, took part as pianist, composer, and conductor.]

Will you please add to the list of your commissions:

The cross of Charles III.

and the cross of Christ of Portugal, large size? You know it is worn on the neck.

Don't lose time and don't be too long in coming.

Yours ever,

F. Liszt

July 23rd, 1845.

Kindest regards to Madame Belloni.—I enclose a few lines for

Benacci, which you will kindly give him.

47. To Madame Rondonneau at Sedan

[Autograph in the possession of M. Etienne Charavay in Paris.]

In spite of rain, snow, hail, and frost, here I am at last, having reached the hotel of the Roman Emperor at Frankfort after forty-eight hours' travelling, and I take the first opportunity of telling you anew, though not for the last time, how much I feel the charming and affectionate reception which you have given me during my too short, and, unhappily for me, too unfortunate stay at Sedan. Will you, dear Madame, be so kind as to be my mouthpiece and special pleader to Madame Dumaitre, who has been so uncommonly kind and cordial to me? Assuredly I could not confide my cause (bad as it may be) to more delicate hands and to a more persuasive eloquence, if eloquence only consists in reality of "the art of saying the right thing, the whole of the right thing, and nothing but the right thing," as La Rochefoucauld defined it; a definition from which General Foy drew a grand burst of eloquence—"The Charter, the whole Charter (excepting, however, Article 14 and other peccadilloes!), and nothing but the Charter."

"But don't let us talk politics any longer," as Lablache so happily remarked to Giulia Grisi, who took it into her head one fine day to criticize Don Juan!

Let us talk once more of Sedan, and let me again say to you how happy I should be to be able one day to show those whose acquaintance I have made through you in what grateful remembrance I keep it.

Will you, Madame, give my best and most affectionate thanks to M.
 Rondonneau, and accept my very respectful and devoted homage?

F. Liszt

Frankfurt, February 11th, 1846

P.S.—Being pressed for time, and owing, perhaps, to a stupid feeling of delicacy, I came away without paying my doctor.

If you think well, would you be so kind as to credit me with a napoleon and give it him from me: Madame Kreutzer will be my banker in Paris. Adieu till we meet again.

48. To Monsieur Grillparzer

[Original, without date, in the possession of the Baroness Mayrhofer-Grunbuhel at Klagenfurt. It might belong to the year 1846, during which Liszt arranged ten concerts in Vienna, from March 1st to May 17th, and lived there during a great part of the summer. From the same year dates a poem of homage to the incomparable magician of the piano from the great poet. This slight and unimportant letter is the only one of Liszt's found among Grillparzer's effects.]

Will you do me the favor, my dear sir, to come and dine, without ceremony, with several of your friends and admirers on Friday next at 3 o'clock (at the "Stadt Frankfurt")? I should be very much gratified at this kindness on your part. M. Bauernfeld leads me to hope that you will not refuse me. Permit me to think that he is not mistaken, and allow me to express once more my high esteem and admiration.

F. Liszt

Tuesday Morning. [1846?]

49. To Franz von Schober, Coucillor of Legation in Weimar

Prague, April 11th, 1846. [According to the postal stamp.]

Dear Friend,

Your commissions have been attended to. The Wartburg has been sent through Bauernfeld to the Allgemeine, and will, I trust, not have to warten [Wait; a play on the words Wartburg and warten. A treatise on the proposed completion of the Wartburg.] too long. I have sent a second copy of this article to Paris, where it is to appear in French garb. The report figures already in the Vienna Theater-Zeitung, a paper with a wide circulation (and none the better on that account!), where it makes quite a good appearance.

You would get the best connection with Frankfort through O. L. B.

Wolff (and through his medium, which is at any rate an honest and proper one, with the German Frankfurtes Journal, or the

Oberpostamts-Zeitung, and even with the Didaskalia).

Talk this over with Wolff!

The same with the "illustrated" Leipzig Journal, in which the article on the Wartburg should appear as soon as possible with an illustration. Wolff can also arrange that, and in case it were necessary, why, in Heaven's name, the sketch can be paid for. The State of Weimar will not be ruined by it. Pereat Philistia and its powerless foolery!!!

You have only to write a line to Brockhaus, and the columns of the Deutsche Allgemeine stand open to you. Your personal and official position in Weimar entitle you to this. Later on, in passing through Leipzig, you can very easily consolidate this connection. My stay in Hungary (Pest) will probably be limited to the first half of May. I shall in any case see Schwab. "Sardanapalus" [An opera planned by Liszt] (Italian) will most probably be produced next season (May) in Vienna.

My stay in Weimar this summer...?? [The continuation of the letter is missing.]

50. To Franz von Schober, Councillor of Legation in Weimar

Castle Gratz (at Prince Lichnowsky's)
May 28th, 1846

You are curious people at Weimar. You stride on towards a possibility, and as soon as the thing is well in train you take fright at it! However that may be, here are the instructions I have received from

Paris, and if you still wish an article on the Wartburg to appear in a French paper you must conform to them, and therefore send to my mother's address (20, Rue Louis le Grand) the indispensable little notice.

The note from my Paris correspondent is as follows:—

"The article in its present form would not be suitable for publication in any French paper; it will be necessary to write another, explaining in a few words in what and how the Wartburg is historically interesting to Europe, and why Europe ought to interest herself in its restoration; then make a short architectural description of the castle; but above all do not forget that the article is to be read by Frenchmen, careless of what is happening in Germany, and utterly ignorant of German history and legend."

I continue:—

1st.—A short account, historical and legendary, of the Wartburg.

2nd.—How it has been allowed to fall into ruins.

3rd.—How it is to be restored.

Finally, plenty of facts and proper names, as M. de Talleyrand so well said. Agreed then! As soon as you have got this sketched out on the lines above mentioned (it will serve also for the illustrated), send it to my mother by Weyland. My mother will already know through me to whom she has to give it.

There is nothing to be done with Schwab. His "Delirium" (as I call it) [It was a "Tellurium"] stood in my room for a week, and we stood there not knowing what to make of it. But never and no how could we bring that good Schwab to try to make us see any basis or proof of his calculation. My opinion is that, in order to take away the incognito from his discovery, he ought to send a sample to the Vienna Academy, and two others to the Berlin and Paris Academies, for trial and discussion. If I can help him in this matter with letters to Humboldt and Arago I will do it right gladly; but it is as plain as day that incompetent private sympathies are of no import in such a sensitive discovery, and therefore can do nothing. Meanwhile they have made a subscription of eight hundred guldens in money, and have bought the machine for the Pest Museum.

The relic with authentic verification is in the locked-up box at Wolff's. Beg the Herr Librarian (it would really make me ill if he is not appointed) to be so good as to find this relic—he will have no difficulty in recognising it—and to send it me to Haslinger's address, Graben, Vienna.

About my law-suit more anon in Weimar. Meanwhile thank my excellent advocate (does he take snuff?) warmly, and beg him to continue to keep me in his good graces.

If I know that it will be agreeable to his Grace [The former Hereditary Grand Duke and present Grand Duke of Saxony.] to see me in Weimar this summer, I shall come, in spite of the upset which this journey will occasion to me. You know how I am, heartily and personally, in his favor without any interest. I should like also to tell him many things, and for this a stay there in the summer with walks (which as a rule I can't abide, as you know) would be pleasanter and more convenient.

My stay in Pest might bear serious fruit, were it not that the Byronic element, which you combat in me, becomes ever more and more predominant.

Farewell and work hard! I cannot arrange any meeting with you. I
am not my own master. In August I mean to make a peregrination to
Oedenburg, and thence to Leo and Augusz (the latter in Szegzard).
If I come to Weimar it will be in July.

Address always to Haslinger's.

Adieu, my dear excellent Schober. Remain as good to me as you are dear!

Yours ever affectionately,

F. Liszt

Remember me most kindly to Ziegesar and Wolff.

51. To Alexander Seroff

[Russian musical critic and composer (1820-71)]

I am most grateful, my dear sir, for the kind remembrance you keep of me since Petersburg, [Seroff was at that time in the Crimea.] and I beg you to excuse me a thousand times for not having replied sooner to your most charming and interesting letter. As the musical opinions on which you are kind enough to enlarge have for long years past been completely my own, it is needless for me to discuss them today with you. There could, at most, be only one point in which we must differ perceptibly, but as that one point is my own simple individuality you will quite understand that I feel much embarrassed with my subject, and that I get out of it in the most ordinary manner, by thanking you very sincerely for the too flattering opinion that you have formed about me.

The Overture to "Coriolanus" is one of those masterpieces sui generis, on a solid foundation, without antecedent or sequel in analogous works. Does it remind you of Shakespeare's exposition of the tragedy of the same name (Act i., Scene I)? It is the only pendant to it that I know in the productions of human genius. Read it again, and compare it as you are thinking of it. You are worthy of those noble emotions of Art, by the fervent zeal with which you worship its creed. Your piano score of the Overture to Coriolanus does all honor to your artist conscience, and shows a rare and patient intelligence which is indispensable to bringing this task to a satisfactory end. If I should publish my version of the same Overture (it must be among my papers in Germany) I shall beg your permission to send you, through Prince Dolgorouki [Prince Argontinski-Dolgorouki, a devoted lover of music. A friend of Liszt's: had rich property in the Crimea.] (I can't tell you half the good I think of him), an annotated copy, which I will beg you to add to the insignificant autograph which you really estimate too highly in attaching so affectionate a price to it! Accept once more, my dear sir, my most affectionate regards.

F. Liszt

Elisabethgrad, September 14th. 1847

52. To Carl Haslinger in Vienna

[The original (without address) in the possession of M. Alfred Bovet at Valentigney.—

There is no doubt that it was written to the above music publisher (son of the well-known Tobias H.), who was a pupil of Czerny, and at the same time a pianist and composer (1816-68), and friend of Liszt]

Woronino, December 19th, 1847

My dear Karolus,

I am delighted to hear from you of the arrival of my box from Galatz. Will you be so good as to send it off speedily and safely to Weymar, so that I may find it when I arrive there (at the end of this month)? and, as I am away, address it to M. le Baron de Ziegesar, Chamberlain to H.R.H. the Hereditary Grand Duchess. Beg Lowy to take the same opportunity of sending me the other boxes belonging to me, which remaincd behind, whether with him or elsewhere, to my Weymar address, unless he prefers to bring them with him when he comes to see me.

In my last letter to my uncle I gave him a commission for you— namely, to beg you to send me the Melodies and Rhapsodies Hongroises complete; also the Schwanengesang and the Winterreise (transcriptions), large size edition, made into a book. As you have had some proofs made of my new Rhapsodies, make up a parcel of it all, which will be an agreeable surprise to me on my arrival.

I have worked pretty well these last two months, between two cigars in the morning, at several things which do not displease me; but I want to go back to Germany for some weeks in order to put myself in tune with the general tone, and to recreate myself by the sight and hearing of the wonderful things produced there by…Upon my word I don't know by whom in particular, if not the whole world in general.

If you want me to…[editor's note: impossible to decipher this word in Liszt's original letter] anything for you, tell me, and give me your ideas as to cut and taste.

Send me also the Schumann Opus (Kreisleriana, etc.) published by yourself and Mechetti, together with Bach's six Pedal Fugues, in which I wish to steep myself more fully. If the three Sonnets (both voice and pianoforte editions) are already re-corrected, kindly send me also an author's copy.

Adieu, dear Karolus. I commend my box to you, and commend myself to you also

As your sincere friend,

F. Liszt

I need not say that of course you shall be repaid immediately for sending the box—only hurry on the sending.

Best regards to your wife.

Lowy will tell you what I wish in regard to the credit for my uncle Eduard.

53. To The Hochwohlgeboren Herr Baron von Dornis, Jena.

[Autograph in the possession of Herr C. Geibel, bookseller in
Leipzig.—The addressee was a sculptor.]

The confidence which you place in me, most esteemed Herr Baron, is naturally very flattering; but in order to meet it according to your wishes, I ought to have quite other means at my disposal than those I have.

It would of course be very gratifying to me to possess one of your valued works; yet I cannot help taking this opportunity of remarking that, in view of the far too many busts, medallions, statuettes, caricatures, medals, and portraits of all kinds existing of my humble self, I long ago resolved not to give occasion to any further multiplication of them.

Accept, esteemed Herr Baron, my expressions of great regret that I cannot meet your kind proposal as you wish, and with the assurance of my highest esteem,

Believe me yours very truly,

F. Liszt

Weymar, March 6th, 1848

54. To Franz von Schober, Councillor of Legation at Weimar.

Castle Gratz, April 22nd, 1848.

My Dear and Honored Friend,

Your dear letter has brought me still nearer to you in the crisis of the estro poetico, which the "Hungaria" [One of Liszt's symphonic poems.] brought forth in me; and, thanks to this good influence, I hope you will not be dissatisfied with the composition.

Since my Beethoven Cantata I have written nothing so striking and so spontaneous. One of these next days the instrumentation will be completed, and when we have an opportunity we can have it performed in Weimar in your honor and that of "Weimar's dead." [Refers to a poem entitled "Weimar's Todten."]

Regardless of the blocking of the Russian frontier the Princess Wittgenstein has safely passed through Radziwillow and Brody with a special official outrider, and established herself at Castle Gratz four days ago with her very charming and interesting daughter. As it is still somewhat early for the German bath season, I should like to persuade her to spend a couple of weeks in Weimar before her Carlsbad "cure" (which, alas! is very necessary for her). If my wishes should be successful I shall arrive at Weimar between the 10th and 15th of May, in order to prepare a suitable house or suite of apartments for the Princess.

I should be so pleased if you had an opportunity of getting to know the P. W. She is without doubt an uncommonly and thoroughly brilliant example of soul and mind and understanding (with immense esprit as well).

It won't take you long to understand that henceforth I can dream of very little personal ambition and future wrapped up in myself. In political relations serfdom may have an end, but the dominion of one soul over another in the region of spirit, is not that indestructible?…You, my dear, honored friend, will assuredly not answer this question with a negative.

In three weeks I hope we shall see each other again. Be so good as to present my respects to our young Duke. What you tell me of him pleases me. As soon as possible you shall hear more, and more fully, from me, but do not write to me till then, as my address meanwhile will be very uncertain. But continue to love me, as I love and honor you.

F. Liszt

55. To Bernhard Cossmann in Baden-Baden

[The addressee became in 1850 solo-violoncellist and chamber virtuoso in Weimar, and, later, in Moscow, and has been, since 1878, a Professor at the Hoch Conservatorium at Frankfort-on- Maine.]

Circumstances! Conditions! My dear sir, these are now the very ceremonious expressions and excuses of theatrical and directorial beings. Unfortunately that is the case here too, although our dear Weymar continuing free, not only from the real cholera, but also from the slighter, but somewhat disagreeable, periodical political cholerina, may peacefully dream by its elm, yet…yet…I am sorry to say I am obliged not to answer your kind letter affirmatively. Should circumstances and conditions, however, turn out as I wish, then the Weymar band would consider it an honor and a pleasure to possess you, my dear sir, as soon as possible as one of its members.

Meanwhile accept the assurance of high regard of yours very sincerely,

F. Liszt

Weymar, September 18th, 1848

56. To Carl Reinecke

[The present conductor of the Gewandhaus Concerts in Leipzig (born 1824), and celebrated composer, pianist, and conductor]

Dear Sir,

Your kind letter has given me much pleasure, and the prospect which you hold out to me, of seeing you soon again at Weymar, is very agreeable to me.

But come soon, and if possible for a few days; I on my side shall certainly do all I can to prolong your stay here and make it seem short to you. The promised Concerto interests me keenly; it will be sure to give us ample material for musical talks, and perhaps after many a talk we shall set to work again and both write a new Concerto.

Would not the best results of criticism altogether be to incite to new creation?

However that may be, do not put off too long taking up your quarters at the Erbprinz, and rest assured that your visit is much desired by me.

Yours very sincerely,

F. Liszt

Weymar, March 25th, 1849

My very best thanks for the splendid stuff for the coat, which will give me quite an important, well-to-do, stately appearance!

57. To Count Sandor Teleky(?)

[The original (without address) in the possession of Count Albert Amadei in Vienna.—The recipient of this letter was presumably Count Teleky, a friend of Liszt's, who often accompanied the latter on his triumphal European journeys, and who was himself an active musician and literary man. He died in June, 1892.]

I have to give you threefold thanks, dear Count, and I feel that I can undisguisedly do so! Your verses, in addition to your prose and music, are three times welcome to me at Weymar, and the Fantaisie dedicated to the royal hours of leisure of H.R.H. has also charmed my leisure hours, as rare as they are modest.

If it would not be a trouble to you to come to Weymar, it would be most kind of you to give us the pleasure of your company for a day or two during our theatrical season, which concludes on the 15th of June. We could then chat and make music at our ease (with or without damages, ad libitum), and if the fantasy took us, why should we not go to some new Fantasie of leisure on the "Traum- lied (dream song) of Tony, [No doubt meaning Baron Augusz, Liszt's intimate friend at Szegzard, who died in 1878.] for instance, at the hour when our peaceable inhabitants are sleeping, dreaming, or thinking of nothing? We two should at least want to make a pair.

May I beg you, dear Count, to recall me most humbly to the indulgent remembrance of your charming and witty neighbor [Nachbarin, feminine.] of the Erbprinz, and accept once more my most cordial expressions for yourself?

F. Liszt

Weymar, May 5th, 1849

58. To Belloni(?)

[The letter written apparently to Belloni (who has already been mentioned) was, like the present one, published by Wilhelm Tappert, in a German translation and in an incomplete form, in the Neue Musik-Zeitung (Cologne, Tonger) of October 1st, 1881. The editor unfortunately could not obtain possession of it complete and in the original. According to Tappert, a Belgian musical paper pronounced it spurious, for reasons unknown to the former.]

Weimar, May 14th, 1849

Dear B.,

Richard Wagner, a Dresden conductor, has been here since yesterday. That is a man of wonderful genius, such a brain- splitting genius indeed as beseems this country,—a new and brilliant appearance in Art. Late events in Dresden have forced him to a decision in the carrying out of which I am firmly resolved to help him with all my might. When I have had a long talk with him, you shall hear what we have devised and what must also be thoroughly realized. In the first place we want to create a success for a grand, heroic, enchanting musical work, the score of which was completed a year ago. [Lohengrin.] Perhaps this could be done in London? Chorley, [Chorley (1808-72) had considerable influence in London as author, critic, and writer in the Athenoeum.] for instance, might be very helpful to him in this undertaking. If Wagner next winter could go to Paris backed up by this success, the doors of the Opera would stand open to him, no matter with what he might knock. It is happily not necessary for me to go into long further discussions with you; you understand, and must learn whether there is at this moment in London an English theater (for the Italian Opera would not help our friend!), and whether there is any prospect that a grand and beautiful work from a master hand could have any success there.

[It was not in London, but in Weimar, as is well known, that the first performance of "Lohengrin" took place (on August 28th, 1850). It was not until twenty-five years later that London made acquaintance with Wagner's work on the stage, in the Italian Opera and with Nicolini in the title-role; and the composer himself heard it for the first time in Vienna on May 15th, 1861.]

Let me have an answer to this as quickly as possible. Later on— that is, about the end of the month—Wagner will pass through Paris. You will see him, and he will talk with you direct about the tendency and expansion of the whole plan, and will be heartily grateful for every kindness. Write soon and help me as ever. It is a question of a noble end, toward the fulfillment of which everything must tend.

59. To Carl Reinecke

Weymar, May 30th, 1849

Thank you much, dear M. Reinecke, for your welcome lines, and I am glad to hope that you are happily arrived at Bremen, which ought to be proud to possess you. The musical taste of that town has always been held up to me, and I feel assured that the inhabitants will have the good taste to appreciate you at your full value, and that you will create a good and fine position for yourself there without many obstacles.

Wagner, who will probably be obliged to lose his post at Dresden in consequence of recent events, has been spending some days with me here. Unluckily the news of the warrant against him arrived the day of the performance of "Tannhauser", which prevented him from being present. By this time he must have arrived in Paris, where he will assuredly find a more favorable field for his dramatic genius. With the aid of success he will end, as I have often said, by being acknowledged as a great German composer in Germany, on condition that his works are first heard in Paris or London, following the example of Meyerbeer, to say nothing of Gluck, Weber, and Handel!

Wagner expressed his regret to me that he had not been able to send a better reply to the few lines of introduction which I had given you for him. If ever you should be in the same place with him do not fail to go and see him for me, and you may be sure of being well received.

I am very much obliged to you for having spoken of me to Schumann in such a manner as he at least ought to think of me. It interested me much to make acquaintance with his composition of the epilogue to "Faust". If he publishes it I shall try to have it performed here, either at the Court or at the theater. In passing lately through Frankfort I had a glance at the score of "Genoveva", a performance of which had been announced to me at Leipzig for the middle of May at latest. I am very much afraid that Schumann will have a struggle with the difficulties and delays which usually occur in trying to get any lofty work performed. One would say that a bad fairy, in order sometimes to counterbalance the works of genius, gives a magic success to the most vulgar works and presides over the propagation of them, favoring those whom inspiration has disdained, in order to push its elect into the shade. That is no reason for discouragement, for what matters the sooner or the later?

A thousand thanks for your exact and obliging packet of cigars. If you should have the opportunity of sending me some samples of a kind neither too thin nor too light, at about twenty to twenty- five thalers the thousand, I shall willingly give an order for some, which might be followed by a larger order.

Schuberth of Hamburg has just sent me your transcriptions of the Schumann songs, which have given me real pleasure. If you publish other things kindly let me know, for you know the sincere interest I feel both in yourself and in your works,— an interest I hope to have the opportunity of showing you more and more.

Meanwhile believe me yours affectionately,

F. Liszt

P.S.—I have not forgotten the little commission you gave me relative to the "Fantasie-Stucke," and in a few weeks I will let you have a copy of the new edition.

60. To Robert Schumann

[original in the Royal Library in Berlin]

Dear, esteemed Friend,

Before everything allow me to repeat to you what, next after myself, you ought properly to have known best a long time ago— namely, that no one honors and admires you more truly than my humble self.

When opportunity occurs we can certainly have a friendly discussion on the importance of a work, a man, even a town indeed. For the present I am specially rejoicing in the prospect of an early performance of your opera, and beg you most urgently to let me know about it a few days beforehand, as I shall most certainly come to Leipzig on that occasion, and then we can also arrange for it to be studied in Weymar as soon as possible afterwards. Perhaps you will also find time there to make me acquainted with your "Faust." For this composition I am anxiously waiting, and your resolution to give this work a greater length and breadth appears to me most judicious. A great subject demands generally a grand treatment. Although the Vision of Ezekiel attains in its small dimensions the culminating point of Raphael's greatness, yet he painted the School of Athens and the entire frescoes in the Vatican.

"Manfred" is glorious, passionately attractive! Don't let yourself be stopped in it; it will refresh you for your "Faust"— and German art will point with pride to these twin productions.

Schuberth has sent me your "Album fur die Jugend" [Album for the Young], which, to say the least, pleases me much. We have played your splendid trio here several times, and in a pretty satisfactory manner.

Wagner stayed some days here and at Eisenach. I am expecting tidings from him daily from Paris, where he will assuredly enlarge his reputation and career in a brilliant manner.

Would not your dear wife (to whom I beg to be kindly remembered) like for once to make a romantic country excursion into the Thuringer Wald [the Thuringian Forest]? The neighborhood is charming, and it would give me great pleasure to see her again at Weymar. A very good grand piano, and two or three intelligent people who cling to you with true sympathy and esteem, await you here.

But in any case there will appear in Leipzig as a claqueur [clapper (to applaud)]

Your unalterably faithful friend,

F. Liszt Weymar, June 5th, 1849

61. To Robert Schumann

[original in the Royal Library in Berlin]

Best thanks, dear friend, for your kind information about the performance of your "Faust" on the 28th of August.

To draw "das Ewig-Weibliche" rightly upwards ["Das Ewig-Weibliche zicht uns hinan" ("The Eternal-Womanly draws us upwards").— Goethe's "Faust"] by rehearsing the chorus and orchestra would have afforded me great pleasure— and would probably have succeeded. ["Gelangen" and "gelingen"—untranslatable little pun.] But unfortunately obstacles which cannot be put aside have intervened, and it will be utterly impossible for me to be present at the Goethe Festival, as I have to betake myself in a few days' time to an almost unknown but very efficacious bath resort, and my doctor's orders are most strict that I must not make any break in my "cure" during six weeks.

Notwithstanding this very deplorable contretemps for me, I immediately informed Herr Councillor A. Scholl, as head of the Goethe Committee, of your friendly proposal. Herewith his answer.

Allow me meanwhile to refresh your memory with an old French proverb, "Ce qui est differe n'est pas perdu" [What is put off is not given up], and give me the hope that soon after my return to Weymar we may occupy ourselves seriously with the performance of your "Faust."…

Hearty greetings to your dear wife, and believe me yours ever most sincerely,

F. Liszt Weymar July 27th, 1849

62. To Robert Schumann

[autograph in the Royal Library in Berlin]

Dear Friend,

A summons which cannot be put off obliges me to be present at the Goethe Festival here on the 28th of August, and to undertake the direction of the musical part.

My first step is naturally to beg you to be so good as to send us soon the score of your "Faust." If you should be able to spare any of the voice or orchestral parts it would be a saving of time to us; but if not we shall willingly submit to getting the parts copied out as quickly as possible.

Kindly excuse me, dear friend, for the manner in which this letter contradicts my last. I am very seldom guilty in such a way, but in this case it does not lie in me, but in the particulars of the matter itself.

For the rest I can assure you that your "Faust" shall be studied with the utmost sympathy and accuracy by the orchestra and chorus.—Herr Montag, the conductor of the Musik-Verein [Musical Union], is taking up the chorus rehearsals with the greatest readiness, and the rest will be my affair!— Only, dear friend, don't delay sending the score and, if possible, the parts.

Sincerely yours,

F. Liszt

Weymar, August 1st, 1849

If your opera is given not later than the 1st of September I shall certainly come to Leipzig.

63. To Carl Reinecke

Heligoland, September 7th, 1849

I am very sorry, my dear M. Reinecke, not to have met you at Hamburg. It would have been such a real pleasure to me to make acquaintance again with your Nonet, and it seems to me, judging from its antecedents in the form of a Concerto, that by this decisive transformation it ought to be a most honorably successful work.

The "Myrthen Lieder" have never been sent to me. If you happen to have a copy I should be very much obliged if you would send it me to Schuberth's address.

With regard to the article which has appeared in "La Musique" I have all sorts of excuses to make to you. The editors of the paper thought fit, I do not know why, to give it a title which I completely disavow, and which would certainly have never entered into my mind. Moreover the printer has not been sparing of changing several words and omitting others. Such are the inevitable disadvantages of articles sent by post, and of which the proof correctors cannot read the writing.

Anyhow, such as it is, I am glad to think that it cannot have done you any harm in the mind of the French public, which has customs and requirements that one must know well when one wishes above all things to serve one's friends by being just to them.

Two numbers of your "Kleine Fantasie-Stucke" have been distributed, up to about a thousand copies, with the paper "La Musique," under the title of "Bluettes,"—a rather ill-chosen title to my idea,—but, notwithstanding this title and the words "adopted by F. Liszt," which the editors have further

110

taken the responsibility of putting, I am persuaded that this publication is a good opening (in material) into the musical world of France, and, looking at this result only, I am charmed to have been able to contribute to it.

I shall return to Hamburg by the last boat from Heligoland on the 27th of September, in order to go to the baths of Eilsen, where I expect to spend all the month of October. In November I shall be back in Weymar for the rest of the winter.

If you would have the kindness to send to Schuberth's address a case of 250 cigars of a pretty good size from the Bremen Manufactory, I should be very much obliged to you, and would take care to let you have the money (which in any case will not be a very great sum) through Schuberth. The samples you sent me to Weymar did reach me, but at a moment when I was extremely occupied, so that I forgot them. Pray let me hear from you from time to time, my dear M. Reinecke, and regard me as a friend who is sincerely attached to you.

F. Liszt

64. To Breitkopf and Hartel

My dear Sir,

The arrival of your piano is one of the most pleasant events in my peacefully studious life at Weymar, and I hasten to send you my best thanks. Although, to tell the truth, I don't intend to do much finger-work in the course of this year, yet it is no less indispensable for me to have from time to time a perfect instrument to play on. It is an old custom that I should regret to change; and, as you kindly inquire after the ulterior destination of this piano, allow me to tell you quite frankly that I should like to keep it as long as you will leave it me for my private, personal, and exclusive use at Weymar. In being guilty of the so-called indiscretion I committed in claiming of your courtesy the continued loan of one of your instruments I thought that, under the friendly and neighborly relations which are established between us (for a long time to come, I hope), it would not be unwelcome to your house that one of its productions should play the hospitable to me, whilst receiving my hospitality at the same time. However retired and sheltered I live from stir and movement at Weymar, yet from time to time it does happen that I receive illustrious visitors, or curious and idle ones who come and trouble one for this or that; henceforth I shall be delighted to be able to do the honors of your piano both to the one and to the other, and that will be, besides, the best proof of the strength of the recommendation that I have had the pleasure of making, for a long time past, of your manufactory. If however, contrary to expectation, it should happen that you were in pressing need of an instrument, very little played upon, the one at Weymar would be at your disposal at any moment.

With regard to the Beethoven Lieder-Cyclus I have just received a letter from Mr. Haslinger which I do not communicate in full because of the personal details it contains, but this is the passage, as laconic as it is satisfactory, with regard to this publication:—

"I give you with pleasure my fullest consent to the edition of the Beethoven Liederkreis by Breitkopf and Hartel."

So by tomorrow's post I shall have the honor

of returning you the proofs of the Lieder-Cyclus, which forms a continuation to the Beethoven Lieder which you have already edited, and which you will publish when you think well. .—.

With the proofs of my third piece on the "Prophete" I will also send you all the pieces on it (piano and voice) which you have been so good as to lend me, as well as the piano score, which I don't require any more; for, unless I should have a success which I dare not hope for (for these three pieces), and an express order from you for another series of three pieces, which I could easily extract from that vast score, I shall make this the end of my work on the "Prophete." I come at last to a question, not at all serious, but somewhat embarrassing for me,—that of fixing the price of the manuscripts that you are so good as to print. I confess that this is my "quart d'heure de Rabelais!" [The "quart d'heure de Rabelais" refers to an incident in his life, and means, in round terms, the moment of paying—i.e., any disagreeable moment.] In order not to prolong it for you, allow me to tell you without further ceremony that the whole of the six works together, which are as follows:—

Lieder of Beethoven, Lieder-Cyclus of Beethoven, Consolations (six numbers), Illustrations of the "Prophete" (three numbers), published by your house, are worth, according to my estimation, 80-100 louis d'or.

If this price does not seem disproportionate to you, as I am pleased to think it will not, and if it suits you to publish other pieces of my composition, I shall have the pleasure of sending you in the course of the year:—

1. A "Morceau de Concert"(for piano without orchestra), composed for the competition of the Paris Conservatoire, 1850.

2. The complete series of the Beethoven Symphonies, of which you have as yet only published the "Pastorale" and the "C minor." (In the supposition that this publication will suit your house, I will beg you to make the necessary arrangements from now onwards with Mr. Haslinger; perhaps it will even be expedient that the Symphony in A (7th), which Haslinger published several years ago from the arrangement that I had made, should reappear in its proper place in the complete series of the symphonies.)

3. Bach's six fugues (for organ with pedals), arranged for piano alone.

In the middle of February I shall send you the complete manuscript of my little volume on Chopin, and a little later in the same month we shall set ourselves to work here on the study of Schubert's opera, the performance of which will take place in the first days of April. If, as I do not doubt, the performance of the "Prophete" draws you to Dresden, I shall certainly have the pleasure of seeing you there, for I have just begged Mr. de Luttichau to be so good as to reserve me a place for that evening, and I shall not fail to be there. Meanwhile, my dear M. Hartel, believe me,

Yours sincerely and affectionately,

F. Liszt Weymar, January 14th, 1850

On the occasion of Schubert's opera I shall probably set to work on the arrangement of the

symphony, of which, meanwhile, I hold the score.—
Compliments and best regards to Madame Hartel,
which I know you will be kind enough to convey to
her.

65. To Breitkopf and Hartel

February 24th, 1850

My dear Sir,

.—. With regard to Schubert's opera ["Alfonso
and Estrella." It was given for the first time on June
24th, 1854, the birthday of the Grand Duke (but not
without some necessary cuts)], a recent experience
has entirely confirmed me in the opinion I had
already formed at the time of the first rehearsals with
piano which we had last spring—namely, that
Schubert's delicate and interesting score is, as it
were, crushed by the heaviness of the libretto!
Nevertheless, I do not despair of giving this work
with success; but this success appears possible only
on one condition—namely, to adapt another libretto
to Schubert's music. And since, by a special fate, of
which I have no reason to complain, a part of
Schubert's heritage has become my domain, I shall
willingly busy myself, as time and place offer, with
the preparatory work and the mise-en-scene of this
opera, for which it would be advantageous, in my
opinion, if it could be first produced in Paris. Belloni
informs me that it will be pretty easy for you to
ensure me the entire rights of this work for France. If
such be the case I would take suitable measures for
the success of this work, on occasion of which I
should naturally have to make a considerable outlay
of time and money, so that I should not be disposed
to run any risk without the guarantee of

proportionate receipts from the sale of the work in France, and author's rights which I shall have to give up to the new poet.

This matter, however, is not at all pressing, for I shall only be able to set to work in the matter in the course of next year (1851); but I shall be very much obliged to you not to lose sight of it, and to put me in possession, when you are able, of the cession of the French and English rights, in consideration of which I will set to work and try to get the best possible chances of success.

Many thanks to you for so kindly sending the score of Schubert's Symphony. That of the "Prophete" not being wanted by me any longer, I enclose it in the parcel of proofs and manuscripts which I beg you to undertake to send off to Mr. Belloni's address in Paris.

On Easter Monday we shall give the first performance of "Comte Ory." [By Rossini] Would you not feel tempted to come and hear it? It is a charming work, brimming over and sparkling with melody like champagne, so that at the last rehearsal I christened it the "Champagner-Oper" ["Champagne Opera."] and in order to justify this title our amiable Intendant proposes to regale the whole theater with a few dozens of champagne in the second act, in order to spirit up the chorus.

"Qu'il avait de bon vin le Seigneur chatelain!"

Cordial remembrances from yours affectionately,

F. Liszt

I should be glad for the publication of No. 3 of the pieces on the "Prophete," and the "Consolations," not to be put off long.

66. To Professor J. C. Lobe in Leipzig

[Autograph in the possession of M. Alfred Bovet at Valentigney.—

The addressee (1797-1881), a writer on music (formerly Court

Musician at Weimar), lived from 1846 in Leipzig.]

My esteemed Friend,

It is with much pleasure I send you the good news that H.R.H. the Grand Duchess has graciously accepted the dedication of your "System of Composition." [Published in 1850.] Our gracious protector [feminine] started yesterday for The Hague, and will not be back till towards the middle of August.

I hope you will be sure not to fail us at the Herder Festival in Weymar (August 25th), as well as at the "Lohengrin" evening (28th); we have been already waiting for you so long!

Between the performances of the "Messiah" and "Lohengrin" (to say nothing of my "Prometheus" choruses) will also be the best opportunity for you to present your work in person to the Grand Duchess.

Remember me kindly to your dear family, and remain my friend as I am yours

Most truly,

F. Liszt Weymar, July 10th, 1850

67. To Friedrich Wieck in Dresden

[published in the "Neue Musik-Zeitung" in 1888.—The addressee was the well-known pianoforte master, the father of Clara Schumann

(1785-1873).]

Esteemed Sir,

It will be a real pleasure to me to welcome you here, and your daughter [Marie Wieck, Hohenzollern Court Pianist in Dresden], whom I have already heard so highly commended. Weymar, as you know it of old, offers no brilliant resources for concerts; but you may rest assured beforehand that I, on my side, shall do everything that is possible in this connection to make things easy for you. To me it seems especially desirable that you should wait until the return of H.R.H. the Grand Duchess, which will be within a fortnight; should you, however, be tied by time and come here before that date, I bid you heartily welcome, dear sir, and place myself at your disposal.

Yours truly,

F. Liszt

Weymar, August 4th, 1850

68. To Simon Lowy in Vienna.

[Autograph in the Royal Library in Vienna. Printed in a German translation, La Mara, "Letters of Musicians during Five Centuries," vol. ii.]

Weymar, August 5th, 1850

Dear Friend,

My cousin Edward writes me word that you are a little piqued at my long silence,—and I, shall I tell you frankly? am a little piqued that you have not yet thought of coming to see me, and of transferring your bath season to some place in the neighborhood of Weymar. Will you make peace with me?—

Accept as a friend the invitation I give you in all friendship. Arrive at Weymar the 23rd of August, and stay till the 30th at least. You will find several of your friends here,—Dingelstedt, Jules Janin, Meyerbeer (?), etc.,—and you will hear, firstly, on the evening of the 24th, a good hour and a half of music that I have just composed (Overture and Choruses) for the "Prometheus" of Herder, which will be given as a Festal Introduction to the inauguration of his statue in bronze by Schaller of Munich, which is fixed for the 25th; secondly, on the evening of the 25th, Handel's "Messiah"; thirdly, on the 28th, the anniversary of Goethe's birth, a remarkably successful Prologue made, ad hoc, for that day by Dingelstedt, followed by the first performance of Wagner's "Lohengrin." This work, which you certainly will not have the opportunity of hearing so soon anywhere else, on account of the special position of the composer, and the many difficulties in its performance, is to my idea a chef-d'oeuvre of the highest and most ideal kind! Not one of the operas which has entertained the theaters for the past twenty years can give any approximate idea of it.

So don't be piqued any longer, or rather, dear friend, be piqued with curiosity to be one of the first to hear such a beautiful thing. Sulk with Vienna, for a few weeks at least, instead of sulking with me, which is all nonsense, and believe me always and ever your most sincerely attached, but very much occupied, very much pre-occupied, and oftentimes very absorbed friend,

F. Liszt

69. To Mathilde Graumann

[Given by the addressee, subsequently

celebrated as Mathilde
 Marchesi, teacher of singing, in "Aus meinem
Leben" (Bagel,
 Dusseldorf)]

Mademoiselle,

Here is the letter for the Grand Master de Luttichau, which M. de Ziegesar has just written in your honor and glory, with all the good grace and obligingness which he keeps for you.

As regards introductions to Berlin there is a provoking contretemps for you. H.R.H. the Princess of Prussia will pass the winter at Coblentz.

Meyerbeer, to whom I beg you to remember me respectfully, will certainly be your best patron with the Court, and I have no doubt that he will receive you with sympathy and interest.

I will also send you, in the course of the week, a letter for the Chamberlain of H.R.H. Princess Charles of Prussia, which Ziegesar has promised me.

As to our concert, fixed for the 19th (Saturday next), I assure you frankly that I should not have ventured to speak to you of it, and that I hardly venture now.

The receipts are to be devoted to some pension fund, always so low in funds in our countries; consequently I am not in a position to propose any suitable terms. Now as, on the occasion of the performance of the "Messiah," you have already been only too kind to us, it really would not do for me to return to the charge, unless you were to authorize me to do so quite directly and positively, by writing me an epistolary masterpiece somewhat as follows:—

"I will sing in a perfunctory manner, but with the best intentions and the best will in the world, the air from…(here follows the name of the piece), and the duet from "Semairamide" with Milde or Mademoiselle Aghte, next Saturday; and in order not to put anybody out, I will arrive at the exact time of the rehearsal, on Friday at four o'clock."

If any such idea as this should come into your head please let me know (by telegram if need be), so that by Monday night, or, at latest, Tuesday midday, I may be able to make the programme, which must appear by Wednesday morning at latest.

With homage and friendship,

F. Liszt

Friday, October 11th, 1850 Be so kind as to give a friendly shake of the hand from me to Joachim; recommend him not to be too late in arriving at Weimar, where we expect him for the evening of the 14th.

P.S.—At the moment when I was going to send my letter to the post the following lines reached me. I send them to you intact, and you will see by them that you could not have friends better disposed towards you than those of Weimar.

Please do not fail to write direct to Ziegesar to thank him for his kindness, of which you have been sensibly informed by me (without alluding to his letter, which you will return to me), and at the same time say exactly which week you will arrive in Berlin; unless, however, you prefer to come and tell him this verbally on Friday or Saturday evening at the Altenburg, after you have again chanted to us and enchanted us. [Literal translation, on account of play on words.]

70. To Carl Reinecke

Dear Reinecke,

Here are the letters for Berlioz and Erard that I offered you. I add a few lines for the young Prince Eugene Wittgenstein, with whom you will easily have pleasant relations; he is an impassioned musician, and is remarkably gifted with artistic qualities. In addition, I have had a long talk about your stay in Paris, and the success which you ought to obtain, with Belloni, who came to me for a few days. You will find him thoroughly well disposed to help you by all the means in his power, and I would persuade you to have complete confidence in him. Go and look for him as soon as ever you arrive, and ask him for all the practical information you require. Make your visit to Messrs. Escudier with him. (N.B. —He will explain why I have not given you a letter for Brandus.)

The greater number of your pieces have hitherto been printed exclusively by Escudier, and in my opinion you would do well to keep well with them in consequence. In your position it is not at all necessary to make advances to everybody—and, moreover, it is the very way to have no one for yourself. Look, observe, and keep an intelligent reserve, and don't cast yourself, German-wise, precipitately into politeness and inopportune modesty.

In one of your leisure hours Belloni will take you to Madame Patersi, who is entrusted with the education of my two daughters, for whom I beg a corner of your kind attention. Play them your Polonaise and Ballade, and let me hear, later on, how their very small knowledge of music is going on. Madame Patersi, as I told you, will have much pleasure in introducing you to her former pupil, Madame de Foudras, whose salon enjoys an excellent reputation.

Need I renew to you here the request of my four cardinal points?- -No, I am sure I need not!— Accept then, dear Reinecke, all my heartiest wishes for this new year, as well as for your journey to Paris. Let me hear of you through Belloni, if you have not time to write to me yourself, and depend in all circumstances on the very cordial attachment of

Yours sincerely and affectionately,

F. Liszt January 1st, 1851 My return to Weymar is unfortunately

again postponed for twenty days, by the doctor's orders, to which

I submit, although not personal to myself. [They referred to

Princess Wittgenstein, who was ill.]

71. To Leon Escudier, Music Publisher in Paris

[autograph in the possession of M. Arthur Pougin in Paris.—The addressee was at that time the manager of the periodical "La France Musicale," in which Liszt's Memoir of Chopin first appeared in detached numbers (beginning from February 9th, 1851).]

Weymar, February 4th, 1851

My dear Sir,

The proofs of the two first articles of my

biographical study of Chopin ought to have reached you some days ago, for I corrected and forwarded them immediately on my return to Weymar. You will also find an indication of how I want them divided, which I shall be obliged if you will follow. Both on account of the reverence of my friendship for Chopin, and my desire to devote the utmost care to my present and subsequent publications, it is important to me that this work should make its appearance as free from defects as possible, and I earnestly request you to give most conscientious attention to the revision of the last proofs. Any alterations, corrections, and additions must be made entirely in accordance with my directions, so that the definitive publication, which it would be opportune to begin at once in your paper, may satisfy us and rightly fulfill the aim we have in view. If therefore your time is too fully occupied to give you the leisure to undertake these corrections, will you be so good as to beg M. Chavee [an eminent Belgian linguist, at that time a collaborator on the "France Musicale"] (as you propose) to do me this service with the scrupulous exactitude which is requisite, for which I shall take the opportunity of expressing to him personally my sincere thanks?

In the matter of exactitude you would have some right to reproach me (I take it kindly of you to have passed it over in silence, but I have nevertheless deserved your reproaches, apparently at least) with regard to Schubert's opera ["Alfonso and Estrella," which Liszt produced at Weimar in 1854]. I hope Belloni has explained to you that the only person whom I can employ to make a clear copy of this long work has been overwhelmed, up to now, with pressing work. It will therefore be about three months before I can send you the three acts, the fate of which I leave in your hands, and for which, by the aid of an interesting libretto, we may predict good luck at the Opera Comique. I will return to this matter more in detail when I am in the position to send you the piano score (with voice), to which, as yet, I have only been able to give some too rare leisure hours, but which I promise you I will not put off to the Greek Calends!

As far as regards my opera, allow me to thank you for the interest you are ready to take in it. For my own part I have made up my mind to work actively at the score. I expect to have a copy of it ready by the end of next autumn. We will then see what can be done with it, and talk it over.

Meanwhile accept, my dear sir, my best thanks and compliments.

F. Liszt

The proofs of the third and fourth articles on Chopin will be posted to you tomorrow.

Has Belloni spoken to you about F. David's "Salon Musical" (twenty-four pieces of two pages each, very elegantly written and easy to play)?—I can warmly recommend this work to you, both from the point of view of art, and of a profitable, and perhaps even popular, success. [Presumably Ferdinand David's "Bunte Reihe," Op. 30, which Liszt transcribed for piano alone.]

72. To Carl Reinecke

My dear Mr. Reinecke,

I am still writing to you from Eilsen; your two

kind and charming letters found me here and have given me a very real pleasure. You may rest quite assured during your life of the sincere and affectionate interest I feel for you, an interest of which I shall always be happy to give you the best proofs as far as it depends on me.

Madame Patersi is loud in her praises both of your talent and of yourself,—and I thank you sincerely for having so well fulfilled my wishes with regard to the lessons you have been so kind as to give to Blandine and Cosima. [Liszt's daughters. Blandine (died 1872) became afterwards the wife of Emile Ollivier; Cosima is the widow of Wagner.] Who knows? Perhaps later on these girls will do you honor in a small way by coming out advantageously with some new composition by their master Reinecke, to the great applause of Papa!

Hiller shows tact and taste in making sure of you as a coadjutor at the Rhenish Conservatorium, which seems to be taking a turn not to be leaky everywhere. Cologne has much good, notwithstanding its objectionable nooks. Until now the musical ground there has been choked up rather than truly cultivated! People are somewhat coarse and stupidly vain there; I know not what stir of bales, current calculations, and cargoes incessantly comes across the things of Art. It would be unjust, however, not to recognize. the vital energy, the wealth of vigor, the praiseworthy activity of this country, in which a group of intelligent men, nobly devoted to their task, may bring about fine results, more easily than elsewhere.

At any rate I approve of what you have done,

and compliment you on having accepted Hiller's offer, [Namely, a position as Professor at the Conservatorium of Cologne, which Reinecke occupied from 1851 to 1854.] and shall have pleasure in sending to your new address some of my latest publications, which will appear towards the end of May (amongst others a new edition, completely altered and well corrected, I hope, of my twelve great Etudes, the Concerto without orchestra dedicated to Henselt, and the six "Harmonies Poetiques et Religieuses"). I have also written a very melancholy Polonaise, and some other trifles which you will perhaps like to look over.

Let me hear from you soon, my dear Mr. Reinecke, and depend, under all circumstances, on the faithful attachment of

Yours affectionately and sincerely,

F. Liszt

Eilsen, March 19th, 1851

73. To Dr. Eduard Liszt in Vienna

[An uncle of Liszt's (that is, the younger half-brother of his father), although Liszt was accustomed to call him his cousin: a noble and very important man, who became Solicitor-General in Vienna, where he died February 8th, 1879. Franz Liszt clung to him with ardor, as his dearest relation and friend, and in March, 1867, made over to him the hereditary knighthood.]

[Weimar, 1851]

Dear, excellent Eduard ,

It will be a real joy to me to take part in your joy, and I thank you very cordially for having thought first of me as godfather to your child. I accept that office very willingly, and make sincere wishes that this son may be worthy of his father, and may help to increase the honor of our name. Alas! it has been only too much neglected and even compromised by the bulk of our relations, who have been wanting either in noble sentiments, or in intelligence and talent—some even in education and the first necessary elements—to give a superior impulse to their career and to deserve serious consideration and esteem. Thank God it is otherwise with you, and I cannot tell you what a sweet and noble satisfaction I derive from this. The intelligent constancy which you have used to conquer the numerous difficulties which impeded your way; the solid instruction you have acquired; the distinguished talents you have developed; the healthy and wise morality that you have ever kept in your actions and speech; your sincere filial piety towards your mother; your attachment, resulting from reflection and conviction, to the precepts of the Catholic religion; these twenty years, in fine, that you have passed and employed so honorably,—all this is worthy of the truest praises, and gives you the fullest right to the regard and esteem of honest and sensible people. So I am pleased to see that you are beginning to reap the fruits of your care, and the distinguished post to which you have just been appointed [He had been made Assistant Public Prosecutor in 1850.] seems to justify the hopes that you confided to me formerly, and which I treated, probably wrongly, as so much naive ambition. At the point at which you have arrived it would be entirely out of place for me to poke advice and counsel out of season at you. Permit me, for the sake of the lively friendship I bear you, and the ties of relationship which bind us together, to make this one and only recommendation, "Remain true to yourself!" Remain true to all you feel to be highest, noblest, most right and most pure in your heart! Don't ever try to be or to become something (unless there were opportune and immediate occasion for it), but work diligently and with perseverance to be and to become more and more some one.—Since the difficult and formidable duty has fallen upon you of judging men, and of pronouncing on their innocence or guilt, prove well your heart and soul, that you may not be found guilty yourself at the tribunal of the Supreme Judge, —and under grave and decisive circumstances learn not to give ear to any one but your conscience and your God!—

Austria has shown lately a remarkable activity, and a military and diplomatic energy the service of which we cannot deny for the re-establishment of her credit and political position. Certainly by the prevision of a great number of exclusive Austrians— a prevision which, moreover, I have never shared—it is probable that the Russian alliance will have been a stroke of diplomatic genius very favorable to the Vienna Cabinet, and that, in consequence of this close alliance, the monarchical status quo will be consolidated in Europe, notwithstanding all the democratic ferments and dissolving elements which are evidently, whatever people may say, at their period of ebb. I do not precisely believe in a state of tranquility and indefinite peace, but simply in a certain amount of order in the midst of disorder for a round dozen of years, the main spring of this order being naturally at Petersburg. From the day in which a Russian battalion had crossed the Austrian frontier my opinion was fixed, and when my friend Mr. de Ziegesar came and told me the news I immediately said to him, "Germany will become Russian, and for the great majority of Germans there is no sort of hesitation as to the only side it remains to them to take."

The Princess having very obligingly taken the trouble to tell you my wishes with regard to my money matters, I need not trouble you further with them, and confine myself to thanking you very sincerely for your exactness, and for the discerning integrity with which you watch over the sums confided to your care. May events grant that they may prosper, and that they may not become indispensable to us very soon.—

Before the end of the winter I will send you a parcel of music (of my publications), which will be a distraction for your leisure hours. I endeavour to work the utmost and the best that I can, though sometimes a sort of despairing fear comes over me at the thought of the task I should like to fulfill, for which at least ten years more of perfect health of body and mind will be necessary to me.

Give my tender respects to Madame Liszt; you two form henceforth my father's entire family; and believe in the lively and unalterable friendship of

Your truly devoted,

F. Liszt

74. To Count Casimir Esterhazy

[Autograph (without address) in the possession

of Herr Albert
 Cohn, bookseller in Berlin.—The addressee was presumably Count
 Esterhazy, whose guest Liszt was in Presburg in 1840.]

Let me thank you very sincerely for your kind remembrance, dear friend, and let me also tell you how much I regret that my journey to Hohlstein cannot come to pass during your short stay there. But as by chance you already find yourself in Germany, will you not push on some fine day as far as Weymar?—I should have very great pleasure in seeing you there and in receiving you—not in the manorial manner in which you received me at Presburg, but very cordially and modestly as a conductor, kept by I know not what strange chance of fate at a respectful distance from storms and shipwrecks!—

For three weeks past a very sad circumstance has obliged me to keep at Eilsen, where I had already passed some months of last winter. The reigning Prince is, as you have perhaps forgotten, the present proprietor of one of your estates,—the Prince of Schaumburg-Lippe. If by chance you are owing him a debt of politeness, the opportunity of putting yourself straight would be capital for me. Nevertheless I dare not count too much on the attractions of the grandeur and charms of Buckeburg! and I must doubtless resign myself to saying a longer farewell to you.

Let me know by Lowy of Vienna where I shall address to you some pieces in print which you can look over at any leisure hour, and which I shall be delighted to offer you. I will add to them later the complete collection of my "Hungarian Rhapsodies," which will now form a volume of nearly two hundred pages, of which I shall prepare a second edition next winter. Hearty and affectionate remembrances from

Yours ever,

F. Liszt

Eilsen, June 6th, 1851

75. To Theodor Uhlig, Chamber Musician in Dresden

[Autograph in the possession of Herr Hermann Scholtz, Chamber virtuoso in Dresden.—The addressee, who was an intimate friend of Wagner's (see "Wagner's Letters to Uhlig, Fischer, Heine"— London: H. Grevel & Co., 1890), gained for himself a lasting name by his pianoforte score of Lohengrin. He died January, 1853.]

The perusal of your most kind and judicious article in Brendel's Musical Gazette on the "Goethe Foundation" [By Liszt, 1850. See "Gesammelte Schriften," vol. v.] confirms me in the belief that I could not fail to be understood by you in full intelligence of the cause. Allow me then, my dear Mr. Uhlig, to thank you very cordially for this new proof of your obligingness and of your sympathy— in French, as this language becomes more and more familiar and easy to me, whereas I am obliged to make an effort to patch up more or less unskillfully my very halting German syntax.

The very lucid explanation that you have made of my pamphlet, as well as the lines with which you have prefaced and followed it, have given me a real satisfaction, and one which I did not expect to receive through that paper, which, if I am not mistaken, had hitherto shown itself somewhat hostile to me personally, and to the ideas which they do me the small honor to imagine I possess. This impression has been still further increased in me by reading Mr. Brendel's following article on R. Wagner, which seems to me a rather arranged transition between the former point of view of the Leipzig school or pupils and the real point of view of things. The quotation Brendel makes of Stahr's article on the fifth performance of "Lohengrin" at Weymar, evidently indicates a conversion more thought than expressed on the part of the former, and at the performance of "Siegfried" I am persuaded that Leipzig will not be at all behindhand, as at "Lohengrin."

I do not know whether Mr. Wolf (the designer) has had the pleasure of meeting you yet at Dresden; I had commissioned him to make my excuses to you for the delay in sending the manuscript of Wiland. Unfortunately it is impossible for me to think of returning to Weymar before the end of July, and the manuscript is locked up among other papers which I could not put into strange hands. Believe me that I am really vexed at these delays, the cause of which is so sad for me.

If by chance you should repass by Cologne and Minden, it would be very nice if you could stay a day at Buckeburg (Eilsen), where I am obliged to stay till the 15th of July. I have not much pleasure to offer you, but in return we can talk there at our ease of the St. Graal...

My pamphlet "Lohengrin and Tannhauser" will appear in French at Brockhaus' towards the end of July. It will have at least the same circulation as the "Goethe Foundation," and I will send you by right one of the first copies.

Kind regards to Wagner, about whom I have written a great deal lately without writing to him; and believe me yours very sincerely,

F. Liszt

Eilsen (Buckeburg), June 25th, 1851.

76. To Rosalie Spohr in Brunswick

[niece of Louis Spohr, and an incomparable harpist,—"The most ideal representative of her beautiful instrument," according to Bulow; after her marriage with Count Sauerma she retired from public life and now lives in Berlin.]

After your amiable authorization to do so, Mademoiselle, I have had your concert announced at Eilsen for Tuesday next, July 8th, and you may rest assured that the best society of Buckeburg and of the Badegaste [visitors who go for the baths] will be present.

The price of the tickets has been fixed for 1 florin, which is the maximum customary in this country. With regard to the programme, I await your reply, in which I shall be glad if you will tell me the four or five pieces you will choose, amongst which will be, I hope, Parish Alvars' Fantaisie on motives from "Oberon" and the "Danse des Fees."

A distinguished amateur, Monsieur Lindemann of Hanover, has promised me to play one or two violoncello solos, and the rest of the programme will be easily made.

As to your route, you had better take the Schnellzug [express] next Monday, which starts about 11 in the morning from Brunswick, and brings you to Buckeburg in less than three hours. From here it will only take you thirty-five minutes to get to Eilsen. The most simple plan for you would be not to write to me beforehand even, but to improvise your programme according to your fancy here. Only let me beg you not to arrive later than Monday evening, so that the public may be free from anxiety, and to set my responsibility perfectly at rest in a corner of your harp- case.

May I beg you, Mademoiselle, to remember me affectionately to your father? and be assured of the pleasure it will be to see you, hear you, and admire you anew, to your sincere and devoted servant,

F. Liszt

Eilsen, July 3rd, 1851

I beg you once more not to be later than next Monday, July 7th, in coming to Eilsen.

77. To Rosalie Spohr

I am deeply sensible of your charming lines, Mademoiselle, the impression of which is the completion for me of the harmonious vibrations of your beautiful talent,—vibrations which are still resounding in the woods and in your auditors at Eilsen. While expressing to you my sincere thanks I should reproach myself were I to forget the piquant and substantial present that your father has sent me, and I beg you to tell him that we have done all honor to the savory product of Brunswick industry. The

Buckeburg industry having a certain reputation in petto in the matter of chocolate, the Princess, who sends her best regards to you and your family, wishes me to send you a sample, which you will receive by tomorrow's post. The chocolate, in its quality of a sedative tonic, will, moreover, not come amiss in the intervals of your study.

May I beg you, Mademoiselle, to give my affectionate compliments to your parents as well as to the clever drawing-historiographer [The younger sister of the addressee, Ida Spohr, at that time sixteen years old, who was a most gifted creature, both in poetry, painting, and music. She died young, at the age of twenty-four] whom you know? and receive once more the best wishes of yours most truly,

F. Liszt

Eilsen, July 22nd, 1851

78. To Breitkopf and Hartel

Allow me, my dear Mr. Hartel, to make known to you, as a kind of curiosity, a very long piece I composed last winter on the chorale "Ad Nos" from the "Prophete." If by chance you should think well to publish this long Prelude, followed by an equally long Fugue, I could not be otherwise than much obliged to you; and I shall take advantage of the circumstance to acquit myself, in all reverence and friendship, of a dedication to Meyerbeer, which it has long been my intention to do; and it was only for want of finding among my works something which would suit him in some respect, that I have been obliged to defer it till now. I should be delighted therefore if you would help me to fill up this gap in the recognition I owe to Meyerbeer; but I dare not press you too much for fear you may think that my Fugue has more advantage in remaining unknown to the public in so far that it is in manuscript, than if it had to submit to the same fate after having been published by your care.

In accordance with your obliging promise, I waited from week to week for the preface that Mr. Wagner has added to his three opera poems. I should be glad to know how soon you expect to bring them out, and beg you to be so good as to send me immediately three copies.

Believe me, my dear Mr. Hartel,

Yours affectionately and most truly,

F. Liszt

Weymar, December 1st, 1851

P.S.—Would it perhaps do to bring out my Fugue on the "Prophete" as No. 4 of my "Illustrations du Prophete"? That was at least my first intention. [It was published in that form by Breitkopf and Hartel.] In the same parcel you will find the piano score of the "Prophete," which I am very much obliged to you for having lent me.

79. To Louis Kohler in Konigsberg

[An important piano teacher and writer on music, and composer of valuable instructive works (1820-86).]

Dear Sir,

The friendly kindness with which you have spoken of a couple of my latest compositions lays me under an obligation of warm thanks, which I must no longer delay having the pleasure of expressing to you. I should be very glad if you find anything that suits you in my next impending piano publication (the new, entirely revised edition of my Studies, the "Harmonies Poetiques et Religieuses," and the two years of "Annees de Pelerinage, Suite de Compositions," etc.). In any case I shall venture to send this work, with the request that you will accept it as a token of my gratitude for the favorable opinion which you entertain of my artistic efforts.

At this moment I have to compliment you also very much on your arrangement of the Hungarian "Volkslieder" [Folk Songs]. For several years past I have been occupied with a similar work, and next winter I think of publishing the result of my national studies in a pretty big volume of "Hungarian Rhapsodies." Your transcriptions have interested me much through the correct perception of the melodies, and their elegant though simple style.

Senff [The well-known Leipzig music publisher.] showed me also in manuscript a book of Russian melodies, that seemed to me most successful. When will it come out?

If by any chance you have a spare copy of your new work, the exact title of which I do not remember, but it is somewhat as follows, "Opern am Clavier" [Operas at the Piano] or "Opern fur Clavierspieler" [Operas for Pianoforte Players] (or, in French, "Repertoire d'Opera pour les Pianistes"), I should be much obliged if you would let me have one.

Accept, dear sir, my best respects, and believe me

Yours truly,
F. Liszt
Weymar, April 16th, 1852

80. To Carl Reinecke

My dear Mr. Reinecke,

A very good friend of mine, Professor Weyden of Cologne, who has just been spending a few days with me here, kindly promises to give you these few lines and to tell you what pleasure your present of the "Variations on a Theme of Bach" has given me. It is a very eminent work, and perfectly successful in its actual form. While complimenting you sincerely upon it, I must also add my thanks that you have joined my name to it.

I should have liked to be able to send you some of my new works for piano, of which I spoke to you before; but, as I have been altering them and touching them up, the publication of them has been delayed; nevertheless, I expect that in the course of this summer the twelve "Grandes Etudes" (definitive edition) and the "Harmonies Poetiques et Religieuses" will successively appear, and in December or January next the "Annees de Pelerinage, Suite de Compositions pour le Piano," and the complete collection of my "Hungarian Rhapsodies." Meanwhile, let me offer you the "Concert Solo" and the two Polonaises which were written at Eilsen shortly after your visit to me there.

Joachim starts tomorrow for London, and I have commissioned him to persuade you to come and see me at Weymar on his return. I have been much attached to him this winter, and I hold his talent as well as himself in high esteem and true sympathy.—

Try not to delay too long the pleasure I should have in hearing your trio; I shall be delighted to make the acquaintance of Madame Reinecke, and would not wish to be among the last to congratulate you on your happiness.

In cordial friendship, yours ever,

F. Liszt

Weymar, April 16th, 1852

81. To Carl Czerny

[Autograph in the archives of the Musik-Verein in Vienna.]

My dearest and most honored Master and Friend,

A melancholy event which has thrown our Court into deep mourning- -the sudden death of the Duchess Bernard of Saxe-Weimar—has not allowed of my presenting your letter to Her Imperial Highness the Grand Duchess until a day or two ago. She has been pleased to receive your letter and your intentions with marked kindness, the expression of which you will find in the accompanying letter which she charged Baron de Vitzthum to write you in her name.

May I beg you then to advise Mr. Schott to send me immediately on the publication of your "Gradus ad Parnassum" a dedication copy, which I will get suitably bound in velvet here, and which I will immediately remit to H.I.H.—As regards the form of dedication, I advise you to choose the most simple:—

Gradus ad Parnassum, etc.,

Compose et tres respectueusement dedie a Son Altesse Imperiale et

Royale Madame la Grande Duchesse de Saxe-Weimar-Eisenach Marie

Paulowna, par Ch. Czerny.

[Composed and most respectfully dedicated to Her Royal and
Imperial Highness Marie Paulowna, Grand Duchess of Saxe-Weimar-
Eisenach by Ch. Czerny.]

Or if the title be in German:—
Componirt und I. kais. kon. Hoheit der Frau Grossherzogin zu Sachsen-Weimar-Eisenach Marie Paulowna, in tiefster Ehrfurcht gewidmet, von C. Cz.
What you tell me of the prodigious activity of your Muse obliges me to make a somewhat shameful acknowledgment of my relative slowness and idleness. The pupil is far from the master in this as in other points. Nevertheless I think I have made a better use of the last three years than of the preceding ones; for one thing I have gone through a rather severe work of revision, and have remodeled entirely several of my old works (amongst others the Studies which are dedicated to you, and of which I will send you a copy of the definitive edition in a few weeks, and the "Album d'un Voyageur," which will reappear very considerably corrected, increased, and transformed under the title of "Annees de Pelerinage, Suite de Compositions pour le Piano-Suisse et Italie"): for another thing I have been continuing writing in proportion as ideas came to me, and I fancy I have arrived at last at that point where the style is adequate to the thought. Unfortunately my outside occupations absorb much of my time. The orchestra and opera of Weymar

were greatly in need of reform and of stirring up. The remarkable and extraordinary works to which our theater owes its new renown—"Tannhauser," "Lohengrin," "Benvenuto Cellini"—required numerous rehearsals, which I could not give into the hands of anybody else. The day before yesterday a very pretty work, in an elegant and simple melodic style, was given for the first time—"Der lustige Rath," [The Merry Councillor (or counsel)] by Mr. de Vesque, which met with complete success. Carl Haslinger, who had arrived for the first performance of "Cellini," was also present at this, and can tell you about it. In the interval between these two works, on Sunday last, he had his Cantata-Symphony "Napoleon" performed, and conducted it himself (as a rather severe indisposition has obliged me to keep my room for several days).

In the course of the month of June my mother, who proposes to pay a visit to her sister at Gratz, will have the privilege of going to see you, dear master, and of renewing to you, in my name and her own, our expressions of sincere gratitude to you for the numerous kindnesses you have shown me. Believe me that the remembrance of them is as lively as it is constant in my heart.

I owe you still further thanks for the trouble you have taken to make Mr. de Hardegg study Schubert's Fantasia, scored by me, and I beg you to give him my best compliments. It is perhaps to be regretted that this work, which contains many fine details, should have been played for the first time in the Salle de Redoute, so "redoutable" and ungrateful a room for the piano in general; in a less vast space, such as the salle of the Musik- Verein, the virtuoso and the work would assuredly have been heard more to advantage, and if I did not fear to appear indiscreet I should ask Mr. de Hardegg to play it a second time, in a concert room of moderate size.

I have inquired several times as to the talent and the career of Mr. de Hardegg, in whom I naturally feel an interest from the fact of the interest you take in him. If by chance he should be thinking of making a journey to this part of Germany, beg him from me not to forget me at Weymar. I shall be delighted to make his acquaintance, and he may be assured of a very affectionate reception from me.

Accept, my dear and honored friend, every assurance of my high esteem, and believe that I shall ever remain

Your very faithful and grateful

F. Liszt

Weymar, April 19th, 1852

82. To Gustav Schmidt, Capellmeister at Frankfort-on-the-Maine

[Autograph (without address) in the possession of M. Alfred Bovet at Valentigney.—The addressee was, in any case, the above- mentioned (1816-82), finally Court-Capellmeister (conductor) at Darmstadt, the composer of the operas "Prinz Eugen," "Die Weiber von Weinsberg," and others.]

Dear Friend,

.—. The idea of a Congress of Capellmeisters is indeed a very judicious one, and from a satisfactory realization of it only good and better things could result for the present divided state of music. There is no question that in the insulation and paralyzing of those who are authorities in Art lies a very powerful hindrance, which, if it continues, must essentially injure and endanger Art. Upon certain principles an union is necessary, so that the results of it may be actively applied, and it especially behooves Capellmeisters worthily to maintain the interests of music and musicians. A meeting such as you propose would be a timely one; only you will approve of my reasons when I renounce the honor of proposing this meeting for Weimar, and indicate Spohr to you as the proper head. The master Spohr is our senior; he has always furthered the cause of music as far as circumstances at Cassel permitted— the "Fliegender Hollander" was given at Cassel under his direction earlier than "Tannhauser" was given at Weymar. Talk it over with him, which from the near vicinity of Frankfort you can easily do, and if, as I do not doubt, he enters into your project, fix the date and let me know. I shall gladly take part in the matter, and will make it my business to do my share towards bringing about the desired results.

"Tannhauser" is announced for the 31st of this month (on occasion of the presence of Her Majesty the Empress of Russia). Beck takes the title-role at this performance. We shall give Schumann's "Manfred" a few days later. For next season the "Fliegender Hollander" and Spohr's "Faust," with the new Recitatives which he wrote for London, are fixed.

Farewell, and happiness attend you, dear friend; remember me kindly to your wife, and believe me ever

Yours most sincerely, F. Liszt

144

Weymar, May 18th, 1852.

83. To Robert Schumann

[Autograph in the Royal Library in Berlin.]

My very dear Friend,

It is with great pleasure that I am able to announce to you the first performance of "Manfred" for next Sunday, June 13th, and to invite you to come to it. ["Manfred" was put on the stage for the first time by Liszt] I hope that, at this time of year, your Dusseldorf duties will allow of your coming here for a couple of days, and that probably you will bring Clara with you, to whom please remember me very kindly. Should you, however, come alone, I beg that you will stay with me at the Altenburg, where you can make yourself perfectly at home. The last rehearsal is fixed for Friday afternoon; perhaps it would be possible for you to be present at it, which of course would be very agreeable to me. Your Leipzig friends will see the announcement of this performance in the papers, and I think you will consider it your bounden duty not to be absent from us at this performance.

Wishing you always from my heart the best spirits for your work, good health, and "every other good that appertains thereto," I remain unalterably

Yours most sincerely, F. Liszt

Weymar, June 8th, 1852.

84. To Robert Schumann

[Autograph in the Royal Library in Berlin.]

My very dear Friend,

I regret extremely that you could not come to the second performance [This might perhaps also be read "first performance."] of your "Manfred," and I believe that you would not have been dissatisfied with the musical preparation and performance of that work (which I count among your greatest successes). The whole impression was a thoroughly noble, deep, and elevating one, in accordance with my expectations. The part of Manfred was taken by Herr Potsch, who rendered it in a manly and intelligent manner. With regard to the mise-en-scene something might be said; yet it would be unfair not to speak in praise of the merits of the manager, Herr Genast. It seems to me therefore that it would be nice of you to write a friendly line of thanks to Herr Genast, and commission him to compliment Herr Potsch (Manfred) and the rest of the actors from you.

One only remark I will permit myself: the introduction music to the Ahriman chorus (D minor) is too short. Some sixty to a hundred bars of symphony, such as you understand how to write, would have a decidedly good effect there. Think the matter over, and then go fresh to your desk. Ahriman can stand some polyphonic phrases, and this is an occasion where one may rant and rage away quite comfortably.

Shall I send you your manuscript score back, or will you make me a lovely present of it? I am by no means an autograph-collector, but the score, if you don't require it any longer, would give me pleasure.

A thousand friendly greetings to Clara, and beg your wife to let me soon hear something of you.

In truest esteem and friendship,

Yours ever,

F. Liszt

Weymar, June 26th, 1852

85. To Peter Cornelius

[The exquisite poet-composer of the operas "The Barber of Baghdad," "The Cid," and "Gunlod," which have at last attained due recognition (1824-74).]

Weymar, September 4th, 1852

It has been a great pleasure to me, my dear Mr. Cornelius, to make the acquaintance of your brother, and I only regret that he passed several days here without letting me know of his stay. Your letter, which reached me through him, has given me a real pleasure, for which I thank you very affectionately. Short though our acquaintance has been, I am pleased to think that it has been long enough to establish between us a tie which years will strengthen without changing the natural and reciprocal charm. I congratulate you very sincerely in having put the fine season to so good a use by finishing the church compositions you had planned. That is an admirable field for you, and I strongly advise you not to give in till you have explored it with love and valor for several years. I think that, both by the elevation and the depth of your ideas, the tenderness of your feelings, and your deep studies, you are eminently fitted to excel in the religious style, and to accomplish its transformation so far as is nowadays required by our intelligence being more awake and our hearts more astir than at former periods. You have only to assimilate Palestrina and Bach—then let your heart speak, and you will be able to say with the prophet, "I speak, for I believe; and I know that our God liveth eternally."

We spoke with your brother about your vocation for composing religious—Catholic music. He enters thoroughly into this idea, and will give you help to realize it under outer conditions favorable to you. Munster, Cologne, and Breslau appeared to us to be the three places for the present where you would find the least obstacles in the way of establishing your reputation and making a position. But before you go to the Rhine I hope you will do me the pleasure of coming to see me here. The room adjoining that which Mr. de Bulow occupies is entirely at your service, and it will be a pleasure to me if you will settle yourself there without any ceremony, and will come and dine regularly with us like an inhabitant of the Altenburg. The theatrical season recommences on Sunday next, September 12th, with Verdi's "Ernani." In the early days of October (at the latest) "Lohengrin" will be given again; and on the 12th of November I expect a visit from Berlioz, who will spend a week at Weymar. Then we shall have "Cellini," the Symphony of Romeo and Juliet, and some pieces from the Faust Symphony.

Kindest regards from yours ever,

F. Liszt

86. To Clara Schumann

Weymar, September 11th, 1852.

It is not without regret that I obey your wish, Madame, in returning to you the autograph score of "Manfred," for I confess that I had flattered myself a little in petto that Robert would leave it with me in virtue of possession in a friendly manner. Our theater possesses an exact copy, which will serve us for subsequent performances of "Manfred;" I was tempted to send you this copy, which, for revision of proofs, would be sufficient, but I know not what scruple of honor kept me from doing so. Perhaps you will find that it is possible generously to encourage my slightly wavering virtue, and in that case you will have no trouble in guessing what would be to me a precious reward...

How is Robert's health? Have the sea baths done him good? I hope he will soon be restored all right to his home circle—and to his composing desk.

——

It would have been very pleasant to me to renew our visit of last year to you at Dusseldorf, and I was indeed touched by the gracious remembrance of it which your letter gives me; but, alas! an unfortunate accident which has happened to my mother, by which she nearly broke her leg in coming downstairs, has obliged her to keep her bed for more than nine weeks, and even now she can only walk with the help of crutches, and it will be some months before she is all right again.

Forced as she was to remain at Weymar, I have not liked to leave her all this summer, and had to give up the pleasure of a holiday excursion.—The Princess Wittgenstein, and her daughter (who has become a tall and charming young girl), desire me to give their very affectionate remembrances to you and Robert, to which 1 add my most sincere wishes for the speedy restoration of our friend, and cordial assurances of my constant friendship.

F. Liszt

87. To Carl Czerny

[Autograph in the archives of the Musik-Verein in Vienna. The date is wanting; it may be placed, judging from Liszt's letter of October 30th, 1852, at the above-mentioned date.]

[September or October, 1852]

My Dear, Honored Master And Friend,

Permit me to recommend particularly to you Professor Jahn [The afterwards celebrated biographer of Mozart], with whose many interesting works of criticism and musical literature you are doubtless familiar (among others his Introduction to the original score of Beethoven's "Leonora," published by Hartel in Leipzig).

Mr. Jahn's object in going to Vienna is to collect documents for a biography of Beethoven, which will, I am persuaded, supply a want so much felt hitherto by the public and by artists. May I beg you—in honor of the great man whom you have had the merit of comprehending and admiring, long before the common herd joined in chorus around his name—to open the treasures of your reminiscences and knowledge to Mr. Jahn, and accept beforehand my sincere thanks for the good service you will render to Art in this matter?

It is with unchangeable attachment that I remain, dear master, your very grateful and devoted

F. Liszt

P.S.—When will the "Gradus ad Parnassum" come out?—You will receive the copy of my Studies, which are dedicated to you, through Mr. Lowy in a few days.

88. To Breitkopf and Hartel

[Autograph in the possession of M. Alfred

Bovet at Valentigney]

Weymar, October 30th, 1852

My Dear Mr. Hartel,

I have given up to a friend the piano which you have been so good as to lend me for some years, and he (as I have already informed you verbally) asks me to let him defer the payment of it till the end of this month. I therefore take this opportunity of proposing to you either to let you immediately have the sum fixed upon for the piano (400 thalers), or else to make a settlement of reciprocal terms up to now, by which we shall be quits towards each other. The pleasure and advantage which I find in my relations with your house are too valuable to me for me not to do all in my power properly to maintain them, by conforming to your wishes and intentions. Of my works published by your house there are, if I mistake not, five—

12 Etudes d'execution transcendante (2 books), 6 Etudes d'apres Paganini (2 books), Grand Concerto Solo, Fantaisie and Fugue on the Chorale from the Prophete (No. 4 of the "Illustrations du Prophete"), Mass (with Pater Noster and Ave Maria) for four male voices with organ accompaniment

—upon which we have deferred putting a price until now. Without trying to deceive myself as to the moderate returns which these (as it happens, rather voluminous) works may bring to your house, I should venture however to flatter myself that they have not been an expense to you, and that they are even works not unsuited to your catalogue. However things may be, I beg you to be so good as to use towards me the same sincerity that I employ towards you, persuaded as I am that sincerity is the only basis of any lasting connection, especially when one has to do with things which divers circumstances may render more delicate and complicated. Allow me then at last, my dear Mr. Hartel, to propose to you to square our accounts by my keeping your piano in exchange for the above-mentioned five manuscripts, which should also acquit me for the works of Marx and Kiesewetter that you have sent me, so that, if my proposition suits you, we should be entirely quits.

I was glad to hear that Mr. Jahn had had occasion to be satisfied with his journey to Vienna, and I beg you to assure him that I am entirely at his disposal with regard to any steps to be taken to help on his work on Beethoven, for which I am delighted to be of any service to him.

In a fortnight's time I am expecting Mr. Berlioz here. The performances of "Benvenuto Cellini" will take place on the 18th and 20th November, and on the 21st the Symphonies of "Romeo and Juliet" and "Faust" will be performed, which I proposed to you to publish. If your numerous occupations would allow of your coming here for the 20th and 21st I am certain that it would be a great interest to you to hear these exceptional works, of which it is a duty and an honor to me not to let Weymar be in ignorance.

Will you, my dear Mr. Hartel, accept this information as an invitation, and also tell your brother, Mr. Raymond, what pleasure a visit from him would give me during the Berlioz week? We shall, moreover, be at that time in good and romantic company of artists and critics from all points, meeting at Weymar.

I will send you shortly my Catalogue, which you will greatly oblige me by bringing out without very much delay. The dispersion and confusion through which my works have had to make their way hitherto have done them harm, over and above any wrong that they already had by themselves; it is therefore of some importance to classify them, and to present to the public a categorical insight into what little I am worth. As I have promised to send this catalogue to many people living in all sorts of countries, I beg that you will put to my account, not gratis, some sixty copies, which I fear will not be enough for me, but which will at least serve to lessen the cost of printing.

In this connection allow me to recur to a plan of which I have already spoken to you—the publication in German of my book on Chopin. Has Mr. Weyden of Cologne written to you, and have you come to terms with him on this subject? The last time he wrote to me he told me that he had not yet had an answer from you. As he is equally master of French and German, and as he thoroughly succeeded in his translation of my pamphlet on "Tannhauser and Lohengrin," I should be glad for the translation of Chopin to be done by him; and in case you decide to publish his work please put me down for fifty copies.

Pray excuse this long letter, my dear Mr. Hartel, and believe me very sincerely,

Yours affectionately and devotedly,

F. Liszt

89. To Breitkopf and Hartel

[Autograph in the possession of M. J.

Crepieux-Jamin at Rouen.]

My dear Mr. Hartel,

I thank you very heartily for the fresh proof of your kind intentions towards me which your last letter gives me, and I hasten to return to you herewith the two papers with my signature by which our little accounts are thus settled. With regard to the extra account of about eighty crowns, which I thank you for having sent me by the same opportunity, I will not delay the paying of it either. Only, as it contains several things which have been got by the theater management (such as "Athalie," the piano scores of "Lohengrin," Schubert's Symphony, etc.), you will allow me to leave it a few days longer, so that I may get back the sum which is due to me,—and which, till the present time, I was not aware of having been placed to my account, thinking indeed that these various works for which I had written for the use of the theater had long ago been paid for by the management.—

I beg that you will kindly excuse this confusion, of which I am only guilty quite unawares.

With regard to the publication of the "Pater Noster" and of the "Ave Maria," please do it entirely to your own mind, and I have no other wish in the matter but that the "Pater" should not be separated from the "Ave," on account of the former being so small a work; but whether you publish these two pieces with the Mass, or whether they appear separately (the two being in any case kept together), either of these arrangements will suit me equally well. For more convenience I have had them bound in one, as having been written at the same time and

154

as belonging to the same style.—Berlioz has just written me word that he will probably arrive here two or three days sooner—and the proprietors of our repertoire have fixed the 17th November (instead of the 18th) for the first performance of the revival of "Cellini." Immediately after he is gone I will put in order the Catalogue that you are kindly bringing out, and which I should be glad to be able to distribute about before the end of the winter. You shall have the manuscript before Christmas.—

As Mr. Weyden has been a friend of mine for several years I may be permitted to recommend him to you, and have pleasure in hoping that your relations with him, on occasion of the translation of the Chopin volume, will be of an easy and agreeable nature. [The German translation of the work was not done until it appeared, by La Mara, in 1880, after the publication of a second edition.]

Pray accept once more, my dear Mr. Hartel, my best thanks, together with every assurance of the sincere affection of

Yours most truly,

F. Liszt

November 10th, 1852

90. To Professor Julius Stern in Berlin

[1820-83; founder of the Stern Vocal Union (which he conducted from 1847-74), and of the Stern Conservatorium (1850), which he directed, firstly with Marx and Kullak, and since 1857 alone.]

November 24th, 1852.

My dear Mr. Stern,

I hope you will excuse my delay in replying to your friendly lines, for which I thank you very

155

affectionately. Mr. Joachim was absent when they reached me, and all this last week has been extremely filled up for Weymar (and for me in particular) by the rehearsals and performance of Berlioz's works. Happily our efforts have been rewarded by a success most unanimous and of the best kind. Berlioz was very well satisfied with his stay at Weymar, and I, for my part, felt a real pleasure in being associated with that which he experienced in the reception accorded to him by the Court, our artists, and the public. As this week has, according to my idea, a real importance as regards Art, allow me, my dear Mr. Stern, to send you, contrary to my usual custom, the little resume that the Weymar Gazette has made of the affair, which will put you very exactly au courant of what took place. You will oblige me by letting Schlesinger see it also, and he will perhaps do me the pleasure of letting the Berlin public have it through his paper (The Echo).

I did not fail to conform to the wish expressed in your last letter, immediately that Joachim returned to Weymar, and I urged him much to accept the proposition you have made him to take part in the concert of the 13th of December. You know what high esteem I profess for Joachim's talent, and when you have heard him I am certain you will find that my praises of him latterly are by no means exaggerated. He is an artist out of the common, and one who may legitimately aspire to a glorious reputation.

Moreover he has a thoroughly loyal nature, a distinguished mind, and a character endowed with a singular charm in its rectitude and earnestness.

The question of fee being somewhat embarrassing for him to enter into with you, I have taken upon myself to speak to you about it without any long comment, and to mention to you the sum of twenty to twenty-five louis d'or as what seems to me fair. If Joachim had already been in Berlin, or if his stay there could take place at the same time with some other pecuniary advantage, I feel sure that he would take a pleasure in offering you his co-operation for nothing; but in the position he is in now, not intending at present to give concerts in Berlin, and not having as yet any direct relations with you, I think you will appreciate the motives which lead me to fix this sum with you...

If, as I hope, you do not consider it out of proportion, please simply to be so good as to write a few lines to Joachim direct, to tell him what day he ought to be in Berlin for the rehearsal of your concert, so that he may ask a little beforehand for his holiday from here.

Will you also please give my best regards to Th. Kullak? I have had the opportunity of talking rather fully about him these last days with two of his pupils, Princesses Anne and Louise (of Prussia), and also with their mother, Princess Charles. Mr. Marx (to whom I beg you to remember me kindly, until I write more fully to him about the performance of his "Moses") will shortly receive a letter from Mr. Montag, whom I have begged to bring with him the arrangements relating to the song parts, which Mr. Marx will be so kind as to lend us. Probably this oratorio can be given here towards the end of next

January or the middle of next February, and as soon as the rehearsals are sufficiently advanced I shall write to Marx to give him positive tidings and to invite him to pay us a short visit at Weymar.

A thousand frank and cordial regards from

Yours ever,

F. Liszt

You probably already know that Joachim is leaving Weymar to settle in Hanover at the beginning of next year.

91. To Wilhelm von Lenz in St. Petersburg

[A well-known writer on music and especially on Beethoven;

Imperial Russian Councillor of State (1809-83).]

I am doubly in your debt, my dear Lenz (you will allow me, will you not, to follow your example by dropping the Mr.?), firstly for your book, ["Beethoven and his Three Styles" (St. Petersburg, 1852).] so thoroughly imbued with that sincere and earnest passion for the Beautiful without which one can never penetrate to the heart of works of genius; and, secondly, for your friendly letter, which reached me shortly after I had got your book, the notice of which had very much excited my curiosity. That I have put off replying to you till now is not merely on account of my numerous occupations, which usually preclude my having the pleasure of correspondence, but chiefly on account of you and your remarkable work, which I wanted to read at leisure, in order to get from it the whole substance of its contents. You cannot find it amiss that it has given me much to reflect upon, and you will easily understand that I shall have much to say to you on this subject—so much that, to explain all my thoughts, I should have to make another book to match yours—or, better still, resume our lessons of twenty years ago, when the master learned so much from the pupil,—discuss pieces in hand, the meaning, value, import, of a large number of ideas, phrases, episodes, rhythms, harmonic progressions, developments, artifices;—I should have to have a good long talk with you, in fact, about minims and crotchets, quavers and semi-quavers,—not forgetting the rests which, if you please, are by no means a trifling chapter when one professes to go in seriously for music, and for Beethoven in particular.

The friendly remembrance that you have kept of our talks, under the name of lessons, of the Rue Montholon, is very dear to me, and the flattering testimony your book gives to those past hours encourages me to invite you to continue them at Weymar, where it would be at once so pleasant and so interesting to see you for some weeks or months, ad libitum, so that we might mutually edify ourselves with Beethoven. Just as we did twenty years ago, we shall agree all at once, I am certain, in the generality of cases; and, more than we were then, shall we each of us be in a position to make further steps forward in the exoteric region of Art.—For the present allow me, at the risk of often repeating myself hereafter, to compliment you most sincerely on your volume, which will be a chosen book and a work of predilection for people of taste, and particularly for those who feel and understand music. Artists and amateurs, professors and pupils, critics and virtuosi; composers and theorists—all will have something to gain from it, and a part to take in this feast of attractive instruction that you have prepared for them. What ingenious traits, what living touches, what well-dealt blows, what new and judiciously adapted imagery should I not have to quote, were I to enter in detail into your pages, so different from what one usually reads on similar subjects! In your arguments, and in the intrinsic and extrinsic proofs you adduce, what weight—without heaviness, what solidity—without stiffness, of strong and wholesome criticism—without pedantry! Ideas are plentiful in this by turns incisive, brilliant, reflected, and spontaneous style, in which learning comes in to enhance and steady the flow of a lively and luxuriant imagination. To all the refinement and subtle divination common to Slavic genius, you ally the patient research and learned scruples which characterize the German explorer. You assume alternately the gait of the mole and of the eagle—and everything you do succeeds wonderfully, because amid your subterranean maneuvers and your airy flights you constantly preserve, as your own inalienable property, so much wit and knowledge, good sense and free fancy. If you had asked me to find a motto for your book I should have proposed this,

"Inciter et initier,"

as best summing up, according to my ideas, the aim that you fulfill by your twofold talent of distinguished writer and musician ex professo. It is really curious to observe how the well-known saying, "It is from the north that light comes to us today," has been verified lately with regard to musical literature. After Mr. Oulibicheff had endowed us with a Mozart, here come you with a Beethoven. Without attempting to compare two works which are in so many respects as different and separate as the two heroes chosen by their respective historiographers, it is nevertheless natural that your name should be frequently associated with that of Mr. Oulibicheff—for each is an honor to Art and to his country. This circumstance, however, does not do away with your right to lecture Mr. Oulibicheff very wittily, and with a thorough knowledge of the subject, for having made of Mozart a sort of Dalai-Lama, [The head of the temporal and spiritual power in Thibet (Translator's note)] beyond which there is nothing. In all this polemical part (pp. 26, 27, etc.), as in many other cases, I am entirely of your opinion, with all due justice to the talents and merits of your compatriot. From a reading of the two works, Mozart and Beethoven, it is evident that, if the studies, predilections, and habits of mind of Mr. Oulibicheff have perfectly predisposed him to accomplish an excellent work in its entirety, yours, my dear Lenz, have led you to a sort of intimacy, the familiarity of which nourished a sort of religious exaltation, with the genius of Beethoven. Mr. Oulibicheff in his method proceeds more as proprietor and professor; you more as poet and lawyer. But, whatever may be said about this or that hiatus in your work, the plan of which has confined you disadvantageously to the analysis of the piano sonatas, and however much people may think themselves justified in cavilling at you about the distribution of your materials, the chief merit, which none could refuse you without injustice, is that you have really understood Beethoven, and have succeeded in making your imagination adequate to his by your intuitive penetration into the secrets of his genius.

For us musicians, Beethoven's work is like the pillar of cloud and fire which guided the Israelites through the desert—a pillar of cloud to guide us by day, a pillar of fire to guide us by night, "so that we may progress both day and night." His obscurity and his light trace for us equally the path we have to follow; they are each of them a perpetual commandment, an infallible revelation. Were it my place to categorize the different periods of the great master's thoughts, as manifested in his Sonatas, Symphonies, and Quartets, I should certainly not fix the division into three styles, which is now pretty generally adopted and which you have followed; but, simply recording the questions which have been raised hitherto, I should frankly weigh the great question which is the axis of criticism and of musical aestheticism at the point to which Beethoven has led us—namely, in how far is traditional or recognized form a necessary determinant for the organism of thought?—

The solution of this question, evolved from the works of Beethoven himself, would lead me to divide this work, not into three styles or periods,— the words "style" and "period" being here only corollary subordinate terms, of a vague and equivocal meaning,—but quite logically into two categories: the first, that in which traditional and recognized form contains and governs the thought of the master; and the second, that in which the thought stretches, breaks, recreates, and fashions the form and style according to its needs and inspirations. Doubtless in proceeding thus we arrive in a direct line at those incessant problems of "authority" and "liberty." But why should they alarm us? In the region of liberal arts they do not, happily, bring in any of the dangers and disasters which their oscillations occasion in the political and social world; for, in the domain of the Beautiful, Genius alone is the authority, and hence, Dualism disappearing, the notions of authority and liberty are brought back to their original identity.—Manzoni, in defining genius as "a stronger imprint of Divinity," has eloquently expressed this very truth.—

This is indeed a long letter, my dear Lenz, and as yet I am only at the preliminaries. Let us then pass on to the Deluge,—and come and see me at Weymar, where we can chat as long and fully as we like of these things in the shade of our fine park. If a thrush chances to come and sing I shall take advantage of the circumstance to make, en passant, some groundless quarrels with you on some inappropriate terms which one meets with here and there in your book,—as, for example, the employment of the word "scale" (ut, fa, la, etc.) instead of arpeggio chord; or, again, on your inexcusable want of gallantry which leads you maliciously to bracket the title of "Mamselle" (!) on to such and such a Diva, a proceeding which will draw down upon you the wrath of these divinities and of their numerous admirers. But I can assure you beforehand that there are far more nightingales than thrushes in our park; and, similarly, in your book the greater number of pages, judiciously thought out and brilliantly written, carry the day so well in worth and valor over any thinly scattered inattentions or negligences, that I join with my whole heart in the concert of praise to which you have a right.

Pray accept, my dear Lenz, the most sincere expressions of feeling and best thanks of

Your very affectionate and obliged

F. Liszt

Weymar, December 2nd, 1852

As Madame Bettina d'Arnim has been passing some weeks at Weymar, I let her know about your book. Feeling sure that the good impression it has made on her would be a pleasure to you to hear, I begged her to confirm it by a few lines, which I enclose herewith.—

92. To Robert Radecke in Leipzig

[Printed in the Neue Berliner Musik-Zeitung, November 20th, 1890.—The addressee, afterwards Conductor of the Royal Opera, and present Director of the Royal Academical Institute for Church Music in Berlin, was formerly Vice-director of the Leipzig "Singacademie" with Ferdinand David, and, intoxicated with the first performance of Berlioz's Faust at Weimar, he had determined to give such another in the Vocal Union of which he was Co-director. With this object he begged Liszt for the score. But the plan was not carried out, as Radecke exchanged his post at New Year, 1853, for that of a Music Director at the Leipzig Town theater.]

Best thanks, dear Radecke, for your letter and

the approved good intention.

The "Faust" score will be at your service with great pleasure as soon as I have got it back from Berlioz. It is probable that the copy which Berlioz will see about for me in Paris will be ready by Christmas, so that I shall be able to send it you soon after New Year.

In the course of the winter I intend also to give a performance of the little oratorio "La Fuite en Egypte," attributed to the imaginary Maitre de Chapelle Pierre Ducre. This graceful and interesting work should meet with approbation in Leipzig, and offers no difficulty either for voice or orchestra. If you keep the secret, and let your Gesangverein [Vocal Union] study it under the name of Pierre Ducre, a composer of the sixteenth century, I am convinced that it will not fail to make an effect.

[Liszt's playful suggestion about the Flight into Egypt was based upon the fact that Berlioz, on its first performance, had mystified the Paris public and brought forward the work under the feigned name of Pierre Ducre, the organist of the Sainte Chapelle in Paris in the year 1679.]

Joachim goes the day after tomorrow to Berlin; Cossmann is in Paris; and Nabich [The first trombone player of the Weimar orchestra, and a most admirable performer on his instrument.] is performing in London, Liverpool, and Manchester. None the less we are giving "Tannhauser" next Sunday (12th) (with subscriptions suspended!), and for this occasion the entire Finale of the second act and the new ending of the third will be studied.

Now farewell, and be active and cheerful, is

the wish of yours most sincerely,

F. Liszt

December 9th, 1852

93. To Bernhard Cossmann

[Weimar, December, 1852.]

[The date and ending of the letter are wanting, but from its contents it may be ascribed to this date.]

Thanks, dear friend, for your kind few lines, which have given me sincere pleasure. Joachim is not yet back from Berlin, and Beck [The chief tenor (hero-tenor) at the Court Opera] has again got his old attack of the throat, and I fear rather seriously, from which these six years of cures, it appears, have not succeeded in curing him radically. In consequence of this dearth of tenors, the performances of Wagner's and Berlioz's operas are going to be put off till February, when I hope that Tichatschek will be able to come from Dresden and sing "Tannhauser," "Lohengrin," and the "Flying Dutchman."

As for Cellini [Berlioz's opera]; we shall unfortunately have to wait until Dr. Lieber, the new tenor engaged for next season, at present at the Cologne theater, has learnt the part. I hear Lieber's voice highly spoken of, and it seems that he possesses also a dose of intelligence sufficient to understand how he ought to behave here.—

In the matter of news I have one small item to give you—namely, that on your return your salary will be raised fifty crowns, to make the round sum of four hundred.—Laub [Ferdinand Laub, a noteworthy violinist, was engaged for the 1st of January, 1853, as Joachim's successor as Concertmeister at Weimar.] will arrive very shortly, and accepts the propositions which have been made to him. He will not be...

94. To Wilhelm Fischer, Chorus Director in Dresden

[Autograph in the possession of Herr Otto Lessmann at
Charlottenburg.—The addressee was an intimate friend of Wagner's
("Letters to Uhlig, Fischer, and Heine"—Leipzig, Breitkopf and
Hartel, 1889).]

Dear Sir,

By today's post I have sent you a minutely corrected copy of the score of the "Flying Dutchman."

As this copy was my own property (Wagner had left it for me after his stay here in 1869) I could not suppose that Uhlig could expect it back from me as a theater score. The last letter from Wagner to me has made the matter clear, and I place this score with pleasure at his further disposal. I have replied to Wagner direct and fully; he is therefore aware that I have sent you my copy. [For fuller particulars about this see the "Wagner-Liszt Correspondence," vol. i., pp. 207-9.]

Allow me to beg you kindly to make my excuses to Herr Heine [Ferdinand Heine, Court actor and costumier, famous through Wagner's letters to him.] that I do not answer his letter just now. His indulgent opinion of our Lohengrtn performance is very flattering to me; I hope that by degrees we shall deserve still better the praise which comes to us from many sides: meanwhile, as the occasion of his writing was just the matter of the "Hollander" score, and as this is now quite satisfactorily settled, it does not require any further writing.

With best regards, yours truly,

F. Liszt

Weymar, January 13th, 1853

Is Tichatschek coming to our "Lohengrin" performance in February? Please beg him to try to do so. On Weymar's side nothing will be neglected, and it will be a real joy to us both.

95. To Edmund Singer

[Formerly Concertmeister at Weimar; at present Court Concertmeister and Professor at the Stuttgart Conservatorium.]

Dear Sir,

I thank you much for your friendly letter, and commission Herr Gleichauf (in whom you will recognize an admirable viola virtuoso) to persuade you not to retract your promised visit to me at Weymar. It would be very pleasant to me to be able to keep you here a longer time, yet I doubt whether you would be satisfied with such a modest post as our administrative circumstances warrant. When we have an opportunity we will talk further of this; meanwhile it will be a pleasure to me to see and hear you again. Laub's acquaintance will also interest you; he has just been playing some pieces with a really extraordinary virtuosity and bravura, so that we have all become quite warm about it.

Come, then, as soon as you have a couple of

spare days, and be assured beforehand of the most friendly reception.

With my very best regards,

Yours truly,

F. Liszt

Saturday, January 15th, 1853

96. To Frau Dr. Lidy Steche in Leipzig

[The addressee sang for two winters in the Gewandhaus concerts (as Frl. Angermann). After her marriage she started a Vocal Union, in the forties, with which, in December 1853, she gave so excellent a pianoforte performance of "Lohengrin" at her own house, and afterwards at the Minerva "lodge," that Hoplit, in his account of stage performances (Neue Zeitschrift fur Musik), spoke of the Steche undertaking as a "model performance." This was before the performance of "Lohengrin" at the Leipzig theater in January 1854.]

My dear Madame,

I have the pleasure of answering your inquiries in regard to the performances of the Wagner operas with the following dates:—

For next Wednesday, February 16th, the birthday of H.R.H. the Grand Duchess, the first performance of the "Flying Dutchman" is fixed. (N. B.—For that evening all the places are already taken, and, as a great many strangers are coming, it will be difficult to find suitable rooms in Weymar.) The following Sunday, February 20th, the "Flying Dutchman" will be repeated; and on the 27th (Sunday) "Tannhauser" is promised, and on March 5th (Saturday) "Lohengrin." Between these two performances of February 27th and March 5th the third performance of the "Flying Dutchman" will probably take place, of which I can give you more positive information at the end of this week. The Wagner week proper begins therefore with February 27th and closes with March 5th, and if it were possible to you to devote a whole week to these three glorious works of art I should advise you to get here by the 27th,—or, better still for you (as you are already quite familiar with "Tannhauser"), to come in time for the third performance of the "Flying Dutchman," the date of which is still somewhat uncertain, but which will probably be fixed for the 2nd or 3rd March. Immediately after the first performance we shall get quite clear about it, and I will not fail to let you know officially the result of the theater Conference here (in which I am not concerned).

Accept, my dear Madame, the assurance of the high esteem of

Yours most truly,

F. Liszt

Weymar, February 4th, 1853

97. To Gustav Schmidt, Capellmeister at Frankfort-On-The-Maine

[Autograph (without address) in the possession of M. Alfred Bovet at Valentigney.—The contents show to whom the letter was addressed.]

Dear Friend,

Berlioz's two symphonies, "Romeo and Juliet" and "Faust," have been twice given here in the course of this winter with the utmost success. Berlioz was so good as to lend me the score and parts,—but with the express condition that they should not go out of my hands. When, at the request of the Leipzig Academy of Singing [Singacademie], I asked him some weeks ago whether he would not allow me to place "Faust" at the disposal of the Leipzig Institute for a proposed performance, he replied to me as follows:—

"Considering the deplorable performances of which my works have often been the victims both in Germany and elsewhere, I have resolved never to lend them in manuscript. Moreover there are enough of my works printed in score and in separate parts (the three Symphonies, several Overtures, the 5th May, the Requiem, etc.) to make it unnecessary to seek for others. If I made an exception for you," ["Pour toi." Showing that Liszt and Berlioz employed the "tutoyer" towards one another.] etc...

Although I was perfectly certain that the Leipzig performance would be a very satisfactory one, as many of my friends took a lively interest in it, and although I have not the least doubt that you would be anxious to give "Faust" its full value in Frankfort, yet you see from the above lines of Berlioz that I, to my regret, dare not risk any further application to him in this matter. "Faust," moreover, will appear in score this year in Paris, and I sent Berlioz his manuscript back a short time ago.

Should you be disposed to perform something or other of Berlioz's in Frankfort, I can recommend you, first of all, most warmly:-

The two Overtures to "Cellini" and the "Carnaval Romain";

Two numbers out of the Symphony "Romeo and Juliet" -the feast at

Capulet's house and the Queen Mab (Scherzo);

And two Marches from the "Harold" Symphony and the "Symphonie Fantastique"-the March of the Pilgrims and the "Marche de Supplice" ["March on the Way to Execution"].

But it will be necessary for you to have several rehearsals—and indeed separate rehearsals for the quartet, and separate rehearsals for the wind instruments.

The effect of Berlioz's works can only be uncommonly good when the performance of them is satisfactory.

They are equally unsuited to the ordinary worthy theater and concert maker, because they require a higher artistic standpoint from the musician's side.

I looked through Kittl's [1809-68. Director of the Prague Conservatorium.] opera some years ago in a piano arrangement, and, between ourselves, I do not think the work will last. Kittl is a personal friend of mine, and I should have been glad to be able to give his work here; but...nevertheless...etc., etc.

Raff's "King Alfred" is a much more successful and important work; and, without wishing to injure Kittl, there is in Raff quite other musical stuff and grist. [Steckt doch in Raff ein ganz anderer musikalischer Kern and Kerl: untranslatable play on words.]

During your last stay in Weymar I spoke to you of Vesque's new opera "Der lustige Rath."

Various local circumstances have delayed the performance at Vienna of this really pretty, nicely worked out opera. The mise-en-scene does not require any special efforts; the piece only requires a somewhat piquant and not unskillful soprano singer. Altogether the opera appears to me to be written in a charming style, not too superficially conservative, and to be one of the best among the new operas mezzo-carattere. In case you still have time and are not indisposed to give the opera in Frankfort, I can send you the score. You would do Vesque an essential service if you could give the opera soon, and would have friendly relations with him, for Vesque is a cultivated, intelligent, and first-rate man. [Vesque von Puttlingen (pseudonym, Hoven), 1803-83, Councillor of the Austrian Foreign Ministry, composer of songs and operas.] There are not too many such!

Yours in all friendship,
F. Liszt
Weimar, February 27th, 1853

98. To Heinrich Brockhaus, Bookseller in Leipzig

[Published in a German translation: La Mara, "Letters of
Musicians during Five Centuries, vol. ii., 1887.]

My dear Mr. Brockhaus,

In thanking you for your kind mention of the notice joined to my name in the Conversations Lexikon, I wish above all things not to go beyond the limits of most scrupulous delicacy, which in these sorts of things have always appeared to me all the more desirable to maintain because they are so very often passed. Consequently I will only allow myself to point out three misstatements of fact in the article about myself: firstly, my supposed title of ex-St. Simonien; secondly, my supposed journey to America; thirdly, my diploma of the University of Konigsberg, which my biographer arbitrarily changes into a diploma of Doctor of Music, which was not the one given to me.—

I have never had the honor of belonging to the association, or, to put it better, to the religious and political family of St. Simonisme. Notwithstanding my personal sympathy with this or that member of it, my zeal has been but little beyond that which Heine, Boerne, and twenty others whose names are in the Conversations Lexikon showed at the same period, and they limited themselves to following pretty often the eloquent preachings of the Salle Taitbout. Among my numerous tailors' bills, I can certify that there is not one to be found of a bleu-barbot coat [The dress of the St. Simonists.]; and, as I have mentioned Heine, I ought to add that my fervor was far short of his, for I never thought of wishing to "Commune through space with the Child-lake Father," by correspondence or dedication, as he has done!—

Further, I can also assure you that my practical course of the geography of Europe has not extended beyond it, and that the four or five other parts of the globe are entirely unknown to me. And when you come to see me at Weymar I can show you, amongst other diplomas, that of the University of Konigsberg, in virtue of which I have the honor to belong, exceptionally, to the class of Doctors in Philosophy, an honor for which I have always been peculiarly grateful to this illustrious University.

As to the summary judgment passed upon my person and my works in this article, you will easily understand that I only accept it as transitory and with due reserve, much obliged though I am besides to the author for his kind intentions. After having attained, according to my biographer, the first aim of my youth,—that of being called the Paganini of the Piano,-it seems to me it is natural that I should seriously have the ambition of bearing my own name, and that I should count somewhat on the results of a desire and of persevering work, so far as to hope that in one of the later editions of the Conversations Lexikon I may have a place more in accordance with my aims. [The article in question, which was published at a time when Liszt's greater works had partly not yet been written, and partly were not yet known in the wider circles, speaks of poverty of invention, and considers his compositions rather those of a virtuoso than of imaginative significance.]

Accept, my dear Mr. Brockhaus, the expression of my most sincere regard, and believe me

Yours very truly,

F. Liszt

Weymar March 22nd, 1853

99. To Dr. Franz Brendel in Leipzig

[Autograph of the letter to Brendel in the possession of Frau Dr. Riedel in Leipzig.—Brendel (born 1811, died November 25th, 1868, in Leipzig) rendered great services to the New German (i.e., the

Wagner-Liszt) musical tendencies, as a writer on music (Geschichte der Musik, History of Music), and as editor of the Neue Zeitschrift fur Musik (founded by R. Schumann). He also, together with Liszt, originated the "Allgemeine Deutsche Musikverein" (the "German Universal Musical Union"), and was its president up to his death.]

Dear Friend,

A little trip to Gotha, where the Duke had invited me to be present at the performance of his opera "Casilda" the day before yesterday, must bear the blame of my delay in writing to you. After duly thinking over and considering your letter, I must tell you first and foremost my exact opinion with regard to the immediate appearance of the proposed paper. In my opinion at least two or three months are requisite to establish the necessary relations with the chief co-operators, and to give due weight to the whole undertaking. Without complete agreement as to means and aims we should compromise rather than help the matter. We must have the positive agreement and assurance of Semper, Stahr, Hettner, Hauenschild, and others (among whom Vischer of Tübingen must be sure not to be forgotten), before the first number appears. We have to struggle for a far higher and more difficult end than, for instance, the Unterhallungen am hausliehen Herd [Entertainments at Home] or the Fliegende Blatter fur Musik. [Fly-leaves for Music.] The most important step for us is the very first, at the house door; and if we do not weigh this step with due reflection we shall run a great risk of winning only imaginary future subscribers for the Art Work of the

Future, and of seeing our best wishes for its feasibility shipwrecked.

Whether also the title Kunstwerk der Zukunft [Art Work of the Future.] should be employed, or what other definition should be the axis of our united efforts in the opening number, I will put on one side for the present. The full discussion of this and other things I will keep for your next visit to Weymar. Raff's opera is announced for this day fortnight (Sunday, April 17th). If it is agreeable to you to come here sooner, you will be most welcome at any moment. This time and every time that you come to Weymar, I beg you to stay with me, both for your own convenience and mine.

Förster's exact address I will send you very soon, although I conclude that letters addressed Herr Hofrath Ernst Forster would be safely delivered by the post office. Stahr is the best person to give you information about Herr von Hauenschild (Max Waldau— not Count, as far as I know), and Hettner is a Professor in Jena.

Further, it is my opinion that you had better not send your communications to these gentlemen until we have settled some of the chief points in this matter.

I shall undertake a security of four hundred thalers on this proposed agreement between us, in return for a receipt from the management which you will give me. I cannot at present hold out the prospect of further support; yet it is possible that I may succeed in getting three to five hundred thalers annually, under certain conditions, for which there is no personal ground whatever (and which I hinted to you in our last conversation in Leipzig), for the pages of The Present and Future.

Remember me kindly to your wife, and be assured of the entire willingness of

Yours truly,

F. Liszt

Weymar, April 3rd, 1853

100. To Dr. Franz Brendel

Dear Friend,

Good advice is seldom cheap, and I must honestly confess that in my present very fluctuating circumstances I am not rich enough to help you efficaciously by lending you a helping hand, however much I might wish to do so. Stahr's refusal is very much to be regretted, for, in order to attain your end and to influence the world of literature, you positively require more literary men of great note to join you. Next to the money question the formation of the nucleus of management is the most important matter in this undertaking. However zealous and self-sacrificing you and Schlonbach [Arnold Schlonbach, journalist, died long ago.] may be in devoting your talents and powers to the paper, yet I doubt whether you will be able to keep it going unless you get some further capable men of talent as co-operators. This brings us, however, again to the money question, which I unfortunately am not in a position to solve. To be obliged to give it up after six months would be a far worse fate than not to begin it at all. Therefore, before everything, the moral guarantee must be forthcoming for its continuance, and for the constantly increasing spread of the paper, and these depend principally on the guarantee which the first five or six co-operators warrant. You remark quite truly that, if Wagner would take an interest in the matter, it would be of the greatest help. Perhaps he might be persuaded to do so, and I will willingly start the subject to him.

The title, size (as well as the limits of the paper, and cover), and fortnightly issue give me thorough satisfaction, and according to my opinion nothing more need be altered in these three particulars. A weekly issue has its advantages— nevertheless I have always thought that two papers per month are on the whole better than four. But whether it is possible and advisable to make the first start as early as July I much question. "Tout vient a point a qui sait attendre," says the French proverb. It certainly is important to seize the right moment, and that must be decided by you. Let me only beg you not to give too much weight to passing and local influences, and only to come forward when you can hold your ground with quiet, deliberate courage. Retreat belongs to the enemy. For us it is "Gradatim vincimus."

The matter of the security remains as promised. If you should not be ready by July, October would be just as favorable, if not more so— only, in Heaven's name, no backward step when once started!— Some articles of provision and ammunition seem to me to be absolutely necessary before you begin. Two months are a short time to get them ready, and I scarcely think it will be possible for you to be ready for action by July. Have you written yet to Wagner? You must not expect much from Hettner without Stahr. But, through Hinrichs or

Franz, Hauenschild might perhaps be won over. I advise you to stick fast to Schwind. One of his last pictures, "Beethoven's Fancy," bought by the King of Greece, points to him above all others as the representative of painting in your paper.

May I beg you also to send a few lines to Kurnberger to tell him that I have given you his manuscript? It would be discourteous if I were to leave him without any answer, and, as I cannot say anything further to him, we should save useless circumlocution if you would be so good as to correspond with him direct.

Incidentally you would also save me another letter about nothing, if you would write to Lenz (on the subject of this conference).

Whilst I am talking with you, Senora Pepita Oliva is doing her favorite tricks at the theater, which are more prized and rated higher than they deserve, so I am assured. "J'aime mieux y croire qu'y aller voir." [I would rather take it for granted than go and see it.] The brothers Wieniawski have also been here some days. The violinist is a virtuoso of importance,—that is to say, in the ordinary, but not quite correct, sense of this word; for Virtuoso comes from Virtu, and should neither be so falsified nor so misapplied.

Yours very truly,

F. Liszt

April 30th, 1853.

101. To Louis Kohler

Dear Friend,

You have again given me a real pleasure by your article on the Romanesca (in the last numbers of the Signale), for which I would gladly requite you. The best way to do this would be by a performance of "Lohengrin"; unfortunately there is very little prospect of that. Still it is not impossible that between the 19th and 26th of this month there may be a performance of this one work by royal command; and, as you are already so kindly disposed towards me, and have promised me to come to Weymar, do make yourself ready, and give me the great pleasure of your company for a few days—if possible, from the 19th to the 26th of this month. The marriage festivities of Princess Amalie of Sachs- Weymar and Prince Henry of the Netherlands, which will take place then, will be the occasion of a grand court concert on the 20th, and the performance of Marx's oratorio "Moses" on the 22nd or 24th, and probably a couple of other musical performances. Joachim is also coming at the same time, and there will be no dearth of entertainment for us. Once more best thanks-and a safe journey—and a revoir—which will be a great pleasure to your very affectionate and obliged.

F. Liszt

Weymar, May 6th, 1853

102. To Louis Kohler

Dear Friend,

A safe journey—and "auf Wiedersehen" next year in Weymar at a chance performance of "Lohengrin"! There is now no probability of a Wagner performance here for a week or ten days, and probably the "Flying Dutchman" will then be chosen.

You ought to keep all my scribblings which

appear henceforth. Meanwhile I send you only the score of the Weber Polonaise, in which the working-out section (pages 19, 20, 21) will perhaps amuse you.

I am writing to Wagner today that he should himself offer you a copy of the "Nibelungen." You ought to receive it soon.

You will find a little packet of Plantaja cigars in your cloak. May it help you to recall your Weymar visit, and think with warm remembrance of

Yours in all friendship,

F. Liszt

Weymar, May 24th, 1853

If you should stay some days in Berlin, ask Dorn why he has not yet sent me his score of the "Nibelungen"? Perhaps he has not had my letter in reply to his in which he mentioned that the score was coming.

When you have half an hour to spare, ask my pupil Winterberger [Composer, piano and organ virtuoso; born at Weimar 1834; was for a long time a Professor at the St. Petersburg Conservatorium; since then lives at Leipzig.] (through Schlesinger) to play you my "Prophete" Fugue on the organ. I consider this opus as one of my least bad productions—if you have not got a copy of it I will send you one on the first opportunity through Hartel.

Your box and cloak are just sent off "Station restante."

103. To Louis Kohler

"Kiraschio! Plimaschio!"

[The refrain of a journeyman's song, given by L. Kohler in his work "The Melody of Speech," in

182

which "The cry of the natural man gives vent to itself in unbridled pleasure."]

Dear friend! Your work [The same work, "The Melody of Speech" (Leipzig, J. J. Weber, 1853).] has given me a refreshing draught to quaff,—not exactly a theoretical "cure" water, such as the people promenading past my window are constrained to take, and which, thank Heaven, I neither require nor take; but a finely seasoned, delightfully comforting May drink,—and I thank you warmly for the lively, pleasant hours I have passed with you in reading and singing your work. The objections with which the Philistines and pedants will arm themselves against you don't interest me in the least. You have certainly brought forth a fresh and exciting little book, and that is a great service not easily attained!—Be satisfied not to please the worse half of brave musicians, among which I might count myself, and write on cheerfully, regardless of shops and shopkeepers!—Specially do I give you my best thanks for the "Weymarasche Zeilen," and the very friendly quotation of my earlier songs. Later on, when I bring out a couple more numbers, I must make a somewhat remodeled edition of these earlier songs. There must, in particular, be some simplifications in the accompaniment. But that you have thought favorably and indulgently of these things, with a due regard to the inner impulse which brought them forth (in my "storm and stress" period), is very pleasant to me. The Lenau concluding song is charmingly composed—only publish some more like that, with or without comment!

I have just received a letter from Wagner for you, which he sends to me as he does not know your address. Take this opportunity of sending me your street and number; for I always address to Putzer and Heimann, which is too formal. At the beginning of July I enjoyed several Walhalla-days with Wagner, and I praise God for having created such a man. Of my further summer projects I will only say that at the end of September I shall conduct the Musical Festival at Carlsruhe, and at the beginning of October shall return to Weymar (where I shall spend the winter).

I have written to Haslinger and Spina to send you the "Hungarian Rhapsodies" and the "Soirees de Vienne" (songs after F. Schubert, in nine parts). The next time I pass through Leipzig I will tell Kistner that you must not fail to have a copy of the "Harmonies Poetiques et Religieuses." The previously mentioned pieces you will have without delay. I have sent my Mass and Ave Maria to Marpurg by Raff. If you approve of these compositions I will gladly get a couple more copies in your honor. My Catalogue will not come out till next winter, as I have not yet had any time to revise it.

Let me hear soon from you, dear friend, and keep ever in friendly remembrance

Yours sincerely and with many thanks,
F. Liszt
Carlsbad, August 1st, 1853
Address to me always at Weymar.
104. To Richard Pohl in Dresden
[Printed in Pohl's pamphlet "The Carlsruhe

Musical Festival in October, 1853" (by Hoplit). Leipzig, Hinze, 1853.—The addressee, a writer on music (born 1826), one of the oldest and most faithful adherents of Liszt and Wagner, lived in Weimar after 1854, his wife Jeanne (nee Eyth) having a post there as a harp virtuosa: after Liszt's departure he was, as he still is, occupied as editor in Baden-Baden.]

In various accounts that I have read of the Festival at Carlsruhe, there is one point on which people seem pretty much agreed—namely, the insufficiency of my conducting. Without here examining what degree of foregone judgment there may be in this opinion, without even seeking to know how much it has been influenced by the simple fact of the choice of myself as conductor, apart from the towns of Carlsruhe, Darmstadt, and Mannheim, it certainly would not be for me to raise pretensions quite contrary to the assertion which it is sought to establish if this assertion were based on facts or on justice. But this is precisely what I cannot help contesting in a very positive manner.

As a fact one cannot deny that the ensemble of the Carlsruhe programme was very remarkably performed, that the proportion and sonority of the instruments, combined with a view to the locale chosen, were satisfactory and even excellent. This is rather naively acknowledged in the remark that it is really surprising that things should have gone so well "in spite of" the insufficiency of my conducting. I am far from wishing to deck myself in the peacock's feathers of the Carlsruhe, Mannheim, and Darmstadt orchestras, and am assuredly more disposed than any one to render full justice to the talents—some of them very distinguished—of the members of these three orchestras; but, to come to the point, whatever may be said to the contrary, it is acknowledged, even by the testimony of my adversaries, that the execution was at times astonishing, and altogether better than there had been reason to expect, considering that I was conductor.

This fact placed beyond discussion, it remains to be seen whether I am so completely a stranger there as they try to make out, and what reasons there can be for thus crying down a conductor when the execution was satisfactory, especially if, as is just, one bears in mind the novelty of the works on the programme for almost the entire audience. For, as every one knew at Carlsruhe, the Ninth Symphony, as well as the works of Wagner, Berlioz, Schumann, etc., were not well known by any one but myself, seeing that they had never been given before in these parts (with the exception of the Berlioz piece, which a portion only of the Carlsruhe orchestra had played under the direction of the composer).—

Now as regards the question of right—to know whether in good conscience and with knowledge of the matter one can justly accuse me of being an insufficient conductor, inexperienced, uncertain, etc.: without endeavoring to exculpate myself (for which I do not think there is any need amongst those who understand me), may I be permitted to make an observation bearing on the basis of the question?

The works for which I openly confess my admiration and predilection are for the most part amongst those which conductors more or less renowned (especially the so-called "tuchtigen Capellmeister" [Qualified conductors.]) have honored but little, or not at all, with their personal sympathies, so much so that it has rarely happened that they have performed them. These works, reckoning from those which are commonly described nowadays as belonging to Beethoven's last style (and which were, not long ago, with lack of reverence, explained by Beethoven's deafness and mental derangement!)—these works, to my thinking, exact from executants and orchestras a progress which is being accomplished at this moment—but which is far from being realized in all places—in accentuation, in rhythm, in the manner of phrasing and declaiming certain passages, and, of distributing light and shade—in a word, progress in the style of the execution itself. They establish, between the musicians of the desks and the musician chief who directs them, a link of a nature other than that which is cemented by an imperturbable beating of the time. In many cases even the rough, literal maintenance of the time and of each continuous bar |1,2,3,4,|1,2,3,4,| clashes with the sense and expression. There, as elsewhere, the letter killeth the spirit, a thing to which I will never subscribe, however specious in their hypocritical impartiality may be the attacks to which I am exposed.

For the works of Beethoven, Berlioz, Wagner, etc., I see less than elsewhere what advantage there could be (which by-the-bye I shall contest pretty knowingly elsewhere) in a conductor trying to go through his work like a sort of windmill, and to get into a great perspiration in order to give warmth to the others.

Especially where it is a question of understanding and feeling, of impressing oneself with intelligence, of kindling hearts with a sort of communion of the beautiful, the grand, and the true in Art and Poetry, the sufficiency and the old routine of usual conductors no longer suffice, and are even contrary to the dignity and the sublime liberty of the art. Thus, with all due deference to my complaisant critics, I shall hold myself on every occasion ulterior to my "insufficiency" on principle and by conviction, for I will never accommodate myself to the role of a "Profoss" [Overseer or gaoler.] of time, for which my twenty-five years of experience, study, and sincere passion for Art would not at all fit me.

Whatever esteem therefore I may profess for many of my colleagues, and however gladly I may recognize the good services they have rendered and continue to render to Art, I do not think myself on that account obliged to follow their example in every particular—neither in the choice of works to be performed, nor in the manner of conceiving and conducting them. I think I have already said to you that the real task of a conductor, according to my opinion, consists in making himself ostensibly quasi-useless. We are pilots, and not mechanics. Well, even if this idea should meet with still further opposition in detail, I could not change it, as I consider it just. For the Weymar orchestra its application has brought about excellent results, which have been commended by some of my very critics of today. I will therefore continue, without discouragement or false modesty, to serve Art in the best way that I understand it—which, I hope, will be the best.—

Let us then accept the challenge which is thrown to us in the form of an extinguisher, without trouble or anxiety, and let us persevere, conscious of right—and of our future.

F. Liszt

Weymar, November 5th, 1853

105. To Wilhelm Fischer, Chorus Director at Dresden

[Autograph in the possession of Herr Otto Lessmann, writer at
Charlottenburg. (Printed in his Allgemeine Musik-Zeitung, 1887,
No. 38.)—The addressee was the well-known friend of Wagner. (See
"Wagner's Letters to Uhlig, Fischer, and Heine."—Grevel & Co.)
Vol. I. 12]

Dear Sir and Friend,

Your letter has given me real pleasure, and I send you my warmest thanks for your artistic resolve to bring "Cellini" to a hearing in Dresden. Berlioz has taken the score with him to Paris from Weymar, in order to make some alterations and simplifications in it. I wrote to him the day before yesterday, and expect the score with the pianoforte edition, which I will immediately send you to Dresden. Tichatschek is just made for the title-role, and will make a splendid effect with it; the same with Mitterwurzer as Fieramosca and Madame Krebs as Ascanio, a mezzo-soprano part. From your extremely effective choruses, with their thorough musicianly drilling, we may expect a force never yet attained in the great Carnival scene (Finale of the second act); and I am convinced that, when you have looked more closely into the score, you will be of my opinion, that "Cellini", with the exception of the Wagner operas, —and they should never be put into comparison with one another—is the most important, most original musical- dramatic work of Art which the last twenty years have to show.

I must also beg for a little delay in sending you the score and the pianoforte edition, as it is necessary entirely to revise the German text and to have it written out again. I think this work will be ready in a few weeks, so you may expect the pianoforte edition at the beginning of February. At Easter Berlioz is coming to Dresden, to conduct a couple of concerts in the theater there. It would be splendid if you should succeed in your endeavors to make Herr von Luttichau fix an early date for the "Cellini" performance, and if you could get Berlioz to conduct his own work when he is in Dresden. In any case I shall come to the first performance, and promise myself a very satisfactory and delightful result. [Dresden did not hear "Cellini" till thirty—four years later.]

Meanwhile, dear friend, accept my best thanks once more for this project, and for all that you will do to realize it successfully, and receive the assurance of the high esteem of

Yours very truly,

F. Liszt

Weymar, January 4th 1841

106. To M. Escudier, Music Publisher in Paris

[Autograph (without address) in the possession of Monsieur Etienne Charavay in Paris.—The contents show to whom it was written.]

My dear Sir,

My time has been so absorbed by the rehearsals of a new opera in five acts, "Die Nibelungen", by Mr. Dorn, musical conductor in Berlin, the first performance of which will take place tomorrow, and also by a heap of small and great local obligations which accumulate for me in particular at the beginning of winter, that I have never yet had a moment in which to send you my very cordial thanks for your biographical notice on occasion of the Alexandre Piano, which [i.e., the biographical notice had just reached me. [A "giant grand piano" with three keyboards and pedals and registers, made according to Liszt's own directions.] I hope you will excuse this delay in consideration of the short time left me, and that you feel sure beforehand how kindly I take it of you for thus taking my part, in divers circumstances, for the honor of my name and of my reputation—a matter in which I will endeavour not to render your task too difficult.

With regard to the Schubert opera of which you again spoke to me in your last letter, I have a preliminary and very important observation to make to you—namely, that the rights of the score of "Alfonso and Estrella," in three acts, were obtained some years ago by Messrs. Hartel of Leipzig. As this work has not hitherto been performed anywhere they have not been in a hurry to publish it, and it was only communicated to me (by a copy) in case of a performance at Weymar. Therefore, before taking any other steps, it is indispensable that you should apply to Messrs. Hartel to obtain their authorization, either for a performance, or for the right to make a foreign edition of this work, and to make conditions with that firm relative to the matter. I do not doubt that Messrs. Hartel will be most obliging in the matter; but you cannot neglect this first step without serious ulterior disadvantages.

Hartel's consent once given, you must think of adapting to this charming music a libretto which is worthy of it,—and, if you are fortunate in doing this, success, and a popular and productive success, is undoubted.

Allow me to beg you once more to send me a copy of the ballet of Gluck's "Don Juan" and of the "Dictionary of Music" which you have just published,—I have already asked Belloni for them, but he is a little subject to distractions in these matters,—and accept, my dear sir, together with my best thanks, the assurance of my affectionate regard.

F. Liszt

Weymar, January 21st, 1854

107. To Monsieur Marie Escudier, Music Publisher in Paris.

[Autograph in the possession of M. Alfred Bovet at Valentigney.]

My Dear Sir,

Mr. Franck [Cesar Aug. Franck, born at Liege in 1822, composer and professor at the Paris Conservatoire, teacher of Faure, Chabrie, and d'Indy, the chief representatives of the new French school of music.] having written to me for a special introduction to you, I have great pleasure in fulfilling his request by writing these few lines to you. For many years past I have had a favorable opinion of Mr. Franck's talent in composition, through having heard his trios (very remarkable, as I think, and very superior to other works of the same kind published latterly).—

His oratorio "Ruth" also contains beautiful things, and bears the stamp of an elevated and well-sustained style. If the opera which he wants to have performed at the Lyric theater answers to these antecedents and to what I expect of Mr. Franck, the Lyric theater could only congratulate itself on its choice, and the best chance of success would be assured. Being unable to judge of it at a distance, and the score of this opera being unknown to me, I confine myself simply to drawing your attention to the very real talent of Mr. Franck, at the same time recommending him affectionately to your kindness.

Pray accept, my dear Sir, the expression of my sincere regard.

F. Liszt

Weymar, January 28th, 1854

108. To Dr. Franz Brendel

Dear Friend,

I have lately been over-occupied, and in addition to that I have been working somewhat, so that I have never had a free half-hour for correspondence.

I send you today the score and pianoforte edition of my "Kunstler-Chor." By next autumn I hope that half a dozen other (longer) scores will be in print. "Ha, der Verruchte!" ["Ah, the wretch!"] we can then say, as in "Tannhauser." Happily, however, no journey to Rome is necessary to obtain my absolution. We only wish to have done with so much outcry and tasteless chatter.

I shall beg David to put off my Leipzig rehearsals for a couple of weeks, as I cannot well get away from here now, and must also have the parts written out afresh. If David does not arrange it otherwise I shall probably come in the latter half of March.—.

Cornelius is telling you more fully, at the same time with this, what I have talked over with him.— Griepenkerl has been here a couple of days, and yesterday read his drama "Ideal and Welt" before our Grand Duke. The company was much the same as at Schlonbach's reading.—.

About your book I am very curious, and beg that you will send it me immediately. With regard to the opportunity for the paper I can tell you something when I come to Leipzig. In the course of next summer a monthly paper will make its appearance here, out of which much might grow. This is between ourselves, for the public will learn about it later.

Remember me most kindly to your wife, and remain good to

Your very sincere and grateful friend,

F. Liszt

Weymar, February 20th, 1854

P.S.—If you see Count Tyskiewicz please repeat my invitation to him to come for a couple of days to Weymar. If he is free next Thursday, that would be a good day. We have a concert here at which the "Kunstler-Chor" and a new orchestral work of mine ("Les Preludes"), the Schumann Symphony (No. 4.), and his Concerto for four horns will be given.

109. To Louis Kohler

My very dear Friend,

I come late—yet I hope you have not forgotten me. I am sending you, together with this, the score and pianoforte arrangement of my chorus "an die Kunstler," ["To the artists."] and also those numbers of the Rhapsodies which have been brought out by Schlesinger. The "Lohengrin" score you have no doubt received two months ago from Hartel, whom I begged to send it you direct—also the "Harmonies" from Kistner, and the last number of the "Rhapsodies" from Haslinger. At the end of the year you shall get some still greater guns from me, for I think that by that time several of my orchestral works (under the collective title of "Symphonische Dichtungen" [Symphonic Poems.]) will come out. Meanwhile accept once more my best thanks for the manifold proofs of your well-wishing sympathy, which you have given me publicly and personally. You may rest assured that no stupid self-conceit is sticking in me, and that I mean faithfully and earnestly towards our Art, which in the end must be formed of our hearts' blood.—Whether one "worries" a bit more or a bit less, as you put it, is pretty much the same. Let us only spread our wings "with our faces firmly set," and all the cackle of goose-quills will not trouble us at all.

That your article has been rudely and spitefully

criticized need not trouble you. You presuppose your reader to have refinement and educated feeling, artistic acuteness, a fine perception, and a certain Atticism. These, my dear friend, are indeed rare things—and only to be found in very homoeopathic doses among our Aristarchuses. Sheep and d[onkeys] have no taste for truffles. "Good hay, sweet hay, has not its equal in the world," as the artist-philosopher Zettel very truly says in the "Midsummer Night's Dream"! Moreover, dear friend, things didn't and don't go any better with other better fellows than ourselves. We need not make any fancies about it, but only go onward quietly, perseveringly, and consistently.

"Lohengrin" will be given here on the Grand Duchess's next birthday, April 8th. Gotze is coming this time from Leipzig, and sings the part of the Knight of the Swan. I hope that in May Tichatschek will undertake the role; he has already been studying the complete work for a long time past, and has had a splendid costume made for it. Perhaps you will be inclined to hear this glorious work here either in April or May. That would be very delightful of you, and I need not tell you how pleased I should be to see you among us again.—

Rafi is working hard at his "Samson," and tells me that he will have finished it by Christmas. Cornelius, whom I think you do not know (a most charming, fine-feeling and distinguished nature), has likewise a dramatic work, poem and music, in readiness for next season. We gave a good performance of Gluck's "Orpheus" lately, and for the last performance of this season (end of June I think we shall still give the Schubert opera "Alfonso und Estrella," if those same theater influences which already made themselves prominent by the "Indra" performance when you were at Weymar do not decide against this work, so interesting and full of intrinsic natural charm!—Farewell, dear friend, and send speedy tidings of yourself to

Yours most sincerely,

F. Liszt

Weymar, March 2nd, 1854

110. To Dr. Franz Brendel

Dear Friend,

Herewith an article which I send you for your paper. "Euryanthe," which I conduct here tomorrow, is the occasion of it. Still a more general question is aroused in it, which I am to a certain extent constrained "to agitate" from Weymar.["Gesammelte Scriften" vol. iii., I.] I flatter myself that our ideas will meet and harmonize in it. At first I had prefaced it by a couple of introductory lines, which I now erase. Will you be so good as to introduce me yourself in the Neue Zeitschrift by a few words? You will be the best one to make up this little preface. My name can be put quite openly with its five letters, as I am perfectly ready to stand by my opinion.

Tuesday morning I go to Gotha. The Duke's opera is to be given at the end of this month, or at latest on the 2nd April, and from the day after tomorrow till the first performance I shall be quartered at Gotha. In consequence of this I must unfortunately give up my excursion to Leipzig for the moment,—but I hope that David will allow another rehearsal in the Gewandhaus in the course of April, after the "Lohengrin" performance here with Gaze (on April 7th and 8th), which I must of necessity conduct. The news, which it appears some papers have published, that I was thinking of arranging a concert in Leipzig, belongs to the generation of ducks [geese?] who amuse themselves in swimming around my humble self. My visit to Leipzig has no other object than to make some of the musicians acquainted with one or two of my symphonic works. Should they be pleased with them, they might perhaps be given there next season. In any case, however, several of them will appear in score next autumn.

My time is exceedingly limited, and I must see about a great many things today which do not put one in the mood for correspondence.

Yours in friendship,

F. Liszt

Saturday, March 18th [1854]

111. To Louis Kohler.

[Weimar, April or May, 1854]

My very dear friend,

I am extremely glad that you liked my article on "Euryanthe" and theater direction, and I thank you most truly for your warm and very encouraging letter. For many weeks past I have been imitating you (as you and others always set me a good example), and am publishing several views on Art-subjects and Art-works in the Weimar official paper. By degrees these articles will swell into a volume, which shall then contain the complete set.

For the present I allow myself to send you my

Sonata, which has just been published at Hartel's. You will soon receive another long piece, "Scherzo and March," and in the course of the summer my "Annees de Pelerinage, Suite de Compositions pour le Piano" will appear at Schott's; two years— Switzerland and Italy. With these pieces I shall have done for the present with the piano, in order to devote myself exclusively to orchestral compositions, and to attempt more in that domain which has for a long time become for me an inner necessity. Seven of the Symphonic Poems are perfectly ready and written out. I will soon send you the little prefaces which I am adding to them, in order to render the perception of them more plain. Meanwhile I merely give you the titles:—

1. "Ce qu'on entend sur la Montagne" (after V. Hugo's poem in the "Feuilles d'Automne").

2. Tasso. "Lamento e Trionfo"

3. "Les Preludes" (after Lamartine's Meditation poetique "Les Preludes").

4. "Orphee."

5. "Promethee."

6. "Mazeppa" (after V. Hugo's Orientale "Mazeppa").

7. "Festklange."

8. "Heroide funebre."

9. "Hungaria."

By Christmas I intend to bring out the scores of all these—which would make about fifteen hundred plates in octavo size.

The post affair in regard to your letter with the article on Raff's "Fruehlingsboten" is very unpleasant to me. Neither has come into my hands, or else I should assuredly have let you know much sooner. What has become of it cannot now be traced; a similar thing happened also with a manuscript sent to me from Dresden, which was never able to be found. Excuse me, dear friend, for the carelessness which you supposed I had shown, of which I am in this case not guilty, as Pohl has already written to you by my request—and continue to keep for me always your sympathetic friendship, with which I remain, in complete harmonious unison,

Yours most truly and gratefully,

F. Liszt

112. To Dr. Franz Brendel

Dear Friend,

Whilst you are trotting about in Leipzig aus Rand und Band,[Uncontrolledly; a pun on the words Rand and Band (edge of the paper and volume), Brendel being editor of a paper.] I have been obliged to keep my bed, owing to a slight indisposition. The reading of your article in the Jahrbuchern [Year-books] has given me a pleasant hour, and I thank you heartily for the value and significance which you accord to my influence and endeavour here, both in this article and in the topographic section of your book. As long as I remain here we will take care that Weimar does not get into a bad way.

I hope to be quite on my legs again in a few days. My present indisposition is nothing but an overstrain and knock-up, which a couple of days' rest and some homoeopathic powder will easily set right. Probably we shall see one another in the early days of next week at Leipzig; but don't let us speak of it before-hand, as I have already been three times prevented from making this little trip.

The Orpheus article was sent to you yesterday. Perhaps it would still be possible to let it appear in the next number of the paper; if not, then it can appear the following week. The order of succession which I gave you by letter appears to me the right one, and begins with the Orpheus. This article is moreover as good as new, for, as your paper allowed me more space, I profited by it to make the earlier articles twice as long.["Gesammelte Schriften." vol. iii., 1.]

There are several points in your writing that we will soon talk over viva voca. I am still really very weak today, and merely wanted to write to thank you, and to tell you of my speedy advent in Leipzig (probably next Tuesday or Wednesday).

Yours in friendship,

F. Liszt

Wednesday, April 26th, 1854

Your commissions to Cornelius and letter to Cotta have been attended to.

113. To Louis Kohler

Dear Friend,

I am going once more to give you a pleasure. By today's post you will receive Richard Wagner's medallion. A friend of mine, Prince Eugene Sayn-Wittgenstein, modeled it last autumn in Paris, and I consider it the best likeness that exists of Wagner.

A thousand thanks for all the kind things you write and think of me. I very much wish that you should be in agreement with my present and my next work. If I could only dispose of my time better! But it is a wretched misery to have to spend one's time upon so many useless things and people, when one's head is quite full of other things!—Well, it must be so. God grant only patience and perseverance! I cannot remember for certain whether I have already sent you the Avant-propos to my Symphonic Poems, which I have in the meantime had printed on the occasion of their performance here. In any case I send them, together with the portrait for which you asked. I am now working at the ninth number (Hungaria)—the eight others are perfectly ready; but it will certainly be next spring before they appear in score.

Of pianoforte music I have nothing more to send you (until the "Annees de Pelerinage" appear at Schott's), except the little "Berceuse," which has found a place in the "Nuptial Album" of Haslinger. Perhaps the continuous pedal D-flat will amuse you. The thing ought properly to be played in an American rocking- chair with a Nargileh for accompaniment, in tempo comodissimo con sentimento, so that the player may, willy-nilly, give himself up to a dreamy condition, rocked by the regular movement of the chair-rhythm. It is only when the B-flat minor comes in that there are a couple of painful accents...But why am I talking such nonsense with you?—Your very perspicuous discovery of my intention in the second motive of the Sonata—

[Here, Liszt illustrates with a 2-measure score excerpt from his
 Sonata]

in contrast with the previous hammer-blows—

[Here, Liszt illustrates with another 2-measure score excerpt from his Sonata, similar to the first excerpt above except the melody is transposed and the rhythm is slightly different]

perhaps led me to it.

Farewell, my dear friend, and remain good to your

F. Liszt

Weymar, June 8th 1854

114. To Dr. Franz Brendel

Dear Friend,

I have had to alter a good deal in the "Robert" article, especially in the division of the subjects. Do not be angry about it. It will only make a very little trouble, and it pleases me better like this. Ergo my present Varianten [various readings] must be printed word for word in the next number.

If you have a couple of hours to spare, come next Saturday to Halle. Schneider's "Weltgericht [Last Judgment] is to be given there by the united Liedertafel [Singing Societies] of Dessau, Magdeburg, Berlin, Halle, etc. (on Saturday afternoon at 3 o'clock), and I have promised to be there. It would give me great pleasure to meet you at Halle; I shall put up at the Englischer Hof there. I hope you will accept my invitation, and therefore I shall say, Auf Wiedersehen [Au Revoir]!

Yours in friendship,

F. Liszt

June 12th, 1854

It will be easy for you to find out for certain about the performance at Halle. In any case I shall come for the day fixed for the "Weltgericht" (a peculiar work, written, as it were, from a pedestal of his own!). At present it is announced for next Saturday. Should there be any alteration, I shall arrange accordingly, and come later.—.

P.S.—The proofs must be very carefully revised, as there are a great many little alterations. Be so good as to revise the whole thing accurately yourself. When the article has appeared, please send me today's proofs back. ["Gesammelte Schriften," vol. iii., I.]

115. To Karl Klindworth in London

[A pupil of Liszt's, eminent both as a pianist, conductor, and musical editor; born at Hanover in 1830, lived in London, Moscow, and America; has, since 1882, been director of a music school in Berlin.]

Best thanks, dear Klindworth, for your nice letter. After the "Lamento" it seems a "Trionfo" is now about to be sounded. That gives me heartfelt pleasure. Your Murl-connection and Murl-wanderings [The Society of "Murls" (Moors, Devil-boys—that is to say, Anti-Philistines) was started at that time in Weimar. Liszt was Padischah (i.e. King or President); his pupils and adherents, Buelow, Cornelius, Pruckner, Remenyi, Laub, Cossmann, etc., etc., were Murls.] with Remenyi [A celebrated Hungarian violinist.] are an excellent dispensation of fate, and on July 6th, the day of your concert at Leicester, the Weimar Murls shall be invited to supper at the Altenburg, and Remenyi and Klindworth shall be toasted "for ever!"—[Liszt writes "for ever hoch leben lassen."]

On July 8th I go from here to Rotterdam. The

days of the performances are July 13th, 14th, and 15th. The last number but one of Brendel's paper (June 16th) contains the complete programme. The principal works will be Handel's "Israel in Egypt," Haydn's "Seasons," the Ninth Symphony, and a newly composed Psalm by Verhulst (the royal conductor of the Netherlands, director of the Euterpe Concerts in Leipzig about twelve years ago, and at present director of the Rotterdam Festivals). Roger, Pischek, Formes, Madame Ney, Miss Dolby, etc., have undertaken the solos, and the programme announces nine hundred members. It would be very-nice if you and Remenyi and Hagen [Theodor Hagen, a writer, known as a witty critic of his time under the name of "Butterbrod" [bread and butter] in the signale; died subsequently in America.] could come; in that case you would have to start at once, for on the 13th it begins, and on the 16th I leave Rotterdam—and go for a couple of days to Brussels, where I shall meet my two daughters.

A couple of Murls would look well in Rotterdam, and would make up to me in the best possible way for a lot of Philistinism which I shall probably have to put up with there (by contact with many honorable colleagues and companions in Art) ...So, if you possibly can, come. We will then have a Murl-Musical Festival in my room. (N.B.—I shall be staying with Mr. Hope, the banker.)

One has to get accustomed to the London atmosphere, and make one's stomach pretty solid with porter and port. For the rest, musical matters are not worse there than elsewhere, and one must even acknowledge some greatness in bestiality. If you can stand it, I am convinced that you will make a lucrative and pleasant position for yourself in London, and also gain a firm footing for the Murl propaganda ("une, indivisible et invincible") on the other side of La Manche, "ce qui sera une autre paire de manches." (In case you don't understand this joke, Remenyi must explain it to you.) So be of good courage and among good things! However things may be, never make capitulation with what is idle, cowardly, or false—however high your position may become-and preserve, under all circumstances, your Murldom!—

The two pieces from Raff's "Alfred" [Arranged by Liszt for the piano.] have been brought out by Heinrichshofcn (Magdeburg), and are dedicated to Carl Klindworth. Write me word how I can send them to you in the quickest and most economical manner—together with the Sonata. [It bore the title, in Liszt's handwriting, "Fur die Murlbibliothek" (for the Murl Library).] The Dante Fantasia will appear in the autumn, with the other pieces of the "Annees de Pelerinage," at Schott's, and I will tell him to reserve a copy for you.

Since you went away I have worked chiefly at my Symphonic Poems, composing and elaborating. The nine numbers are now quite ready, and seven of them entirely copied out. Next winter I intend to publish the scores, which ought to make about a thousand engraved plates. Immediately after my return from Rotterdam I shall set to work on the Faust Symphony, and hope that I shall have it ready written out by February.

Hartel is publishing also a couple of

transcriptions from

"Lohengrin" (the Festal March before the third act, with the

Bridal Chorus, Elsa's Dream and Lohengrin's rebuke to Elsa),

which I wrote lately.

A propos of Hartel, haven't you heard anything of your arrangement of the Schubert Symphony? The matter is being delayed rather long, and when I go to Leipzig I will inquire at Hartel's. [The arrangement for two pianos of the C major Symphony was brought out by them.] I have nothing new to tell you of Wagner. Joachim and Berlioz came to see me in May. Hoffmann von Fallersleben has settled here, and we see each other pretty often. His last poems, "Songs from Weymar," are dedicated to me.

Mason went to London a fortnight ago, and will probably come to Rotterdam. Laub is getting married in Bohemia, and brings his wife here in September. Schulhoff was also with me for a day.

Of Rubinstein I will tell you more when there is an opportunity. That is a clever fellow—the most notable musician, pianist, and composer, indeed, who has appeared to me from among the newer lights, with the exception of the Murls. Murlship alone is wanting to him still. But he possesses tremendous material, and an extraordinary versatility in the handling of it. He brought with him about forty or fifty manuscripts (Symphonies, Concertos, Trios, Quartets, Sonatas, Songs, a couple of Russian Operas, which have been given in Petersburg), which I read through with much interest during the four weeks which he spent here on the Altenburg. [Liszt's home] If you come to Rotterdam you will meet him there.

Now farewell, my dear Klindworth, and let me soon hear from you.

Your

F. Liszt

July 2nd, 1854

From the 10th to the 15th of July letters will find me in Rotterdam—Poste restante. N.B.— Remenyi gives me no reply about the manuscript of Brahms' Sonata (with violin). Probably he has taken it with him, for I have, to my vexation, rummaged through my entire music three times, without being able to find the manuscript. Don't forget to write to me about this in your next letter, as Brahms wants this Sonata for printing.

116. To Dr. Franz Brendel

Dear Friend,

I send you herewith a long article on "Harold" and Berlioz, which
Pohl will translate, and adopt in his intended book on Berlioz.
Be so good as to see that Pohl gets the manuscript as soon as
possible, as he is probably in Leipzig now.

[The article appeared in the "Neue Zeitschrift" in 1855 (afterwards "Gesammelte Schriften," vol. iv), whereas it did not appear in Pohl's book on Berlioz, which only saw the light thirty years later, in 1884.]

Tonight I go to Rotterdam for the Musical Festival, and thence for a couple of days to Brussels. On the 22nd—24th of July I shall come to Leipzig for a few hours, before I get back to Weimar.

I suppose you have given up your Rotterdam journey. If you have anything to send for from there, write me a line immediately to Poste restante, Rotterdam.

Two articles are ready for your paper, "Die weisse Frau" [The White Lady] and "Alfonso and Estrella." As soon as the "Montecchi" and the "Favorita" appear you shall receive them [the complete "Gesammelte Schriften," vol. iii, 1]. The "Fliegender Hollander" is also ready, but must be copied.["Gesammelte Schriften," vol. iii., 2.] This article is a very long one, and will take up several of your numbers.

Remember me kindly to your wife, and bear me in friendly remembrance as your willing collaborator and attached friend,

F. Liszt

Weymar, July 7th, 1854

117. To Anton Rubinstein.

[Rubinstein (born 1830, at Wechwotynetz in Russian Bessarabia) gave concerts as early as 1839 in Paris, and Liszt, who was there, welcomed in the boy the future "inheritor of his playing," and helped him in his studies, both during his stay in Paris, and during his stay in Vienna later on, by giving him lessons. When Rubinstein, in 1854, after a long sojourn in Russia, came back to Germany, Liszt gave him a most hospitable reception at the Altenburg at Weimar.]

What are you doing with yourself, my dear Van II.? [From Rubinstein's likeness to Beethoven Liszt jokingly called him Van II. (that is, Van Beethoven)] Are you settled according to your liking at Bieberich, and do you feel in a fine vein of good-humor and work, or are you cultivating the Murrendo[This must refer to some witty joke.] of your invention?

Your luggage van of manuscripts was sent off to you the day after my return, and will have reached you in good condition, I think. I acquit myself herewith of my little debt of one hundred thalers, with many thanks for your obligingness, until the case arises again. A propos of obligingness, will you please send me the letter of introduction for Cornelius's sister, who is about to begin her theatrical career in the choruses of the Italian opera at St. Petersburg? I told Cornelius that you had promised it to me. And I should be very glad to send it him without too much delay. His sister is an excellent young person, not too pretty, but well brought up, and whom one can introduce with a good conscience. It is to be feared that she will feel herself very isolated there, and will get "Heimweh" [homesickness]!

Let me hear from you soon. As regards myself I have very little to tell you at this moment. Weymar is deserted, as the Court is absent. Schade alone is radiant, for he has already got a heap of subscribers to his "Weymar'sche Jahrbucher" [Weimar Year-books], the first number of which is half printed and will definitely appear on the 28th August. Mr. de Beaulieu will not be back for three weeks; in spite of this send me your scenario of the Russian opera as soon as ever you have finished it, for I will see that he has it, and, if there is no political obstacle (which is a very exceptional circumstance in these matters), your work shall be given next November. [The opera "The Siberian Hunters" was, in point of fact, given at Weimar through Liszt's instrumentality.] When you have sufficiently enjoyed the charms of Bieberich, come and see me at the Altenburg. It seems to me that you will be at least as comfortable here as elsewhere (Baden-Baden with Madame * * * excepted!), and Van II may be certain of being always welcome

To his very affectionate friend,

F. Liszt

Weymar, July 31st, 1854

For the translation of your opera I again recommend Cornelius, but you will have to pass some weeks here to hasten the work.

118. To Dr. Franz Brendel

You would have greatly deceived yourself, dear friend, if you had attributed any sort of personal aim to my last intimation regarding the conduct of the critical part of your paper. By no means could that be the case, and I think I even said to you in the course of conversation that, so long as my set of articles on various operas, which provisionally closes with the "Flying Dutchman", is going on in the Neue Zeitschrift, it seems to me more becoming not to bespeak any other musical productions of mine. None the less do I consider it desirable and quite in the interest of our cause that, for the future, the more important productions, especially the works of R. Schumann, Hiller, Gade, etc., should be brought into consideration more fully and oftener than has been the case of late years. The bookseller's views, as regards the sending or non-sending of works, appear to me unimportant and even injurious for the higher position which your paper maintains.

—

I send you herewith Cornelius's article on the Prize Symphony and the "Girondistes" Overture. It is very nicely written, and will probably suit you. If possible put it into your next number.

I cannot now undertake the discussion about the Schumann collective writings, as I am prevented by musical work for a long time. Still, if I write later on a couple of articles on the work, that need not prevent you from bringing out very soon one or more articles discussing the same work. There is much to take in and to bring out in it, which one critic alone is scarcely capable of conceiving. The best plan of all would be if you yourself will undertake the discussion of the Schumann writings. Should you, however, not have time for it, then Pohl would be the best man for this work. His predilection for Schumann, and his familiarity with Schumann's views, qualify him thoroughly for this.

My articles on the "Flying Dutchman" must not wait so long as you propose to me in your letter. I wish explicity that the two articles on the "Weisse Dame" and "Alfonso and Estrella" should appear as soon as possible, and immediately afterwards the "Flying Dutchman", so that by the end of September this series of twelve opera discussions may have all appeared in the Neue Zeitschrift.

At the same time with the proofs of the article on the "Weisse Dame" you will receive the "Alfonso and Estrella" article, and, as soon as these are out, the "Flying Dutchman", which must be published in September—for various reasons, which cannot well be explained in a letter.

Raff's book "Die Wagnerfrage" [The Wagner Question] has arrived here today, and I have already read it. The author is so pleased with himself that it would be a miracle if his readers were joined to him in the same proportion, and Raff is specially at variance with miracles!—

This book makes on me the effect of a pedagogic exuberance. Even the occasional good views (on harmony, for example) that it contains are obscured by a self-sufficiency in the tone and manner of them, of which one may well complain as insupportable. What Raff wishes to appear spoils four-fifths (to quote the time which he adapts so ridiculously to "Lohengrin" of what he might be. He is perpetually getting on scientific stilts, which are by no means of a very solid wood. Philosophic formulas are sometimes the envelope, the outside shell, as it were, of knowledge; but it may also happen that they only show empty ideas, and contain no other substance than their own harsh terminology. To demonstrate the rose by the ferule may seem a very scientific proceeding to vulgar pedants; for my part it is not to my taste; and without being unjust to the rare qualities of Raff's talent, which I have long truly appreciated, his book seems to me to belong too much to the domain of moral and artistic pathology for it to help in placing questions of Art in their right light.

I beg you, dear friend, not to repeat this to anybody, for I could not go against Raff in any but the most extreme case, for which I hope he will not give me any occasion. Against the many charges to which he has exposed himself I even intend to shield him as far as possible, but I am very much grieved that he has mingled so much that is raw and untenable in his book with much that is good, true and right.

Farewell, dear friend, and give most friendly greetings to your wife from

Yours most sincerely,

F. Liszt

August 12th, 1854

In the "Favorita" article a great error has been allowed to remain. "No lover, no knight behaves thus"—and not "A lover behaves thus," etc. Send me at once the proofs of the "Weisse Dame", and in September bring the "Fliegende Hollander", which must not wait any longer.

I am now working at my Faust Symphony. The three-keyboard instrument arrived yesterday from Paris. It might be well to take the opportunity of my Catalogue appearing at Hartel's to see about a special article on it in your paper.

119. To Anton Rubinstein

[August, 1854]

My dear Van II.,

Whatever scruple I may have in making the shadow of an attempt on the liberty of your determinations and movements,—a scruple of which I gave you a pertinent proof by not insisting any

214

further on your choosing Weymar instead of Bieberich as your villegiatura during this last month, —yet duty (and a theatrical duty!) obliges me to snatch you from your Rhine-side leisure, to set yourself to work afresh at your business on the banks of the Ilm,—

"Non piu andrai, farfalone," etc. [Aria from Mozart's "Figaro"]

We have to hunt the Siberian bear; ["The Hunters of Siberia", an opera of Rubinstein's.] and whether it is the season or not, I don't trouble myself about that. Mr. de Beaulieu has just answered me in the affirmative about the proposition I made to him to give your "Hunters of Siberia" at the beginning of November (the 9th, a date already made famous by the "Homage to Art" a Prologue which will be again given this season), and asks me particularly to push on as fast as possible the copying of all the parts. Now one must kill the bear before selling his skin— that is to say, translate the libretto, fit it to the music, and arrange the score for the performance at Weymar.

According to what we arranged verbally, I spoke about it to Cornelius, who accepts the work of translator with pleasure, and will fulfill it promptly, and, I am persuaded, to your satisfaction. The only thing wanting is for you to come at once, and spend a fortnight at Weymar to finish everything. I give you then rendez-vous at the Altenburg, where your former quarters await you. No one will bother you there, and you can give yourself up to cultivating murrendos [La Mara thinks there was a joke in connection with this; I cannot help thinking it is a

215

corruption of morendo, and that perhaps Rubinstein joked about cultivating a particular touch or nuance. —Translator's note] to your heart's content whenever the fancy takes you. Try therefore not to be too long over your farewells to the Tannhausers of the banks of the Rhine (and if by chance Madame S. is there, pack yourself off secretly so as not to provoke a scene of too much frenzy), so as to get to Weymar by 1st to 3rd September, for your score must be given to be copied by the 15th to the 20th. I will keep your three books till you come, and will give them you back at the Altenburg, and I take great pleasure in advance in your success on our stage.

A revoir then, my dear Rubinstein, in a week's time.

Yours ever in friendship,

F. Liszt

Write me simply a word to fix the date of your arrival, so that I may let Cornelius know, as he is gone for a week to his mother, a few hours away from here.

In the matter of news I will tell you that my instrument with three keyboards is installed in the second etage of the Altenburg, and that I have finished the first part of my Faust Symphony (a third of the whole)—the two other parts will be ready in November, I hope.

I shall also have a little friendly quarrel to pick with you, which I reserve for our after-tea conversations.

A bientot!

120. To Alexander Ritter in Dresden.

[Ritter at this time joined the Weimar

Hofcapelle (Court orchestra); was afterwards music director at Stettin, and lives now in Munich; is celebrated as the composer of the operas "Der Faule Hans" and "Wem die Krone."]

Hearty good wishes on your marriage, dear friend. I reproach myself for disturbing you in your honeymoon. Well, a little music to it won't hurt anybody. So come as soon as it is agreeable to you. The matter is not so very pressing; I only beg you to send a few lines in reply to Herr Jacobi, the secretary of the Court theater, who wrote to you previously, and to tell him the date of your arrival in Weymar. As your marriage takes place on the 12th of this month, you are quite justified in asking for a few days' respite. If it suits you to stay a fortnight longer in Dresden, then fix the 1st of October for your coming to Weymar. With regard to your quarters, I am quite ready to help you in word and deed.

In case Pohl is in Dresden you can tell him that his wife is also engaged from the 15th of September (on which date the theater here reopens). I wrote yesterday to Brendel, in order to get Pohl's exact present address. I expect the answer tomorrow, and Herr Jacobi will immediately write to Frau Pohl.

Meanwhile remember me most kindly to your wife, and dispose entirely—without ceremony—of

Yours most sincerely,

F. Liszt

Weymar, September 6th, 1854

121. To Bernhard Cossmann, Schloss Chanceaux bei Loches in Touraine

Weymar, September 8th, 1854

Dear Friend,

Whilst you are promenading at your leisure beneath the fine oaks, beeches, birches, horse-chestnuts, etc., of Chanceaux, I have the sotte chance [Silly opportunity] of gaping chanceusement [doubtfully] to the crows of Weymar, where we have certainly no Chanceaux, but pretty well of gens sots [stupid people] im Loch [In this hole. All plays upon words, and given therefore in the original.] (near Loches!!). This almost attains to the height of punning of our friend Berlioz, does not it?—I should not be able to keep on such heights, and therefore I hasten to descend to more temperate regions (des regions plus temperees),-"le Clavecin bien tempere of J. S. Bach," for example, or to some "Beau lieu" with or without marque au nez (Marconnay). [A play on words. The name of the Intendant of the Weimar Court theater was Beaulieu- Marconnay.] (I implore you to keep this execrable improvisation to yourself, for, in my position as Maitre de Chapelle, I should run the risk of being fined by the "Hofamt" [office in the royal household] for allowing myself such an application of Berlioz's treatise on instrumentation—but I really don't know what tarantula of a pun is biting me at this moment!)

Mr. de Beaulieu has just done two graceful acts for me, for which I am very grateful. Madame Pohl is engaged as harpist to the Weymar Kapelle, and A. Ritter of Dresden—the brother of Hans de Bulow's friend—as violinist in place of little Abel, who is leaving us to go and probably assassinate some Cain at a second or third desk in an orchestra, somewhere!

A. Ritter is going to marry Mdlle. Wagner on

the 12th of this month (the sister of Johanna), who has played in comedy at the Breslau theater, and who, by her husband's orders, will not continue playing when she has her home to keep. Let us hope so at least! These two new engagements are a great pleasure to me, and I shall willingly console myself for the loss of the innocent Abel.

And as Mr. de Beaulieu is just in such a good temper, I advise you to profit by the circumstance to write him a letter, artistically turned, to beg for a prolongation of your holiday, which he will grant you with a good grace, I am sure.

The theater will reopen the 15th September. The 16th "Ernani" will be given. In the course of October we shall have the "Huguenots", with a new singer from Prague, Mdlle. Stoger, of whom one hears wonders.

For the 9th October (fiftieth anniversary of the entry of H.I.H. the Grand Duchess Marie Paulowna into Weymar) a rather curious performance will be arranged:—

1st. The Homage to Art by Schiller.

2nd. One of my Poemes Symphoniques.

3rd. "The Hunters of Siberia", Opera in one Act—Music by Rubinstein.

4th. The Finale of "Lorelei" by Mendelssohn.

For the winter season they are thinking of giving the two

"Iphigenies", "in Aulis" and "in Tauris", by Gluck, and

Schumann's "Genoveva".

Rubinstein and Wasielewski (of Bonn) have

been here some days. Raff has published his volume "The Wagner Question." I would neither answer nor vindicate it!—My monster instrument with three keyboards has also arrived a fortnight ago, and seems to me to be a great success—and on your return I shall pretty nearly have finished my Faust Symphony, at which I am working like a being possessed.

This is all my news from here, to which I add the expression of the old and sincere friendship of your very affectionate

F. Liszt

P.S.—I, on my side, will also write to Mr. de Beaulieu about you, but it is the thing for you to write him a few lines. The matter in itself will not present any difficulty.

122. To Gaetano Belloni in Paris

[autograph in the possession of M. Etienne Charavay in Paris]

[September 9th, 1854]

My dear Belloni,

Will you do me the kindness to tell Mr. Escudier that on my last visit to H.R.H. the Duke of Gotha I gave Monseigneur the volume on Rossini, and spoke to him at the same [time] of the desire that Mr. Escudier had mentioned to me in his last letter to be admitted into the order of H.R.H., before putting himself at his command? It goes without saying that I warmly recommended Mr. Escudier to the Duke; but nevertheless he seemed to turn a little deaf, at any rate with one ear, to the side of the ribbon. In the course of this month I shall probably see the Duke again, and will speak to him again about it. On your side do not neglect Oppelt [a Belgian writer; translated the Duke's opera], who frequently corresponds with Gotha, and rest assured that I shall not fail to be agreeable to your friends on this occasion.

Yours ever,

F. Liszt

Nothing new here. The theatrical season will open with "Ernani" on the 16th September at latest; they talk of mounting "Rigoletto" or the "Foscari." Unfortunately the German translations of Verdi's operas are not worth a straw, and we are great purists at Weimar. In November the "Huguenots" will also be given, for the first time at Weymar, the late Grand Duke never having permitted the performance of this work on account of his respect for Luther, whom his ancestors had specially protected.

Hartel is going to engrave several of my scores. Four or five of them will appear in the course of the winter ("Tasso"—the "Preludes"—"Orphee"—"Mazeppa" will be printed first) under the title of "Poemes Symphoniques."

I won't write to Escudiers—it will be enough if you let them know of my good intentions in regard to them. You know that I am overdone with correspondence, and, unless it is absolutely necessary for me to write, I abstain from it, so as not to interrupt my work of composition, which is my first raison d'etre.

123. To Eduard Liszt in Vienna

What affliction and what desolation, my very dear friend! [Eduard Liszt, then member of the provincial Court of Justice in the Civil Senate, had lost his wife from cholera.] Alas! in trials such as these even the sympathy felt by those who are nearest to us can do but little to alleviate the overwhelming weight of the cross which we have to bear. And yet I wish to tell you that in these days of sorrow my heart is near to yours, sympathizing with your suffering, and trusting that "the peace of the Lord," that peace which the world can neither give nor take away, may sustain you.

Ever yours,

F. Liszt

October 10th, 1854

P.S.—Try to come and see me soon!

124. To Anton Rubinstein

Weimar, October 19th, 1854

Schott makes me ashamed, my dear Rubinstein. Here come the new proofs of the "Kamenoi-Ostrow," [Rubinstein had written a number of short pianoforte pieces named after the Emperor's summer residence near St. Petersburg.] which he addresses to me for you, and I have not yet sent you the previous ones! To excuse myself I must tell you that I am frightfully busy (especially at the theater), and that I did not want to put the proofs in a wrapper without writing and thanking you for your charming and clever letter from Leipzig. Well, here is the whole packet at last, which you can send direct to Schott. Nevertheless, I am in your debt for the carriage (which please beg Redslob to put to my account), and for ten crowns which I borrowed from you at the railway. As you are coming back here at the beginning of November we shall have plenty of time to settle these little matters.

The rehearsals of your "Chasseurs de Siberie" begin in the course of next week. You may trust in my zeal, and be assured that your work will be suitably prepared. I only beg you to be here about the 4th November, in order to give us your own ideas at the final rehearsals. If you decidedly prefer to be a spectator at the performance, I will willingly conduct the work—but perhaps at the general rehearsals the fancy may take you to mount the conductor's chair, as I proposed to you at first: whatever you definitely decide in this matter will only be agreeable to me. Therefore just do as you generally do, I beg you, without ceremony or bother of any kind.

How do you find yourself as regards the musical atmosphere of Leipzig? Has your "Ocean" obtained the suffrages of the Areopagus which must be its first judge? At which Gewandhaus Concert will Mr. Van II. be heard? If you already know anything positive as to your debuts in Leipzig, write it to me, with a continuation of the commentaries which amused me so much in your former letter. We have nothing of special news here which can interest you. Madame Wagner returns to Weymar the day after tomorrow, and next Sunday "Lohengrin" will be given. The Wednesday after that a new singer (Mdlle. Stoger, the daughter of the director at Prague), who possesses a beautiful voice and appears to be highly endowed, will make her debut in "Lucrezia Borgia." On the 24th October I expect Madame Schumann, whom you will already have seen and heard at Leipzig. When you have an opportunity please tell her not to delay her journey to

Weymar, for I have made all the arrangements with Mr. de Beaulieu, etc., from the 24th to the 26th, for the Court Concert and for the one which will take place at the theater in her honor.

My "Faust" is finished, and I am going to give it to the copyist in a couple of days. I am very curious to make acquaintance with yours, and to see in how far the beaux-esprits differ whilst meeting on common ground! Your "murrendos" at Leipzig will have proved favorable to your conversations with the Muse, and I look forward to a fine Symphony. A revoir then, dear friend; on the 4th November, or the 5th at latest, we have the first performance of an unpublished tragedy, "Bernhard von Weymar," for which Raff has written a grand Overture and a March, and on the following days your general rehearsals.

Yours in all friendship,

F. Liszt

125. To Dr. Franz Brendel

[Beginning of November, 1854]

Dear Friend,

Pohl's article on Lieder und Spruche, etc. (Songs and Sayings), appears to me to be of general interest to the public—therefore I begged you to put it in your paper.

Touching what you have reserved of Raff's, I am quite of opinion that you should also make room for him in his critical examinations of the Minnesingers. [The German poet-singers of the Middle Ages.] The ground is an interesting and attractive one— and if a rather warm discussion should ensue later on between Raff and Pohl, the field of the Minnegesang (love-song) is by far the most agreeable for both, as well as the more entertaining for your readers. Ergo, put Pohl's article into your next number. Raff can then spring his mines in honor of the Minnegesang when he pleases. This may make a quite pleasant and harmless joke— perchance a crown of lilies will mingle with it in the end and shape the affair into a University concern... Your paper, in any case, will not suffer. Therefore set to work and go through with it!

In Bussenius [Bussenius, under the pseudonym W. Neumann, published the set of biographies "The Composers of Recent Times" (Balde, Cassel).] you have rightly found the man of whom I previously foretold you somewhat. I think that by the New Year he will settle at Gotha, and carry on there with his firm (Balde) greater literary and publishing undertakings. Meanwhile don't speak of this. When the outlook is more certain, and things are favorably settled, I will tell you more.

I gladly accept your friendly invitation to write an article for your New Year's number. In the course of the next few days you will receive the article on Clara Schumann, and shortly afterwards the second half of "Robert Schumann."

Cornelius has been rather unwell for several days, which has delayed the translation. [Peter Cornelius translated the articles written in French by Liszt—with the collaboration of the Princess Wittgenstein—for the Neue Zeitschrift; those which are published in vols. iii. to v. of the "Gesammelte Schriften."]

Will you, dear friend, be so good as to give my

special thanks to Herr Klitzsch for his article in today's number? By the favorable manner in which he enters into the intentions of my Mass, and the artistic sympathy he shows for my endeavour, he has given me a very great pleasure. Probably a good opportunity will present itself, later on, for me to undertake a further work in the religious style, as I feel and conceive it, by the composition of a "Missa Solemnis" for mixed chorus and orchestra...For the present I cannot, however, occupy myself with this; but aufgeschoben soll nicht aufgehoben heissen. [A German proverb— "Put off is not given up."]

When I come to Leipzig I shall have the pleasure of calling on Klitzsch and giving him my best thanks in person. If you think I ought to write him a few lines before then, let me know.

Litolff was here several days, and we have come nearer together both from a friendly and an artistic standpoint. His fourth Concerto (Conzert-Symphonie) is a marked advance on the previous ones. He played this, as well as the third Concerto, the day before yesterday, in a truly masterly and electric, living manner. Frau Dr. Steche will have told you about it. Perhaps in your next number you will put in a short appreciative notice of Litolff's appearance here.

Rubinstein left for Leipzig at midday today. The performance of his Symphony ["Ocean"; given for the first time, November 16th, 1854, at the Gewandhaus Concert for the Poor.] is fixed for the 16th at the Gewandhaus, and later on he will also appear as a pianist. Hartel, Hofmeister, and Schott have already taken about thirty of his manuscripts, which is about the smaller half of his portfolio!—

About the Berlin "Tannhauser" affair I cannot for the moment say more than that I have always made Wagner feel perfectly at liberty to put me on one side, and to manage the matter himself, according to his own wishes, without me. But so long as he gives me his confidence as a friend, it is my duty to serve him as a discreet friend—and this I cannot do otherwise than by giving no ear to transactions of that kind, and letting people gossip as much as they like. Don't say anything more about it for the present in your paper. The matter goes deeper than many inexperienced friends of Wagner's imagine. I will explain it to you more clearly by word of mouth. Meanwhile I remain passive— for which Wagner will thank me later on.

Yours most truly,

F. Liszt

N. B.—Pohl wishes his Minnesinger article not to be signed with the name Hoplit, but with the letters R. P., when it appears in your paper.

126. To Anton Rubinstein

Your "Dialogue Dramatique" a propos of your "Ocean" is a little chef-d'oeuvre, and I shall keep it, in order, later on, to put it at the disposal of some future Lenz, who will undertake your Catalogue and the analysis of the three styles of Van II. We laughed with all our hearts, a deux, in the little blue room of the Altenburg, and we form the most sincere wishes that Gurkhaus, [Principal of the music firm F. Kistner in Leipzig.] the deus ex machine, may have come to put you out of the uncomfortable state of suspense in which the Gewandhaus public did you the honor to leave you. To tell the truth, this decrescendo of applause, at the third movement of your Symphony, surprises me greatly, and I would have wagered without hesitation that it would be the other way. A great disadvantage for this kind of composition is that, in our stupid musical customs, often very anti-musical, it is almost impossible to appeal to a badly informed public by a second performance immediately after the first; and at Leipzig, as elsewhere, one only meets with a very small number of people who know how to apply cause and effect intelligently and enthusiastically to a piece out of the common, and signed with the name of a composer who is not dead. Moreover I suspect that your witty account is tainted with a species of modesty, and I shall wait, like the general public, for the accounts in the newspapers in order to form an opinion of your success. Whatever may come of it, and however well or ill you are treated by the public or criticism, my appreciation of the value that I recognize in your works will not vary, for it is not without a well-fixed criterion, quite apart from the fashion of the day, and the high or low tide of success, that I estimate your compositions highly, finding much to praise in them, except the reservation of some criticisms which almost all sum up as follows—that your extreme productiveness has not as yet left you the necessary leisure to imprint a more marked individuality on your works, and to complete them. For, as it has been very justly said, it is not enough to do a thing, but it must be completed. This said and understood, there is no one who admires more than I do your remarkable and abundant faculties, or who takes a more sincere and friendly interest in your work. You know that I have set my mind upon your "Ocean" being given here, and I shall beg you also to give us the pleasure of playing one of your Concertos. In about ten days I will write and tell you the date of the first concert of our orchestra.

Meanwhile your "Chasseurs de Siberie" will be given again on Wednesday next (the 22nd). I will tell Cornelius to give you tidings of it, unless the fancy takes you to come and hear it, in order to make a diversion from your "Voix interieures" [internal voices] of Leipzig.

Write to me soon, my dear Van II., and believe me wholly your very affectionate and devoted friend,

F. Liszt

November 19th, 1854

127. To Dr. Franz Brendel

Dear Friend,

Kahnt [The subsequent publisher, for many years, of the Neue Zeitschrift.] is only known to me by name, as an active and not too moderately Philistine publisher. Personally I have never met him, and therefore I cannot give a decided opinion as to his fitness and suitability for the post of publisher of the Neue Zeitschrift—yet, on the grounds you give me, it seems quite right. Nothing is to be expected from Bussenius until he has made a firm footing at Gotha, which can only come to pass in the course of the next months; besides this, he has such gigantic plans for his new establishment in Gotha that the affairs of the Neue Zeitschrift might be left somewhat in the background. I entirely agree with you on this point, that you cannot put the Neue Zeitschrift in the market and offer it to just any publisher who has shown himself up to now hostile to our tendencies. To do such a thing as that could never lead to a satisfactory result. I would, however, remark that the next few years will probably set our party more firmly on their legs; the invalidity of our opponents vouches pretty surely for that, apart from the fact, which is nevertheless the principal point, that powerful talent is developing in our midst, and many others who formerly stood aloof from us are drawing near to us and agreeing with us. Consequently it seems to me that it is not to your interest to conclude at once a contract for too many years with Kahnt, unless, which is scarcely likely, he were to make you such an offer that you would be satisfied with it under the most favorable conditions. If Kahnt shows the necessary perception and will for the matter, try to get him to have a consultation with me about it at Weymar. As he is also a music publisher I could tell him some things, and make others plainer, which would not be without interest to him. He need not be afraid that I shall belabor him with manuscripts or urge him to untimely or useless sacrifices...(I need not waste more words over the purity of my intentions!) But I think it is desirable that, if Kahnt consents to become editor of the Neue Zeitschrift, I should put him on his guard about several things beforehand which do not come exactly within the sphere of your activity, but which may essentially help to the better success of the undertaking. A couple of hours will be ample for it, and as I shall not be absent from Weymar during the coming weeks Kahnt will find me any day. Perhaps it could be arranged for you to come to Weymar with him for a day, and then we three can make matters perfectly clear and satisfactory.

Although it is very difficult to me to make time for the more necessary things, yet I am quite at your service with a short article for the trial-number on Wagner's "Rheingold." I had arranged the article so as to do for the New Year's number—you shall have it in four to five days. Dispose of it as suits you best. In case the "Clara Schumann" article does not appear in the next number of the paper, and we do not have to wait too long for the trial-number, it would be well perhaps to put it in there. Possibly it might also be reprinted in the trial-number.

I am glad that you, dear friend, after some "jerks and wrenches," have come together again with the pseudo-Musician of the Future, Rubinstein. He is a clever fellow, possessed of talent and character in an exceptional degree, and therefore no one can be more just to him than I have been for years. Still I do not want to preach to him—he may sow his wild oats and fish deeper in the Mendelssohn waters, and even swim away if he likes. But sooner or later I am certain he will give up the apparent and the formalistic for the organically Real, if he does not want to stand still. Give him my most friendly greetings; as soon as our concert affairs are settled here I shall write and invite him to give one of his orchestral works here.

Do not let yourself be grieved at the ever-widening schism in Leipzig about which you write to me. We have nothing to lose by it; we must only understand how to assert our full rights in order to attain them. That is the task, which will not be accomplished in a day nor in a year. Indeed, it is as it is written in the Gospel, "The harvest truly is plentiful, but the laborers are few!" Therefore we are not to make ourselves over- anxious—only to remain firm, again to remain firm—the rest will come of itself!—

I will do my utmost for Fraulein Riese, [Pianoforte teacher in Leipzig, who for years went every Sunday to Weimar to study with Liszt; died 1860] that she may not repent the somewhat trying journey. It is a splendid and plucky determination of hers to come regularly to Weymar, and I hope she will gain thereby much pleasure and satisfaction.

Nauenburg's proposal of a Tonkunstler-Versammlung (meeting of musicians) in Weymar is very flattering to me; the same was written to me from several other sides. Hitherto I have always abstained from it, because I thought it was more prudent not to sell the bear's skin before the bear is shot. Moreover the ordinary fine talk without deeds ["much cry and little wool"] is very distasteful to me: let friend Kuhmstedt [Professor at a school, and Music Director at Eisenach; died 1858] sing that kind of philosophical fiortures in Eisenach; I have no talent for it. None the less we can return to the Nauenburg proposition at a convenient opportunity, and see how it could be best carried out. According to my opinion, Leipzig would be the most suitable place—and the summer a good time for it.

I consider Raff's polemic entirely harmless.

Your readers will get a lesson in history from it, for which they can but be grateful to you—and we need not be anxious about Pohl. It will not puzzle him to eat his way out suitably and wittily.

Yours ever,

F. Liszt December 1st, 1854

128. To J.W. von Wasielewski in Bonn

[Formerly Conductor of the Town Vocal-Union at Bonn (born 1822), afterwards at Dresden; then again in Bonn as Music Director, and living since 1884 in Sondershausen. Widely known as a literary man through his biographies of Schumann and Beethoven, and also through his book "The Violin and its Masters," etc.]

Dear Friend,

Owing to the somewhat long detour of the "Pesther Lloyd," in which the friendly lines of remembrance have been reprinted which you dedicated to the "Altenburg" in the Cologne paper, I only heard of these a few days ago. [Written on the occasion of a week's visit to Liszt at the Altenburg at Weimar, at which time A. Rubinstein was also the Master's guest.] Please therefore to excuse the delay in my thanks, which are none the less sincere and heartfelt.

I have heard many accounts of your most successful concert performances in Bonn, all of which unite in giving you due praise for your excellent conducting. At the beginning of January concert affairs here, which have hitherto been in a vacillating and fluctuating condition, owing to various local circumstances, will take a more settled turn; I will send you the complete programme shortly. By today's post you will receive the "Songs and Sayings" from the last period of the "Minnesang," arranged for four voices by W. Stade (of Jena). It is an interesting work, and the editors would be very much indebted to you if you would have the kindness to give a couple of numbers of them at your concerts. The little pieces make quite a pretty effect, and one peculiar to themselves, which will prove still more intense with the beautiful Rhine Voices. Perhaps you would also find time and inclination to make the public favorably disposed towards the work by a few lines in the Cologne paper.

How is Hiller? Has his "Advocate" [an opera, "The Advocate." It had no success, and was publicly ridiculed at the Cologne Carnival.] won his requisite suit, as I wish from my heart may be the case? It would be very kind of you to let me know your plain, unvarnished opinion of the performance. I should like to recommend an early performance of the opera in Weymar if Hiller has nothing against it. As you frequently have occasion to see Hiller I beg you to ask him whether it would be agreeable to him to send me the text-book and the score, so that I may make the proposal to the management to give the opera here very soon.— Should the matter be then so arranged that he himself conducts the first performance I should be very glad indeed, and I will write to him more fully about it.

The opera Repertoire here will be rather at a stand-still this winter. Frau von Milde is in an interesting condition: consequently there can be no Wagner operas from three to four months; for Frau von Milde is for us, and for these operas in particular, not to be replaced. Berlioz's "Benvenuto Cellini" must also be left unperformed; all the more because Beck, the tenor, has entirely lost his upper notes, and is less able than ever to sing the part of Cellini. But Berlioz will come here in January to conduct his oratorio "L'Enfance du Christ," etc. (German translation by Cornelius), and his "Faust." I on my side have also finished my "Faust Symphony" (in three parts—without text or voice). The entity or non-entity has become very long, and I shall in any case have the nine "Symphonic Poems" printed and performed first, before I set "Faust" going, which may not be for another year. Rubinstein's "Ocean Symphony" is to figure in one of our next programmes. If it were not the rule to keep these concerts exclusively instrumental, I should have begged Hiller for his "Loreley." Probably a good opportunity will occur for giving this work when he himself comes to Weymar, as he promised me he would do.

Joachim sent me, together with his Hamlet Overture, which is in print, two others—to "Demetrius" (by Hermann Grimm), and to "Henry IV." (of Shakespeare)—two remarkable scores composed with lion's claws and lion's jaws!—

Have you any news of Schumann? Give me some good tidings of his recovery. "Genoveva" will be given here in April at latest.—

Once more best thanks, dear friend, for the very pleasant days you gave us here, which the inhabitants of the Altenburg most agreeably remember; they send you most friendly greetings. I have not forgotten about the Weimar orchestra matter—a half-prospect has already appeared of realizing my wish, which is in accord with your own. I cannot help, however, always doubting whether it will be for your advantage to exchange Bonn for Weymar, for your position in Bonn appears to me to offer you decidedly improving chances from year to year, and in these regions so much is wanting…that I am constrained to be satisfied with small things. Well, what must be will be. Meanwhile keep in kind remembrance

Yours in sincere friendship,

F. Liszt

Weymar, December 14th, 1854

129. To William Mason in New York

[A pupil of Liszt's, born 1828 at Boston, esteemed as a first- rate piano virtuoso in America]

My dear Mason,

Although I do not know at what stage of your brilliant artistic peregrinations these lines will find you, yet I want you to know that I am most sincerely and affectionately obliged to you for the kind remembrance you keep of me, and of which the papers you send me give such good testimony. "The Musical Gazette" of New York, in particular, has given me a real satisfaction, not only on account of the personally kind and flattering things it contains about me, but also because that paper seems to ingraft a superior and excellent direction on to opinion in your country.

Now you know, my dear Mason, that I have no other pride than to serve, as far as in me lies, the good cause of Art, and whenever I find intelligent men conscientiously making efforts for the same end I rejoice and am comforted by the good example they give me. Will you please give my very sincere compliments and thanks to your brother, who, I suppose, has taken the editorship-in- chief of, the Musical Gazette, and if he would like to have some communications from Weymar on what is going on of interest in the musical world of Germany I will let him have them with great pleasure through Mr. Pohl, who, by the way, no longer lives in Dresden (where the numbers of the Musical Gazette were addressed to him by mistake), but in the Kaufstrasse, Weymar. His wife, being one of the best harpists whom I know, is, now among the virtuosi of our orchestra, which is a sensible improvement both for opera and concerts.—

A propos of concerts, I will send you in a few days the programme of a series of Symphonic performances which ought to have been established here some years ago, and to which I consider myself in honor as in duty bound to give a definite impetus at the beginning of the year 1855.—Toward the end of January I expect Berlioz. We shall then hear his trilogy of "L'Enfance du Christ," [The Childhood of Christ] of which you already know "La Fuite en Egypte," [The Flight into Egypt] to which he has added two other little Oratorios called "Le Songe d'Herode" [Herod's Dream] and "L'Arrivee a Sais." [The Arrival at Sais]—His dramatic Symphony of Faust (in four parts, with solos and chorus) will also be given entire while he is here.

As regards visits of artists last month which were a pleasure to me personally, I must mention

Clara Schumann and Litolff. In Brendel's paper (Neue Zeitschrift) you will find an article signed with my name on Madame Schumann, whom I have again heard with that sympathy and thoroughly admiring esteem which her talent commands. As for Litolff, I confess that he made a great impression on me. His Fourth Symphonic Concerto (in manuscript) is a very remarkable composition, and he played it in such a masterly manner, with so much verve, such boldness and certainty, that it gave me very great pleasure. If there is something of the quadruped in Dreyschock's marvelous execution (and this comparison should by no means vex him: is not a lion as much a quadruped as a poodle?), there is certainly something winged in Litolff's execution, which has, moreover, all the superiority over Dreyschock's which a biped with ideas, imagination, and sensibility has over another biped who fancies that he possesses a surfeit of them all—often very embarrassing!

Do you still continue your intimate relations with old Cognac in the New World, my dear Mason? —Allow me again to recommend you measure, which is an essential quality for musicians. In truth, I am not very much qualified to preach to you the quantity of this quantity; for, if I remember rightly, I employed a good deal of Tempo rubato in the times when I was giving my concerts (a business that I would not begin again for anything in the world), and again, quite lately, I have written a long Symphony in three parts entitled "Faust" (without text or vocal parts), in which the horrible measures of 7/8, 7/4, 5/4, alternate with C and 3/4.—

In virtue of which I conclude that you ought to limit yourself to 7/8ths of a small bottle of old Cognac in the evening, and never to go beyond five quarters!—

Raff, in his first volume of the "Wagner-Frage," has realized something like five quarters of doctrinal sufficiency; but that is an example that can hardly be recommended for imitation in a critical matter, and especially in Cognac and other spirituous matters.

Pardon me, my dear Mason, for these bad jokes, which however my good intentions justify, and try to bear yourself valiantly both morally and physically, which is the heartfelt wish of

Your very affectionate

F. Liszt

Weymar, December 14th, 1854

You did not know Rubinstein at Weymar. [Liszt was mistaken about this. Mason had even done the principal honors to Rubinstein at his first visit to Weimar, in the absence of the Master.] He stayed here some time, and notoriously cuts himself off from the thick mass of so-called pianist composers who don't know what playing means, and still less with what fuel to fire themselves for composing—so much so that with what is wanting to them in talent as composers they think they can make themselves pianists, and vice versa.

Rubinstein will constantly publish a round fifty of works— Concertos, Trios, Symphonies, Songs, Light pieces—and which deserve notice.

Laub has left Weymar; Ed. Singer has taken his place in our orchestra. The latter gives great pleasure here, and likes being here also.

Cornelius, Pohl, Raff, Pruckner, Schreiber, and all the new school of new Weymar send you their best remembrances, to which I add a cordial shake hand. [Written thus in English by Liszt]

F. L.

130. To Rosalie Spohr

Pray pardon me, dear artist and friend, that I am so late in expressing the hearty sympathy which your Weymar friends take in the joyful event of your marriage. [To Count Sauerma.] You know well that I am a poor, much-bothered mortal, and can but seldom dispose of my time according to my wishes. Several pressing pieces of work, which I was obliged to get ready by this New Year's Day, have prevented me up to now from giving you a sign of life—and I am employing my first free moment to assure you that the changing date of the year can bring with it no variation in my sincere, friendly attachment. Remember me most kindly to the papa and sister, and write to me when you can and tell me where you are going to live henceforth. Possibly I might happen to be in your neighborhood, in which case I should hasten to come and see you.

I have but little news to give you of Weymar. That Litolff has been to see me here, and played his two Symphony-Concertos capitally, you doubtless know. Probably he will come back after his journey to Brussels, in the course of next month, when I also expect Berlioz here. Our orchestra now also possesses a very first-rate harpist, Frau Dr. Pohl, with a good double-movement harp of Erard. It seems that poor Erard is no better, and his "cure" at Schlangenbad has not had the desired result. I frequently get very sad tidings of his condition through my daughter.

I thank you warmly for the friendly reception you accorded to Herr Wolf as a Weymarer. I hope he did not inconvenience you by too long visits. His wife brought me some weeks ago the original sketch of your portrait, which is to become my possession.

The Frau Furstin [Princess] and Princess Marie commission me to give you their most friendly greetings and wishes, to which I add once more the expression of my friendly devotion.

A thousand respects and homage.

F. Liszt

January 4th, 1855

131. To Alfred Dorffel in Leipzig

[Writer on music, born 1821; custodian of the musical section of the town library of Leipzig: the University there gave him the degree of Dr. phil. honoris causa.]

Dear Sir,

Allow me to express to you direct my most cordial thanks for the conscientious and careful pains you have taken in regard to my Catalogue. ["Thematic Catalogue of Liszt's Compositions."] I am really quite astonished at the exactitude of your researches, and intend to repeat my warm thanks to you in person in Leipzig, and to discuss with you still more fully the motives which lead me not entirely to agree with your proposal, and only to use a part of your new elaboration of my Catalogue. To avoid diffuseness, I can for today only state a couple of points.

The standpoint of your new arrangement is, if I have rightly understood you, as follows:—There are still being circulated in the music-shops a certain number of copies of my works, especially of the "Studies," "Hungarian Rhapsodies," and several "Fantasiestucke" (under the collective title of "Album d'un Voyageur"), etc., that I have not included in my Catalogue, which I gave into Dr. Hartel's hands for printing;—and you have taken upon yourself the troublesome task of arranging these different and somewhat numerous works in what would be, under other circumstances, a most judicious manner.

However gratifying to me this interest of yours in the production of a suitable Catalogue can but be, yet I must declare myself decidedly for the non-acceptance of the portions added by you (with certain exceptions).

1. The Hofmeister edition of the twelve Studies (with a lithograph of a cradle, and the publisher's addition "travail de jeunesse"!) is simply a piracy of the book of Studies which was published at Frankfort when I was thirteen years old. I have long disowned this edition and replaced it by the second, under the title "Etudes d'execution transcendante," published by Haslinger in Vienna, Schlesinger in Paris, and Mori and Lavener in London. But this second edition has now been annulled several years ago, and Haslinger has, by my desire, put aside my copyright and plates, and bound

himself by contract not to publish any more copies of this work henceforth. After a complete agreement with him I set to work and produced a third edition of my twelve Studies (very materially improved and transformed), and begged Messrs. Hartel to publish it with the note "seule edition authentique, revue par l'auteur, etc.," which they did. Consequently I recognize only the Hartel edition of the twelve Studies as the SOLE LEGITIMATE ONE, which I also clearly express by a note in the Catalogue, and I therefore wish that the Catalogue should make no mention of the earlier ones. I think I have found the simplest means of making my views and intentions clear by the addition of the sign (+).

2. It is the same case with the Paganini "Etudes" and the "Rhapsodies Hongroises;" and after settling matters with Haslinger I completely gained the legal right to disavow the earlier editions of these works, and to protest against eventual piracy of them, as I am once more in possession both of the copyright and the entire engraving plates.

These circumstances will explain to you the reappearance (in a very much altered conception and form) of many of my compositions, on which I, as piano player and piano composer, am obliged to lay some stress, as they form, to a certain extent, the expression of a closed period of my artist-individuality.

In literature the production of very much altered, increased, and improved editions is no uncommon thing. In works both important and trivial, alterations, additions, varying divisions of periods, etc., are a common experience of an author.

In the domain of music such a thing is more minute and more difficult— and therefore it is seldom done. None the less do I consider it very profitable to correct one's mistakes as far as possible, and to make use of the experiences one gains by the editions of the works themselves. I, for my part, have striven to do this; and, if I have not succeeded, it at least testifies to my earnest endeavour.

3. In the "Annees de Pelerinage" (Schott, Mainz) several of the pieces are again taken from the "Album d'un Voyageur." The Album brought out by Haslinger must not be quoted in the Catalogue, because the work has not been carried out according to its original plan, and Haslinger has given me back, in this case also, the copyright and plates.

As the natural consequence of what I have said I beg you therefore, dear sir, not to undertake any alteration in the disposition and arrangement of my Catalogue, and only to add the various enlargements and improvements, for which I have to thank your overlooking and corrections, as I have now given them and marked them.—

The title of the Catalogue might sound better thus in German:—

F. Liszt

"Thematischer Catalog." ["Thematic Catalogue"]

And the letters of the headings "Etudes— Harmonies—Annees de
 Pelerinage—Ungarische Rhapsodien—Fantaisies on Airs from
 Operas, etc.," must be rather large, and these headings separated

from the special title of the works.

I cannot agree with the admission of a supplementary Opus- number,—but it is of consequence to me that the Catalogue should come out speedily, in order to get as clear a survey as possible of my works up to the present time (which, however, are by no means sufficient for me).

Accept once more my best thanks, dear Sir, as also the assurance of high esteem of

Yours most truly,

F. Liszt

January 17th, 1855.

P.S.—I take the liberty of keeping your edition of the Catalogue here meanwhile, as it cannot be used for the arrangement of the Hartel edition.

132. To Anton Rubinstein

Your fugue of this morning, my dear Rubinstein, is very little to my taste, and I much prefer to it the Preludes that you wrote at an earlier date in this same room, which, to my great surprise, I found empty when I came to fetch you for the Berlioz rehearsal. Is it a fact that this music works on your nerves? And, after the specimen you had of it the other time at the Court, did the resolution to hear more of it seem to you too hard to take? Or have you taken amiss some words I said to you, which, I give you my word, were nothing but a purely friendly proceeding on my part? Whatever it may be, I don't want any explanations in writing, and only send you these few lines to intimate that your nocturnal flight was not a very agreeable surprise to me, and that you would have done better in every way to hear the

"Fuite en Egypte" and the "Fantaisie sur la Tempete" of Shakespeare.

Send me tidings of yourself from Vienna (if not sooner), and, whatever rinforzando of "murrendo" may happen, please don't do a wrong to the sentiments of sincere esteem and cordial friendship invariably maintained towards you by

F. Liszt

Weymar, February 21st, 1855.

133. To Louis Kohler

My very dear Friend,

Hans von Bulow will bring you these lines. You must enjoy yourself in the artist who, above all other active or dying out virtuosi; is the dearest to me, and who has, so to speak, grown out of my musical heart.—When Hummel heard me in Paris more than twenty-five years ago, he said, "Der Bursch ist ein Eisenfresser." [The fellow is a bravo."] To this title, which was very flattering to me, Hans von Bulow can with perfect justice lay claim, and I confess that such an extraordinarily gifted, thorough-bred musical organism as his has never come before me.

Receive him as an approved and energetic friend, and do all you can to make his stay in Konigsberg a pleasant one.

Yours in friendship,

F. Liszt

Weymar, March 16th, 1855

The engraving of my Symphonic Poems is in progress, and in the course of this summer five or six of them will be ready. There is a good bit of work in it.

At the present time I am exclusively engaged in the composition of a "Missa Solemnis." You know that I received, from the Cardinal Primate of Hungary, the commission to write the work for the consecration of the cathedral at Gran, and to conduct it there (probably on the 15th of August).

134. To Dr. Franz Brendel

Sunday, March 18th, 1855

A few words in haste, dear friend, for I am over head and ears in work. First and foremost, my best thanks for your communications, with the request to continue them, even if I cannot always answer the different points thoroughly.

I send you herewith the title of "The Captive" [Song, by Berlioz, for alto voice with orchestra or piano.]—the words must be written under the notes both in French and German. There can be no copyright claimed for this Opus in Germany, as it appeared years ago in Paris. It is to be hoped, however, that Kahnt will not lose by it, as he has only to bear the cost of printing—and in any case it is a suitable work for his shop..—.

To be brief—Panofka's [A well-known teacher of singing and writer on music (1807-88); collaborator of the Neue Zeitschrift.] letter, in your last number, must be regarded as a mystification. In the first few lines a glaring falsehood, founded on facts, is conspicuous, for the Societe de Ste. Cecile has been in existence for years, and was formerly [1848-54] conducted by Seghers [Pupil of Baillot (1801-81)]—not to mention that Berlioz conducted the Societe Philharmonique, where "many Symphonies were performed," for at least a season (of something like four years)—and then as regards Scudo, [Musical critic and journalist in Paris (1806-64)] it must appear incredible to see a man like that mentioned with approval in your paper. It is well known that Scudo has, for years past, with the unequivocal arrogance of mediocrity, taken up the position of making the most spiteful and maliciously foolish opposition, in the revue des Deux Mondes (the "Grenzboten" only gives a faint impression of it), to our views of Art, and to those men whom we honor and back up. (I can tell you more about this by word of mouth.) If Panofka calls that "persuasion and design," I give him my compliments…on his silliness.—

Your views on the characteristic motives are right, and for my part I would maintain them very decidedly against the bornes attacks which they have to bear—yet I think it is advisable not to discuss Marx's book ["The Music of the Nineteenth Century," 1855.] at present.

Yours ever,

F. Liszt

135. To Dr. Franz Brendel

April 1st, 1855

Dear Friend,

The question of criticism through creative and executive artists must some time come on the tapis, and Schumann affords a perfectly natural opportunity for it. [Liszt's article on Robert Schumann, "Gesammelte Schriften," Vol. iv.] By the proofs of the second article (which I thank you much for having corrected with the necessary exactitude) you will observe that I have modified several expressions, and have held them in more just bounds. Believe me, dear friend, the domain of artists is in the greater part guilty of our sluggish state of Art, and it is from this side especially that we must act, in order to bring about gradually the reform desired and pioneered by you.

Tyszkiewicz's [Count Tyszkiewicz, writer on music, collaborator of the Neue Zeitschrift.] letter gave me the idea of asking you to make him a proposal in my name, which cannot be any inconvenience to him. In one number of Europe artiste he translated the article on "Fidelio." [By Liszt, "Gesammelte Schriften," Vol. iii., I.] Should he be disposed to publish several of my articles in the same paper, I am perfectly ready to let him have the French originals, [Liszt's articles were, as already mentioned, written in French and translated into German by Cornelius.] whereby he would save time and trouble. He has only to write to me about it; for, after his somewhat capricious behaviour towards me, I am not particularly inclined to apply to him direct, before he has written to me. I am in perfect agreement with his good intentions; it is only a question how far he is able and willing to carry them out, and how he sets about it. His "Freischutz-Rodomontade" is a student's joke, to which one can take quite kindly, but which one cannot hold up as a heroic feat. If he wishes to be of use to the good cause of musical progress, he must place and prove himself differently. For my part I have not the slightest dislike to him, only of course it seemed rather strange to me that, after he had written to me several times telling me that he was coming to see me at Weymar, and had also allowed Wagner to write a letter of introduction for him, which he sent to me, he should ignore me, as it were, during his long stay in Leipzig. This does not of course affect the matter in hand, and I am not in the least angry at his want of attention, but I simply wait till it occurs to him to behave like a reasonable man.

I thank you for your tidings about Dietrich— although I am accustomed to expect less, rather than more, from people.

On the 9th April Schumann's "Genoveva" will be given here—and I think I may venture to promise before-hand that the performance will be a far better one than that at Leipzig. Fraulein Riese will tell you about the "Transfiguration of the Lord." [Oratorio by Kuhmstedt] Of this kind there should certainly be no more [oratorios The word is missing in the original, as the corner of the letter is cut off] composed.

Yours in friendship,

F. Liszt

136. To Anton Rubinstein

My dear Rubinstein,

Gurkhaus has just sent me a copy of your "Persian Songs," on the title-page of which there is a mistake which I beg you to get corrected without delay. The Grand Duchess Sophie is no longer "Hereditary Grand Duchess," but "Grand Duchess" pure and simple, and I think it would not do to send her the dedicatory copy with this extra word. Please write therefore to Gurkhaus to see to it.

In the number of the Blatter fur Musik which has come to me I have read with great pleasure and satisfaction Zellner's article on your first concert in

Vienna. It is not only very well written but thoroughly well conceived, and of the right tone and manner to maintain for criticism its right and its raison d'etre. I second it very sincerely for the just eulogy it gives to your works; and, if you have the opportunity, make my compliments to Zellner, to whom I wrote a few lines the other day. This article coincides rather singularly with that which appeared in the Neue Zeitschrift (No. II.) on Robert Schumann, in which I probed rather deeply into the question of criticism. If you believe me, my dear Rubinstein, you will not long delay making yourself of the party; for, for the few artists who have sense, intelligence, and a serious and honest will, it is really their duty to take up the pen in defense of our Art and our conviction—it matters little, moreover, on which side of the opinions represented by the Press you think it well to place yourself. Musical literature is a field far too little cultivated by productive artists, and if they continue to neglect it they will have to bear the consequences and to pay their damages.

With regard to Weymar news, I beg to inform you that this evening Kulhmstedt's oratorio "The Transfiguration of the Lord" will be given at the theater, under the very undirecting direction of the composer. I cannot, unfortunately, return him the compliment he paid you at Wilhelmsthal—"Young man, you have satisfied me"; for, after having heard it at three rehearsals, I found no satisfaction in it either for my ears or my mind: it is the old frippery of counterpoint—the old unsalted, unpeppered sausage, [Figure: Musical example]

etc., rubbish, to the ruin of eye and ear! I will

try to leave it out in my Mass, although this style is very usual in composing Church music. In five or six weeks I hope to have finished this work, at which I am working heart and soul (the Kyrie and Gloria are written). Perhaps I shall still find you at Vienna (or in the outskirts, which are charming), when I come to Gran in the month of July.

If not, we shall see each other again at Weymar, for you owe me a compensation for your last fugue, which is no more to my taste than Kuhmstedt's counterpoint. When are you going to send me the complete works of Anton Rubinstein that you promised me, and which I beg you not to forget? Your idea of a retrospective Carnival seems to me excellent, and you know how to write charming and distinguished pieces of that kind.

Farewell, dear friend; I must leave you to go and have a rehearsal of Schumann's "Genoveva," which is to be given next Monday. It is a work in which there is something worthy of consideration, and which bears a strong impress of the composer's style. Among the Operas which have been produced during the last fifty years it is certainly the one I prefer (Wagner excepted— that is understood), notwithstanding its want of dramatic vitality—a want not made up for by some beautiful pieces of music, whatever interest musicians of our kind may nevertheless take in hearing them.

A thousand cordial greetings, and yours ever,

F. Liszt

Weymar, April 3rd, 1855

When you write to me, please add your address. I beg you will also return my best compliments to Lewy. [Pianist in St. Petersburg; a friend of Rubinstein's.]

A thousand affectionate messages to Van II. from the Princess.

137. To Freiherr Beaulieu-Marconnay, Intendant of the Court theater at Weimar

[Autograph in the possession of Herr Hermann Scholtz, Kammer-
Virtuosos in Dresden. The addressee died in Dresden.]

Dear Baron,

It is not precisely a distraction, still less a forgetfulness, with which I might be reproached as regards the programme of this evening's concert. The indications which Her Royal Highness the Grand Duchess condescends to give me are too precious to me for me not to be most anxious to fulfill at least all my duties. If, then, one of Beethoven's Symphonies does not figure in today's programme, it is because I thought I could better satisfy thus the intentions of H.R.H., and that I permitted myself to guess that which she has not taken the occasion to explain this time. The predilection of His Majesty the King of Saxony for Beethoven's Symphonies assuredly does honor to his taste for the Beautiful in music, and no one could more truly agree to that than I. I will only observe, on the one side, that Beethoven's Symphonies are extremely well known, and, on the other, that these admirable works are performed at Dresden by an orchestra having at its disposal far more considerable means than we have here, and that consequently our performance would run the risk of appearing rather provincial to His Majesty. Moreover if Dresden, following the example of Paris, London, Leipzig, Berlin, and a hundred other cities, stops at Beethoven (to whom, while he was living, they much preferred Haydn and Mozart), that is no reason why Weymar—I mean musical Weymar, which I make the modest pretension of representing —should keep absolutely to that. There is without doubt nothing better than to respect, admire, and study the illustrious dead; but why not also sometimes live with the living? We have tried this plan with Wagner, Berlioz, Schumann, and some others, and it would seem that it has not succeeded so badly up to now for there to be any occasion for us to alter our minds without urgent cause, and to put ourselves at the tail—of many other tails!—

The significance of the musical movement of which Weymar is the real center lies precisely in this initiative, of which the public does not generally understand much, but which none the less acquires its part of importance in the development of contemporary Art.

For the rest, dear Baron, I hasten to make all straight for this evening by following your advice, and I will ask Messrs. Singer and Cossmann to play with me Beethoven's magnificent trio (in B- flat— dedicated to the Archduke Rudolph), as No. 3 in the programme.

A thousand affectionate compliments, and
Yours ever,
F. Liszt
Monday, May 21st, 1855
138. To Anton Rubinstein

My dear Rubinstein,

On my return from the Musical Festival at Dusseldorf, where I hoped to meet you, I found the parcel of oeuvres choisies and the portrait, which is very successful, of Van II. I hasten to give you my best thanks for this first sending, begging you not to forget your promise to complete, in the course of their publication, the collection of your works, which have for me always a double interest of Art and friendship. This morning we had a taste, with Singer and Cossmann, of the Trio in G minor, of which I had kept a special recollection—and afterwards Princess Marie Wittgenstein (who commissions me to give all her thanks to you, until she can have the pleasure of giving them to you in person) demanded the pieces dedicated to her, which had complete success. A propos of dedications, the Grand Duchess Sophie is enchanted with the "Persische Lieder" ["Persian Songs"], and this she has probably already intimated to you. Shortly before her departure for Dusseldorf she sang several of them over again, taking more and more liking to them. Decidedly the first impression that these "Lieder" made on me, when you showed them to me, and when I begged you to publish them without delay, was just, and I have not been deceived in predicting for them a quasi-popular success. Mdlle. Genast, who has returned from Berlin, tells me that she made a furor there with "Wenn es doch immer so bliebe!" ["Oh, could it remain so for ever!"] But, unfortunately, as an older song has it, "it cannot remain so for ever under the changing moon!" The last time I was passing through Leipzig (where they gave my "Ave

Maria" exceedingly well at the Catholic Church), I told Gotze to appropriate to himself three or four of your "Persische Lieder," which he will sing splendidly; and, as he comes here pretty often, I will beg him to give us the first hearing of them at some Court concert. The Grand Duchess Olga is expected for the day after tomorrow; and if, as is probable, they treat her to a little concert, I shall take advantage of the opportunity to make her become better acquainted with the Trios you dedicated to her, and which I consider as among your best works. In the parcel I noticed the absence of "L'Album de Kamennoi-Ostrow," which I should like to make known, or, better still, to offer from you to H.I.H. the Dowager Grand Duchess, and which I want you to send me for this purpose.

If by chance you pass through Bonn, do not forget to go and see Professor Kilian, who has been interested in you from very old times, and with whom we talked much of you and your works during the journey from Cologne to Dusseldorf.

Write me word soon what you are doing now. I, for my part, shall spend the summer at Weymar, up to the time of my journey to Gran (June-August). I count on your promise to come and see me in the autumn, unless your road should lead you into these parts sooner. You may be very sure of being always most welcome at the Altenburg—and, even if a number of those holding our musical opinions should meet still less often than in the past, that would not in any way influence the very sincere feelings of friendship and esteem which I bear towards you and keep towards you invariably. When we see each other again, you will find my "Divina Commedia" pretty far advanced; I have sketched a plan of it (a Symphony in three parts: the two first, "Hell" and "Purgatory," exclusively instrumental; the third, "Paradise," with chorus): but I cannot set myself entirely to this work until I have finished the new score of my choruses from Herder's "Prometheus," which I am rewriting in order to have it printed shortly after the publication of my Symphonic Poems, six of which will come out next October.

I am very curious to see what your new case of manuscripts will contain. Have you set to work on "Paradise Lost"? I think that would be the most opportune work for taking possession of your fame as a composer.

A thousand cordial expressions of friendship, and

Yours ever,
F. Liszt
June 3rd, 1855
139. To Dr. Franz Brendel
[Weimar, June 1855]
Dear Friend,

Best thanks for your munificence. The weed [Cigars] is very welcome, and you will have to answer for it if it induces me to importune you with some more columns. Meanwhile I send you the proofs of the second Berlioz article, together with a fresh provision of manuscripts, and with the next proofs you will get the end.

I will also send you very soon a report of the Dusseldorf Musical Festival (not by me), the authorship of which I beg you to keep strictly anonymous. Probably he will be piquant and forcible. On the whole, and also in detail, the Dusseldorf Musical Festival can only be described as a great success, and I, for my part, rejoice in this and every success without particularly envying it. My task is quite a different one, the solution of which is by no means troubled thereby.

If you should by any chance have read that I am going to America (!—there are many people who would be glad to have me out of sight!), and that a Leipzig virtuoso (in Leipzig such animals as virtuosi are seldom to be met with!) is going to take my place here, you can simply laugh, as I have done, at this old canard— but don't say anything to contradict it in your paper; such bad jokes are not worth noticing, and are only good as finding food for inquisitive Philistines. In a few days I hope to be able again to do something serious with my work, and shall not leave Weymar until my journey to Hungary (at the end of August). Gutzkow's appointment is still in suspense, but is not impossible. Have you read Frau Marr's (Sangalli's) brochure, brought out by Otto Wigand? The pages which she devotes to my work here may perhaps interest you, and I have absolutely nothing to complain of in them, especially in view of the fact that I have not hitherto been able to go "hand in hand" with Marr. Marr has, moreover, according to what he told me, given in his resignation as artistic Director, [At the Weimar Court theater] and one cannot get clear about the entire theater-management for some weeks to come. I keep myself very passive in the matter, and don't fish in troubled waters. Thus much is certain—that if Weymar wants to do anything regular, it cannot do without my ideas and influence. About the rest I don't need to trouble myself. Last Sunday we held a satisfactory performance of "Tannhauser" in honor of the Princess of Prussia—and next Monday the opera will be repeated.

Friendly greetings to your wife from your almost too active fellow-worker and friend,

F. Liszt

I am writing to Fraulein Riese one of these next days, to invite her to the performance of my Mass at Jena. [The Mass for male voices was performed there in the latter half of June.]

140. To Dr. Franz Brendel.

[The first sheet of the original is missing]

Evers' [Doubtless Carl Evers (1819-75), composed Sonatas, Salon pieces, etc.] letter has amused me, and it will cost you but little diplomacy to conciliate the sensitive composer. You know what I think of his talent for composition. From people like that nothing is to be expected as long as they have not learned to understand that they are uselessly going round and round in what is hollow, dry, and used up. That good Flugel [Music writer and composer; at that time teacher in a school at Neuwied; now organist at the Castle at Stettin.] has also little power of imagination, although a little more approach to something more earnest, which has at least this good in itself—that it checks a really too naive productiveness…His letter on the Dusseldorf Musical Festival is again a little bit of Barenzucker [Liquorice.] (reglisse in French), and

259

W.'s article in comparison with it quite a decent Pate Regnault. When we see each other again I will make this difference clear to you—meanwhile make the Rhinelanders happy with the latter, and don't be afraid of the whispers which it may perhaps call forth; for, I repeat, it contains nothing untrue or exaggerated, and in your position of necessary opposition it would be inconsistent if you were to keep back views of that kind from the public.

With the most friendly greeting, your

F. Liszt

June 16th, 1855.

My Mass for male voices and organ (published by Hartel two years ago) will be given next week at the church in Jena. As soon as the day is fixed I will let Fraulein Riese know.

Once more I recommend you to keep the W. article strictly anonymous.

141. To Concertmeister [Leader of orchestra] Edmund Singer.

Dear Singer,

If I write but seldom to my friends there is, besides other reasons, one principal cause for it, in that I have but seldom anything agreeable or lively to tell them. Since your departure very little has happened here that would interest you. One half of our colleagues of the Neu-Weymar-Verein [New Weymar Union] is absent—Hoffmann in Holland, Preller in the Oldenburg woods, Pruckner and Schreiber at Goslar, etc., etc.—so that our innocent reunions (which finally take place in the room of the shooting-house) are put off for several weeks. Cornelius is working at a Mass for men's voices—on the 15th of August we shall hear it in the Catholic Church. I, on my side, am working also at a Psalm (chorus, solos, and orchestra), which will be ready by your return, in spite of all interruptions which I have to put up with by constant visits. An exceptionally agreeable surprise to me was Hans von Bulow, who spent a couple of days here, and brought with him some new compositions, amongst which I was particularly pleased with a very interesting, finely conceived, and carefully worked-out "Reverie fantastique." Until the 15th of August (when his holidays end) he remains in Copenhagen, where he will certainly meet with a friendly reception. Perhaps next summer you would be inclined to go there. You would find it a very pleasant neighborhood, and many pleasant people there, who have also been agreeably remembered by me. If I had time, I would gladly go there again for a couple of weeks, to find a little solitude in the Zoological Gardens and to forget somewhat other bestialities. [Probably a play on the words Thiergarten (beast-garden) and Bestialitaten] This satisfaction is not so easily attainable for me elsewhere.

I envy you immensely about Patikarius [Hungarian gipsy orchestras] and Ketskemety. [Hungarian gipsy orchestras] This class of music is for me a sort of opium, of which I am sometimes sorely in need. If you should by chance see Kertbeny, who has now obtained a logis honoraire, please tell him that my book on the Gipsies and Gipsy Music is already almost entirely translated by Cornelius, and that I will send it to him by the autumn. But beg him at the same time not to write tome, as it is impossible for me to start a detailed correspondence with K.

I sent the pianoforte arrangement (with the voices) yesterday to Herr von Augusz, with the request that he would present them, when he had an opportunity, to His Eminence Cardinal Scitowsky. The Mass [Liszt's Graner Messe.] will not take up an excessively long time, either in performance or studying. But it is indispensable that I should conduct the general rehearsal as well as the performance myself; for the work cannot be ranked amongst those in which ordinary singing, playing, and arrangement will suffice, although it offers but small difficulties. It is a matter of some not usual trifles in the way of accent, devotion, inspiration, etc.

When are you coming back, dear Singer? Only bring home with you an orderly packet of manuscripts, that is to say to Weymar, where I hope that you will feel yourself more and more at home.

The members of our Club who are still here send you the most friendly greetings by me, to which I add a cordial "auf baldiges Wiedersehen" ["May we soon meet again!"].

Yours ever,

F. Liszt

August 1st, 1855

P.S.—Joachim is going to make a walking tour in Tyrol. I hope he will come and see us on his return. Berlioz proposes to give some concerts in Vienna and Prague next December. I shall probably postpone my journey to Wagner (at Zurich) until November. I shall remain here for the next few months, in order to write several things in readiness for the winter.

142. To Bernhard Cossmann In Baden-Baden
Wilhelmsthal, August 15th, 1855

Here am I really on the road to Baden-Baden, dear friend; but that does not advance matters at all, and in spite of myself I must resign myself to remain en route. Tomorrow morning I return to Weymar, where I have promised to meet my two daughters, as well as Mr. Daniel [Liszt's son], who has pretty well distinguished himself at the general competition. After passing ten days or so with me the girls will take up their abode with Madame de Bulow at Berlin, who is good enough to take charge of them, and Daniel will return to Paris to continue his studies there. I was hoping also to be able to spend a week or two there- -but that cannot possibly be arranged, and on reflection I was obliged to limit myself to conducting the Princess W[ittgenstein] as far as Eisenach, whence she has continued her journey to Paris with her daughter (with the special view of seeing the exhibition of pictures there); and for my exhibition I shall content myself with that to the north, which I can enjoy from the windows of my room!—This picturesque solemnity is almost up to the height of the musical solemnities of Baden which you describe to me in such bright and lively colors, but with this difference, that at Wilhelmsthal we are very much favored by the element of damp, whereas at Baden the artists who give concerts are drained dry.

At Weymar all the world is out of doors, and the town is pretty full of nothing, offering to the curiosity of travelers only the trenches and practical circumvallations in honor of gas-lighting which they are going to start in October. Singer is bathing in the Danube (at Ofen), and tells me he shall be back by the roth of September; Raff is promenading amid the rose and myrtle shrubberies of his "Sleeping Beauty" at Wiesbaden; Stor is returning with his pockets full of new nuances which he has discovered at Ilmenau, where he has composed (as a pendant to my Symphonic Poem) "Ce qu'on entend dans la vallee"! ["What is heard in the valley." Liszt's work bears the title "Ce qu'on entend sur la montagne" ("What is heard on the mountain.")] Preller [Friedrich Preller, the celebrated painter of the Odyssey pictures] has found beautiful trees in the Duchy of Oldenburg which serve him as a recovery of the "Recovery" [Or a "recreation of the Recreation." I do not know which is meant. The original is "qui lui servent d'Erholung von der 'Erholung.'"—Translator's note.]; Martha Sabinin [A pupil of Liszt's, a Russian] is haunting the "Venusberg" in the neighborhood of Eisenach in company with Mademoiselle de Hopfgarten; Bronsart [Hans von Bronsart, Liszt's pupil, now General-Intendant at Weimar] is gone to a sort of family congress at Konigsberg; and Hoffman [Hoffmann von Fallersleben, the well-known poet] is running through Holland and Belgium to make a scientific survey of them; whilst Nabich is trying to gain the ears of England, Scotland, and Ireland with his trombone!

I, for my part, am in the midst of finishing the 13th Psalm (for tenor solo, chorus, and orchestra), "How long wilt Thou forget me, O Lord?" which you will hear this winter; and I shall not leave Weymar till November to go and pay a few days' visit to Wagner at Zurich. Don't altogether forget me, my dear Cossmann, in the midst of your solemnities ——[The end of the letter was lost.]

143. To August Kiel, Court Conductor in Detmold

[Autograph (without address) in the possession of M. Alfred Bovet, of Valentigney. The contents lead to the conclusion that the above was the addressee (1813-71).]

I have been prevented until now, by a mass of work and little outings, from sending you my warmest thanks for your kind forwarding of the opera text of "Sappho," and I beg that you will kindly excuse this delay. The manner in which Rietz's composition to the Schiller dithyramb is to be interwoven with the poem I cannot venture fully to explain. I confess also that the dramatico-musical vivifying of the antique is for me a sublime, attractive problem, as yet undecided, in the solution of which even Mendelssohn himself has not succeeded in such a degree as to leave nothing further to be sought for. Some years ago "Sappho" (in three acts—text by Augier, music by Gounod) was given at the Paris Opera. This work contains much that is beautiful, and Berlioz has spoken of it very favorably in the Journal des Debats. Unfortunately it did not appear in print, and up to the present time no other theater has performed it, although it made a sensation in Paris and ensured a first-rate position to the composer. If it would interest you, dear sir, to get to know the score, I will willingly write to Gounod and beg him to give me the work to send to you.

I have repeatedly heard the most gratifying tidings of the sympathy and care which you bestow in Detmold upon the works of Wagner and Berlioz. Regardless of the many difficulties, opposition, and misunderstandings which meet these great creations, I cherish with you the conviction that "nothing truly good and beautiful is lost in the stream of Time," and that the pains taken by those who intend to preserve the higher and the divine in Art do not remain fruitless. In the course of this autumn (at the end of November at latest) I am going to see Wagner, and I promise to send you from Zurich a little autograph from his hand. I would gladly satisfy your wish sooner, but that the letters which Wagner writes to me are a perfectly inalienable benefit to me, and you will not take it amiss if I am more than avaricious with them.

Accept, my dear sir, the assurance of my highest esteem, with which I remain

Yours most truly,

F. Liszt

Weymar, September 8th, 1855

Enclosed are Berlioz' letter and the manuscript of "Sappho."

144. To Moritz Hauptmann

[The celebrated theorist and cantor of the Thomashirche in
 Leipzig (1792-1868)]

Very dear Sir,

By the same post I send you, with best and

warmest thanks for your friendly letter, the volume of Handel's works which contains the anthems. The second of them, "Zadok the Priest and Nathan the Prophet anointed Solomon King," is a glorious ray of Handel's genius, and one might truly quote, of the first verse of this anthem, the well-known saying, "C'est grand comme le monde." ["It is as great as the world."]—

The cantata "L'Allegro, il Pensieroso," etc., enchants me less, yet it has interested me much as an important contribution to imitative music; and, if you will kindly allow me, I want to keep the volume here a few days longer and to send it back with the two others.

I agree entirely, on my side, with your excellent criticism of Raimondi's triple oratorio ["Joseph," an oratorio by the Roman composer, consisting of three parts, which was given with great success in the Teatro Argentina in Rome in 1852]. There is little to seek on that road, and still less to find. The silver pfennig (in the Dresden Art-Cabinet), on which ten Pater Noster are engraved, has decidedly the advantage of harmlessness to the public over such outrages to Art, and the Titus Livius, composed by Sechter, will probably have to moulder away very unhistorically as waste-paper. Later on Sechter can write a Requiem for it, together with Improperias over the corruption of the taste of the times, which have found his work so little to their taste.

With the pleasant expectation of greeting you soon in Leipzig, and of repeating to you my best thanks, I remain, my dear sir, with the highest esteem,

Yours truly,

F. Liszt

Weymar, September 28th, 1855

145. To Eduard Liszt

I have just received your last letter, dearest Eduard, and will not wait till Vienna to give you my warm thanks for your faithful friendship, which you always prove to me so lovingly on all possible occasions. The Mozart Festival seems to me now to have taken the desired turn—that which I suggested from the beginning—and to shape itself into a festival of "concord, harmony, and artistic enthusiasm of the combined Art-fellowships of Vienna." [Liszt was invited by the magistrate of the city of Vienna to conduct two concerts on the 27th and 28th of January, 1856, for the celebration of the centenary of Mozart's birth.]

It is to be hoped that I shall not stick fast in my task, and shall not let this opportunity go by without attaining the suitable standpoint in Vienna.

Meanwhile I rejoice at the satisfactory prospects which present themselves for the Mozart Festival, and greet you heartily.

F. L.

Berlin, December 3rd, 1855

You will have the most favorable news from Berlin.

146. To Frau Meyerbeer in Berlin

[The wife of the composer of the Huguenots

(1791-1864), with whom
 Liszt stood all his life in such friendly relations that it is
 very extraordinary that there are no Liszt letters extant among
 Meyerbeer's possessions.]

Madame,

Your gracious lines only reached me at the moment of my leaving Berlin, so that it was no longer possible for me to avail myself of the kind permission you were good enough to give me. Nevertheless, as it is to be presumed that neither the brilliant departure of which I was the hero a dozen years ago, nor the less flattering dismissal with which the infallible criticism of your capital has gratified me this time, will prevent me from returning from time to time, and without too long an interval, to Berlin (according to the requirements of my instructions and of my artistic experiments), I venture to claim from your kindness the continuation of your gracious reception, and thus venture to hope that the opportunity will soon arise for me to have the honor of renewing viva voce, Madame, the expression of my respectful homage.

Your very devoted servant,

F. Liszt

Weymar, December. 14th, 1855

The Princess Wittgenstein is much pleased with your remembrance, and would be delighted to have the opportunity of thanking you personally.

147. To his worship Dr. Ritter von Seiler, mayor of the city of Vienna, etc.

[Autograph in the possession of M. Alfred Bovet, of Valentigne—.
VOL. I.]

Your worship and dear Mr. Mayor,

The willingness which I had already expressed, at the first mention of the impending Mozart Festival, becomes to me, by your kind letter of the 19th of December (which I only received yesterday, owing to the delay from its having gone to Berlin), a duty, which it is equally my honor and pleasure to fulfill. With the utmost confidence and conviction that the resolution of the Town Council will meet with the fullest assent and most gratifying recognition among all circles of society—the resolution is as follows: "That all undertakings in connection with the Mozart Secular Festival shall be conducted and carried out in the name of the city of Vienna,"—and in agreement with the honorable motives of the Town Council "to lend to the festivities the worthy and higher expression of universal homage," I, for my part, undertake with the most grateful acknowledgments the commission to conduct the Festival Concert on the 27th January, 1856, and its repetition on the 28th according to your desire; and I hope to fulfill quite satisfactorily every just claim which is made on the musical director of such a celebration.

Although the excellent orchestra, chorus, and staff of singers in Vienna—long intimate with Mozart's works—afford the complete certainty of a most admirable performance, yet I think it is desirable that I should come a couple of weeks

270

before the concert is to take place, in order to have time for the necessary rehearsals; and immediately on my arrival. I shall have the honor of paying my respects to you, dear Mr. Mayor, and of placing myself at the service of the Festival Committee.

In the programme which has been sent to me, the music of which will take about three hours in performance, I am pleased with the prospect before us, that the glories which Mozart unfolds in the different domains of Art—Symphony, Opera, Church, and Concert music-are taken into account, and that thus the manifold rays of his genius are laid hold of, as far as is possible in the limits of a concert programme. Whilst thoroughly agreeing with the performance of the different items as a whole, I have nevertheless one request to make—namely, that you would be good enough to excuse me from the performance of the Mozart Pianoforte Concerto which has been so kindly designed for me, and that this number may be given to some other pianist of note. Apart from the fact that for more than eight years I have not appeared anywhere in public as a pianist, and that many considerations lead me to adhere firmly to my negative resolve in this respect, the fact that the direction of the Festival will require my entire attention may prove, in this case, my sufficient excuse.

Accept, Your Worship, the assurance of the high esteem with which
I have the honor to remain,

Dear Mr. Mayor, yours very truly,
F. Liszt

Weymar, December 26th, 1855.

148. To Eduard Liszt

My very dear Eduard,

Scarcely had I returned to Weymar [From the Mozart Festival at Vienna.] when I again put on my travelling coat to help in Berlioz' concert at Gotha, which took place the day before yesterday—and the whole day yesterday was spent in rehearsals of "Cellini;" followed by a Court concert in the evening (in honor of H.R.H. the Prince Regent of Baden); so that this morning is the first leisure moment I have had to take up my pen again and my position…at my writing-table. I profit by it first of all to tell you how happy I am in this earnest intimacy, as sincerely felt as it is conscientiously considered—this real intimacy of ideas and feelings at the same time—which has been cemented between us in these latter years, and which my stay in Vienna has fully confirmed. All noble sentiments require the full air of generous conviction, which maintains us in a region superior to the trials, accidents, and troubles of this life. Thanks to Heaven, we two breathe this air together, and thus we shall remain inseparably united until our last day!

I am sending you after this the document which serves as a basis to the Bach-Gesellschaft [Bach Society], from which it will be easy to make out an analogous one for the publication of Mozart's complete works. I earnestly invite and beg you to carry out this project to its realization.

According to my ideas, the "Friends of Music in Austria" should constitute and set the matter going, and the Royal State Press should be employed for it, especially as one can foresee that special favors might be obtained from the Ministry. Probably the whole Festival Committee of the Mozart Celebration will also consent to this undertaking, in the sense that, by an edition of Mozart's works, critically explained, equally beautifully printed, and revised by a committee appointed for it, a universally useful, lasting, and living monument to the glorious Master will be formed, which will bring honor and even material gain to all Austrian lovers of music and to the city of Vienna itself. Without doubt, if the matter is rightly conducted, it will also pay well and be pretty easy to carry through. In about twelve years the whole edition can be completed. In the composition of the Committee of Revision I stipulate to call your attention to a few names. Spohr, Meyerbeer, Fetis, Otto Jahn, Oulibicheff, Dr. Hartel—among foreigners these ought especially to have a share in the matter; and a special rubric must be given to the cost of revision. The work of proof-correcting, as well as the special explanations, commentaries, comparisons of the different editions, ought not to be expected gratis; therefore a fixed sum should be applied to it. Haslinger, Spina, and Gloggl, being Vienna publishers, ought specially to be considered, and would be the best to direct the propagation and regular sending out of the volume, which is to appear on the 27th of January every year.

At Spina's you would find several volumes of the Bach- Gesellschaft, to which is always added a list of the subscribers and a statement of accounts for the past year.

I advise you to keep on good terms with Zellner, who was the first to air the subject in his paper (after I had invited him to do so), and to get him into the proposed Committee, if the matter be taken up in earnest. In the Committee of Revision Schmidt (the librarian) and Holz must not be forgotten. With regard to my humble self, I don't want to be put forward, but simply to take my place in alphabetical order; but please explain beforehand that I am ready to undertake any work which they may think fit to apportion to me. I likewise undertake to invite the Grand Duke of Weimar, the Duke of Gotha, etc., to become subscribers.

The whole affair must bear the impress of an Art enterprise—and in this sense the invitation to a Mozart-Verein [Mozart Union] must be couched. (I leave you to decide whether you prefer the word Mozart-Gesellschaft [Mozart Society] or Mozart-herein for the Publication of the Complete Works of Mozart, or any other title.) Together with this I repeat that certainly there is no need to fear any loss in this matter, but that probably there will be a not insignificant gain. This gain, according to my ideas, should be formed into a capital, until the edition is completed, to be then employed, or perhaps not till later, by the Society of Austrian Lovers of Music for some artistic purpose to be decided upon.

.—. Be so good as to give Herr Krall the sum (24 florins) for the four seats kindly placed at my disposal for the two concerts of the Mozart Festival. Although I have only paid in cash six gulden of the amount, because the other gentlemen insisted on sending me several gulden, yet I expressly wish that the receipts should not be any smaller through me—any more than that the performance should suffer by my conducting!—Therefore please don't forget the twenty-four gulden.

Berlioz arrived here yesterday evening, and I shall be over head and ears in work with Cellini, the great Court concert on the 17th, and the performance of Berlioz' Faust in the course of next week, the preparations for which I have undertaken.

Cellini I shall conduct—with the two others I only direct the rehearsals.

In faithful friendship thy Saturday, February 9th, 1856.

F. Liszt

149. To Dr. von Seiler, Mayor of Vienna. [Autograph in the possession of M. Alfred Bovet, of Valentigney.]

Dear Sir,

As it was not permitted me to see Your Worship again at home before my departure, I venture to express once more in these few lines my warmest thanks for the very great kindness shown to me during my stay in Vienna, the remembrance of which will not fade from my grateful thoughts.

The worthy example which you, dear Mr. Mayor, and the Town Council of Vienna have given on the occasion of the Mozart Festival, guaranteed and attained the desired prosperity and success of the affair. This example will doubtless bring forth fruit in other places, so that the whole artist society will owe you the most grateful acknowledgments for it. As regards myself and my modest services on that occasion, I am very happy to think from the kind letter signed by yourself and Herr Councillor Riedel von Riedenau, that what I did so gladly was well done—and I only cherish the wish that coming years may offer me an opportunity of devoting my poor, but seriously well-intentioned services in the cause of music to the city of Vienna, whose musical traditions shine forth so gloriously. Accept, dear sir, the assurance of high esteem with which I have the honor to remain

Your most obliged

F. Liszt

Weymar, February 10th, 1856

150. To Dr. Franz Brendel

Dear Friend,

Before everything else I must give you my warmest thanks for the manifold proofs of your friendship and attachment which you have given me lately; especially has the article in the last number but one of the paper, taken from the concluding chapter of your musical history, truly rejoiced me, and I should have written you at once a couple of lines in grateful acknowledgment had I not been so very much engaged, on my return here, that I have had no leisure hour until now. In Leipzig I could only stay from the time of one train to the other, and could not go to see any one except Hartel, whom it was necessary for me to see. Scarcely had I arrived here than I had to go to Gotha (where I was present at Berlioz' concert), and the previous week we had enough to do with the preparations and rehearsals of "Cellini" and the Court concert. The performance this time was really capital. Caspari had studied his part admirably, and made a good thing of it; the opera, thanks to him, made quite a different impression from what it did formerly, when poor Beck (now the proprietor of a cafe in Prague, where I saw him lately) had to fit himself as best he could into the Cellini jacket!—Probably Pohl will send you a full account, and also mention the concert which took place the day before yesterday at the Castle. Berlioz conducted it, and Fraulein Bianchi very much pleased the nobility as well as the rest of the audience—so that she is again engaged for a small concert next Thursday.

In contrast to many other artists of both sexes, Fraulein Bianchi is well-bred, without being stupidly stuck up, and, in addition, a pleasant and well-trained singer whom one can safely recommend.

The few lines which she brought me from you were her best introduction to me—only I will beg you, another time, not to be in doubt as to "whether I still think of you with the old friendship." Once for all, you may be perfectly certain on this point, that I shall not develop any talent for Variations towards you, but be always ready to give a proof, on every opportunity, of how highly I prize your services in matters musical, and how sincerely friendly I am to you personally.

F. Liszt

February 19th, 1856

Next Sunday "Lohengrin" will be given (with Fraulein Marx from Darmstadt as Ortrude)—and on Thursday, the 28th February, the entire "Faust" of Berlioz.

151. To Dionys Pruckner in Vienna

[Liszt's pupil; has been a professor at the Stuttgart
Conservatorium since 1858.]

Dearest Dionysius,

The joyful tidings of your success ever find the most joyful echo in Weymar, and I thank you much for the pleasant tidings in your letter. Haslinger, on his side, was so kind as to write me a full account of your first concert, as well as the Court soiree at H.R.H. the Archduchess Sophie's—and yesterday evening v. Dingelstedt gave me also full details of your concert ravages in Munich. All this plainly shows dass man Bock-Bier trinken kann, ohne deswegen Bocke zu schiessen! [A play on words: that one may drink "Bock" beer, without thereby making blunders.]

I entirely approve of your intention of spending some months in Vienna and its charming environs—also of your closer intercourse with the Master Czerny, whose many-sided musical experiences may be of the greatest use to you practically and theoretically. Of all living composers who have occupied themselves especially with pianoforte playing and composing, I know none whose views and opinions offer so just an experience. In the twenties, when a great portion of Beethoven's creations was a kind of Sphinx, Czerny was playing Beethoven exclusively, with an understanding as excellent as his technique was efficient and effective; and, later on, he did not set himself up against some progress that had been made in technique, but contributed materially to it by his own teaching and works. It is only a pity that, by a too super-abundant productiveness, he has necessarily weakened himself, and has not gone on further on the road of his first Sonata (Op. 6, A-flat major) and of other works of that period, which I rate very highly, as compositions of importance, beautifully formed and having the noblest tendency. But unfortunately at that time Vienna influences, both social and publishing, were of an injurious kind, and Czerny did not possess the necessary dose of sternness to keep out of them and to preserve his better ego. This is generally a difficult task, the solving of which brings with it much trouble even for the most capable and those who have the highest aims.

When you see Czerny remember me to him as his grateful pupil and devoted, deeply respectful friend. When I pass through Vienna this summer, I shall rejoice to have a couple of hours with him again. I shall probably find you still there. According to what has been written to me, the consecration of the Gran Cathedral will take place at the beginning of September, in which case I shall start from here at the beginning of August.

Excuse me for not having been willing to send you the orchestral parts to the "Turkish Capriccio." It seemed to me, on the one hand, unsuitable to ask Hans for it—apart from the fact that the sending of the parts backwards and forwards from Berlin to Vienna is very roundabout—and, on the other hand, I could not but suppose that you would find first-rate copyists in Vienna, who would do the copying for you far better in a fortnight. Principles of economy are UTTERLY WORTHLESS in copying, and, if you will believe my experience, always choose therefore the best, and consequently most expensive, copyists for transcribing the parts that you want. Recommend them, into the bargain, to do them with great care, and to add the cues (which are a great help towards a good performance).

Bronsart wrote to you at my direction, to let you know in good time that you should get the parts copied out in Vienna yourself, and should look them over carefully with the copyist before the rehearsal —a work which I have often done in earlier years, and in which I generally make a rule of not sparing myself.

Please find out for me at Spina's, on a convenient opportunity, how far the engraving of the Schubert Fantasia [Fantasia in C major, on the Wanderer.] (instrumented by me) has progressed, and whether he can soon send me the proofs. Bronsart played the Fantasia with orchestral accompaniment lately at Jena.

Fare you well, dearest Dionysius, and send soon some good tidings of yourself to

Yours in all friendship,

F. Liszt

Weymar, March 17th, 1856.

152. To Breitkopf & Hartel

Dear Sir,

Whatever fate may be in store for my Symphonic Poems, however much they may be cut up and pulled to pieces and found fault with through their performances and reviews everywhere, yet the sight of the beautiful manner in which these first six numbers are published and got up will always be a pleasant satisfaction to me, for which I give you my warmest and heartiest thanks..—. The two scores still wanting (Nos. 1 and 9) I will send you at the end of this month, and will request you to publish them in the same size and manner. Although there is somewhat of the SPECULATIVE in these things, yet [I] by no means seek

to make a speculation of it, and only expect your friendly favor in so far as a favorable pecuniary result may arise from it in future years. I am expecting next time the proofs of the two- piano arrangements, and you shall receive the two remaining piano arrangements at the same time as the two last scores..—.

In the matter of the Handel-Gesellschaft, [Handel Society] the scheme of which you have sent me, pray be assured of my most complete readiness. The choice of Messrs. Hauptmann, Dehn, Chrysander (Otto Jahn?), as the musical directors proper, I consider thoroughly suitable—as also of Messrs. Gervinus and Breitkopf and Hartel as members of the committee—and, as soon as the pecuniary basis of the undertaking is fixed, I shall not fail to get you some subscriptions, as I did for the Bach- Gesellschaft.

With warm thanks and esteem,
Yours very truly,
F. Liszt
Weymar, May 15th, 1856
If it is possible to you to send me soon the proofs of the five piano arrangements I shall be glad, as they make the comprehension and spread of the

scores easier.

153. To Louis Kohler

Dear Friend,

After I had seen about your commission to Dr. Hartel, and he had sent me your Methode, [Systematic method of teaching for pianoforte playing and music, 1857 and 1858.] I delayed writing to you, because the result (favorable, as might be expected) of the little business had been already communicated to you through Hartel, and I wished at the same time to send you somewhat of my wares. Unfortunately, I have been hindered by multifarious occupations from getting through the proofs of my Symphonic Poems quickly; and, besides this, these proofs have taken up a great deal of my time; for although I had not omitted, in the first proofs, to have things altered in the scores many times, yet many things looked different to me in print from what I wished them to be, and I had to try them over again plainly with the orchestra, have them written out again, and ask for fresh proofs. At last the six first numbers have come out, and even if they are very badly done I can no longer do them otherwise or better. No doubt you have already received from Hartel the copy destined for you, and within a short time you will receive the somewhat freely arranged pianoforte edition—for two pianos— of the same things. I tried at first a four-hand arrangement of them, which would be much more practicable for sale, but gave up this mutilation, as I saw that in four-hand pieces the working into one another of the hands stands too much in the way of my tone-picture. The two- piano arrangement sounds passable, if I mistake not. Bulow, Bronsart, Pruckner, etc., have played it several times, and you will assuredly find in Konigsberg a partner (masculine or feminine) who will beguile you into it. I shall be very glad if the things please you somewhat. I have labored too much in order to realize the requisite proportion and harmony, for them to be able to give me any other pleasure if some sympathy, and also some understanding of the spirit of them on the part of my few friends, does not fall to my share. However that may be, tell me, dear friend, quite candidly, without any compliments, what impression the pieces have made on you. The three numbers which will appear next are still longer, worse, and more venturesome. But I cannot let matters rest there, for these nine numbers serve only as Prolegomena [Prologue, preface] to the "Faust" and "Dante" Symphonies. The former is already settled and finished, and the second more than half written out. "Away, away," [Written in English.] with Mazeppa's horse, regardless of the lazy hack that sticks in the mud of old patterns!

Let me soon hear from you how you dispose of your time in Konigsberg. In Frau Knopp you have got an excellent Ortrude. What have you been giving this winter? Do you keep on a good understanding with Marpurg? Is Pabst remaining in K.?

Don't forget also to let me have your Methode (I forget the exact title) through Hartel. Although I have grown too old and too lazy to improve my piano-playing, yet I will get some good out of it for my pupils, amongst whom are two or three really brave, earnest fellows. Beyond that I have very little to tell you of Weymar. Since Berlioz' stay here, which gave occasion for the Litolff cudgel-smashing newspaper rubbish, Carl Formes and Johanna Wagner have been playing here; the latter with well-deserved and extraordinary success in Gluck's "Orpheus" and "Iphigenia in Aulis" (in Wagner's translation and arrangement). This evening the "Sleeping Beauty" (a fairy-tale epic), by Joachim Raff, will be given. According to my opinion, this is Raff's most successful and grateful work.

Farewell, dear friend, and bear in friendly remembrance

Your very sincere and obliged

F. Liszt

Weymar, May 24th, 1856

154. To Louis Kohler

My Very Dear Friend,

At last I have come out of my "Purgatory"—that is to say that I have come to the end of my symphony to Dante's "Divina Commedia." Yesterday I wrote the final bars of the score (which is somewhat smaller in bulk than my "Faust" Symphony, but will take pretty nearly an hour in performance); and today, for rest and refreshment, I can allow myself the pleasure of giving you my friendliest thanks for your friendly letter. The dedication of your work "Systematic Method of Teaching for Pianoforte Playing and Music" (the latter must not be forgotten!) pleases me much, and you will allow me to take a modest revanche [revenge] shortly, in dedicating one of my latest works to you. Probably Schlesinger will bring out several books of my songs next winter, in which you will perhaps find much that is in sympathy with your ideas of the melody of speech. Hence I wish that you would not refuse me the pleasure of using your name in connection with them, and of letting it precede them, as an interpretation, as it were, of the intention of the songs. Hartel will send you in a couple of days the first seven numbers of the arrangements for two pianofortes of my Symphonic Poems which have already appeared. An arrangement of that kind is not so easy to make use of as a four-hand one. Nevertheless, after I had tried to compass the score of Tasso plainly into one pianoforte, I soon gave up this project for the others, on account of the unadvisable mutilation and defacement by the working into and through one another of the four-hand parts, and submitted to doing without tone and color and orchestral light and shade, but at any rate fixing an abstract rendering of the musical contents, which would be clear to the ear, by the two-piano arrangement (which I could arrange tolerably freely).

It is a very agreeable satisfaction to me that you, dear friend, have found some interest in the scores. For, however others may judge of the things, they are for me the necessary developments of my inner experiences, which have brought me to the conviction that invention and feeling are not so entirely evil in Art. Certainly you very rightly observe that the forms (which are too often changed by quite respectable people into formulas) "First Subject, Middle Subject, After Subject, etc., may very much grow into a habit, because they must be so thoroughly natural, primitive, and very easily intelligible." Without making the slightest objection to this opinion, I only beg for permission to be allowed to decide upon the forms by the contents, and even should this permission be withheld from me from the side of the most commendable criticism, I shall none the less go on in my own modest way quite cheerfully. After all, in the end it comes principally to this—WHAT the ideas are, and HOW they are carried out and worked up—and that leads us always back to the FEELING and INVENTION, if we would not scramble and struggle in the rut of a mere trade.

When is your Method of teaching coming out? I rejoice beforehand at all the incitement and forcible matter contained in it. You will shortly receive a circular with a letter from E. Hallberger (Stuttgart), who asks me to undertake the choice of pieces to appear in his edition of the "Pianoforte." Do send something soon to it; it is to be hoped that the establishing and spreading of this collection will prove quite satisfactory.

Fare you well in your work, dear friend, and think affectionately of

Yours ever sincerely,

F. Liszt

Weymar, July 9th, 1856.

P.S.—In your next letter send me your exact address.

155. To Hoffmann von Fallersleben

[The well-known poet (1798-1874), who was living at that time in Weimar; was an intimate friend of Liszt, and in 1854 founded, with him, the Neu-Weimar-Verein, which, under the presidency of Liszt, was joined by all the most distinguished musicians, authors, and painters of Weimar.]

Dear Friend,

In your [The second person singular is employed in this letter] pleasant villeggiatura, where you will find no lack of the Beautiful and Good, let yourself also be welcomed by a friend of the New-Weymar

School, who is truly yours. It is true I have nothing new to tell you. You already know that the Grand Duke received your poem on the morning of his birthday, and said the kindest things about it to me later on. Most of our colleagues of the Neu-Weimar-Verein are away and scattered in various countries;—Singer in Pesth; Soupper [Eugen v. Soupper, concert singer, a countryman of Liszt's, was in Weimar in 1855-56.] in Paris, where he is trying the solitude of a crowd (according to Chateaubriand's expression, "the crowd, that vast desert—not dessert—of men"); Stor [Music director in Weimar; died 1889.] at the bathing-place Heringsdorf, probably drawn there by a secret affinity between his herring form and the name of the place; Winterberger in Holland, to inspect the Haarlem and other organs, which he will certainly do in a masterly way; and Preller goes today to Kiel. On the Altenburg no change worth mentioning has taken place: visits of strangers to me fail not summer or winter, and, still less, works which have become my life's task. I might almost sing, like Hoffmann von Fallersleben,

"Hier sitz ich fest, ein Fels im Meer, Woran die Wellen toben; 's geht drunter, dran and druber her— Ich bleibe fortan oben"—

["Here firm I sit, a rock sea-girt, On which the waves are dashing, But I remain above, unhurt, Nor heed the waters' lashing."]

if only there were more waves and less marsh!

—

My travelling plans are still somewhat vacillating, because I cannot yet decide whether I shall go to Hungary or not. In any case I shall go and see R. Wagner, in the middle of September at latest, at Zurich, where Stahr at present is with his wife (Fanny Lewald). Stahr will shortly publish a new volume of Paris Letters (about the Exhibition), and is translating Suetonius for the Classical Library coming out at Stuttgart. He told me that there is a passage in Suetonius which one can quite apply to the baptism of the Prince Imperial in Paris! After this precedent, why might not everything in the Horoe belg, and the Weymar Year- Book be proved as referring to something?

Remember me most warmly to your dear Amphitrion, whom I unfortunately did not manage to see again before her departure, and, if the Mildes are in the same house as you, give them my best greetings, woven into a toast.

Fare thee well, dearest friend, and do not remain too long away.

Thine in heartfelt friendship,

F. Liszt Weymar, July 14th, 1856

156. To Wilhelm wieprecht, General Music Director of the Military Corps of the State of Prussia

[Autograph in the possession of Herr Otto Lessmann at Charlottenburg. The addressee (1802-72) was one of the inventors of the bass-tuba, and improved many of the wind instruments.]

Dear Friend, I learn from several Berliners, who have passed through here, that you have had the great kindness to instrument my march "Vom Fels zum Meer" ["From the Rock to the Ocean."] splendidly, and have had it performed several times. Permit me to express my warmest thanks to you for this new proof of your friendship, and at the same time to remind you of a promise the fulfillment of which is very much desired by me.

It is that, in my last visit to Berlin, you were so kind as to say that the Symphonic Poem Tasso would not be amiss arranged by you for a military band, and you, with your well-known readiness for action, expressed your willingness to arrange the instrumentation accordingly. Allow me today to lay claim to half your kind offer, and to beg you to strike out forty-two pages of this long score, and so to dispose your arrangement that, after the last bar of page 5 (score), you make a skip to the second bar of page 47 (Lento assai), by this means shortening the lamento of Tasso and of the public also.

[Here, Liszt illustrates with a musical score excerpt of the last bar of page 5.]

[Here, Liszt illustrates with another musical score excerpt, from the second bar of page 47.]

By the same post I send you the score and the piano arrangement (for two pianofortes) for convenience in looking it over. If the concluding figure (Letter M., Moderato pomposo) seems to make a better effect in the instrumentation by following the piano arrangement with the simple quaver figure [Liszt illustrates with a brief musical score excerpt] instead of the triplets, according to the score, I have not the slightest objection to it, and beg you altogether, dear friend, to feel quite free to do as you like in the matter. The flattering thing for me would be just this— that the work should please you sufficiently for you to be allowed to take what liberties you wish with it.

Some years ago Dahlmann gave a lecture at Bonn upon immature enthusiasm. God preserve us rather from untimely pedantry! Certainly no one shall have to suffer from this from my side!

I am sending you, together with the "Tasso" score, that of
 "Mazeppa" also. Take an opportunity of looking at the concluding
 "March" (beginning page 89 of the score):—

[Here, Liszt illustrates with a musical score excerpt]

(N.B—It must begin with the 4/6 chord, perhaps after a couple of introductory bars roll on the drum—without any distinct tone.)

Perhaps the subject may suit for some occasion or other.

Forgive me, dear friend, for being so pressing, and behold in this only the joy which the fulfillment of your promise will give me. Next winter I hope to give you my thanks in person in Berlin.

Meanwhile accept the expression of high esteem of yours truly and with all friendly acknowledgments,

F. Liszt

Weymar, July 18th, 1856

If, as I imagine, the Finale from "Tasso" could be so arranged that moderate military bands could play it fairly well, I should of course be glad. However I leave it entirely in your hands to do with it whatever seems best to you, and give you my best thanks beforehand for your kindness.

157. To Concertmeister Edmund Singer

Dear Friend,

In consequence of the definite decision which was made known to me yesterday by T. R. the Titular Bishop and the Cathedral Cantor Fekete, my Mass is to be performed on the day of the consecration. [Of the Cathedral of Gran] I shall therefore get to Pest by the 11th or 12th August, as I had previously arranged, and shall be very glad to see you and two or three others of my friends again. I am also reckoning on you for certain as leader of the orchestra at the rehearsals and performance of the Mass. I am writing tomorrow to Winterberger, who is making a tremendous sensation in Holland, to beg him to undertake the organ part, and to be in Pest by the middle of August.

While speaking of Holland, I may add that Herr Vermeulen (General Secretary of the "Maatschappy" ["Maatschappy tot bevordering der toonkunst."]) is coming to see me here early in August. This offers me a good opportunity of being of service to you in regard to your concert arrangements in Rotterdam and Amsterdam, etc., of which I will not fail to make use. More of this viva voce. Meanwhile, it would be better for you not to write there.

I enclose several notes of acknowledgment for

E., Dr. F., B. and
K., to which I beg you will kindly attend.

And now one more commission, which you can easily fulfill through Rosavoegly, [Music publisher in Budapest] with my best greetings to him. In my reply to the official letter of H. R. von Fekete yesterday I forgot to repeat that, in order to avoid loss of time, it is easy to have the voice parts (solos and chorus) written out before my arrival, and as carefully as possible, clean and clearly. I will willingly discharge the copyist's fee, and the orchestral parts I will bring with me together with the score, so that the rehearsals may begin as soon as the performers taking part in it are assigned to me.

I confidently hope that we shall have a very fine performance, without trouble and worry, and one in which musicians as well as audience will find pleasure and edification. The length of the Mass will also fulfill the required dimensions, and yesterday I hunted out a couple of "cuts," which could be made, if necessary, without any essential harm to the work. You know, dear Singer, that I am a special virtuoso in the matter of making cuts, in which no one else can easily approach me!—

I am simply not disposed, in spite of much prudent advice, to cut my Mass and myself altogether, all the less so as my friends and countrymen have on this occasion shown themselves so kind and good to me. I therefore owe it to them to give them active proof that their confidence and sympathy in me are not wholly undeserved—and with God's help this shall be irrefragably proved!

For the rest I want to keep very quiet and private this time in Pest. Composers of my sort write, it is true, plenty of drum and trumpet parts, but by no means require the too common flourish of trumpets and drums, because they are striving after a higher aim, which is not to be attained by publicity.

"Auf baldiges Wiedersehen," ["To a speedy meeting"] dear friend— I leave here by the 9th August at latest. Meanwhile best thanks for your letter,—and

Ever yours,

F. Liszt

July 28th, 1856.

158. To Joachim Raff

[Raff (1822-82) lived, as is well known, for some years in Weimar (first of all as Liszt's secretary), and at that time joined the Liszt tendencies as a composer, afterwards going other ways.]

Dear Sir and Friend,

It is very pleasant to me to find from your letter that you have taken aright the recognition in my article on the "Sleeping Beauty," and see unequivocally in its attitude a fresh proof of the high estimation in which I hold your artistic powers, as well as of my readiness to be of use to you as far as my insight and loyalty in Art matters will permit me. In this first discussion of a work so much thought of and so widespread, it was most important that I should draw the attention of Art-fellowship to your entire works and higher endeavors during the past six years. You will still give me the opportunity, I hope, later on, of spreading much deserved praise and of placing more in the shade any chance differences in our views. If I have not placed you this time so completely as I should have wished among the musical fellowship of the time, like a Peter Schlemihl,[The man without a shadow— German fable.] this was partly in consequence of your own oft-repeated advice that "one should not exclusively praise men and works if one wishes to be useful to them."[Neue Zeitschrift fur Musik. Later "Gesammelte Schriften," vol. v.]

I do not always agree with you in this view, but on this occasion
I hope I have hit the happy medium.

Accept my best thanks for the friendly interest you have shown in my orchestral compositions in the concert direction of Wiesbaden. Whether I shall be able to comply with several invitations for concerts in the coming winter depends on a good many circumstances which I cannot quite settle beforehand. But in any case I shall be glad if my compositions become more widely spread, and perhaps during your present stay in Wiesbaden the opportunity may offer of conducting one or two numbers of the Symphonic Poems, in accordance with your previous intentions.

At the end of next week at latest I set out for Gran, to conduct my Mass on the 31st of August (in celebration of the consecration of the Basilica). Toward the middle of September I go to Zurich, where, if I am not prevented by any special hindrances, for which I always have to be prepared, I think of spending a couple of weeks with Wagner.

Fare you well, dear Raff, and send soon some tidings of yourself to

Yours most truly,

F. Liszt

Weymar, July 31st, 1856.

Hans von Bulow has been with me a couple of days, and goes to Baden-Baden the day after tomorrow. Winterberger is scoring an extraordinary triumph by his organ-playing in Holland, and played the Prophete and BACH Fugue [Fugue on the name of Bach] before an audience of two thousand people with immense success.

Do not forget to give my friendly greetings to Genast [the celebrated Weimar actor, afterwards Raff's father-in-law] and my homage to Mademoiselle Doris [Afterwards Raff's wife, an excellent actress].

159. To Anton Rubinstein

It is a very great regret to me, my dear Rubinstein, to have to miss your visit the day after tomorrow, of which you sent me word by Mr. Hallberger. You know what a sincere pleasure it always is to me to see you again, and what a lively interest I take in your new works. This time in particular I am at high tension about the completion of your Paradise Lost. If the continuation and the end correspond with the beginning which you showed me, you have reason to be really and truly satisfied with yourself, and you may sleep in peace conscious of having written a grand and beautiful work.

Unfortunately, whatever curiosity I have to be quite assured of this, I cannot stay here any longer, and must start tomorrow morning for Gran, where, in spite of a lot of useless talk, the thread of which you have perhaps followed in the papers, they will end after all by giving my Mass on the 31st of August (the day of the consecration of the Basilica). You see that I have only just time to set the thing on foot, and cannot, without the risk of unpleasantness, defer my arrival beyond the day which, moreover, I officially fixed about a week ago.

Please excuse me then, my dear Rubinstein, for my involuntary fugue, and allow me to make up for it without too much delay. On my return from Hungary I shall come through Stuttgart (towards the middle of September). Perhaps I shall find you still there, which would be a very great pleasure. We would sing together the choruses, solos, and orchestra of your new score with all our might! And Winterberger (who has just had a fabulous success at Rotterdam, Haarlem, etc., where he has given several organ concerts largely attended) might also be one of the party, for I expect to make the journey from Zurich with him, and on our way we shall explore the organs of Ulm, Stuttgart, Friburg, and Winterthur.

Will you let me know by a few lines what your plans are for the end of the summer and autumn? Shall you return to Leipzig? Will it suit you to try your Oratorio first at Weymar? In this latter case, which you may be sure will be the most agreeable to me, I will try to facilitate the arrangements that have to be made as regards copies, and to save you the expense of copying. Toward the end of October, at latest, I shall be back here; and, if we do not meet before, I count on your not letting this year elapse without coming again for a few days to your room at the Altenburg, where you are certain of being always most cordially welcome, for we shall make no changes.

If you have a quarter of an hour to spare do write a piece of a few pages for Hallberger, without making him wait any longer, for I especially want one of your loose works to appear in the first copy of the "Pianoforte."

The Princess bids me give you her best compliments, to which I add the expression of frank and cordial friendship of your very devoted

F. Liszt

August 6th, 1856.

Have you received my things in score?
Continue to address me at
 Weymar.

160. To Joachim Raff

You would be making a great mistake if you put any mistrust in my conduct, and I can assure you with a perfectly good conscience that to me there is nothing more agreeable and more to be desired than to rely entirely on one's friends. With regard to the Wiesbaden affair, I must necessarily await a definite invitation from the concert directors before I can give a definite answer. I think I have too often shown that I am ready and willing, for it to be necessary for me to say more on that point. I was again at Sondershausen last Sunday, and promised to go there again in the course of next winter. The orchestra there, under its conductor Stein (whose acquaintance

I had not made until now), has performed two of my Symphonic Poems—"Les Preludes" and "Mazeppa"—with really uncommon spirit and excellence. Should there be a similar willingness in Wiesbaden, it will of course be a pleasure to me to accept the invitation of the concert directors; so also I am greatly obliged to you for being so helpful toward the spread and sympathetic understanding of my works. But from your letter I see that you will not be staying much longer in Wiesbaden, and as I am not acquainted with the present circumstances there I cannot reckon beforehand on the friendly reception without which public performances always prove very unfruitful for composers. According, therefore, to whether these circumstances show themselves favorable or unfavorable to my honest endeavors, I will come, or I will remain at home.

I give you my heartiest good wishes for the performance of your "King Alfred" [an opera of Raff's]. Your two "Tanz-Capricen" (bolero and valse) have been sent me by Hallberger, and I have already recommended a speedy edition of both.

This afternoon I start for Gran. In the middle of September I shall get to Stuttgart and go to Zurich. Letters can be always addressed to me at Weymar, and before the end of October I shall be back here again.

With best greetings and thanks, yours very truly,

F. Liszt

Weymar, August 7th, 1856

161. To Anton Rubinstein

I much regret, dear Rubinstein, to have missed

your visit to Weymar, and, while thanking you most sincerely for your kind intention, I am going to beg you to grant me full reparation by a second visit when I return.

By the news which reaches me from the Altenburg I learn that you think of spending part of the winter in Berlin, and will there give your "Paradise Lost," which will doubtless be a piece well found, and from which you will derive benefit. Please do not fail to let me know in good time which day it is to be performed, for I am set upon being present at this first performance, and shall certainly come to Berlin unless anything absolutely unavoidable prevents me.

I expect to be back at Weymar towards the end of October, and to set seriously to work again, a thing which is not possible elsewhere. The rehearsals of my Mass are going on here admirably, and I expect we shall have a very fine performance at Gran on the 31st, where, moreover, there will be so many other things and people of quite a different importance to be seen and heard, that they will scarcely hear three bars of my Mass. Happily my work has the good luck to have two general preliminary rehearsals, public ones, at Pest next week, and a final rehearsal at Gran itself. Zellner will probably be there, and you will hear about it from him. Possibly also the same Mass will be given on the 28th September (the day of St. Wenceslas, the patron saint of Bohemia) at Prague, whence they have just written to me to that effect. You will give me great pleasure, my dear Rubinstein, if you will write me something about your autumn and winter plans; and if by chance I can be of use to you in any way show me the friendship of disposing entirely of me, as of one who is your very sincerely affectionate and devoted

F. Liszt Pest, August 21st, 1856

Address always to Weymar.

I am still expecting to go by Stuttgart to Zurich towards the middle of September, but it is possible that Prague may occasion me a fortnight's delay.

162. To Eduard Liszt

[Pest,] Friday, September 5th, 1856

Dearest Eduard,

Yesterday's performance of my Mass was quite according to my intentions, and was more successful and effective by far than all the preceding ones. Without exaggeration and with all Christian modesty I can assure you that many tears were shed, and that the very numerous audience (the church of the Stadtpfarrei [I.e., the parish church] was thronged), as well as the performers, had raised themselves, body and soul, into my contemplation of the sacred mysteries of the Mass…and everything was but a humble prayer to the Almighty and to the Redeemer! —I thought of you in my heart of hearts, and sought for you—for you are indeed so very near and dear to me in spirit!—Next Monday, the 8th September, at the consecration of the Hermine-Kapelle (which the Cardinal Prince Primate of Hungary will consecrate), my Mass for four men's voices will be sung. Winterberger will accompany it on a Physharmonica of the organ genus. On the same evening (Monday) the concert for the benefit of the Pension Fund will take place at the theater: Singer and Pruckner will play at it, and two of my Symphonic Poems—"Les Preludes" and "Hungaria" (Nos. 3 and 9)- -will be given.

On the 14th September at latest I shall get to Vienna, and I will write to Haslinger more definitely about it. Meanwhile will you please tell Haslinger, as I cannot write to him until the concert in the Hungarian theater is over.

.—. I expect to leave here before the end of next week.

God be with you and with your

F. L.

At the rehearsal this morning I was told that you have got such an excellent article on the Mass in the Wanderer. I suppose you sent the number to Weymar? If possible let me have one here also.

163. To Louis Kohler

Bravo, dear friend, for the three very graceful and charmingly conceived melody-dialogues! I have pleasure in them, and am certain of the success of this charming selam. [Meaning a musical bouquet.] As an old laborant [Worker in a laboratory] at piano music allow me merely to lay before you a slight alteration in the two bars before the return of the motive (No. I). According to my conception one bar more would have a beneficial effect there, thus:—

[Here Liszt writes out a 5-measure excerpt of piano music]

If you agree with this version, write me simply Yes to the address of Richard Wagner, Zeltweg,

Zurich. I shall get there next Sunday, and stay some days with our great friend. At the beginning of November I shall be back in Weymar.

Hearty greetings from yours in all friendship,

F. Liszt

Stuttgart, October 8th, 1856.

In No. 3 (in the first two bars) the F seems to me the right sound in the bass, and that was what you had first written:—

[Here, Liszt illustrates with a musical score excerpt]

instead of:—

[Here, Liszt illustrates with another musical score excerpt]

Will you leave these little alterations to me in the proof?

164. To Dr. Gille, Councillor of Justice at Jena

[An ardent friend of Liszt's, a promoter of musical endeavors, a co-founder and member of the Committee (General Secretary) of the Allgemeine Deutsche Musikverein, is at the head of the Liszt Museum in Weimar, and lives in Jena, where he is Prince's Council and Councillor of Justice.]

Zurich, November 14th, 1856

My very dear Friend,

I am heartily rejoiced at the honorable proof of the sympathy and attachment of our Circulus harmonicus Academiae Jenensis, which was prepared for me for the 22nd October by your kindness, and I give you my warmest thanks for it, begging you to be so good as to pass them on also to our friends Stade and Herr Schafer, whose names strengthen the diploma.

It touches me deeply that you join the Gran Basilica and my "Missa Solemnis" in this diploma. You may be sure, dear friend, that I did not compose my work as one might put on a church vestment instead of a paletot, but that it has sprung from the truly fervent faith of my heart, such as I have felt it since my childhood. "Genitum, non factum"—and therefore I can truly say that my Mass has been more prayed than composed. By Easter the work will be published by the Royal State Printing Office at the cost of the Government, thanks to the kind instructions of His Excellency Minister von Bach, and I am looking forward to the pleasure of presenting one of the first copies to the Circulus harmonicus. The Mass has been given a second time at Prague since I left, and, as Capellmeister Skraup writes, "with increasing interest"; a couple more performances, in Vienna, etc., are pending.

Pray excuse me, dear friend, for not having sent you my thanks sooner. Your letter found me in bed, to which I am still confined by a somewhat protracted illness, which will delay my return to Weymar some weeks. Next week I am to begin to get out into the air again, and I hope to be able to get away in about ten days. At the beginning of December I shall be at Weymar, and shall then soon come to you at Jena.—

I shall have a great deal to tell you verbally about Wagner. Of course we see each other every day, and are together the livelong day. His "Nibelungen" are an entirely new and glorious world, towards which I have often yearned, and for which the most thoughtful people will still be enthusiastic, even if the measure of mediocrity should prove inadequate to it!—

Friendly greetings, and faithfully your

F. Liszt

165. To Dr. Adolf Stern in Dresden

[Poet and man of letters, now professor at the Polytechnikum at
Dresden, a member of the Committee of the Allgemeine Deutsche
Musikverein since 1867.]

Very Dear Sir and Friend,

A long and protracted illness has kept me in bed for a fortnight past—and I owe you many apologies for my delay in sending you my warmest thanks for the very kind remembrance with which you adorned the 22nd of October. The beautiful poem, so full of meaning, and soaring aloft with its delicately powerful flight, goes deeply to my heart, and my dreams hear the charm of your poetry through Lehel's magic horn tones! Perhaps I shall be able shortly to tell you what I have heard, when the disjointed sounds have united in shaping themselves harmoniously into an artistic whole, from which a second part of my Symphonic Poem "Hungaria" might well be formed.

Meanwhile I have ventured to send your poem to a couple of my friends in Pest, who will delight in it like myself.

In spite of my illness I am spending glorious days here with Wagner, and am satiating myself with his Nibelungen world, of which our business musicians and chaff-threshing critics have as yet no suspicion. It is to be hoped that this tremendous work may succeed in being performed in the year 1859, and I, on my side, will not neglect anything to forward this performance as soon as possible—a performance which certainly implies many difficulties and exertions. Wagner requires for the purpose a special theater built for himself, and a not ordinary acting and orchestral staff. It goes without saying that the work can only appear before the world under his own conducting; and if, as is much to be wished, this should take place in Germany, his pardon must be obtained before everything.—I comfort myself with the saying, "What must be will be!" And thus I expect to be also standing on my legs again soon, and to be back in Weymar in the early days of December. It will be very kind of you if you will not let too long a time elapse without coming to see me. For today accept once more my heartfelt thanks, and the assurance of sincere friendship of your

F. Liszt

Zurich, November 14th, 1856

166. To Louis Kohler

Enclosed, dear friend, is a rough copy of the Prelude to "Rheingold," which Wagner has handed me for you, and which will be sure to give you great pleasure.

After having been obliged to keep my bed for a couple of weeks, which has lengthened out my stay here, I am now making ready to go with Wagner the day after tomorrow to St. Gall, there to conduct a couple of my Symphonic Poems with a very respectable orchestra (twenty violins, six double basses, etc.). Toward the middle of December I shall be back in Weymar, and shall continue to write my stuff!—

A thousand friendly greetings.

F. Liszt

Zurich, November 21st, 1856

167. To Eduard Liszt

St. Gall, November 24th, 1856

.—. A really significant concert took place yesterday at St. Gall. Wagner conducted the Eroica Symphony, and I conducted in his honor two of my Symphonic Poems. The latter were excellently given —and received. The St. Gall paper has several articles on the subject, which I am sending you.

By Christmas I will send you the new copies of my Mass (which I think I have considerably improved in the last revision, especially by the concluding Fugue of the Gloria and a heavenward-soaring climax of the subject.

[Here, Liszt illustrates with a vocal score excerpt at the point where the singer sings: "et u-nam sanctam catho-li-camet a-po - sto - - - - li-cam"]

Probably the work will be ready to appear by Easter. If you write by return of post, you can send the ministerial answer to my letter to Bach to me here. The contents, of which you have told me, please me much, and I reckon with confidence that the publishing of the score will fix the sense and meaning of my work in public opinion. The work is truly "of pure musical water (not in the sense of the ordinary diluted Church style, but like diamond water) and living Catholic wine."

.—. Farewell, dearest Eduard, and remain true

306

to me in heart and spirit, as is also to you your

F. Liszt

168. To Alexander Ritter, Music Director in Stettin

Munich, December 4th, 1856

Dear Friend,

I received your letter on a day when I again greatly missed your presence. We were together with Wagner at St. Gall, and the Musical Society there had distinguished itself by the production of an orchestra of ten first, ten second violins, eight violas, six celli and double basses. Wagner conducted the Eroica, and I two of my Symphonic Poems —"Orpheus" and "Les Preludes." The performance and reception of my works were quite to my satisfaction, and the "Preludes" had to be repeated (as they were in Pest). Whether such a production would be possible in Stettin I much doubt, in spite of your friendly advances. The open, straightforward sense of the public is everywhere kept so much in check by the oft-repeated rubbish of the men of the "But" and "Yet," who batten on criticism, and appear to set themselves the task of crushing to death every living endeavour, in order thereby to increase their own reputation and importance, that I must regard the rapid spread of my works almost as an imprudence. You desire "Orpheus," "Tasso," and "Festklange" from me, dear friend! But have you considered that "Orpheus" has no proper working out section, and hovers quite simply between bliss and woe, breathing out reconciliation in Art? Pray do not forget that "Tasso" celebrates no psychic triumph, which an ingenious critic has already denounced (probably mindful of the "inner camel," which Heine designates as an indispensable necessity of German aestheticism!), and the "Festklange" sounded too confusedly noisy even to our friend Pohl! And then what has all this canaille to do with instruments of percussion, cymbals, triangle, and drum in the sacred domain of Symphony? It is, believe me, not only confusion and derangement of ideas, but also a prostitution of the species itself!

Should you be of another opinion, allow me at least to keep you from too greatly compromising yourself, so near to the doors of the immaculate Berlin critics, and not to drag you with myself into the corruption of my own juggling tone-poems. Your dear wife (to whom I beg you to remember me most kindly) might be angry with me for it, and I would not on any account be put into her bad books. Instead of conducting my Symphonic Poems, rather give lectures at home of the safe passport of Riehl's "Haus-Musik," and take well to heart the warning,

"Ruckkehr zum Mass." ["A returning within bounds." A footnote by Liszt follows: "Dabei wird naturlich das Mass der Mittelmassigkeit als einzig massgebend verstanden." ("By this is of course understood the bounds of mediocrity as the one limitation.") A play on the words, "Mass," "Massigkeit," and "Massgebend."]

On this road alone can you soon attain a conductor's post, and the "esteem" due to you as a music director, both from musicians and people of rank.

For the rest you would entirely misconstrue

my good advice if you thought you could see in it only a pretext for not keeping my former promise of coming to see you at Stettin. I shall most certainly come to you on the first opportunity, and shall be delighted to spend a couple of days with such excellent friends. But first of all I must stop in Weymar for a while, in order to finish some works begun, and to forget altogether my lengthy illness in Zurich.

I had some glorious days with Wagner; and "Rheingold" and the
"Walkure" are incredibly wonderful works.

To my great sorrow, I only saw your brother Carl [A musician, a friend of Wagner's.] a couple of times in the early days of my stay in Zurich. I will tell you vaud voce how this happened, so entirely against my wish and expectation, through a provoking over-sensitiveness on the part of your brother. I am sure you don't need any assurance that I did not give occasion in any way to this. But for the future I must quietly wait till Carl thinks better and more justly of it.

Farewell, dear friend, and let me soon hear from you again.

Yours in all friendship,

F. Liszt

Bronsart is going shortly to Paris, where he will stay some time. Cornelius is working at a comic opera [This would be the Barber of Baghdad.—Translator's note.] in the Bernhard's-Hutle. Raff is to finish his "Samson" for Darmstadt. Tausig is giving concerts in Warsaw. Pruckner will spend the winter in Vienna and appear at several concerts. Damrosch composed lately an Overture and Entre- acte music to the "Maid of Orleans." Stor plunges himself into the duties of a general music director. Thus much have I learned of our Neu-Weymar-Verein.

169. To Professor L. A. Zellner in Vienna

[General Secretary of the Gesellschaft der Musikfreunde ("Society of Lovers of Music") in Vienna; composer and writer on music.]

To my letter of yesterday I have still to add a postscript, my dear friend, concerning the information in your new Abonnement,[The Blatter fur Musik, Theater, and Kunst ("Pages of Music, theater, and Art"), edited by Z.] in which I was struck with the name of Bertini among the classics, which does not seem to me suitable. As far as I know, Bertini is still living, [He did not die till 1876.] and according to the common idea, to which one must stick fast, only those who are dead can rank as classic and be proclaimed as classic. Thus Schumann, the romanticist, and Beethoven, the glorious, holy, crazy one, have become classics. Should Bertini have already died, I take back my remark, although the popularity of his Studies is not, to me, a satisfactory reason for making his name a classic.—Moscheles' and Czerny's Studies and "Methods" would have a much more just claim to such a thing, and your paper has especially to set itself the task of counteracting, with principle and consistency, the confusion of ideas from which confusion and ruin of matters arise. Hold fast then to this principle, both in great and small things, for the easier understanding with the public, that the recognition of posterity alone impresses the stamp of "classical" upon works, in the same way as facts and history are established; for thus much is certain, that all great classics have been reviled in their own day as innovators and even romanticists, if not bunglers and crazy fellows, and you yourself have commented on, and inquired into, this matter many times..——.

In your number of today I read an extract from my letter to Erkel, [A well-known Hungarian composer ("Hunyadi Laszlo")] in which, however, the points are missing. Erkel shall show you the letter on the first opportunity, for he has not left it lying idle in his desk. Of course no public use is to be made of it.

Yours ever, F. L.

January 2nd, 1857

170. To Herr von Turanyi, Musical Conductor of the Town of Aix- la-Chapelle

[Published in the Allgemeine Musikzeitung, July 11th, 1890]

Weymar, January 3rd, 1857

Dear Herr Capellmeister,

Although I am still kept to my bed by a long-continued indisposition, yet I will not delay giving you my warmest thanks for the active pains you have so kindly taken to place my endeavors in the cause of Art in a better light than I could otherwise have expected in your neighborhood.

The result of the choice of myself as conductor of the Musical Festival at Aix-la-Chapelle this year —a result which was notified to me yesterday by the letter of the Committee of the Lower-Rhine Musical

Festival—is a welcome sign to me of the gradual recognition which an open and honestly expressed, consistent, and thoroughly disinterested conviction may meet with in different places. Whilst feeling myself especially indebted to you for having brought about this result, I would express to you at the same time the fact of my readiness to answer your very flattering wishes to the best of my powers, and to put aside any hindrances that may be in the way, in order to fulfill the task entrusted to me, if the following remarks are brought to the attention of the Committee, as I consider them essential to the success and also to the importance of the Musical Festival.

My conducting in Aix-la-Chapelle can only have such significance as attaches to the less-known and newer works, and those which are more nearly allied to the Art-interests of today; its justification would be strengthened by an excellent performance of such works. I was on this account completely in accordance with the programme you so kindly sent me (with the addition of one or two numbers), as I am unable to be with the other programme, received in the letter of the Committee yesterday. The latter is as follows:—

First day: Messiah by Handel.—Second day: Mass (in D major) by
Beethoven.

The former as follows:—
First day: Mass by Beethoven (preceded by one of the shorter works of Handel—or possibly by a Cantata by Bach [?]).

Second day: Schubert's Symphony (in C); one of the larger choral works of Schumann (say, perhaps, "The Rose's Pilgrimage"—or one of the Ballades), and, as I should propose, one of the longer scenes from Berlioz' "Faust," and one or other of my Symphonic Poems.

You will not expect of me, dear Herr Capellmeister, that I should go off into a great panegyric about Handel and, if you caught me doing it, you might stop me immediately with the words of the ancient Greek who did not want any more praises of Homer—"You praise him, but who is thinking of blaming him?" The fullness and glory of this musical majesty is as uncontested as the pleasant, emulating, easily attainable performance of the "Messiah," a chef-d'oeuvre, which has been for years the "daily bread," so to speak, of great and small vocal societies both in England and Germany. With the exception of Haydn's "Creation" there is scarcely a work of that kind existing which could show such countless performances. I, for my part, chose the "Messiah" for performance again in Weymar (in August 1850)—partly because Herder had interested himself in the preparation of the German text—and in the previous August they celebrated the Middle-Rhine Musical Festival at Darmstadt with it. This latter circumstance enhances my general consideration as to the artistic judiciousness of a repeated performance of the Messiah, up to a special point in regard to the Aix-la-Chapelle Festival, and therefore I should like the question put to the Committee "whether they consider that, in the interests of the 'fresher life of the Musical Festival

313

there,' it can be advantageous for the Lower-Rhine to repeat it after the Middle-Rhine."

The sentence in the letter of the Committee, in which the hope is cherished and expressed that "the celebrated Frau Lind- Goldschmidt may be engaged," leads me to an almost more serious consideration.—

Do not be alarmed, dear sir, and do not be in the least afraid that I am going to struggle, in the usual style of our unchivalrous Don Quixote of musical criticism, with the windmill of virtuosity. You could not fairly expect this of me either, for I have never concealed that, since the grapes of virtuosity could not be made sour for me, I should take no pleasure whatever in finding them sour in somebody else's mouth.

Frau Land-Goldschmidt stands as incomparable in her glittering renown as a singer as Handel in his as a composer, with the difference—which is in Frau Lind's favor to boot—that Handel's works weary many people and do not always succeed in filling the coffers, whereas the mere appearance of Frau Lind secures the utmost rapture of the public, as well as that of the cashier. If, therefore, we place the affairs of the Musical Festival simply on the satisfying and commercial debit and credit basis, certainly no artist, and still less any work of Art, could venture to compete with, and to offer an equal attraction to, the high and highly celebrated name of Frau Lind. Without raising the slightest objection to this, I must express my common-sense opinion that with this magnet all others would be quite superfluous, which, however, cannot be quite so indifferent to me; for, as Louis XIV. represented the State, so Frau Lind would constitute the Musical Festival proper. This avowal (for which I deserve, at the very least, stoning with the usual ingredients of operations of that kind in our civilized age, if I did not happen to implore grace of the divine Diva herself)—this avowal I already made last year, on occasion of the Dusseldorf Musical Festival, to my esteemed friend of many years, Ferdinand Hiller. What is the use of orchestra and singers, rehearsals and preparations, pieces and programmes, when the public only want to hear the Lind, and then hear her again—or, more correctly speaking, when they must be able to say they leave heard her, in order to be able to wallow at ease in their enthusiasm for Art? What I foresaw then was also confirmed to a hair, for it proved, as everybody knows, that all the sympathy of the public went in favor of whatever Frau Lind did, so that the so-called Artist- concert on the third day was the most fully attended, because in it there were an aria from "Beatrice di Tenda" and Swedish songs as special attraction—for which marvels the very simplest pianoforte accompaniment was no doubt sufficient. —Should the Committee of Aix-la-Chapelle be minded to take to heart the motto of Hiller's Symphony, "Es muss doch Fruhling werden," ["The spring will surely come."] in all its artistic endeavour, and, as you write, to steer clear towards the goal of a "fresher rekindling of the Musical Festival," we shall be obliged, alas! to do without the Swedish Nightingale and Europe's Queen of Song.

In short, the point of the matter of this year's

Musical Festival at Aix-la-Chapelle is, as concerns myself, as follows:-

If they decide on having the "Messiah," I must beg to be pardoned for having to excuse myself from coming. [Liszt finally dropped his objection to the "Messiah." He had it performed at the Musical Festival, conducted by him.]

If the Committee accepts the programme I have drawn (Schubert Symphony, etc., including the last numbers) for the second day, then it will be a pleasing duty to me to accept the honor of the invitation, always supposing that the means for a brilliant performance of the Beethoven Mass and the other works are forthcoming, as one cannot doubt will be the case in Aix-la- Chapelle—if my share in the Festival does not in any way give offence to the neighboring towns, in which case I should of course gladly and quietly retire, in order not to occasion any disturbance, or unsatisfactorily prepared discord in the customs of the musical Rhine-lands. I think there is no need for me to accentuate the fact that a musical conductor cannot blindly subscribe to just every programme that is put before him, and I hope that the honorable Committee will not consider that there is any assumption in my proposition to place the Aix-la-Chapelle programme more in accord with my own collective endeavors.

I am writing a few lines of thanks by the next post to President Herr Van Houten for the distinction shown to me about the consideration contained in this letter, which I beg that you will communicate to him verbally.

Awaiting further communications from the

Committee, I remain, dear Herr Capellmeister, with warm acknowledgements and high esteem,

Yours very truly,

F. Liszt

171. To J. W. von Wasielewski in Dresden

Dear Friend,

Your letter reached me, after some delay, in Zurich, where I had to keep my bed for several weeks—and today I write to you still from my bed, and sulking because the geographical change which I have made has not brought about any improvement in my pathological condition (which, by the way, is quite without danger).

How are you, dear Wasielewski? Have you settled yourself pleasantly in Dresden? Are you working at music industriously and methodically?— How far have you got in your biography of R. Schumann? With regard to this work, the publication of which I am awaiting with great interest, I am sorry to be unable to follow the wish you so kindly express. Many letters addressed to me by Schumann in earlier years are lost, and since my residence in Weymar (from the year 1848) we certainly wrote to one another from time to time, but only when theater or concert performances of his works gave a sort of business occasion for it. Weymar does not deserve the reproach of having kept itself too much in the background in this respect. At the Goethe Festival in 1849 I had the great closing scene to the second part of "Faust" given, which was, later on, repeated; at the beginning of 1852 the music to Byron's "Manfred," with a stage performance of the drama such as he desired, was given several times, and, as far as I know, up to now no other theater has made this attempt. [Liszt was actually the first.] The Weymar theater is likewise the only one which contains in its repertoire Schumann's "Genoveva" (which was indeed given here for the first time in April 1855). It goes without saying that, during the years of my work here, most of his chamber music— Quartets, Trios, Sonatas—as well as his Symphonies, Overtures, and Songs, have been cherished with particular preference and love, and have been frequently heard in various concerts, with the exception of one of the most important; but the very slight amount of public activity of our Vocal Union has prevented, as yet, any performance of the "Peri," which, however, has already been partly studied, and will ere long be given at last.

As a contribution to your biographical studies, dear Wasielewski, I should like to tell you truly with what sincere, heartfelt, and complete reverence I have followed Schumann's genius during twenty years and faithfully adhered to it. Although I am sure that you, and all who know me more intimately, have no doubt about this, yet at this moment the feeling comes over me—a feeling which I cannot resist—to tell you more fully about my relations with R. Schumann, which date from the year 1836, and to give them you here plainly in extenso. Have a little patience, therefore, in reading this letter, which I have not time to make shorter.

After the buzz and hubbub called forth by my article in the Paris Gazette Musicale on Thalberg (the meaning of which, be it said in passing, has been quite distorted), which was re-echoed in

German papers and salons, Maurice Schlesinger, the then proprietor of the Gazette Musicale, took the opportunity of asking me to insert in his paper a very eulogistic article on anything new that came out in the world of Art. For months Schlesinger sent me with this object all sorts of novelties, among which, however, I could not find anything that seemed to me deserving of praise, until at last, when I was at the Lake of Como, Schumann's "Impromptu" in C major (properly variations), the "Etudes symphoniques," and the "Concert sans orchestre" [Concerto without orchestra] (published later, in the second edition, under the more suitable title Sonata in F minor) came into my hands. In playing these pieces through, I felt at once what musical mettle was in them; and, without having previously heard anything of Schumann, without knowing how or where he lived (for I had not at that time been to Germany, and he had no name in France and Italy), I wrote the critique which was published in the Gazette Musicale towards the end of 1837, and which became known to Schumann.

Soon afterwards, when I was giving my first concerts in Vienna (April to May 1838), he wrote to me and sent me a manuscript entitled "Gruss an Franz Liszt in Deutschland" ["Greeting to Franz Liszt in Germany"]. I forget at this moment under what title it was afterwards published; the opening bars are as follows:—

[Here, Liszt hand-writes the score for the opening bars. It is the beginning of the second Novelette Op. 21, but not quite correctly quoted by Liszt]

At about the same time followed the publishing of the great "Fantasia" (C major) in three movements, which he dedicated to me; my dedication to him in return for this glorious and noble work was only made three years ago in my "Sonata" in B minor.

At the beginning of the winter of 1840 I traveled from Vienna back to Paris by way of Prague, Dresden, and Leipzig. Schumann paid me the friendly attention of welcoming me immediately on my arrival in Dresden, and we then travelled together to Leipzig. Wieck, afterwards Schumann's father-in-law, had at that time a lawsuit against him to prevent his marriage with Clara. I had known Wieck and his daughter from Vienna days, and was friendly with both. None the less I refused to see Wieck again in Dresden, as he had made himself so unfriendly to Schumann; and, breaking off all further intercourse with him, I took Schumann's side entirely, as seemed to me only right and natural. Wieck without delay richly requited me for this after my first appearance in Leipzig, where he aired his bitter feelings against me in several papers. One of my earlier pupils, by name Hermann Cohen—a native of Hamburg, who in later years aroused much attention in France, and who, as a monk, had taken the name of Frere Augustin (Carme dechausse [Barefooted Carmelite])—was the scapegoat in Leipzig for Wieck's publicly inflamed scandal, so that Cohen was obliged to bring an action for damage by libel against Wieck, which action Hermann won with the assistance of Dr. Friederici, barrister-at-law.

In Leipzig Schumann and I were together every day and all day long—and my comprehension of his works became thereby more familiar and intimate. Since my first acquaintance with his compositions, I have played many of them in private circles in Milan, Vienna, etc., but without being able to win over my hearers to them. They lay, happily, much too far removed from the insipid taste, which at that time absolutely dominated, for it to be possible for any one to thrust them into the commonplace circle of approbation. The public did not care for them, and the majority of pianists did not understand them. In Leipzig even, where I played the "Carneval" at my second concert in the Gewandhaus, I did not succeed in obtaining my usual applause. The musicians, together with those who were supposed to understand music, had (with few exceptions) their ears still too tightly stopped up to be able to comprehend this charming, tasteful "Carneval," the various numbers of which are harmoniously combined in such artistic fancy. I do not doubt that, later on, this work will maintain its natural place in universal recognition by the side of the "Thirty-three Variations on a Waltz of Diabelli" by Beethoven (to which, in my opinion, it is superior even in melodic invention and importance). The frequent ill-success of my performances of Schumann's compositions, both in private circles and in public, discouraged me from including and keeping them in the programmes of my concerts which followed so rapidly on one another— programmes which, partly from want of time and partly from carelessness and satiety of the "Glanz-

Periode" ["Splendor period"] of my pianoforte-playing, I seldom, except in the rarest cases, planned myself, but gave them now into this one's hands, and now that one, to choose what they liked. That was a mistake, as I discovered later and deeply regretted, when I had learned to understand that for the artist who wishes to be worthy of the name of artist the danger of not pleasing the public is a far less one than that of allowing oneself to be decided by its humors

—and to this danger every executive artist is especially exposed, if he does not take courage resolutely and on principle to stand earnestly and consistently by his conviction, and to produce those works which he knows to be the best, whether people like them or not.

It is of no consequence, then, in how far my faint-heartedness in regard to Schumann's pianoforte compositions might possibly be excused by the all-ruling taste of the day, but I did without thinking of it thereby set a bad example, for which I can hardly make amends again. The stream of custom and the slavery of the artist, who is directed to the encouragement and applause of the multitude for the maintenance and improvement of his existence and his renown, is such a pull-back, that, even to the better- minded and more courageous ones, among whom I am proud to reckon myself, it is intensely difficult to preserve their better ego in the face of all the covetous, distracted, and—despite their large number—backward-in-paying We.

There is in Art a pernicious offence, of which most of us are guilty through carelessness and fickleness; I might call it the Pilate offence. Classical doing, and classical playing, which have become the fashion of late years, and which may be regarded as an improvement, on the whole, in our musical state of things, hide in many a one this fault, without eradicating it:—I might say more on this point, but it would lead me too far.

For my part I need not, at least, reproach myself with having ever denied my sympathy and reverence for Schumann; and a hundred of the younger companions in Art in all lands could bear witness that I have always expressly directed them to a thorough study of his works, and have strengthened and refreshed myself by them.

If these particulars have not wearied you, dear Wasielewski, I will gladly continue them, and tell you about everything from my second visit to Leipzig (at the end of 1841) which was brought about by Schumann, up to my last meeting with him at Dusseldorf (in 1851). Friendly greetings

From yours most sincerely,

F. Liszt

Weymar, January 9th, 1857.

172. To General Alexis von Lwoff in St. Petersburg

[1799-1877; in addition to his military position, he was a celebrated violinist, and conductor of the Imperial Court-Singers at St. Petersburg.]

Your Excellency and My Honored Friend,

Permit me to think that I am not quite effaced from your recollection, and to avail myself of the medium of Mdlle. Martha de Sabinin to recall myself to you more particularly. It being her wish to find herself in pleasant relations with the chief representatives of music in St. Petersburg, it was natural that I should introduce her in the first instance to you, and recommend her to you first and foremost as the protegee of Her Imperial Majesty the Grand Duchess Marie Pawlowna, as well as of the reigning Grand Duchess of Saxe-Weymar (in whose service she has been for several years as Court Pianist and Professor at the Institute for Young Ladies of the Nobility),—and, secondly, as a clever woman and excellent musician and pianist, who, after having gone through the most conscientious study, is perfectly fitted to teach others in a most agreeable manner. She especially excels in her execution of classical music and ensemble; and, this side of music being, from what I hear, more and more cultivated at St. Petersburg, especially through your care, I am pleased to think that Mdlle. de Sabinin will easily find an opportunity of coming out advantageously in this line. I much regret that you have, as yet, neglected Weymar since I have been settled here. It would have been a pleasure to me to place at your disposal a musical personnel, which has been justly spoken of with praise, for the performance of your "Stabat Mater" and other of your compositions, which we should have great pleasure in applauding. Let me hope that you will not always be so rigorous towards us, and pray accept the expressions of high esteem and respect with which I shall always be, dear and honored friend,

Your Excellency's very obedient servant,
F. Liszt

Weymar, January 10th, 1857

173. To Johann Von Herbeck in Vienna

[Hofcapellmeister (Court conductor), and an excellent conductor (1831-1877).—The above letter, as well as a later one addressed to the same musician, was published in "Johann Herbeck. Ein Lebensbild von seinem Sohne Ludwig." Vienna, Gutmann, 1885.—Date in Herbeck's handwriting.]

[Received January 12th, 1857]

Dear Sir,

On my somewhat delayed return to Weymar I find your friendly letter, for which I send you my

sincere and warmest thanks. I am very much pleased to learn from you that you have succeeded, thanks to your careful and intelligent preparation, in making such a good effect with the "Faust" (Student) Chorus. [It was the first choral composition which was conducted by Liszt in Vienna, and with the very same Mannergesangverein which Herbeck conducted.] This light little piece has been pretty successfully given several times by Mannergesangvereinen [Vocal societies of male voices] in Cologne, Berlin, etc., and even in Paris. When I published it fifteen years ago, I did not think much about making allowance for any possible laxity in the intonation of the singers; but today, when my experience has taught me better, I should probably write the somewhat steep and slippery passage as follows:—

[Here, Liszt illustrates with a vocal score musical excerpt at the point where the singer sings "Die Ko-chin hat ihr Gift gestellt, da ward zu eng ihr in der Welt, etc."]

Probably this version would also be more effective—with the alteration in the last verse (in honor of prosody!):—

[Here, Liszt illustrates with a vocal score musical excerpt at the point where the singer sings "ha, sie pfeift auf dem letzten Loch."]

I shall venture shortly to send you (by Herr Haslinger), my dear sir, a couple of other Quartets for male voices to look through. If, after doing so, you think you may risk a public performance of them, I leave the matter entirely in your hands.

There is not the slightest hurry about the Mass, [For men's voices. On the occasion of the Mozart Festival in Vienna in 1856, conducted by Liszt, he had played portions of this Mass to Herbeck, and the latter felt himself, as he wrote to Liszt, "electrified by the spirit of this work and its creator," and set himself "at the same time the artistic duty of a worthy rendering of this Song of Praise."] and I fear that the preparation of this work will cost you and your singers some trouble. Before all else it requires the utmost certainty in intonation, which can only be attained by practicing the parts singly (especially the middle parts, second tenor and first bass)—and then, above all, religious absorption, meditation, expansion, ecstasy, shadow, light, soaring—in a word, Catholic devotion and inspiration. The "Credo," as if built on a rock, should sound as steadfast as the dogma itself; a mystic and ecstatic joy should pervade the "Sanctus;" the "Agnus Dei" (as well as the "Miserere" in the "Gloria") should be accentuated, in a tender and deeply elegiac manner, by the most fervent sympathy with the Passion of

Christ; and the "Dona nobis pacem," expressive of reconciliation and full of faith, should float away like sweet-smelling incense. The Church composer is both preacher and priest, and what the word fails to bring to our powers of perception the tone makes winged and clear.

You know all this at least as well as I do, and I must apologize for repeating it to you. If the extent of the chorus allows of it, it might perhaps be desirable to add a few more wind instruments (clarinets, bassoon, horns, indeed even a couple of trombones) to support the voices more. If you think so too, please send me a line to say so, and I will at once send you a small score of the wind instruments. [Herbeck himself undertook, at Liszt's desire (which, as he wrote, filled him with joy and pride), to write the instrumental accompaniment to the Mass.] You shall have the vocal parts from Jena immediately. For today accept once more my best thanks, together with the assurance of the highest esteem of

Yours ever,

F. Liszt

174. To Professor Franz Gotze in Leipzig

[The celebrated singer in Leipzig (1814-88); was a pupil of Spohr's, and was first violinist in the Weimar Hofcapelle, then went on to the stage, and both as a lyric tenor and as a singer of Lieder was incomparable. He was the first who publicly went in for Liszt's songs, in which his pupils imitated him.]

Dear Friend,

In consequence of an invitation of the directors, I shall have the honor of having several of my works performed at the concert on the 26th

February for the Orchestral Pension Fund in Leipzig, and very much wish that you would do me the kindness to sing two of my songs ("Kling leise, mein Lied" and "Englein du mit blondem Haar"), and to rejoice the public with your ardent and beautifully artistic rendering of these little things.

Fraulein Riese is so good as to bring you the new edition of my six first songs (amongst which is the "Englein" in A major)—a couple more numbers will shortly follow.

Grant me my request, dear friend, and rest assured beforehand of the best thanks, with which I remain,

Yours in most sincere friendship, F. Liszt

Weymar, February 1st, 1857

175. To Dionys Pruckner in Vienna

Weymar, February 11th, 1857

From all sides, dearest Dionysius, I hear the best and most brilliant accounts of you. Without being surprised at this I am extremely pleased about it. To make a firm footing in Vienna as a pianoforte player is no small task, especially under present circumstances! If one succeeds in this, one can, with the utmost confidence, make a name throughout Europe. It is very important for you, dear friend, to appear often in public, so as to make yourself feel at home with them. In production the public have far more to care about the artist than he has to care about them, or indeed to let himself be embarrassed by them. At home, our whole life through, we have to study and to devise how to mature our work and to attain as near as possible to our ideal of Art. But when we enter the concert-room the feeling ought not to leave us, that, just by our conscientious and persevering striving, we stand somewhat higher than the public, and that we have to represent our portion of "Menschheits-Wurde," [Manhood's dignity] as Schiller says. Let us not err through false modesty, and let us hold fast to the true, which is much more difficult to practice and much more rare to find. The artist—in our sense— should be neither the servant nor the master of the public. He remains the bearer of the Beautiful in the inexhaustible variety which is appointed to human thought and perception—and this inviolable consciousness alone assures his authority.

Through your father I learn that you are thinking of going to Munich in the course of the spring. I, on my side, had also the intention of giving you a rendez-vous there. But yesterday I definitely accepted the conductorship of the Musical Festival of the Lower-Rhine, which will take place this year in Aix-la- Chapelle at Whitsuntide, on the 31st May, and could not undertake a long journey before then, in order not to break in on my work too much.

At the beginning of September we shall have grand festivities here in honor of the centenary of Carl August. Rietschel's Schiller and Goethe group will then be put up, and there will be a great deal of music on this occasion at the theater, for which I must prepare. I hope we shall see each other before then.

Bronsart is in Paris. You shall have his Trio very soon. Bulow is playing in Rostock, Bremen, and Hamburg. The Aix-la-Chapelle Committee have also invited him to the Musical Festival. Singer goes next week to Rotterdam, and on the 26th February a couple of my Symphonic Poems will be given at the Gewandhaus (directed by myself). I yesterday finished the score of another new one, Die Hunnenschlacht, [The Battle of the Huns] which I should like to bring out in Vienna when there is an opportunity.

Yours in all friendship,

F. Liszt

176. To Joachim Raff

[February 1857]

You may rest assured, dear friend, that it was very much against the grain to me that I could not accept the kind invitation of the Wiesbaden Concert Committee, for which I have to thank your intervention; and your letter, in which you explain to me some other circumstances, increases my sincere regret. But for this winter it is, frankly, impossible for me to accept any invitations of that kind, and I think I have told you before now that I have had to excuse myself in several cities (Vienna, Rotterdam, etc.). Even for Leipzig, which is so near me (although I might appear somewhat far-fetched to many a one there!), it was difficult to find a day that would suit me. On the 26th of this month the "Preludes" and "Mazeppa" are to be given in the Gewandhaus under my direction (for the Orchestral Pension Fund Concert). Perhaps this performance will serve as a definite warning for other concert-conducting, which might have been thought of, to question my "incapability as a composer," so often demonstrated (see the proof number of the "Illustrirte

Monatsheft" of Westermann, Brunswick, the National Zeitung, and the "thousand and one" competent judges who have long since been quite clear on the matter!).

How far are you in your Opera? When will one be able to see and hear something of it? As far as I have heard, you intend to perform "Samson" first in Darmstadt. If this does not happen at too awkward a time for me I shall come.

After having twice renounced the honor of conducting the approaching Musical Festival of the Lower-Rhine (to be held this year at Aix-la-Chapelle) a deputation of the Committee arrived here yesterday. In consideration of their courtesy I shall therefore go to Aix-la-Chapelle at Whitsuntide, and perhaps you will let yourself be beguiled into visiting me there. By that time also the Mass [The Gran Festival Mass] will probably have already come out, and you must have a copy of it at once. By the many performances, which have been of great use to me in this work, many additions, enlargements, and details of performance have occurred to me, which will enhance the effect of the whole, and will make some things easier in performance. An entirely new concluding fugue of the "Gloria," with this motive:—

[Here, Liszt illustrates with a vocal score musical excerpt at the point where the singer sings "Cum sanc-to spi-ri-tu, in Gloria."]

may not be displeasing to you.

Very shortly I will send you also the three numbers still wanting (1, 8, and 9) of the Symphonic Poems, so that you may again have some (for you) light reading as a rest from your work. The "Berg" Symphony was given, in its present form, a short time ago at Bronsart's farewell concert. Bronsart played the same evening a Trio of his own composition in four movements, which I esteem as a successful and very respectable work.

Once more best thanks for the fresh proof of your friendly attachment which your letter gives me, and don't let too long a time elapse without sending good news to

Yours most sincerely,

F. Liszt

177. To Concertmeister Ferdinand David in Leipzig

[Printed in Eckardt's "F. David and the Mendelssohn Family,"
 Leipzig, Dunker & Humblot, 1888.]

Leipzig, February 26th, 1857, 10 o'clock

[Preceding the body of the letter, Liszt illustrates with a vocal score musical excerpt with the words "Away! Away!" written in English by Liszt. It is a quotation from Liszt's Symphonic Poem "Mazeppa," which he had conducted in the Leipzig Gewandhaus on the same day as the "Preludes," and with which he had had ill- success. David, who was present as leader of the orchestra, "disapproved"—according to Eckardt—of Liszt's composing tendency, but continued, till his life's end, "filled with admiration for the incomparable artist and genial man," in the friendliest relations with Liszt.]

Before I go to bed let me give you my most sincere and heartfelt thanks, my very dear friend, which I owe you for this evening. You have proved yourself anew such a thorough gentleman [Gentleman, put in English by Liszt] and high-standing artist at this evening's concert.

That is nothing new in you, but it gives me pleasure, as your old friend, to repeat old things to you, and to remain ever yours most gratefully,

Franz Liszt

178. To Wladimir Stassoff in St. Petersburg

[A Russian writer, a musical and art critic, at present director of the Imperial Public Library at St. Petersburg.]

An illness, not in the least dangerous, but very inconvenient, since it obliges me to keep my bed rather often (as at this moment), has deprived me of the pleasure of replying sooner to your very kind letter, firstly to thank you for it, and also to tell you how delighted I shall be to make acquaintance with Mr. Scroff's manuscripts, which you kindly introduce to me in so persuasive a manner. Many people who have the advantage of knowing Mr. Seroff, among others Mr. de Lenz and Prince Eugene Wittgenstein, have spoken of him to me with great praise, as an artist who unites to real talent a most conscientious intelligence. It will be of great interest to me to estimate the work to which he has devoted himself with such praiseworthy perseverance, and thus to avail myself of the opportunity offered to me of hearing those sublime works of the LAST PERIOD (I purposely put aside

the inappropriate word MANNER, and even the term STYLE) of Beethoven—works which, whatever Mr. Oulibicheff and other learned men may say who succeed more easily in POURING FORTH in these matters than in being well versed [A play on words—verser and verse.] in them, will remain the crowning point of Beethoven's greatness.

With regard to the edition of these scores of Mr. Seroff's for two pianos, I will willingly do what you wish, though at the same time confessing to you that my credit with the editors is not worth much more than my credit with the above-mentioned learned men, as these latter do their best to keep all sorts of cock-and- bull stories going, which prevent the editors from running any risk in mad enterprises they have so peremptorily been pointed out to be! And, more than this, you are not ignorant that arrangements for two pianos—the only ones adapted to show the design and the grouping of ideas of certain works—are but little in favor with music-sellers and very unsaleable, as the great mass of pianists is scarcely capable of PLAYING ON the piano, and cares very little (except sometimes for form's sake and human respect) for the interest of intelligence and feeling which might attach to the promenades of their fingers. In spite of all this, please rest assured, sir, that I shall neglect nothing that can justify the confidence you place in me, and pray accept the very sincere regards of

Yours most truly,

F. Liszt

Weymar, March 17th, 1857

I am awaiting with impatience the parcel you promise me, and beg you to make it as large as possible, so that I may make a thorough acquaintance with Mr. Seroff's work. Especially be so good as not to forget the arrangement of Beethoven's latter Quartets.

179. To Wilhelm von Lenz in St. Petersburg

For pity's sake, dear friend, don't treat me like Moscheles; don't think I am dead, although I have given you some little right to think so by my long silence. But there are so many "demi"-people, and demi-clever people (who are at least as dangerous to Art as the demi-monde is to morals, according to Alexandre Dumas), who say such utter stupidities about me in the papers and elsewhere, that I really should not like to die yet, if only not to disturb their beautiful business. You were even complaining of one single whistling blackbird [Merle; means also a whistling or hissing fellow.] pastorally perched on your book— what shall I say then of the croaking of that host of ravens and of obliques hiboux [Oblique owls; the term is repeated afterwards, and evidently refers to some joke, or else to some remark of Lenz's.—Translator's note.] that spreads like an "epidemic cordon" all the length of the scores of my Symphonic Poems?—Happily I am not made of such stuff as to let myself be easily disconcerted by their "concert," and I shall continue steadfastly on my way to the end, without troubling about anything but to do what I have to do—which will be done, I can promise you. The rest of your "Beethoven," of which you speak, has never reached me, and for six months past I have not had any news of B., who, I am afraid, finds that he is clashing with some rather difficult editorial circumstances, but from which I presume he will have the spirit to free himself satisfactorily. A propos of Beethoven, here is

Oulibicheff, who has just hurled forth a volume which I might well compare with the dragons and other sacred monsters in papier-mache, with which the brave Chinese attempted to frighten the English at the time of the last war.—The English simply replied by bombs, which was the best mode of procedure. If I find time in the course of the summer, I shall answer Oulibicheff very respectfully in a brochure which may be a pretty big one. For the moment I am still pinned to my bed by a lot of boils which are flourishing on my legs, and which I consider as the doors of exodus for the illness which has been troubling me rather violently since the end of October.

Mr. Stassoff, having written to me about Mr. Seroff, I wrote him word quite lately that I should have real pleasure in making acquaintance with the arrangement for two pianos of Beethoven's later Quartets, etc. As soon as he lets me have them I will examine them with all the attention that such a work merits, and will write him my opinion, such as it is, with sincerity. As to the question of the edition, that is not so easy to solve as you seem to think. I wrote to Mr. Stassoff that arrangements for two pianos, which are the only ones that give a suitable idea of certain works, have very little currency with the public, as it is very rare to find two instruments with most amateurs. In spite of this, if, as I am inclined to think, Mr. Seroff's work answers to the eulogies you pronounce on it, I shall try to find him a publisher, and ask you only to get Mr. Seroff to let me know what sum he expects.

Why, dear friend, don't you decide to make a

trip to Germany, and to come and see me at Weymar? I asked you this three years ago, and I again assure you that such a journey would not be without use to you. It is in vain for you and Oulibicheff to enumerate the advantages and improvements of Russia in musical matters; people who know anything of the matter will beware of taking you literally. Art at Petersburg can only be an accessory and a superfluity for a long time to come, in spite of the very real distinction and, if you will, even the superiority of some persons who work at it with predilection, and who reside there. Proofs abound in support of this opinion, and could not be so soon changed.

Believe me, my dear Lenz, if you wish to get to know the heart of the musical question, come to Germany and come and see me.

Meanwhile don't trouble yourself any more than I do about either "merles" or "obliques hiboux"; go on familiarizing yourself with the smiles and glances of your "chimera," and believe me your most sincerely affectionate and devoted

F. Liszt

Weymar, March 24th, 1857

180. To Eduard Liszt

Best and excellent Eduard,

At last I send you the pianoforte edition of the Mass, which I could not get in order sooner, much as I wished to do so, partly owing to the excess of matters, letters, and business which have been pressing upon me, and partly also on account of my illness, which has obliged me to keep my bed for more than three weeks past. As regards the edition, which can be got up in two styles, according to whether one wants it to be economical or luxurious, I send you word of all that is necessary on the accompanying note-sheet (first page of the score—written by my hand), and beg you, best friend, to use your influence to get the proofs sent to me and to get the work published as quickly as possible. [The Gran Mass.]

Your last letter was again a great pleasure to me, owing to your loving comprehension of my works. That in composing them I do not quite work at haphazard and grope about in the dark, as my opponents in so many quarters reproach me with doing, will be gradually acknowledged by those among them who may be honest enough not to wish entirely to obstruct a right insight into the matter through preconceived views. As I have for years been conscious of the artistic task that lies before me, neither consistent perseverance nor quiet reflection shall be wanting for the fulfillment of it. May God's blessing, without which nothing can prosper and bear fruit, rest on my work!—

I have read with attention and interest the discussions in the Vienna papers, to which the performance of the Preludes and the concert gave rise. As I had previously said to you, the doctrinaire Hanslick could not be favorable to me; his article is perfidious, but on the whole seemly. Moreover it would be an easy matter for me to reduce his arguments to nil, and I think he is sharp enough to know that. On a better opportunity this could also be shown to him, without having the appearance of correcting him. I suppose the initials C. D. in the

Vienna paper mean Dorffl—or Drechsler? No matter by whom the critique is written, the author convicts himself in it of such intense narrowness that he will be very welcome to many other people less narrow than himself. His like has already often existed, but is constantly in demand. The musician nowadays cannot get out of the way of all the buzzing. Twenty years ago there were hardly a couple of musical papers in Europe, and the political papers referred only in the most rare cases, and then only very briefly, to musical matters. Now all this is quite different, and with my "Preludes," for instance (which, by the way, are only the prelude to my path of composition), many dozen critics by profession have already pounced on them, in order to ruin me through and through as a composer. I by no means say that present conditions, taken as a whole, are more unfavorable to the musician than the earlier conditions, for all this talk in a hundred papers brings also much good with it, which would not otherwise be so easy to attain;—but simply the thinking and creative artist must not allow himself to be misled by it, and must go his own gait quietly and undisturbed, as they say the hippopotamus does, in spite of all the arrows which rebound from his thick skin. An original thinker says, "As one emblem and coat of arms I show a tree violently blown by the storm, which nevertheless shows its red fruit on all the boughs, with the motto, Dum convellor mitescunt; or also, Conquassatus sed ferax."

When you have an opportunity I beg you to give my best thanks to my old friend Lowy for the letter he wrote me directly after the performance of the "Preludes." I know that he means well towards me, in his own way, which, unfortunately, cannot be mine, because, to me, friendship without heart and flame is something foreign; and I cannot understand, for instance, why at the concert in question he did not take his customary place, but kept back in a corner, as he tells me. Pray when have I given him any occasion to be ashamed of me? Do I not then stand up in the whole world of Art as an honest fellow, who, faithful to his conviction, despising all base means and hypocritical stratagems, strives valiantly and honorably after a high aim? Given that I, deceived by my many-sided experiences (which really cannot be estimated as very slight, since I have lived and worked through the periods—so important for music—of Beethoven, Schubert, Mendelssohn, as well as Rossini and Meyerbeer), led astray by my seven years' unceasing labour, have hit upon the wrong road altogether, would it be the place of my intimate friend, in the face of the opposition which is set up against me because I bring something new, to blush, hide himself in a corner, and deny me? You did otherwise and better in this, dearest Eduard, and your conduct with Castelli was, as ever, perfectly right. My few friends may take a good example from you, for they assuredly need not let themselves be frightened by the concert which the bullies and boobies raise against my things. I have, as usual, thought over your musical remarks and reflections. The fourth movement of the Concerto, [No. I, in E flat major.] from the Allegro marziale,

[a score appears here]

corresponds with the second movement, Adagio:—

[a score appears here]

It is only an urgent recapitulation of the earlier subject-matter with quickened, livelier rhythm, and contains no new motive, as will be clear to you by a glance through the score. This kind of binding together and rounding off a whole piece at its close is somewhat my own, but it is quite maintained and justified from the standpoint of musical form.

The trombones and basses

[a score appears here]

take up the second part of the motive of the Adagio (B major):—

[a score appears here]The pianoforte figure which follows

[a score appears here]

is no other than the reproduction of the motive which was given in the Adagio by flute and clarinet,

[a score appears here]

just as the concluding passage is a Variante [various reading] and working up in the major of the motive of the Scherzo,

[a score appears here]

until finally the first motive

[a score appears here]

on the dominant pedal B flat, with a shake accompaniment,

[a score appears here]

comes in and concludes the whole.

The Scherzo in E flat minor, from the point where the triangle begins, I employed for the effect of contrast.

[a score appears here] As regards the triangle I do not deny that it may give offence, especially if struck too strong and not precisely. A preconceived disinclination and objection to instruments of percussion prevails, somewhat justified by the frequent misuse of them. And few conductors are circumspect enough to bring out the rhythmic element in them, without the raw addition of a coarse noisiness, in works in which they are deliberately employed according to the intention of the composer. The dynamic and rhythmic spicing and enhancement, which are effected by the instruments of percussion, would in more cases be much more effectually produced by the careful trying and proportioning of insertions and additions of that kind. But musicians who wish to appear serious and solid prefer to treat the instruments of percussion en canaille, which must not make their appearance in the seemly company of the Symphony. They also bitterly deplore, inwardly, that Beethoven allowed himself to be seduced into using the big drum and triangle in the Finale of the Ninth Symphony. Of Berlioz, Wagner, and my humble self, it is no wonder that "like draws to like," and, as we are treated as impotent canaille amongst musicians, it is quite natural that we should be on good terms with the canaille among the instruments. Certainly here, as in all else, it is the right thing to seize upon and hold fast [the] mass of harmony. In face of the most wise proscription of the learned critics I shall, however, continue to employ instruments of percussion, and think I shall yet win for them some effects little known.

I hear from Paris that at all the street corners there they are selling a little pamphlet for a sou entitled "Le seul moyen de ne pas mourir le 13 Juin a l'apparition de la Comete." ["The only means how not to die on the 13th of June at the appearance of the comet."] The only means is to drown oneself on the 12th of June. Much of the good advice which is given to me by the critics is very like this seul moyen. Yet we will not drown ourselves—not even in the lukewarm waters of criticism—and will also for the future stand firm on our own legs with a good conscience.

I had still much more to say to you, but the letter has become so long that I should not like to take up any more of your time. It is to be hoped that we shall see each other in the course of this summer, when we shall be able again to talk over everything to our hearts' content. Meanwhile I thank you again warmly for your friendship, and remain yours from my heart.

F. Liszt

What you tell me of your idea for Daniel [Liszt's son] is very agreeable and soothing. I must beg the Princess to correspond with you in reference to the matter. My decision to send D. to Vienna, in order to finish his law there, and to entrust him to your protection, is pretty much unchanged.

Weymar, March 26th, 1857

In the next number of Brendel's paper appears a long letter from R. Wagner on my individuality as a composer, which will be of interest to you.

181. To Georg Schariezer, Vice-President of the Church Musical Society at the St. Martin's

Coronation Church in Pressburg

[From a copy of Herr Stadthauptmann Johann Batka in Pressburg.— The Church Musical Society, which has been in existence since 1833, and which undertakes the performance of classical instrumental Masses during the service every Sunday and saint's day, performed Beethoven's Grand Mass as early as 1835, and many times since, and has given Liszt's Gran Mass every year since 1872.]

Dear Sir,

The friendly intention of the highly renowned Pressburg Kirchenmusikverein [Church Musical Society] to give a performance of my "Missa Solemnis" is an uncommon pleasure to me, and I send Your Honor my special thanks for the kind letter with which you have honored me in the name of the Kirchenmusikverein. Much as I should like to meet your wishes without any ceremony, and to send you the score and parts at once, yet I am constrained to beg for a long delay, for the reason that the score, together with the pianoforte arrangement, is obliged to remain for some months longer in the Royal State Printing House in Vienna, and I cannot get the parts copied out afresh until the publication of the work next September. The copies which were used at Gran and Prague have been lost, and several essential alterations which I have finally made in the score necessitate the making of an entirely new copy.

I hope, however, that you, dear sir, as well as the K.-M.-V, will continue your kind intention towards me, whereby I may have the prospect of my Mass being performed by you later on. If I am not quite mistaken, the Church element, as well as the musical style of this work, will be better understood and more spiritually felt after frequent performances than can be the case at first in the face of the prevailing prejudice against my later compositions, and the systematic opposition of routine and custom which I have to meet with on so many sides. Thus much I may in all conscientiousness affirm, that I composed the work, from the first bar to the last, with the deepest ardor as a Catholic and the utmost care as a musician, and hence I can leave it with perfect comfort to time to form a corresponding verdict upon it.

As soon as the score comes out I shall have the pleasure of sending Your Honor a copy; and should your present design perhaps come to pass in the spring, I shall be delighted to be present at the performance, and to conduct the final rehearsals myself.

Accept, dear sir, my best thanks, together with the expression of my high esteem.

Yours most truly,

Franz Liszt

Weymar, April 25th, 1857

182. To Eduard Liszt

Dearest Eduard,

I have been thinking over the matter of supporting the voices by some wind instruments and brass in my Mass for men's voices, without being able to make up my mind to write out this accompaniment. I ought properly to hear the Vienna chorus in order to hit the right proportion, which is very various, according to the size of the church, and also the class of instruments, and the less or greater ability of the musicians. It would be very agreeable to me if Herbeck, who appears to take an interest in my work, would take the decision upon himself according to what he thinks best, and would either keep in the printed organ accompaniment, or write a small additional score as support to the voices. In the latter case I think that horns, clarinets, oboes, and bassoons cannot be dispensed with, and that probably trombones would also make a good effect in the Kyrie and Credo.

Remember me most kindly to Herbeck, and tell him my idea as well as my request. In the studying of the Mass he will best ascertain which passages most require a supplement-accompaniment.

Owing to my long-continued illness, which obliges me for the most part to keep my bed, I have not yet been able to hear his Quartet, which he was so good as to send me; but I shall shortly give it over to our excellent Quartet Society (Singer, Cossmann, Stor, Walbruhl) for a performance.

By today's post I send you an alteration in the Agnus Dei of my Gran Mass, which I beg you to hand to the compositor. The voice parts remain as before, but in the pauses I make the first subject come in again in the basses, which makes the movement more completely one whole. The compositor must work by this proof for the whole Agnus Dei, and only revert to the general score where the "Dona nobis pacem" (Allegro moderato) comes in.

Wagner's letter has been published in a separate form, and you will receive several copies of it, as I believe you take interest in it, and will make a good use of it.

The Princess has been a prisoner to her bed for more than three weeks, and is suffering from acute rheumatism. Princess Marie has also been poorly, so that the whole house has been very dismal. The last few days I have pulled myself together, and have had my choruses to Herder's "Prometheus" performed, which have unexpectedly made a very good impression, and were received with unusual sympathy. In the course of the summer I shall have the whole work printed. The eight choruses, together with the [spoken] text, which has been skillfully compiled after Herder and Aeschylus [By Richard Pohl], and the preliminary Symphonic Poem (No. 5 of those published by Hartel), take about an hour and a half in performance. If I am not mistaken, the work will, later on, approve itself in larger concerts.

About the 15th May I shall be going to Aix-la-Chapelle, to conduct the Musical Festival there at Whitsuntide. That will be another good opportunity for many papers to abuse me, and to let off their bile!—If the programme which I shall put forward is realized at the September Festival you must come here and hear it with me.

My mother writes from Paris that Blandine has been living with the Countess d'A. since the 20th of this month. Cosima's marriage with H. von Bulow will probably take place before September. About Daniel the Princess will write to you fully when she is better.

God be with you and yours. Yours from my heart,

F. Liszt

Weimar, April 27th, 1857
183. To Frau von Kaulbach

[The letter, together with the following one, written by Kaulbach to Liszt in the fifties, was published in the Tagliche Rundschau [Daily Review], and afterwards in the Neue Berline Musikzeitung [Berlin New Musical Paper] of March 19th, 1891. It is well known that Liszt derived his inspiration to write the Hunnenschlachl [Battle of the Huns] from Kaulbach's celebrated picture on the staircase of the New Museum in Berlin. He intended to work up the six pictures of Kaulbach's which are there, in a similar symphonic manner, probably for theatrical performance in Weimar. Dingelstedt appears also to have planned an after-poem in verses. Kaulbach's letter to his friend is as follows: "Your original and spirited idea—the musical and poetic form of the historical pictures in the Berlin Museum—has taken hold of me completely. I much wish to hear yours and Dingelstedt's ideas of this performance. The representation of these powerful subjects in poetical, musical, and artistic form must constitute a harmonious work, rounded off into one complete whole. It will resound and shine through all lands!!—I shall therefore hasten to Weimar, as soon as my work here will let me free.—With the warmest regards to the Princess, that truly inspired friend of Art, and to her charming daughter, from myself and my wife, I remain, in unchangeable respect and friendship, Your faithful, W. Kaulbach."]

Dear Madam,

I have been encouraged to send you what indeed truly belongs to you, but what, alas! I must send in so shabby a dress that I must beg from you all the indulgence that you have so often kindly shown me. At the same time with these lines you will receive the manuscript of the two-pianoforte arrangement of my Symphonic Poem "Die Hunnenschlacht" (written for a large orchestra and completed by the end of last February), and I beg you, dear madam, to do me the favor to accept this work as a token of my great reverence and most devoted friendship towards the Master of masters. Perhaps there may be an opportunity later on, in Munich or Weymar, in which I can have the work performed before you with full orchestra, and can give a voice to the meteoric and solar light which I have borrowed from the painting, and which at the Finale I have formed into one whole by the gradual working up of the Catholic chorale "Crux fidelis," and the meteoric sparks blended therewith. As I already intimated to Kaulbach in Munich, I was led by the musical demands of the material to give proportionately more place to the solar light of Christianity, personified in the Catholic chorale "Crux fidelis," than appears to be the case in the glorious painting, in order thereby to win and pregnantly represent the conclusion of the Victory of the Cross, with which I, both as a Catholic and as a man, could not dispense.

Kindly excuse this somewhat obscure commentary on the two opposing streams of light in which the Huns and the Cross are moving; the performance will make the matter bright and clear— and if Kaulbach finds something to amuse him in this somewhat venturesome mirroring of his fancy I shall be royally delighted.

Through Dingelstedt, whom our Grand Duke is taking away from Munich, you have heard the latest news from Weymar, and I have, alas! only bad news to give you of the Princess W. For many weeks she has been confined to bed with acute rheumatism, and it is hardly likely that she will be restored to health before my departure for Aix-la-Chapelle towards the middle of May. Allow me, my dear lady, to beg you to give Kaulbach my warmest and most hearty thanks for the wonderful sketch of Orpheus with which he has honored and delighted me; and once more begging you to pardon me for the dreadful scrawl of my manuscript, I remain yours with all respect and devoted friendship,

F. Liszt

Weymar, May 1st, 1857

184. To Fedor von Milde, Kammersanger

[A singer in the service of a prince] in Weimar [An   excellent Wagner singer. The first Telramund in Lohengrin.]

Dear Friend,

I cannot refuse myself the pleasure of letting you know of the really extraordinary success, not made up, but thoroughly effectual and brilliant, of your wife. [Rosa, nee Agthe, trained by Franz Gotze.] Cologne, Dusseldorf, Bonn, Elberfeld, and the entire neighborhood agree with Aix-la-Chapelle that your wife made the festivity of the Musical Festival; and although success cannot as a rule be considered as a criterion of artistic worth, yet if it be attested so truly and de bon aloi as in this case, and follow that artistic worth, it has something refreshing and strengthening in which we, in trio, can fully rejoice.

A speedy meeting to us, and friendly greetings and thanks from

Yours ever,

F. Liszt

Aix-La-Chappelle, Wednesday, June 3rd, 1857

185. To Johann von Herbeck

Weymar, June 12th, 1857

Dear Sir and Friend,

On my return from the Aix-la-Chapelle Musical Festival—which may be considered successful on the whole, from the very fact that opponents do not conceal their dissatisfaction—I find here your kind letter, for which I send you my warmest thanks. My excellent cousin and friend, Dr. Eduard Liszt, had already informed me of your kind willingness to undertake the instrumentation of my Vocal Mass: I am entirely in accord with the various sketches you so kindly lay before me in your letter, and only beg you, dear sir, to complete this work according to your own best judgment, without any small considerations. I certainly should not wish the organ to be absent from it, but it is a perfectly correct idea to give those passages in the Kyrie, Suscipe deprecationem, Crucifixus, and others besides,

[A score appears here]

to the wind exclusively. When I expressed to my cousin my wish to place the instrumentation of the Mass in your hands, it was because I was convinced beforehand of the excellence of your work. The examples which you have given me in your letter show me that I was not wrong, and I shall rejoice most sincerely when the moment arrives for us to go through the whole score together. Eduard intends to visit me here towards the end of August, and if it is possible for you to come to Weymar at the same time with him, and to stay a few days in my house, it will be very agreeable to me.

On the 3rd, 4th, and 5th September the Jubilee festivities of the Grand Duke Carl August will take place here, on which occasion I propose to perform several of my later orchestral compositions, and also the chorus "An die Kiinstler." ["To Artists."] Eduard will give you a more detailed programme of the Festival later on. Should you, however, be prevented from being present at it, it needs no special assurance to you that your visit will be very welcome to me any day, and I will do my best that you shall not suffer from ennui in Weymar. [Herbeck accepted the invitation.]

May I also beg you to send me, when you have an opportunity, and if possible very soon, the parts of your Quartet, [D minor, unpublished] which pleases me so much, and which, both in its mood and in its writing of the different parts, is so eminently noble and finely sustained. In case you have not been able to arrange for the copying of the parts, it will be a pleasure to me to get them copied here. Our Weymar quartet, Messrs. Singer, Stor, Walbruhl, and Cossmann, is competent for this work, and you will, I trust, be satisfied with the performance. Unfortunately Cossmann's illness has prevented our usual quartet-productions for some months past, and

Cossmann was also unable to take part in the Aix-la-Chapelle Musical Festival. But yesterday he told me that in a few days he should be able to take up his bow again, and therefore I want them to set to work on your Quartet at once.

To our speedy meeting then, and once more best thanks from yours in all friendship,

F. Liszt

186. To Countess Rosalie Sauerma, nee Spohr

Your letter gave me great pleasure, dear Countess and admirable artist, and, though still obliged to keep my bed (which I have been able to leave so little during the whole winter), I hasten to reassure you entirely about my state of health. As a fact, I have never done my obstinate illness the honor of considering it serious, and now less than ever, for I hope to have entirely got over it by the end of the week. So do not let us talk about it any more, and let me tell you at once how sincerely I rejoice in your projects of being, so to say, in the neighborhood of Dresden, for it seems to me that, among the towns of Germany, it is the one in which you will find most charm. I shall certainly come and pay you my visit there in the course of the winter, and I hope also that you will not altogether forget your friends of Weymar.

When you come back here, you will find very little change, but simply three more Weymarers—Goethe, Schiller, and Wieland—whose statues will be inaugurated next September, on the occasion of the celebration of the Jubilee fetes of the Grand Duke Carl August. They are also planning music for the occasion; and I predict to you beforehand that you will be able to read all sorts of unflattering things on this subject, as the music in question will be in great part my composition. However that may be, I shall try to have always something better to do than to trouble myself with what is said or written about me.

How delighted I shall be to hear you again, and to rock myself as in a hammock to the sound of your arpeggi. You have not, I am sure, broken off your good habits of work, and your talent is certain to be more magnificent than ever. Quite lately Madame Pohl, who played Parish Alvars' Oberon Fantaisie charmingly, recalled most vividly the remembrance of the delightful hours at Eilsen and Weymar, which I hope soon to resume at Dresden... Be so kind as to present my best compliments to your husband and all your dear ones, and pray accept, dear Countess, the expression of most affectionate homage from yours very sincerely,

F. Liszt

Weymar, June 22nd, 1857

The Princess W. has been very seriously ill for more than two months; she is only just convalescent, and bids me give her best remembrances to you.

187. To Ludmilla Schestakoff, nee Glinka, in St. Petersburg

[sister of the celebrated Russian composer Glinka]

Madame,

I wish I were able to tell you how much I have been touched by the letter you have done me the honor to address to me. Thank you for having thought of me as one of the most sincere and zealous admirers of the fine genius of your brother, so worthy of a noble glory for the very reason that it was above vulgar successes. And again thank you for the grace which prompts you to wish to inscribe my name on one of his orchestral works, which are certain to be valued and to obtain a sympathetic preference from people of taste.

I accept with a real gratitude the dedication with which you honor me, and it will be at once my pleasure and duty to do my best towards the propagation of Glinka's works, for which I have always professed the most open and admiring sympathy. Of this I beg you, Madame, to receive anew my assurance, and to accept the most respectful homage of

Yours very truly,

F. Liszt

Weymar, October 7th, 1857

I am writing by the same post to Mr. Engelhardt in Berlin to thank him for his letter, and to tell him that I feel quite flattered at seeing my name attached to a score of Glinka's.

188. To Carl Haslinger

[autograph without address in the possession of M. Alfred Bovet in Valentigney—The above was presumably the addressee.]

Dear Friend,

The writing of notes [music] draws me more and more away from the writing of letters, and my friends have already much to pardon me in this respect. With the best will in the world to fulfill my obligations, it is nevertheless impossible for me, owing to the countless claims that are made on me, to find time to do so. So do not scold me, dear friend, for having left your last letter unanswered. I had given myself a great deal to do with some manuscripts; the final proofs of the Faust and Dante Symphonies, in particular, which will now soon be engraved, had occupied me much longer than I expected. The two works are now as well finished as I am in a position to make them, and will, I hope, hold their POSITION.

I congratulate you most warmly on the performance of your opera. You may safely expect various disagreeables in connection therewith, which are inseparable from musical work. The great thing is to remain cheerful, and to do something worth doing. The cuckoo take the rest!—

Let me have a talk with you about the Zellner matter in Vienna, if, as seems likely, I have to go there at the end of May for the performance of my Mass. Meanwhile thank you very much for the pains you have taken over the proof-sheets of this long-protracted work, and I should be glad if the whole were ready to come out by the time I reach Vienna.

Tausig, who is to come out in Berlin at the beginning of January,
will probably come with me. There is again a real "bravo,"
[Literally, iron-eater.] as Hummel said of me when he heard me in
Paris in the twenties.

Will you be so kind as to give the enclosed letters to Winterberger and Rubinstein? How is our friend Winterberger getting on in the not very suitable atmosphere of Vienna? Let me know something about him soon. Yours ever,

F. Liszt

Weymar, December 5th, 1857.

189. To Hofcapellmeister Stein In Sondershausen.

[Autograph in the possession of M. Alfred Bovet at Valentigney.— The addressee, a first-rate conductor (born 1818), lived from 1853 in Sondershausen; died 1864.]

Let me give you once more my hearty thanks, dear friend, for the delightful day you gave me at Sondershausen, which continues so brightly and pleasantly in my recollection. The rare consummation with which your orchestra solved one of the most difficult tasks, and brought "what one hears on the mountains" [Liszt's Mountain Symphony] to the impressive understanding of the ears in the valley (if not indeed under the water and worse still), strengthens me in my higher endeavors, —and you, dear friend, will have to bear some of the responsibility if I go on writing more such "confused," "formless," and, for the every-day critic, quite "fathomless" things.

Singer [A letter from this first-rate violinist is on the same sheet with Liszt's.] needs no further recommendation from me, as he is already known to you as an eminent virtuoso. Especially at Court concerts his own refined and brilliant qualities are placed in their most favorable light.

If it is possible for you to take an opportunity of bringing out my dear and extraordinary budding genius Carl Tausig ["The last of the virtuosi;" as

Weitzmann called him; born at Warsaw 1841; died at Leipzig 1871.] at the Court, I promise you that he will do honor to your recommendation.

In all esteem and devotion, yours ever,

F. Liszt

Weymar, December 6th, 1857

190. To Alexander Ritter in Stettin.

Dear friend,

Your tidings sound as incredible as they are pleasant. And I must admit, what has long been proved to me, that you are a valiant and excellent friend, and prove your friendship splendidly by the success of your venturesome undertaking. Specially do I give you my best thanks for the pregnant and poetic form which you gave to the Tasso programme. Later on, as you have broken the ice in so happy a fashion, we can push on with

[Here, Liszt illustrates with a musical score excerpt of the beginning of the Symphonic Poem "Festklange."

and other such corrupt things in Stettin!—

I was not able to attend to your letter about the matter of the parts of the Flying Dutchman until after my return to Weymar. Herr von Dingelstedt spoke to me about the idea in regard to the fee for Wagner (from the Stettin Directors), and the reply to you from the Secretary Jacobi will be to that effect. If, as I presume, you can so arrange that this idea is carried out, and that Wagner receives his fee, the parts shall be sent you from here.

I visited your dear sisters many times in Dresden, and had some delightful chats with them.

In Carl's Sonatas [Carl Ritter], which I have

read with much interest, there is a decidedly musical germ; only I hope that by degrees more juicy fruit may spring from it.

Cornelius is bringing his completed opera back to Weymar at the end of this month. [Doubtless "Der Barbier von Baghdad."] Lassen, who is getting on splendidly with his ("Frauenlob "), has composed several exquisite songs between whiles. "Landgraf Ludwig's Brautfahrt" ["Landgrave Ludwig's Bridal Journey," an unpublished opera of Lassen's.] will again be given next Sunday, and from New Year (1858) Lassen will act as Grand Ducal Music Conductor of Weymar. Gotze is retiring from work, and your friend Stor undertakes his post as First Music Conductor. Damrosch, your successor, has composed a quite remarkable Violin Concerto with a Polonaise Finale, with which you will be pleased.

Recall me most kindly to your wife's remembrance, as one who remains ever

Yours in all affection and devotion,

F. Liszt

Weymar, December 7th, 1857

191. To Capellmeister Max Seifriz At Lowenberg

[Autograph in the possession of Herr Alexander Meyer Cohn in
 Berlin. The addressee (1827-85) was, after 1854, conductor to
 Prince Hohenzollern-Hechingen at Lowenberg in Silesia, until the
 latter's death in 1869, when he became Court Conductor in
 Stuttgart.]

Dear Herr Capellmeister,

With my very best thanks for your friendly letter I send you, according to your wish, the score of the "Prometheus" choruses. For the present I am not requiring it, and send it you with great pleasure, so that you may be able to read it through at your ease. I fear, alas! that the difficulty of some of the intonation in the first choruses may make the studying of it a rather detailed matter to you. Such irksomeness unfortunately attaches to all my works, not excepting the Ave Maria, which I might nevertheless venture to recommend to you next, if you have any intention of performing a vocal work of my composition. It was published by Breitkopf & Hartel (score and parts), and has been pretty favorably received at various performances of it.

I wrote yesterday to His Royal Highness, and expressed my special thanks for the kind attention in inviting Herr von Bulow during my stay at L. I rejoice immensely at the thought of these days, in which musical matter will by no means be wanting to us. Meanwhile remember me most kindly to your orchestra, which preserves so well its high renown, and accept, my dear sir, the assurance of high esteem with which I remain

Yours in all friendship,

F. Liszt

Weymar, December 24th, 1857

In the early part of April you shall hear when I am coming to
Lowenberg.

192. To Alexander Seroff

My dear Sir,

By what I said in the Neue Zeitschrift fur Musik, [1858, No. 1, in the article "Oulibicheff and Seroff."] on New Year's Day, of your remarkable articles on Oulibicheff, you will have seen to what point I take your ideas into consideration, and how closely we meet in our musical convictions. To the sincere eulogies which I have had much pleasure in addressing to you in public, it remains to me to add those which I owe you for the conscientious work that you have had the kindness to communicate to me by sending me the pianoforte score of Beethoven's Quartet in C sharp minor. Without the least exaggeration, I don't think anything of its kind could have been better done, as much on account of the intelligent division of the parts between the two pianos, as by the skill with which you have appropriated to the piano the style of this Quartet, without forcing or disfiguring anything.

In this latter task there are without doubt some impossibilities which one cannot fail to recognize, and, whatever effort we may make, we shall never succeed in rendering on our instrument either the intensity or the delicacy of the violin bow. In the same manner the coloring, and the fine nuances of the violin, viola, and violoncello will always escape us—but in spite of this it is due to you in justice to recognize that your work identifies itself as far as possible with the sentiment and thought of the original, and that you have frequently succeeded in supplementing the poverty and defects inherent in such an arrangement.

About six weeks ago I sent your manuscript to Mr. Schott, the editor, at Mainz, recommending him to publish your arrangement. Up to the present time I have received no reply, which, however, seems to me a good sign. As soon as ever I hear his determination I will let you know. Possibly in the course of the summer you will find a few weeks' leisure to make a journey into these parts and to bring us the complete collection of your arrangements of Beethoven's latter instrumental works. In that case let me beg of you, my dear sir, not to forget me, and to rest assured beforehand of the lively interest that I shall take in your work, which it would be doubly interesting to me to go through with you. Bearing in mind the original, we should probably find, between us, some details to modify previous to a definite publication.

For today allow me to thank you once more, my dear sir, very cordially for having associated me in thought with your beautiful work, and pray accept the expression of very sincere and affectionate regard of

Yours very truly,

F. Liszt

Weymar, January 8th, 1858

193. To Basil von Engelhardt

[A very intelligent musical amateur, a friend of Glinka's, and publisher of several of his works]

Sir,

Whilst giving you my very sincere thanks for so kindly sending me the Glinka scores published by your friends, I am much pleased to be able at the same time to inform you that the Capriccio on the melody of the "Jota Aragonese" has just been performed (on New Year's Day) at a grand Court concert with most complete success. Even at the rehearsal the intelligent musicians whom I am proud to count among the members of our orchestra had been both struck and delighted by the lively and piquant originality of this charming piece, so delicately cut and proportioned, and finished with such taste and art! What delicious episodes, cleverly joined to the principal subject (Letters A and B)! What fine nuances and coloring divided among the different timbres of the orchestration (Letters C to D)! What animation in the rhythmic movement from one end to the other! How the happiest surprises spring constantly out of the logical developments! and how everything is in its right place, keeping the mind constantly on the watch, caressing and tickling the ear by turns, without a single moment of heaviness or fatigue! This is what we all felt at this rehearsal; and the day after the performance we promised ourselves to hear it again speedily, and to make acquaintance, as speedily as possible, with Glinka's other works.

Will you, my dear musician, be so kind as to renew the expression of my gratitude to Madame Schestakoff for the honor she has done me in dedicating this work to me? And when you have time, do come and hear it with your own ears at Weymar. I can assure you that you will not have occasion to regret the troubles of a little journey; and were it only the rhythm

[FIGURE: Music example in 2 staves, the upper 'wind and brass', the lower 'string quartet']

that would be enough to make ample amends for them. I beg you, sir, to accept the assurance of my sincere regard.

F. Liszt

Weymar, January 8th, 1858

P.S.—I shall be much obliged if you will send me two supplementary parts of the quartet (first and second violin, viola, and bass) of each of Glinka's works.

194. To Felix Draseke

[Now professor at the Dresden Conservatorium, a well-known composer of importance, also a writer on music (born 1835)]

Your articles [Published in the paper started by Brendel, "Hints" (or "Suggestions")], which were so universally suggestive, my dear and valiant friend, have given great pleasure to us on the Altenburg. I hope to have an opportunity of showing you my gratitude in a lasting and abiding fashion. Meanwhile be satisfied with a good conscience in having strengthened and sustained an honest man in his better purpose.

I have received through Brendel an invitation to Prague, which I shall probably accept for the beginning of March. I am delighted to think of seeing you again, dear friend, in passing through Dresden, and perhaps you might make it possible to accompany me to Prague. The "Dante Symphony" and the "Ideale" are again to be given there, and, if I am not mistaken, you will rather like the former work in its present shape. The Dresden performance was a necessity to me, in order to realize its effect. As long as one has only to do with lifeless paper one can easily make a slip of the pen. Music requires tone and resonance!—I cannot at first lay claim to effectual results, because I have to meet too much opposition. The chief thing is that my present works should prove themselves to be taking a firm footing in musical matters, and should contribute something towards doing away with what is corrupt…

What is Reubke [A pupil of Liszt's.] doing, and how does he like Dresden?—Take him most friendly greetings from me. By-the-by ask him also to give me tidings as soon as possible (through Herr Menert) about the copying of the orchestral parts of the Rubinstein Oratorio "Paradise Lost," and to get Herr Menert to send me these parts to Weymar by the end of this month at latest. It is to be hoped that Reubke won't have left the score in his box like Pohl! But if by chance he has committed such a transgression I beg that he will make amends as speedily as possible.

Fischer (the organist) wrote to me lately, to ask me for a testimonial to his musical ability, as he wants to have one to show in Chemnitz. Please to make my friendly excuses to him for not fulfilling his wish—possibly, in view of the enmity which I have to bear on all sides, such a document would do him more harm than good; apart from the fact that I very unwillingly set about drawing up such testimonials. He must not, however, misconstrue this disinclination on my part, and may rest assured of my readiness to be of use to him.—

I would still draw your attention to Bronsart's concert in Leipzig. It will take place in a few days, and if you can get free I invite you to it. Bronsart is a very dear friend of mine; I value him as a character and as a musician. If you go to Leipzig go and see him; he will please you, and will receive you in the most friendly manner. He is a friend of Bulow's. Both names have the same initials, and for a long time Bronsart signed himself "Hans II." in his letters to me.—

In the virtuoso line we have lately been hearing Sivori and Bazzini here several times. The latter is now in Dresden; I told him that Reubke would perhaps call on him. Get Reubke to do so, and assure him that he will be most friendlily received. A well- known piece of Bazzini's, "La Ronde des Lutins," was, by a printer's error, called "Ronde des Cretins!" ["Rondo of Idiots."] What an immeasurably large public for such a "Rondo"! If only half of them would become subscribers to the Anregungen (Hints)!

Once more a thousand thanks, dear friend, for your courageous battling; I on my side will endeavour not to let us have to acquiesce with too overpowering a modesty! [An untranslatable pun on the words "beseheiden" and "Bescheidenheit."

Yours ever,

F. Liszt

[Weimar,] Sunday, January 10th, 1858

195. To Louis Koehler

My very dear friend,

A few days ago I received a letter from Koenigsberg, signed by a gentleman unknown to me. By chance this letter has got lost, and I cannot myself remember the exact name. But, as your name was mentioned in it, I beg you to be so good as to let

Herr * * * know that I do not possess the arrangement of the second movement of my Faust Symphony made by Zellner in Vienna for pianoforte, violin, harp, and harmonium, and that consequently I cannot hand it over to him. Besides this, I do consider such a fragmentary performance of this work of mine, which stands in such bad credit with the critics, as rather unsuitable, and would not advise any concert-giver, and still less any concert-directors, to smuggle into a programme my name so challenged as a composer. How long this curious comedy of criticism will last I am unable to determine; anyhow I am resolved not to trouble my head about the cry of murder which is raised against me, and to go on my way in a consistent and undeterred fashion. Whether I shall be answerable for the scandal, or whether my opponents will entangle themselves in the scandal, will appear later. Meanwhile they can hiss and scribble as much as they please. In the course of the summer my "Faust" and "Dante" Symphonies will be published by Hartel, together with a couple of new Symphonic Poems. The "Faust Symphony" is dedicated to Berlioz, and the "Dante" to Wagner. I am sending them to you, dear friend, with the two pianoforte arrangements, with the risk that nothing will please you in them, which however will not prevent us from being good friends. You may rest assured that I shall always be grateful to you for the friendliness you have shown me in past years, and that I would never attempt to compromise you with my future. For the latter I alone can and must care.

Please then make my best excuses to Herr * *

*, whose kind letter has, alas! cost me much useless searching, and continue your personal well-wishing to your ever faithful friend (though fallen in musical esteem and under your ban),

F. Liszt

Weymar, February 1st, 1858

196. To Professor L. A. Zellner in Vienna

You may believe me, dear friend, when I tell you that all the disagreeables and vexations which the preparations for the performance of my Mass [The Gran Festival Mass.] draw upon you are the most acutely felt by myself. Do you really think it is desirable to go against trifles of this sort and openly to fight them? I should not like to decide this "a distance"; but I promise you that I will not leave you in the lurch if in the end the indispensable invitation to me follows. The concert at Prague is to take place on the 12th of March, and I invite you to it. Then after that I can travel with you on the 14th to Vienna or return to Weymar. But I hope the former. I have nothing whatever to say against the invitation of the Pest singers, because the four persons have remained in my friendly remembrance. Yet I must remark that the performance of the solos in my Mass offers no special difficulties, and that consequently it could be quite suitably and satisfactorily given by Vienna singers, which seems both simpler and pleasanter. Herr Dr. Gunz, Herr Panzer, and Fraulein Huber are quite satisfactory to me as soloists, as also Fraulein Friedlowsky, of whom I have heard the highest praise as Elizabeth. The tenor and alto are the chief people concerned, as they have the principal subject in the Kyrie and Benedictus. If we have two rehearsals with pianoforte, which I shall have great pleasure in holding with the ladies and gentlemen myself, we shall thoroughly get to the bottom of it; and if the singers have steadfastness enough to make an effect with their part the thing will go of itself.

With regard to the chorus and orchestra I reserve it to myself to express my thanks to Hellmesberger and the chorus-directors in writing, as soon as I have definite tidings. But to you, dear friend, I can only repeat that he who will understand me loves me also—and that I remain,

Yours in all friendship,

F. Liszt

Weymar, February 8th, 1858

197. To Peter Cornelius in Mainz

[Weimar,] February 19th, 1858

It is very bad, dearest Cornelius, that you have so long forsaken us! Much as I must approve of your decision to finish writing your Opera ["Der Barbier von Baghdad"] completely, yet I am dreadfully sorry to be without you for so many months. I did hope that you would be with us on the 18th of February for certain; now you announce yourself for the middle of March, at which time I shall probably not be here. On the 12th of March I conduct a concert at Prague, at which the "Ideale" and the "Dante Symphony" will be given. Thence I proceed to Vienna, and later to Loewenberg (in Silesia) to my noble and most amiable patron Prince Hohenzollern-Hechingen, who, in spite of political changes, has not only retained his Hechingen orchestra, but has also increased it by fresh members.

I wish I could give you better tidings of my

work, best friend, than I am able to do. The last few months have passed without my being able to do any steady work at my writing. I have merely sketched and patched.

By May will appear a new edition of the Kuenstler-Chor (with some important simplifications and improvements), and shortly after that the volume of my "Gesammelte Lieder" ["Collected Songs."] (about thirty), one or two of which will not be displeasing to you. I shall not be able to set to the working out of my Elizabeth till my return from Vienna.

The three songs [by Cornelius] (dedicated to Princess Marie) [Princess Wittgenstein, now Princess Hohenlohe in Vienna.] are charming and excellent. There is in them such a refined and true proportion in union with such fervent and ardent mood that other people besides the author must love them.

In order to make no break in my wonted fault-finding, I observe that in the fifth bar of the first song the A-flat is more agreeable than G.

[Figure: Music example showing the passage in question.] The carrying out of the motive in the second song:

[Figure: Here Liszt writes 2 bars of music to illustrate.]

(page 2, last line, and page 3) you have done most happily—also the moonlight conclusion of it,

[Figure: Here Liszt writes 3 bars of music to illustrate.]

and the poetic delineation of the last verse in the third song (in which the rests in the voice part and the motive in the accompaniment, enlivened by the rhythm [Here follows in the original an illegible sign. In the song there come in here, in place of the quaver movement which has prevailed hitherto, some long-sustained chords in the accompaniment, which are again interrupted by the quaver movement.], make an excellent effect):- -

"Wenn mein Lied zu Ende geht, Sing ich's weiter in Gedanken,
 Wie's im Wald verschwiegen weht, Wie die Rosen sich umranken!"

["When my song is ended quite, Yet in thought I still am singing,
 As the wood at silent night Echoes from the day is bringing!"]

Well and good, dearest Cornelius, and now some more soon, let me beg of you! Don't make too long pauses in your hermitage, and allow us to tell you and prove to you how truly we love you.

F. Liszt

P.S.—About two months ago I at last sent Schott the proofs of the second year of the "Annees de Pelerinage," together with the manuscript of Seroff's arrangement for two pianofortes of Beethoven's C-sharp minor Quartet. Will you be so good as to get Schott to let me know the fate of the C-sharp minor Quartet? Although two-piano arrangements are somewhat thankless articles of sale, yet perhaps Schott may manage to bring out this Quartet, of which I should be very glad.

Don't forget, dearest friend, to remind him that

he has left my letter about this matter hitherto unanswered—and I should be glad to let Seroff know something definite.

198. To Dionys Pruckner in Munich

"Lohengrin" be thanked that I hear something from you again, dear Dionysius, and I give you my best thanks that you wrote to me directly after the first performance, and thus gave me fresh good tidings [Namely after the first performance of Lohengrin in Munich, on February 28th, 1858]. What criticism will emit about it by way of addition troubles me little—in our present circumstances its strength consists mainly in the fear which people have of it; and, as the Augsburg gentlemen renounce all claim "to wash to teach us," nothing remains for us but to teach ourselves better than they can do it.

Ad vocem of the severe gentlemen of Augsburg, I will send you in a few days Bronsart's brochure "Musikalische Pflichten" ["Musical Duties." Leipzig, Matthes, 1858] (in answer to the "Musikalische Leiden" ["Musical Sufferings." In Nos. 353-55 of the supplement to the Augsburg Allgemeine Zeitung, 1857.], etc.). The A[llgemeine]Z[eitung] only made a couple of extracts from it in its columns, and from these the point was missing. Bronsart exquisitely accuses our opponents of ill-will, unfairness, and calumniation. Since they have not succeeded in silencing us in a conspicuous manner, they would like to kill us insignificantly, for which, however, other weapons would be necessary than those which they have at their command.

Meanwhile Bronsart's form of argument will

give you a pleasant hour, and if, as you tell me, you have found in Munich a few comrades of the same mind, let the "Musikalische Pflichten" be recommended in their circle.

Amongst other things the assumption of the reporter of the A. Z. that Wagner himself had never conducted his Lohengrin better than Franz Lachner, appeared to me very droll. It is well known that Wagner has never heard this work, let alone conducted it!— Ignorance of this kind is, moreover, not the worst on the other side, where intentional and unintentional ignorance and lies (not to mince the matter) are continually being directed against us.

But enough of that. Let us continue to go on our own way simply and honorably, and let the tame or wild beasts on our right and left behave as they like!—

I have not kept your last letter (during my stay in Dresden). Address, up to the 25th of this month, to Haslinger in Vienna. I shall get there by the beginning of next week, and shall conduct the Gran Mass in the Redouten-Saal [Ball-room] on the 22nd and 23rd. Next Thursday the "Dante Symphony" and the "Ideale" will be given here—and on Sunday "Tasso" (in a Conservatorium Concert). Tausig and Pflughaupt [A pupil of Henselt and Liszt (1833-71)] play my two Concertos.

In the E-flat major (No. 1) I have now hit on the expedient of striking the triangle (which aroused such anger and gave such offence) quite lightly with a tuning-fork—and in the Finale (Marcia) I have pretty nearly struck it out altogether, because the ordinary triangle-virtuosi as a rule come in wrong and strike it too hard.

Rubinstein and Dreyschock came to see me in Weymar before I left. The latter is intending to go to Munich. Go and see him and give him greetings from me.

Write and tell me, dear Dionysius, if I can be of use to you in any way, and you may always dispose of Yours in all friendship,

F. Liszt

Prague, March 9th, 1858

P.S.—Give me some tidings about your stay in Munich. With whom do you have most intercourse? Do you see many of my friends there—Kaulbach, Frau Pacher, etc.? Do you give lessons? Are you thinking of settling there, or do you intend to make a concert tour, and if so, where?—Send me also your exact address.

199. To Eduard Liszt

Dearest Eduard,

Hearty thanks for your few lines.

The letter of invitation has not yet arrived. It goes without saying that I shall accept it; and as soon as I know in what form and to whom I have to reply, I shall write at once. Meanwhile I intend to reach Vienna on Monday, or Tuesday at latest. After tomorrow's concert (with "Dante" and the "Ideale") there is still a Conservatorium Concert to come off on Sunday at midday, at which I shall conduct "Tasso," and also my first Concerto will be played by Herr Pflughaupt. I shall either start for Vienna at once that same evening, or else on Tuesday early. Will you be so good as to order me rooms, as before, in the Kaiserin von Oesterreach [Empress of

Austria.] hotel? I am bringing Tausig with me, whose acquaintance you will like to make.

Yours in spirit, and by the ties of flesh and blood,

F. Liszt

Prague, Wednesday early, March 10th, 1858

I received the five hundred gulden all right—and also the big bill, which was a pleasant surprise to me, for when I left Weymar I had made up my mind to give up all claim to it. Now that it has come, however, it must be something good!—I promise you this, that we shall not disgrace ourselves, and shall even surpass the expectations of our very few friends!—

200. To Frau Dr. Steche in Leipzig

Vienna, March 20th, 1858

How many excuses I owe you, my dear lady and kind friend, for all the trouble and disagreeables that the "Preludes" have occasioned you! I can really scarcely pardon myself for having written the piece! —When the Princess informed me of your kind intention I wrote to her that a performance of my things in Leipzig appeared to me untimely, and that I was resolved to let them fall into oblivion rather than to importune my friends with them. Hence the heterogeneousness of the letters and telegrams to you, dear madam, which I beg you kindly to excuse. Candidly, I still think it is better not to have the "Preludes" performed now in Leipzig;[As there had already been a performance of this on the 26th of February, 1857, this can only refer to a performance in the "Euterpe" Concerts.] but I thank you none the less warmly for the kind interest you take in my compositions—in spite of their bad name—and take this opportunity of repeating to you the expression of high esteem and friendly devotion with which I remain

F. Liszt

201. To Professor L. A. Zellner in Vienna

Pest, April 6th, 1858

Dear Friend,

With the

[Here Liszt writes a musical score excerpt of a whole note A falling to quarter note D, in octave below middle C, with the word 'Cre - do' under the notes]

Cre-do we will conclude this time in Vienna! We must not give certain gentlemen any occasion to imagine that I concern myself about them more than is really the case. Faust and Dante can quietly wait for the due understanding of them. I must send them next to Hartel, so that they may be published by the end of this year. Give my very best thanks to Hellmesberger for the kind way in which he meets me; he will forgive me if I cannot as yet put it to use. Under existing circumstances it is wise and suitable for me "to strive with earnest consistency for my high aim, regardless of adverse circumstances and small-minded people."

At the end of next week I go to Lowenberg, and thence back to Weymar. Therefore no concert in Vienna for this season—what may happen later on remains meanwhile undecided.

The Pest concert has also not been given; but possibly my Symphonic Poems may obtain a hearing in Pest sooner than in Vienna, because I may expect much more susceptibility to them here. When I have got my Opera finished, [This must be "Sardanapalus."] I must in any case stay here a couple of month— and on that occasion, perhaps, I may be able to bring in my Symphonic things in three or four concerts. But there is no hurry whatever for this; the "Elizabeth" and the Opera must be finished first…

My intention had been to get to Vienna yesterday, and to be satisfied with calling only on our four solo-singers and Count Raday in Pest to express my thanks. But I was pressed on all sides in so kind a manner to let my Gran Festival Mass be heard again that I willingly acquiesced. The articles in the Austrian p[aper], and your brochure, have done the most towards stirring up the general wish. The public is like this—that they only know what they ought to think of a work when they see it printed in black and white!—You have therefore to answer for it if the Mass is performed here a second time—on Friday afternoon in the Museum-Saal (for the benefit of the Conservatorium) and on Sunday in the Parish Church. On Monday evening I shall be in Vienna. I wrote to Tausig yesterday that we would decide on the evening of our musical meeting at your house after Countess Banffy has chosen on the evening for her soiree (at which Tausig will play). If I hear anything further about it Tausig shall let you know at once, so that you may be able to make your invitations in advance. On Thursday or on Saturday at latest I leave Vienna. All further particulars viva voce.

Yours ever,

F. Liszt

There is no truth in the idea of a private concert. I will tell you in what way I might be able to realize it another time—and will take counsel and consent about it from you.

202. To Eduard Liszt

Dearest Eduard,

It is not enough that I have already been in all sorts of trouble here in connection with the two performances of the Gran Mass, which will take place next Friday and Sunday (for which four to five rehearsals at the least are indispensable)—but now the post from Vienna brings me bad tidings, for which indeed I was prepared, but which, nevertheless, are by no means desired by me. I had a long letter yesterday from our friend Z., which I am answering with a decided refusal as regards a nearly impending performance of my Symphonic Poems in Vienna. For this time we will stop at the two performances of the Gran Mass—neither a note more nor less. Later on we will consider how we shall stand on the next occasion, and I shall take counsel with you about it, because I have the conviction that you not only intend and act for the best and kindest as regards me, but also the most judiciously!—

On Monday evening I shall be back in Vienna—and will expect you directly I reach home. If possible I shall start from Vienna on Thursday evening—but at the latest on Saturday early. I have written to Tausig to take my old rooms for me. Much as I should like to come to you, yet this time it is simpler for me to stay at an hotel.

To our speedy meeting, which, alas! will be a good deal clouded for us by these various obstructions. But in Vienna it can't be otherwise. On this account you must soon come again to Weymar, where we can belong to ourselves.

Heartfelt greetings in sincere friendship and loving devotion from

F. Liszt

Pest, April 7th, 1858

203. To Adolf Reubke, Organ-Builder at Hausneinsdorf in the Harz.

[Written on the death of his son Julius Reubke (died June 3rd, 1858), a favorite pupil of Liszt's.]

Dear Sir,

Allow me to add these few lines of deepest sympathy to the poem by Cornelius, ["Bein Tode von Julius Reubke" ("On the Death of Julius Reubke"). Cornelius, Poems. Leipzig, 1890.] which lends such fitting words to our feelings of sorrow. Truly no one could feel more deeply the loss which Art has suffered in your Julius, than the one who has followed with admiring sympathy his noble, constant, and successful strivings in these latter years, and who will ever bear his friendship faithfully in mind—the one who signs himself with great esteem

Yours most truly,

F. Liszt

Weymar, June 10th, 1858

204. To Prince Constantin von Hohenzollern-Hechingen

[Autograph in the possession of Herr Alexander Meyer Cohn in Berlin.—This very musical Prince was for years Liszt's patron, and often invited the latter to stay with him at his Silesian residence at Lowenberg, where he kept up an orchestra.]

Monseigneur,

When Your Highness was kind enough to express your views to me respecting your noble design of encouraging in an exceptional manner the progress of musical Art, and to question me as to the best mode of employing a certain sum of money for this object, I think I mentioned to you Mr. Brendel, the editor of the Neue Zeitschrift fur Musik, as the best man to make your liberal intentions bear fruit. As much on account of the perfect uprightness of his character, which is free from all reproach, as for the important and continuous services which his paper and other of his works have rendered to the good cause for many years past, I consider Mr. Brendel entirely worthy of your confidence.

It is not lightly that I put forward this opinion —and I venture to flatter myself that my antecedents will be a sufficient guarantee to Your Highness that in this matter, as in any others in which I may have the honor of submitting any proposition to you, I could follow no other influences, no other counsels, than those of a scrupulous conscience. Putting aside all considerations of vanity or personal advantage foreign to the end in view, my sincere and sole desire is to make Your Highness's intentions and capital the most productive possible. It is with this view that I have openly spoken of the matter to Brendel, whose letter, which I venture to enclose herewith, corresponds, as it seems to me, with the programme in question.

I venture to beg you, Monseigneur, to look into this attentively, and to let me know whether you will grant permission to Brendel to enter into these matters more explicitly by writing to you direct. In the event of the propositions contained in his letter meeting with the approval of Your Highness, as I trust they may do, it would be desirable that you should let him know without too much delay in what manner you would wish your kind intentions carried out.

In order to fulfill its task of progress, the Neue Zeitschrift fur Musik has not spared its editor either in efforts or sacrifices. By the fact that it represents, in a talented and conscientious manner, the opinions and sympathies of my friends and myself, it is in the most advanced, and consequently the most perilous, position of our musical situation; therefore our adversaries lose no opportunity of raising difficulties for it. Our opinions and sympathies will he sustained, I doubt not, by their worth and conviction; but if Your Highness condescends to come to our aid, we shall be both proud and happy—and it is by spreading our ideas through the Press that we can best strengthen our position.

In other words, I am convinced that, in granting your confidence to Mr. Brendel, the sum that Your Highness is pleased to devote to this matter will be employed in the most honest manner, and that most useful to the progress of Art—and that all the honor and gratitude which your munificence deserves will spring from it—as is the earnest desire of him who has the honor to be, Monseigneur, Your

Highness's most devoted and humble servant,

F. Liszt

Weymar, August 18th, 1858

205. To Frau Rosa von Milde

[Court opera-singer in Weimar, nee Agthe; the first Elsa in

Lohengrin; a refined and poetical artist]

Weymar, August 25th, 1858

My honored and dear Friend,

If the outward circumstances which you mention in your kind letter are not exactly of the kind that I could wish for you, yet I am egotist enough to be much pleased at its friendly contents towards myself. Accept my warmest thanks for them —and let me tell you how anxious I am that you should like me very much, and how desirous I am to deserve this—as far as it can be deserved; for the best part of a harmonious intimacy must ever remain a free gift.

The "wanton, ragged garments of the Muse," which you abandon with strict generosity, make a show and please almost everywhere. Her sensual charm is not unknown to me; yet I think I may say that it was given me to lay hold of a higher and a pure ideal, and to vow to it my whole endeavors for many years past. You, dear friend, have, through your singing, often led me to this in the best way, without thinking of it. Moreover it always does me so much good when we meet in unity in the same path.—

Owing to a heap of visits (among which were several of deep interest, such as Kaulbach,

Varnhagen, Carus, etc.), I have been much interrupted in the completion of the "Elizabeth." Still, I hope to be ready with it by February. You will then again do the best part for it, and must practice works of artistic mercy!— What is the good of anything that is written on paper, if it is not comprehended by the soul and imparted in a living manner?— But among the works of mercy I am not desirous that you should have to bury a still-born Oratorio!—

My heartfelt, twofold greetings to Milde, as friend and as artist. I am writing the part of Landgrave Ludwig for him—and, as the Landgrave is very speedily got out of the way, I will ask him to undertake, in addition, two other parts (those of a Hungarian magnate and a bishop).

The day after tomorrow I accompany the Princess to the mountains and cascades of the Tyrol. On our return journey we shall spend a couple of days in Munich, and shall be back here by the end of September. Will you allow me to conduct "Alceste" on the 2nd of October?—Sobolewski's "Comala" [Opera by Sobolewski.] is fixed for the 12th. I shall give over to our common friend Lassen (to whom please remember me warmly) the pianoforte rehearsals during my absence.

I hope you will get quite strong and enjoy yourself much at the seaside, dear friend, and return in good spirits to us at Weymar, where you are quite indispensable to

Yours most truly and devotedly, F. Liszt

P.S.—Possibly Fraulein * * * (whose name at this moment I forget) will come from Berlin to

Weymar during my absence. I recommend her again to Milde and yourself. Preller will introduce her to you, and I beg that Milde will help her with good teaching. If I am not mistaken, she would stand proof well in mezzo-soprano parts.

I have trustworthy tidings of the brilliant success of the first performance of "Lohengrin" in Vienna (on the 19th of this month). Rienzi was also taken up again in these days as before.

206. To Dr. Franz Brendel

Dear honored Friend,

The memorandum is excellent, and I agree with it in all points. I have noted this, according to your wish, at the end by the words vu et approuve [Seen and approved.] (a perfectly correct formula in French). The Prince's address is as follows:—

To His Highness Prince Constantin Hohenzollern-Hechingen, Lowenberg, Silesia. I should not be able for the present to find you a Paris correspondent. But, as I understand, Bülow intends to go to Paris in the course of this winter, and would then be best able to tell you of a colleague there. There is no hurry about the article on theater curtains. As soon as I am somewhat through the mass of arrears in correspondence I will take an opportunity of sending it to you, but whether it will be in time to appear in the first number of the "Anregungen" I cannot say.

I told Pohl yesterday that I wish the Dresden Weber concerto affair in the meantime not to be mentioned in the paper. The whole affair has for the moment made an extraordinary stir, and I will tell you about it later on. For the present there is nothing to be said about it on our side, even if other papers mix themselves up in it in an incompetent manner. Very likely the winter will slip away before the intended concert comes off. [The Dresden theater directors intended, as M. M. v. Weber tells us in his biography of his father (vol. ii., p. 721), to arrange a concert for the benefit of the Weber Memorial which was to be erected. Liszt was equally desirous of doing something publicly for the Master whom he so highly esteemed; but "because they could not agree whether he should take part in the directors' concert or use the personnel of the Royal Opera at his own concert, neither of the concerts was given."]

Sobolewski (who has been detained this time by his theater work in Bremen) will come here for the second performance of "Comala". I will let you know about it.

The work is worth your hearing and interesting yourself in. Owing to the acting of the two Schmidts (husband and wife), as guests here, ["Das Gastspiel"—the playing as guests at a theater—is an expression used when actors or singers other than those attached to the theater of the place come to act or sing there for a time] the second performance has been postponed until towards the middle of this month.

I will send Riedel the pianoforte edition of my Mass very shortly.

With heartfelt greetings,

Yours,

F. Liszt

November 2nd, 1858

207. To Johann von Herbeck

Dear Friend,

Your three splendid fellows, my high-minded and honorable gipsies, ["Die drei Zigeuner" ("The Three Gipsies"), by Lenau, for voice with pianoforte accompaniment.] are most excellently lodged on the Altenburg. First of all the song was played on the violin, then with cello—another time I tried it alone, and yesterday Caspari sang me the song, so full of pith and beauty and intrinsic worth, to the delight of us all and of myself in particular. It will remain as a brilliant repertoire piece amongst us, and I shall very soon introduce it to Tichatschek, who will assuredly give it with inspiration and will make it widely known. Please forgive me, dear friend, for not having expressed my warm thanks to you sooner.—I only got home a few weeks ago from my journey to the Tyrol and Munich, and have scarcely been able to sit down to write, owing to all the business pressing upon me from every side. If Lessing says "One must not must," nevertheless the saying of Kladderadatsch, "Bien muss," ["The bee must"—referring to a joke in the German Punch (Kladderadatsch).] is, for ordinary mortals, much more applicable—and over this "bee must" one at last becomes quite idle from sheer weariness.

I will take the first opportunity of sending you your manuscript of the score of the Mass for men's voices to Vienna. The Gloria, which was performed at the University Jubilee Festival of Jena last August, was made most effective by your excellent instrumentation. You will observe a slight alteration at the conclusion (six bars instead of five, and a slightly less risky modulation), which I beg you to follow at any performance there may chance to be in Vienna.

As regards the choruses to "Prometheus," I confess to you candidly that, much as I thank you for thinking about them, I think it is wiser to wait a little bit. I am not in the slightest hurry to force myself on to the public, and can quietly let a little more of the nonsense about my failure in attempts at composition be spread abroad. Only in so far as I am able to do something lasting may I place some modest value upon it. This can and will be decided by time alone. But I should not wish previously to impose on any of my friends the disagreeables which the performance of my works, with the widespread presuppositions and prejudices against them, brings with it. In a few years I hope things will go better, more rationally, and more justly with musical matters.

Until then we will go forward composedly and contemplatively on our way! Once more best thanks and greetings from yours in all friendship,

F. Liszt

Weymar, November 22nd (St. Cecilia's Day), 1858

208. To Felix Draseke

My very dear Friend,

Herewith the piano edition of the two first acts of "Sigurd." [Opera by Draseke.]—Imagining that you may also want the score of the first act, which had remained here, I send it also, sorry as I am to part from this monumental work. Under present existing circumstances, which on my side are passive and negative, as I intimated to you after the performance of Cornelius's Opera, there is no prospect of putting Sigurd on the boards at present. But I promise myself the pleasure and satisfaction of letting all your "Tamtis" and "Beckis" be heard, when I have again resumed my active work at the Weymar theater, for which there may probably be an opportunity next season.

After you left Weymar we had to swallow a kind of second piece or supplement to the performance of the "Barber of Baghdad," on occasion of Madame Viardot's performance as "guest" here. But I will not weary you with tales of our local miseries and crass improprieties. I will only intimate thus much—that, under the present Intendant régime, to my sorrow, the inviting of Frau Schroder-Devrient to play here as guest is met by almost unconquerable difficulties from within. Tell our excellent friend Bronsart this, and tell him into the bargain that a concert (in the room in the Town Hall), at which he and Frau Schroder- Devrient should appear without any other assistance, would certainly be very welcome to the public, and I should look upon this as in any case a practical introduction to the performance as guest. This matter lies outside my present sway, but it goes without saying that I will not fail to let my slight influence towards a favorable solution of the matter be felt.—

The day before yesterday I heard at Gotha your countryman's new opera (Diana von Solange) for the second time. The work was received with great approval, and is shortly to be given in Dresden, where you will be best able to judge of it. Mitterwurzer and Frau Ney have some very effective moments in it.

The concerts of the joint Weymar and Gotha orchestras (a matter which I broached long ago) again came under discussion, and possibly this March an attempt will be made to set them going. Meanwhile let us look after our cordial [Magen-Starkung] "mentre che il danno e la vergogna dura," ["Whilst prejudice and shame last."] as Michael Angelo says.—

Friendly greetings from your faithful and devoted

F. Liszt

January 12th, 1859

Will you give the enclosed letter to Bronsart?

209. To Heinrich Porges In Prague

[Now Royal music-director and conductor of a first-rate Gesang- verein [vocal union] in Munich, where he has lived since 1867. Born 1837. Is also a writer on music.]

Dear Sir and Friend,

Owing to your affectionate understanding of what I have striven after in the "Dante Symphony" and the "Ideale", you have a special right to both works. Allow me to offer them to you as a token of my sincere attachment, as also of the grateful remembrance which I keep of the Prague performance. [At Porges' initiative the medical students had invited Liszt, in 1858, to a concert, at which his Dante Symphony and the Icdeale were given. In 1859 Bulow was also invited at Porges' inducement.] Taking your kindness for granted, I beg you to give the other two copies to Herr Professor Mildner and Herr Dr. Ambros with my best thanks.

It is to be hoped that this year's "Medical" Concert will have favorable results. My valiant son-in-law, H. von Bulow, cannot fail to be recognized among you as an eminent musician and noble character. I thank you and Herr Musil (to whom I beg you to remember me most kindly) for offering Bülow this opportunity of doing something in Prague.—There is no doubt that he will fulfill all your expectations.

For the next "Medical" Concert I willingly place myself at your disposal. Possibly we might on this occasion venture on the Symphonic Poem No. I "Ce qu'on entered sur la Montagne"—the chorus "An die Kunstler," and the "Faust Symphony?"—The respected medical men would thus take the initiative in the new musical pathology!—

For the Tonkunstler-Versammlung, etc. [Meeting of Musicians], in Leipzig at the beginning of June Dr. Brendel is expecting you, and I rejoice at the thought of meeting you again there. If the affair is not too much hampered in its natural course by local miseries and malevolence, it may do much for the bettering of our suffering musical position. In any case we will not fail in doing our part towards it.

With highest esteem, yours most truly,

F. Liszt

Weymar, March 10th, 1859

210. To Capellmeister Max Seifriz in Lowenberg

[Autograph in the possession of Herr Alexander Meyer Cohn in
Berlin.]

Dear Friend,

I feel the most heartfelt sympathy with you in your sad days at Lowenberg, and trust with you that they will not last much longer. When there is a suitable opportunity, express to our Prince my heartfelt, grateful devotion. Then tell me quite openly and candidly whether my visit to Lowenberg, in the course of next month, will be welcome and will make no trouble. I had planned to spend the Easter week there, and only await preliminary tidings from you to announce myself by letter to His Highness. Dr. Brendel wished at the same time to pay his respects to the Prince. The press of work upon him just now especially will only allow him to stay a couple of days with you; but I for my part, if I am assured that my visit will not come inopportunely, should like to prolong my stay a little. Perhaps, as you are so kindly intending to invite Damrosch, it might be arranged for him to come at the same time. It would be a great pleasure to me to see the valiant friend and comrade in Art again with you.

I give you once more my best thanks for the kind attention which you have caused to be bestowed on my works. The many attacks on me which I have to bear enhance still more the value I place on the sympathy and concurrence of my friends.

By today's post I send you the scores of the Dante Symphony, the "Ideale," and the Goethe March, which have just come out—the former merely to read through (as a memento of the Dresden performance, which served as a rehearsal to me, after which several alterations in the score occurred to me)-but the other two might not be wholly unsuitable for a performance with your gallant orchestra, to whom I beg you to remember me most kindly.

May the things be welcome to you, dear friend, as a token of the very high esteem of

Yours in all friendship,

F. Liszt

Weymar, March 22nd, 1859

211. To Eduard Liszt

Warmest thanks for all you have done, said, and felt, dearest Eduard. I hope that I am only going a few steps in front of you, and that in a couple of years the same distinction will fall to your lot, in which I shall then have the same pleasure as is granted to you today. [This would be the bestowing of the title of nobility on Liszt, who, however, as is well known, never used it.]

Herewith my letter of thanks to S. E. von Bach. [Austrian Minister of the Interior.] Perhaps you would think it well to deliver the letter yourself. Take the opportunity of remembering me to Wurzbach, who has always been most friendly to me. I will write to Daniel one of these next days. The Princess goes tomorrow to Munich, where Kaulbach is painting the portrait of Princess Marie. On the 30th of this month I again make a visit to Prince Hohenzollern at Lowenberg (Shlesia), and shall then soon take up my quarters at Leipzig, where we shall have to live through some rather warm days on the 1st, 2nd, and 3rd June. For the rest there are good prospects for us there; and, even if dishonesty and malevolence make the utmost exertions (as we may expect they will do), this can do us but very little injury (where it does not help us).

You have possibly already heard that the Schiller Festival in Weymar has been frustrated by the imprudence of Dingelstedt. In spite of that I am composing the Introduction to the Festival by Halm, which may find its use here or elsewhere. With heartfelt thanks and greetings, your

F. Liszt

[Weimar,] April 5th, 1859

212. To N. N., Music-Director at Weimer

[Autograph in the possession of Herr Gille, Privy Councillor in
Jena.]

Dear Herr Music-Director,

I learn today by chance of the measures which have been taken a posteriori against the concert conducted and arranged by Herr Gotze [Carl Gotze, chorister, afterwards music-director.] and sincerely regret that a Weimar music-director and Weymar Court musician could deem such a thing suitable.

I, with my exceptional and only occasional dealings with the orchestra here, can only draw your attention to the fact of how deplorably such occurrences run counter to a nice feeling of decorum, and still more to the nobler artist feeling.

With compliments,

F. Liszt

April 17th, 1859

213. To Peter Cornelius In Vienna Weymar

May 23rd, 1859

Dearest Friend,

I learn with joy from your letter (which has just crossed mine from Lowenberg), that things are going well and comfortably with you in Vienna. It is easy to see that your stay there, when once you have made a firm footing, will become very advantageous —and whatever I can do towards helping this you may be sure I shall do. Herewith a few lines for Herr von Villers, Secretary of the Saxon Embassy (where you will learn his address). He is one of my older friends who has remained very dear to me. In his refined poetic and musical feeling many kindred tones will sound for you. Tell him all about Weymar and play him something from the "Barbier". [Cornelius' Opera] Although he lives somewhat a part, he can prove himself agreeable to you in many things,—firstly, by his own personal intercourse— and then also by his relations with Baron Stockhausen (the Hanoverian Ambassador), at whose house there is frequently really good music, etc.—Don't delay, therefore, looking up Villers.

For today I must beg you also to get the Prologue for the Leipzig days [The Leipzig Tonkunstler-Versammlung (Meeting of Musicians), from which the Allgemeine Deutsche Musikverein (Universal German Musical Society) sprang] ready as quickly as possible. I shall settle down at the end of this week (Saturday) in Leipzig—Hotel de Pologne. It would be very good of you if you could send me the Prologue to Leipzig within eight days. Address to Brendel, Mittelstrasse, 24. I still do not possess a single copy of my Mass, because I sent on the two or three that had been previously sent to me

394

at once to M[usic]-D[irector] Riedel for studying the work. But my cousin, Dr. Eduard Liszt, will certainly be delighted to give you your copy at once. You have only to tell Daniel to bring it to you, if you have not time to call on Eduard.

Frau von Milde, Bulow, Bronsart, Draseke, Lassen, etc., etc., etc., are coming to Leipzig from Monday, 30th May, until Sunday, 4th June. You must not fail us, dearest friend, and we await you with open arms and loving hearts. Your

F. Liszt

The Princess stays a little longer in Munich, and will not get to Leipzig till towards the end of this month. Remember me most respectfully and warmly to Hebbel.

Best greetings to Catinelli.

Once more, please send the "Prologue".

214. To Dr. Franz Brendel

[Autograph in the possession of Herr A.O. Schulz, bookseller in
 Leipzig.]

Herewith is an answer to the nine points of your letter of today, my dear friend [Referring to the Tonkunstler-Versammlung in Leipzig, in June, 1859].

1. The Mildes have got leave of absence from Monday, 30th April, till Friday, 3rd June, inclusive. Your programme remains as already fixed. Duet from the "Flying Dutchman", "Cellini Aria", Songs by Franz and Schumann (etc. ad libitum).

2. I will bring all the orchestral parts that there are with me, or, better still, I will send you the whole

lot tomorrow. For "Tasso" the whole set is complete —but for the "Duet" from the "Dutchman", and the "Cellini Aria" and "Overture" a couple of copies of the quartet will have to be written out afresh in Leipzig.

3. I do not possess the "Overture to the Corsair" [By Berlioz] (and would not recommend it for performance), and the "Prelude to Tristan" Bülow will see after.

4. I expect more particulars from Bülow in the course of the week.

5. I am writing today to Cornelius about the Prologue affair.

6. Herewith is the German text of the Mass, [Lizst's "Gran Festival Mass."] which is to be printed in Leipzig in the same manner as in Vienna— namely, with the addition of the Latin text- -and which belongs to the General Programme of the Festival. This programme we will settle and revise together next Sunday.

7. Leave of absence for Frau Pohl will be attended to.

8. I reserve to myself the matter of deciding on what pianists shall accompany the Ballads, and undertake the piano part of the "Trios" that are to be given. If possible I want Bronsart to take a part in it.

9. I will send off the definite invitations to the nobility next Sunday (at latest) from Leipzig to Gotha and Meiningen. I am coming to you on Saturday afternoon, 21st May [Must be 28th May, as the letter is dated the 23rd], and shall then stay in Leipzig till the end of the Festival. For the present a suitable room (without sitting-room) will satisfy me,

and I beg you to bespeak this for me in the Hotel de Pologne for Saturday. My ministering spirit should have his room close to mine, because looking for him and calling is highly disagreeable to me.

Goodbye till Saturday. Your

F. Liszt

Monday, May 23rd, 1859

P.S.—The performance of "Judas Maccabaeus" (for the Handel Festival) is announced here for next Wednesday, 25th May. Tomorrow, Tuesday, there will be a similar Handel celebration in Erfurt with a performance of the "Messiah." Frau von Milde will sing the soprano part there. Let Pohl know this—perhaps he may like to hear "Judas."

The rehearsals of Rietz's little Opera are in progress,   and
 Pasque (who has written the libretto for it) told me yesterday
 that the first performance will take place next week. Probably
 Rietz will undertake to conduct it, as I proposed.

215. To Felix Draseke

Where, my dear, excellent friend, have you got hold of the extraordinary idea that I could be angry with you? How to begin such a thing I really should not know. You are far too good and dear to me for me not to remain good to you also in all things!—Herewith are a few lines for Wagner, which however you don't in the least need. I am glad that you are not putting off this journey any longer. But before you set out WRITE to Wagner (you can add my lines to your letter extra), and inquire whether he will be staying at Lucerne still, so that your Swiss pilgrimage may not be in vain.—You will be certain to get an answer from Wagner by return of post, and will thus be sure of your object.

Schuberth tells me that "King Helge" will ride into his shop almost immediately...to Sigrun, the ever blooming delicious sorrow!—How scornfully, "without greeting or thanks," will "King Helge" look down upon all the other wares in Schuberth's shop. Somewhat as the hippopotamus looks on toads and frogs.—But it is quite right to let the Ballade come out, and I am impatiently awaiting my copy.—[Liszt subsequently formed out of Draseke's song the melodrama of the same name.]

I hope it may be possible for me to come to Lucerne at the end of
August. But send some tidings of yourself before then to

Your sincere and faithful
F. Liszt
[Weimar,] July 19th, 1859
216. To Peter Cornelius in Vienna
Dearest Friend,

You are quite right in setting store upon the choice and putting together of the three Sonatas. The idea is an excellent one, and you may rest assured of my readiness to help in the realization of your intention as well as of my silence until it is quite a settled thing. If Bronsart could decide on going to Vienna, his cooperation in that matter would certainly be very desirable. Write about it to him at Dantzig, where he is now staying with his father

(Commandant-General of Dantzig). Tausig, who is spending some weeks at Bad Grafenberg (with Her Highness the Princess von Hatzfeld), would also adapt the thing well, and would probably be able to meet your views better than you seem to imagine. As regards Dietrich, I almost fear that he does not possess sufficient brilliancy for Vienna—but this might, under certain circumstances, be an advantage. He plays Op. 106 and the Schumann Sonata capitally—as also the "Invitation to hissing and stamping," as Gumprecht designates that work of ill odor—my Sonata. Dietrich is always to be found in the house of Prince Thurn and Taxis at Ratisbon. He will assuredly enter into your project with pleasure and enthusiasm, and the small distance from Ratisbon makes it not too difficult for him. You would only have to arrange it so that the lectures come quickly one after the other.

Where Sasch Winterberger is hiding I have not heard. Presupposing many things, he might equally serve your purpose.

In order to save you time and trouble, I will send you by the next opportunity your analysis of my Sonata, which you left behind you at the Altenburg.

Draseke is coming very shortly through Weymar from Lucerne. I will tell him your wish in confidence. It is very possible that he would like to go to Vienna for a time. I have not the slightest doubt as to the success of your lectures, in conjunction with the musical performance of the works.—I would merely advise you to put into your programme works which are universally known—as, for instance, several Bach Fugues (from "Das wohltemperierte Clavier"), the Ninth Symphony, the grand Masses of Beethoven and Bach, which you have so closely studied, etc. [The proposed lectures did not come off.]

Well, all this will come about by degrees. First of all a beginning must be made, and this will be quite a brilliant one with the three Sonatas. Later on we will muster Quartets, Symphonies, Masses, and Operas all in due course!

A propos of operas, how are you getting on with the "Barbier" and the publication of the pianoforte edition? Schuberth told me for certain that printing would begin directly they had received the manuscripts. Don't delay too long, dearest friend— and believe me when I once more assure you that the work is as eminent as the intrigue, to which it momentarily succumbed, was mean-spirited.

Schuberth has no doubt told you that I want to make a transcription of the Salamaleikum. But don't forget that another Overture is inevitably NECESSARY, in spite of the refined, masterly counterpoint and ornamentation of the first. The principal subject

[Figure: Musical example of the principal subject.]

must begin, and the "Salamaleikum" end it. If possible, bring in the two motives together a little (at the end). In case you should not be disposed to write the thing I will do it for you with pleasure—but first send me the complete piano edition for Schuberth. The new Opera can then afford to wait a while, like a "good thing"—only may weariness at it remain long absent [Untranslatable play on the words Weile and Langeweile]!—In order that you may not have a fit of it in reading this letter, I will at once name to you the magic name of Rosa [Rosa von Milde, the artist and friend of Cornelius, who wrote poetry upon her]…

In consequence of an insinuating intimation of our mutual patroness, I have still to add the excuses of our good friend Brendel to you. When I have an opportunity I will tell you in person about the Prologue disturbances at the Leipzig Tonkunstler Versammlung. Pohl had also supplied one—but the choice was given over to Frau Ritter, and she chose her good "Stern," whose prologue was indeed quite successful and made a good effect. But oblige me by not bearing any grudge against Brendel, and let us always highly respect the author of "Liszt as a Symphonic Writer"!—

A thousand heartfelt greetings from your faithful

F. Liszt

Weymar, August 23rd, 1859

Princess Marie will thank you herself for the Sonnet, and at the same time tell you about the musical performances of the 15th August. Lassen's song, "Ave Maria," of which you gave him the poem long ago, was especially successful. The Quartet:

"Elfen, die kleinen,
Wollen dich grussen,
Wollen erscheinen
Zu deinen Fussen"

["Elfin world greeting

To thee is sending,
Fairy forms lowly
At thy feet bending."]

composed by Lassen), and
"Wandelnde Blume, athmender Stern,
Duftende Bluthe am Baum des Lebens"

["Swift-changing flowers, pulsating star,
Sweet-scented blossoms on life's living tree."]

(composed by Damrosch), which we had sung together two years ago, rejoiced us anew and most truly this time.

217. To Dr Franz Brendel

[In this letter, the programme refers to some theater concerts, which were to be arranged according to Brendel's design. The sketch was as follows:—

"1st Concert: Paradise and the Peri.

2nd Concert: Eroica, Prometheus.

3rd Concert: Overture of Wagner. Solo (Bronsart). Overture of
        Beethoven.
        2nd part: L'enfance du Christ of Berlioz.

4th Concert: Festival Song of Liszt. Solo. Draseke. Chorus for
        men's voices from his Opera.
        2nd part: Walpurgisnacht of Mendelssohn.

5th Concert: Overture of Berlioz, Wagner, or Beethoven.

Solo. Preludes.

2nd part: Manfred.

6th Concert: Overture. Solo. Tasso.
  2nd part: B-flat major Symphony."

To this Liszt adds, besides some remarks about getting the parts for
No. 5:

"An orchestral work of Hans von Bulow (possibly the Caesar Overture) would be suitable for this concert. I would also recommend that Bronsart's "Fruhlings-Phantasie" ["Spring Fancy"] should be included in one of the programmes.
    "Of Berlioz' works I should recommend the following as the most acceptable for performance:—
    "The festival at Capulet's house (Romeo),
  The Pilgrims' March (from Harold),
  Chorus and Dance of Sylphs (Faust),
  Terzet and Chorus (from Cellini), with the artists' oath,
  Overture to Lear.

    "N.B.—We can bring out the Terzet from Cellini at the next
  Tonkunstler-Versammlung. It is a very important and effective piece."]

    Dear Friend,
    The sketch for your programme is excellent, and if I have some doubts as to the entire project, yet your proposed programme seems to me in any case the most suitable, both as regards choice of works and their order and grouping. With regard to the doubts which I have so often mentioned I will only

make the general remark that a competition with the Gewandhaus in Leipzig brings a good deal of risk with it, and for this winter a passive attitude on our side would not specially injure our cause (at least not according to my opinion). Whether Wirsing and Riccius will be able to give the requisite support to the theater concerts, or are willing to do so, I cannot undertake to say, as the ground of Leipzig lies in many ways too far removed from me. In this I rely entirely on your insight and circumspection, dear friend. In case you end by deciding in the affirmative I will willingly do something to help—as, for instance, to undertake the conducting of the "Prometheus." I would rather not let myself in for much more than that, because conductings in general become more burdensome to me every year, and I don't in the least desire to offer further active resistance to the ill-repute with which I am credited as a conductor. Indeed I owe my friend Dingelstedt many thanks for having (without perhaps exactly desiring to do so) given me the chance of freeing myself from the operatic time- beating here, and I am firmly resolved not to wield the baton elsewhere except in the most unavoidable cases! Bülow must now often mount the conductor's desk. He has the mind, liking, talent, and vocation for this. If the theater concerts should be arranged, be sure to secure his frequent co-operation. He will certainly bring new life into the whole affair, and possesses the necessary amount of experience and aplomb, [Employed in French by Liszt] to be their solid representative.

I have just written to Klitzsch [Music-conductor at Zwickau] and promised him to conduct the "Prometheus" in Zwickau. The concert will take place at the end of October (perhaps on my birthday, the 22nd). Although you have heard the Prometheus choruses in Dresden, I wish very much that you could come to Zwickau this time. I have again worked most carefully at it, have amplified some things, and have arranged others in a simple and more singable manner, etc. Now I hope that it will thoroughly hold its ground and stand the test of proof. So do come to Zwickau.

I have still one more request to make to you today, dear friend. P. Lohmann [A music colleague of the Neue Zeitschrift fur Musik, living in Leipzig] was so kind as to send me his drama some weeks ago. I have read The Victory of Love with much interest, but I have not yet been able to get so far as the other, and as little have I been able to express my thanks to him in writing. Kindly undertake my excuses to him, and tell him that I am exceedingly obliged by his letter and what he sent me. On the occasion of my journey to Zwickau I will call on Lohmann in Leipzig, and tell him personally what an impression his dramas make on me. I specially take notice of his article in the paper.

I thank you most truly for the kindness which you have shown to B. He is in many things somewhat awkward, impractical—and almost looks as though he could not devote himself to any productive and consistently carried-out form of activity. None the less is there in him a certain capacity and worth which, in a somewhat more regular position than he has yet been able to attain, would make him appear worth more. A more frequent application of a few utensils such as soak tooth-brush, and nail brush might also be recommended to him!—I expect much good to result from your influence on B.'s further work and fortunes, and hope that your store of patience will not be too sorely tried by him.

With heartfelt greetings, your

F. Liszt

Weymar, September 2nd, 1859

Herewith the programme scheme with two or three little remarks appended. Weigh again the pros and cons of the matter, and keep the right balance between the risk and the possible gain. Motto: "First weigh, then risk it!"—[The nearest English equivalent seems to be "Look before you leap."

.—. I have had so much of notes [musical] to write lately that my writing of letters [of the alphabet] has got still worse. But where you can't read what I have written, you can guess it all the easier.—

218. To Louis Koehler

Dear Friend,

Your letter was a real joy to me, for which I thank you heartily. You are far too honorable, brave, and admirable a musician for our paths to remain long sundered. For the very reason that people cannot (as you so wittily remark) immediately "label and catalogue me correctly and place me in an already existing drawer," I am in hopes that my efforts and working will eventually prove in accordance with the spirit of the time, and will fructify. I promise you also that I am not wanting in pains and labour in honor of my friends. But I certainly cannot recognize weaklings and cowards as such. It is only with high- minded, brave, and trusty comrades that we move forwards, no matter though the number remain small. In matters of intelligence the majority always follows the minority, when the latter is sufficiently strong to hold its own.— Welcome, therefore, dear friend, welcome most truly. If there is still a lot of scandal which we have to bear quietly and without mortification, we will by no means let ourselves be confounded by it!

I have written at once to Hartel to send you the arrangements for two pianofortes of the Symphonic Poems that you wished for. But there is a better way for the scores than that of a bookseller. Fraulein Ingeborg Stark is going to St. Petersburg on the 20th of this month, and will stay a day in Konigsberg. She will bring you the Dante Symphony, etc., and if there should be an opportunity she will play the things through with Bronsart (who is also going to Konigsberg at the same time). I have grown very much attached to Fraulein Stark, as hers is a very particularly gifted artistic nature. The same will happen to you if you hear her striking Sonata. Ingeborg composes all sorts of Fugues, Toccatas, etc., into the bargain. I remarked to her lately that she did not look a bit like that. "Well, I am quite satisfied not to have a fugue countenance," was her striking answer.

The Pohls are both still in Baden-Baden (whence I hear the excerpts from Berlioz' manuscript opera Les Troyens [The Trojans] spoken of with enthusiasm). Madame Viardot sang a grand scena and a duet from it in the concert conducted by Berlioz—and Fraulein Emilie Genast is staying a couple of weeks longer with her sister Frau Raff in Wiesbaden. On her return I will give her your greetings, and Emilie will certainly be glad to make known the concert song which you mention to her. In her performance a beautiful and sympathetic "melody of speech" is reflected. As I write this word I can't help at the same time wishing that you may find in my "Gesammelte Lieder" something that appeals to your feelings, which you have so cleverly represented in the "melody of speech." You will receive a proof-copy of the six numbers at the same time as the Dante Symphony. I wanted to dedicate the last number, "Ich mochte hingehn" (poem by Herwegh), specially to you, and when next you have occasion to come to Weymar, I will look for the manuscript for you on which your name is put. But as I have left out all other dedications in this complete edition, I propose to dedicate something else to you later—probably some bigger and longer work.

A Ballade of Draeseke's—"Koenig Helge"—has just appeared, which pleases me extremely. You must look closely into this wonderful Opus 1.

In conclusion one more request, dear friend. Do me the kindness to be perfectly free and open and regardless of consequences in the discussion of my works. Do not imagine that the slightest vanity comes over me or impels me. I have long ago done with all that sort of thing. So long as you allow that I possess the necessary musical equipments to create freely in Art, as I gather from your letter that you do,

I can but be grateful to you for all else, even were it severe blame. I have often expressed my opinion to my friends that, even if all my compositions failed to succeed (which I neither affirm nor deny), they would not on that account be quite without their use, owing to the stir and impetus which they would give to the further development of Art. This consciousness so completely satisfies me that I can consistently persevere and go on composing.

With all respect and attachment I remain,

Yours most sincerely,

F. Liszt

Weymar, September 3rd, 1859

If the Koenigsberg Academy does not take alarm at my name (as has indeed been the case in other places, owing to the foolish prattle of the critics), they might try the "Prometheus" choruses there by-and-by. They are to be given almost directly (at the end of October) at Zwickau, and probably later on in Leipzig, where I shall then also have them published.

In the matters of the prize-subject we will wait and see what comes. You very justly remark that it hinges now upon enharmony.

It is a pity that you do not bring something. Perhaps you will still find time to do so.

219. To Dr. Franz Brendel

Dear Friend,

I beg you to send me by return of post a copy of the intricate biography ("Liszt's Life and Work"—if I am not mistaken) by Gustav Schilling. Siegel and Stoll in Leipzig have taken the work from the Stuttgart publisher, and there will surely be some way of getting a copy in Leipzig. Ask Kahnt to be so good as to see after one and to send it me immediately by post, for I require the work in connection with a special and pressing question which I can best answer by a quotation from Schilling's book.

With friendliest greetings, your

F. Liszt

Weymar, September 8th, 1859

Why does not Schuberth send me my dedicatory copy of Draeseke's
Ballade "Koenig Helge"?

220. To Johann von Herbeck

Dear Friend,

Warmest thanks for your persevering and well-wishing sympathy. It is a great pleasure to me that you are bringing about the performance of the Mass for men's voices on the 23rd October, and I hope that, as you have once "made your way through it," we shall also not succeed ill.

The "sneaking brood" (as you well name the people) can henceforth growl as much as they like. What does that matter to us, so long as we remain true and faithful to our task? In the performance last year at Jena (at the secular celebration of the University) I had the opportunity of convincing myself how capital your instrumentation of the Mass sounds, and I especially beg that you will not leave out one iota of it in the oboes or trombones. The organ alone is not sufficient, especially if there is a large chorus, and the completion of the accompaniment could not have been better accomplished than you have done it.

N.B.—At the Jena performance I hit upon the following alterations at the conclusion of the Gloria:

[Here, Liszt illustrates with a vocal score musical excerpt]

If you are agreed with this, then let this simplification serve for Vienna. I can only send you the score and parts of the "Prometheus" choruses towards the middle of November, as Klitzsch (in Zwickau) has arranged a performance of this work on the 12th to the 14th November, and I have already placed the parts at his disposal. If this delay does not hinder your kind intention of having the "Prometheus" choruses performed in Vienna, I will send the whole packet of parts to your address in Vienna, free, immediately after the Zwickau Concert. For the poem belonging to it, which I will also send with the rest, it is desirable that you should get an adequate tragic declaimer. In Dresden Davison undertook this, and in Zwickau Frau Ritter will declaim it. I am writing today to Herr von Bulow, but rather doubt whether he will be able to accept your invitation for this winter. According to what he told me lately, he thinks of going to Warsaw and Paris in the latter part of the winter. With regard to the eventual choice of a piece you may, moreover, pacify the strict gentlemen of the Committee. In case Bulow should make his appearance at the Philharmonic Concert he will, on my advice, not play my A major Concerto (nor any other composition of mine), but just simply one of the Bach or Beethoven Concertos. My intimate friends know perfectly well that it is not by any means my desire to push myself into any concert programme whatever…With regard to the scores and parts that you want, I have noted on a separate sheet which ones I have at my disposal, and where you can obtain the rest. In conclusion allow me once more to beg you kindly to let me have a couple of lines about the performance of the Mass. Perhaps some things may occur to you which might still be altered and simplified. Do not deprive me, dear friend, of your good advice, which I shall be glad to make use of in the score edition of the Mass which must shortly ensue. Naturally your name will stand on the title-page, and the responsibility of the instrumentation will be remitted to you.

With friendly thanks and highest regard, I am
Yours most truly,
F. Liszt
Weymar, October 11th, 1859
221. To Felix Draseke
Dear excellent friend,

Your surmise that I could not go away from Weymar at present was quite correct. The Altenburg is indeed very deserted, as Princess Marie went away directly after her marriage on the 15th October, and the Princess went to Paris yesterday for several days —yet I will not leave my own hearth so soon, even if my outward activity be much limited henceforth (as I have already intimated to you) both here and elsewhere.—I require my whole time for my further works, which must go on incessantly—consequently I have resolved to keep at a distance all the delights of conductorship, and to give the baton a rest equally with the piano.—

On the 9th November the festival play by Halm, "A Hundred Years Ago," will be given here with the music I have composed to it— and on the 11th the "Kuenstler-Chor" is to introduce the Festival-oration by Kuno Fischer at Jena. Damrosch writes to me also from Berlin that he intends to include the "Kuenstler-Chor" in the programme of the Schiller Festival there. The Zwickau Concert is fixed for the 15th November—and I am delighted to think of meeting the Ritters there. By the way, I am of opinion that Sasch [Sasch, i.e., Alexander, Ritter's Christian name] will undertake two numbers of the programme, and will fulfill Klitzsch's wish with the "Chaconne" as well as mine with the original Concerto, on the same evening. Zwickau chances to belong to the few towns where the "Chaconne" (so Klitzsch writes me word) has never been heard in public. Sasch can take this fact into consideration, and without doing anything derogatory can grant the public the enjoyment of the "Chaconne." The assured success which he will have with it may also act beneficially on the receptiveness of the audience in connection with his Concerto. Tell our dear friend this, with the proviso that, if he only undertakes one number on the programme, I advise him in any case to choose his Concerto. The piece has much that is interesting and effective in itself, and it will be useful to Sasch to test the relation of the orchestra to the solo part by a public production. If necessary, therefore, force him to do it, by my order.

With regard to the causes and excuses for your pretended "obstinacy, dogmatism," and imaginary "arrogance," I beg you, dearest friend, to rest assured that you will never find any such suspicion in me. What you think, feel, compose, is noble and great— therefore I take a sympathetic interest in it.—The next time we are together I will merely endeavour to make "amputation" more bearable to you by chloroform!—

With highest esteem I remain,
Yours in all friendship,
F. Liszt
[Weimar,] October 20th, 1859
222. To Heinrich Porges in Prague.
Dear Friend,

Your letter for the 22nd October gave me heartfelt pleasure, and you need not be in doubt as to the correctness of the affectionate and deep perception of my endeavour, which "has proceeded both from man's need of freedom as well as of love," and which, by and with the grace of God, has been impelled to raise itself toward the "Divine."—I cannot say much on this subject; but may my works only remain no dumb witnesses, and may your intimate understanding of them give you some satisfaction.

I send you herewith Dingelstedt's Festal Song for the Schiller Celebration, which I have purposely composed in a very simple, national manner. Perhaps there might be an opportunity of bringing the thing to a hearing during the Schiller Festival in Prague. Will you ask Apt whether he would be disposed to do it? The studying of it would not give the least trouble. It requires only a baritone or bass for the solo part, and an ordinary chorus of men's voices without any accompaniment.—

Leaving it entirely in your hands to act about it as you may think best, and either to promote the performance or to let it alone, I remain, with best thanks and high esteem,

Yours very truly,

F. Liszt

October 30th, 1859

My composition to Halm's festival play has been sent through H. von Dingelstedt to Herr Thome, and will probably be performed on the 9th or 10th November. [The festival play was given in Prague under the theater conductor Thome. The music to it was never published. The Weimar archives probably possess the score.] Write and tell me how the matter is settled.

223. To Ingeborg Stark

[A pupil of Liszt's, who afterwards married Liszt's pupil Hans von Bronsart, now General Manager of the Weimar Court theater: she was also known as a composer.]

It is very charming and graceful of you, dear Mademoiselle Inga, to remember the 22nd October so kindly, and I should have thanked you sooner for your letter, which gave me sincere pleasure, had I not been kept to my bed for nearly a week in consequence of much emotion and fatigue.

Through our friend Bronsart I have had some preliminary good tidings of you; you have fulfilled your role of charmer in the best possible manner, and Bronsart is full of raptures about you. But all this is ancient history for you, something like a chapter of Rollin on the history of the Medes,—after whom come the Persians, the Greeks, and the Romans...

For the present it is the turn of Russia, which you are in the way of conquering, and I see from here the enchantment of your admirers of St. Petersburg, who are all ears and all eyes around the piano where you are enthroned.

Will you remember me affectionately to Prince Odoyewski, and give a friendly shake hand [Written in English by Liszt] from me to Mr. Martynoff. As for our dear Tartar, [The composer Alexander Seroff] tell him how much I am attached to him; he will be all the more agreeably persuaded of this if you tell him. Ask him also to write to me after your first concert, for I would not risk offending your modesty so far as to beg you to send me an exact account of your undoubted successes. But I don't intend on that account to let you stand still as regards letter-writing, and you will give me great pleasure if, for example, you will continue your history of the musical prowess of Rubinstein (that you have begun so well).

You know that I am truly interested in what he is doing, considering that he has all that is wanting to compose good and beautiful things, provided that he does not persist in writing straight off too hurriedly, and guards a little against excess in the very exercise of these grand qualities.

The "Ocean" of which Rubinstein has sung might serve as his model in this; he knows how to restrain his waves in their liberty and power—and I hope Rubinstein would not be offended by the comparison!—Let me know then about his artistic actions and attitudes, of which, I presume, he will have every occasion to be satisfied and proud. Our little Weymar has remained, as usual, pretty tame since you left; but in a week's time we shall be celebrating here the centenary of Schiller's birth with all the enthusiasm of which we are susceptible (which is not saying much).

On the 9th November the music that I have composed for Halm's Festival-play, "A Hundred Years Ago," will be given at the theater, and Jena has put on its festival programme my chorus "An die Kuenstler," which will terminate the ceremony of the 11th (Friday next).

In addition you will find in the Schiller number of the Leipzig Illustrirte Zeitung, which will appear on the 12th November, a Festival song "im Volkston" [In the style of a folk-song] of my composition. Do not be shocked at the extreme simplicity of this song; it was not the occasion to make a display of musical knowledge—but simply to write forty bars or so which could be quite easily sung and remembered by tutti quanti. In order to do this I had to dress my Muse in a blouse, or, if you prefer a more German comparison, "ich habe der Dame eine bayrische Joppe angezogen!" ["I have dressed the lady in a Bavarian jacket."]

How are you getting on with your truly Samsonic Variations—and with your Fugue "Martha"? Don't make too great a martyr of yourself over it, and reserve for yourself also the better part... that of Mary. [She had written a fugue on the musical letters of the names Martha and Maria [Mary]—the names of her friends, the sisters Von Sabinin.]

As I have mentioned this name I will tell you that Princess Marie

Hohenlohe will spend her winter in Vienna.

I, for my part, shall not stir from the Altenburg, where I am reckoning on finishing my Elizabeth, and on living more and more as a recluse—indeed, even a little like a bear—but not in the style of those estimable citizens of the woods, whom the impresarii of small pleasures degrade by making them dance in the market-places to the sound of their flutes and drums! I shall rather choose a model ideal of a bear—be sure of that—and the flutes and drums which might lead me into the slightest future temptation of cutting capers have still to be invented.

Will you be so good, dear Mademoiselle Inga, as to present my very affectionate respects to Madame, your mother, as well as my best remembrances and compliments to la Sagesse Olivia —[Liszt's name for the sister of Ingeborg Stark] and believe me invariably

Your very devoted

F. Liszt

Weymar, November 2nd, 1859

224. To Johann von Herbeck.

Dear Friend,

I only returned a few hours ago from Zwickau, and find your friendly letter here, in reply to which I must excuse myself for not having been able to fulfill your wish so soon as I had intended, in respect to the Schubert Marches. This delay, which was very unpleasant to me, was occasioned by an indisposition which obliged me to keep my bed for a whole week at the end of October. The Weymar and Jena Schiller Festivals, following on the top of that, made it utterly impossible for me to get on with the instrumentation of the Marches. But I promise you that you shall have the score by Christmas at latest.

"Prometheus" will present himself to you by the end of this month. If after looking through the score, dear friend, you think the work suitable for a performance in Vienna, I shall be glad. If not, I beg you to tell me so with perfect candor, and without the slightest scruple of thereby wounding my vanity. Whether the stomach of the critics and of the public will be able to digest such a liver cut out of the vulture as this of my "Prometheus," or whether at the very first bars all will not be lost, I cannot determine; but still less would I prepare superfluous disagreeables for you by the performance of my "Tonschmiererei;" [Tone-daubing] of such ill-odor from the beginning!

Decide therefore entirely according to your own judicious opinion—and, whatever that may be, rest assured of the sincere acknowledgment and esteem with which I remain

Yours in all friendship,

F. Liszt

November 18th, 1859

225. To Dr. Franz Brendel

Dear Friend,

Of the three prize essays (which I return to you herewith) the one with the motto "Try all things and maintain the best" is, according to my opinion, very significant and suitable to the definite solving of the question. The writer develops his thesis with so safe, so rightly apprehending, and so far grasping a logic that it shows convincingly that the now indispensable practice is in complete union with the results of the theory. It is to be hoped that our excellent colleague and friend Lobe will also give his weighty judgment in favor of this prize essay, and will also scientifically explain his motives for doing so—for I cannot suppose that Lobe is in agreement with the opponents of the enharmonic system, whose theory would make us have to do musical penance.

In the two other essays with the mottoes "Our eyes see, but they require the light to do so," and "Look, this is what man has done!" there is much that is true and worthy of consideration (especially in the former), which might be made prominent after reading through all the essays sent in.

Come to an understanding next with Lobe about the final business of the causes for the award of the prize, and let me have a draft of it. It cannot be otherwise than profitable if the affair is treated somewhat exhaustively and thoroughly, which you, dear friend, in conjunction with Lobe and Weitzmann, are much better able to do than my humble self, since I, as Hauptmann justly observes, should appear to be too much prejudiced by my own practice. In matters of harmony, as in other greater matters, I believe also that Nature is in everlasting union with Genius.

"What one promises, the other surely performs." And Beethoven was quite right to assert his right to allow that which was forbidden by Kirnberger, Marpurg, Albrechtsberger, etc.!— Science must only investigate more and more the nature of things and the freedom of genius, and become experienced in their further development.

———- ——-

Ever faithfully yours,

F. Liszt

[Weimar,] December 1st, 1859

I quite agree with your project of giving two prizes. The first prize will be awarded to the above-mentioned treatise, unless, which I doubt, a still more successful one should be sent in.

226. To Anton Rubenstein

Certainly, my very honored friend, I shall not leave off taking a very sincere and loyal part in the unfolding of the career that you are pursuing with such rare prowess, and all that you can tell me of your doings in composition and musical conducting will always find in me a lively interest. Thank you, therefore, for your nice letter, which contains also a promise which I shall be very much pleased to see you fulfill—namely, that of your visit next spring, in company with your Opera in four acts—and probably also with your "Song of Songs," which you do not mention to me, but which I am none the less desirous, on that account, of knowing.

Have you thought well to give your "Paradise Lost" at St. Petersburg? I urged you strongly to do so, for it is a capital work, which does you great honor, and the place of which seems fixed in your concerts. And on this subject allow me to compliment you very sincerely upon the idea (all the less frequent as it is just) which has been uppermost in the distribution of the programme of these concerts. If it continues to predominate, and if in effect they take it into their heads at St. Petersburg to do justice (as you tell me) "to all the masters of all schools and of all times" (not excepting our own!), the famous verse

"'Tis from the North that light comes to us today"

will be justified, and even by Music! In France and Germany we are far from this—and classical Pharisaism swells its voice there to make a diversion to Mercantilism, that rich disgraceful one, who succeeds perfectly well in making the principal papers and their numerous readers dance to the sounds of his harsh flute, whilst his antagonist (Pharisaism) only ends in "Improperias" and "Jeremiads"…not composed by Palestrina!

Your choice of the introduction to the second act of the Fliegender Hollander seems to me an excellent one, and I shall get the score (of this scene) copied for you, as it is very difficult to get a complete score of the Opera, and as I only possess the autograph, with which it would be a matter of conscience to me to part. In about a fortnight I will send you what you want for your programme.

Princess Marie Hohenlohe is at the present time at St. Petersburg, and will be much delighted to see you again. Her husband does a good deal in the way of music, and plays several "Lieder ohne Worte" of his own composition very nicely. He and his wife will assuredly have pleasure in being amongst the first to applaud at the time of the performances of your Opera in Vienna.

A revoir then, my dear Rubinstein, in the spring—and ever yours in sincere esteem and affection,

F. Liszt

Weymar, December 3rd, 1859

P.S.—When you see Mademoiselle Ingeborg Stark, please give her my very affectionate remembrances. If her journey from Paris should bring her back by Weymar she would be sure to find me there; for, in spite of what the papers say, which, among other fancies, have taken it into their heads to make me travel hither and thither, I shall not stir from here for several months, but continue to work my best—if only to prove to the "kindly critic" and the idlers that it is very much to be regretted that I should have taken it into my head to turn composer! —This recalls the proverb, "On devient cuisinier, mais on nait rotisseur!"

[There does not seem to be any equivalent to this proverb in English: the nearest approach to it is, perhaps, "A poet is born, not made."]

227. To Dr. Franz Brendel

Dear Friend,

It is of great consequence to me not to delay any longer the publication of my "Gesammelte Lieder." Forgive me, therefore, if today I am somewhat troublesome to your friendship..—.

It seems to me that the best plan would be if, before you confer with Herr Schulze, you would first have a consultation with Klemm, and come to a thorough understanding on the matter with him. [Liszt evidently wished to have the songs engraved first at his own cost, and to let Klemm undertake the sale on commission.] Beg him also, in my name, to show a friendly sympathy to the work. The songs can hold their ground in their present form (regardless of the criticism of our choking and quarrelling opponents which will infallibly follow!); and if a few singers could be found, not of the raw and superficial kind, who would boldly venture to sing songs by the notorious non-composer, Franz Liszt, they would probably find a public for them.

I think I told you that a couple of them made a furore in certain salons which are very much set against me, as posthumous songs of Schubert, and were encored!—Of course I have begged the singer to carry the joke on further.

Klemm need not therefore be in the least ashamed of undertaking the publication of the work in a friendly spirit.

Best thanks beforehand for your kind trouble in this matter—and ever faithfully yours,

F. Liszt

Weymar, December 6th, 1859

P.S.—I have just received your letter. The two K.'s—Kompel and Kahnt—shall be made most welcome. Pohl had already told me of Kahnt's coming; it will be a pleasure to me not to verlangweilen [To make the time hang heavily] his visit here (if that word is not quite German, still I consider it is comprehensible!). Julius Schuberth had also the intention of rescuing something [Namely, Liszt's composition] from Kuehn. [Music publisher] Your idea of giving Bronsart the conductorship of the Euterpe Concerts is a most excellent one. I suppose the letter which I wrote about this to P. Fischer (to your address) came to hand (?). The day before yesterday I also let Bronsart know that possibly some favorable openings might occur for him in Leipzig, and recommended him not to neglect them. Bronsart would be just in his right post in Leipzig, and I do not doubt that he would in every respect maintain it in the most honorable manner. In addition to this, it would be especially agreeable to me to begin constant intercourse with him as my next neighbor. He is now working at his Opera, and sent me a little while ago the libretto which he has himself composed to it, and which seems to me very successful in the most important scenes, as well as in the dialogue. [It was afterwards composed by his wife ("King Hiarne").]

Address your letters to "Herr von Bronsart, c/o Herr General von
Bronsart, Commandant of Dantzig, Dantzig."

In consequence of the performance of my Mass in Munich (on the King's birthday, at the end of November), which, as I am told on many sides, was well given and—which seems wonderful—was acknowledged by many musicians there to be a work of importance— so that even Lachner spoke favorably of it—the "Allgemezne" Zeftung again breathes forth poison and gall (supplement of 3rd December), without forgetting therewith the "Neue Zeitschrift fur Musik." I should like to take the opportunity of making this pack of critics, such as W., B., G., B., and whatever all the assistants' assistants are called, understand the following thoughts as Xenie:—[Epigram]

"Ye break your staff over me, but your staff has indeed long since become rotten from all the dust and dirt that stick to it, and it scarcely serves any longer to cut the air!"

Tell this idea to Lohmann—perhaps he may be inspired with a happy rhyme for it.

I cannot say anything better to you about Pohl than what you tell me.—

Herewith, for your private delectation, is a copy of some lines from my letter to Herr Gustav Eggers (in Berlin), brother of the well-known Art-journal Eggers, now very much concerned in the Prussian paper. Gustav E. was here at the September Festival (1857), when he heard the Faust Symphony, and sent me lately a very pretty book of songs, begging me to recommend them to Hartel.—Send me the little paper back soon.

228. To Eduard Liszt

By the loving friendship which you have shown me, especially during the last decade in which so many trials have been laid on me, our close relationship in heart and character has been for ever firmly sealed, dearest Eduard. You are, and will ever be to me, a support and a courage-giving comforter in the battles and straits of my life. God grant me grace to go through them without wavering, as a faithful servant of the truth in Christ!

You have decided upon just what is most right and suitable in the arrangement of the funeral ceremony of my son. [He died in Vienna, where he was studying law.] The selection of Terziani's Requiem was a very suitable one under the existing conditions. I thank you for everything from the depths of my soul!

I shall write a couple of lines to Herbeck tomorrow, and send him at the same time the score and parts of the "Prometheus," as well as two Marches of Schubert which I have instrumented for him. The sending off of this parcel has been delayed by the circumstance that it was necessary to have the whole score of the "Prometheus" written out afresh, and to make some alterations in the parts. The earlier score was indeed sufficient for me—but any strange conductor would scarcely find his way through it. I hope Herbeck will be pleased with the instrumentation of the Schubert Marches. I fancy I have been successful in this little work, and I shall continue it further, as it offers much attraction to me. The four other Marches will follow shortly, which should make the half- dozen complete.

Cornelius arrived here the day before yesterday. His friendly attachment to you is a very warm and sincerely devoted one. On me Cornelius's pure mind and thoroughly honorable disposition always have the most beneficial effect; but it is especially welcome to me just now to hear more of you from him, and thus to be more with you.

Be as good to me as you are dear to my heart!

F. Liszt

Weymar, December 28th, 1859

229. To Josef Dessauer

[Autograph in the possession of Herr Von Hannen, painter in Venice.—The addressee ("Maitre Favilla," as George Sand named her friend) was known as the composer of refined songs (1798-1876). Three of these Liszt transcribed (1847, Berlin, Schlesinger).]

Dear honored Friend,

It is possible that the delicacy of your

427

perception may have brought you much trouble, but it assures you a soft place in the better region of the heart of your friends. This I again felt in reading your dear letter.

Accept, therefore, the heartfelt thanks of your old friend, whose "manly formed nature" must further prove itself; he has still many duties to fulfill and more than one battle to fight. May the Cross remain his support, his strength, and his shield!

Whatever fatality also may hang over me, be assured of the faithful attachment of your

F. Liszt

Weymar, December 30th, 1859

The crucifix from you (after the Gran Mass) has grown still dearer to me!—

When I have finished with some works which cannot be postponed any longer, Daniel shall receive his Requiena.

230. To Wilkoszewshi, Secretary of the Concerts of the "Hofcapelle" in Munich.

[From a copy in Liszt's own handwriting (amongst the letters to
 Brendel)]

Dear Sir,

The performance of new works on the part of so renowned an orchestra as that of Munich must ever remain a mark of special attention for the composers. But I must rate it still higher that, in face of the strong prejudice against my name, one of my ill-famed Symphonic Poems should have been included in the programme of the concerts of the Munich Hofcapelle.

It is ill preaching to deaf ears, and it is well known that there is no worse deafness than that of people who will not hear. Hence it is that the Festklange, as well as the Mass and everything that I and others better than my humble self have been able to compose, is prejudiced. But the more unseemly and malicious factiousness may show itself against new works, the more am I laid under a grateful obligation to those who do not accept as their artistic criterion the injustice inflicted on me.

Time levels all things, and I can quietly wait until people are more occupied in learning to know and to hear my scores than in condemning and hissing them. Mean-spirited, blackguard tricks, even when played in concert-rooms and newspaper reports, are no arguments worthy of a lasting import.

I beg you, dear sir, to convey to General Music-Director Lachner my best thanks for his well-meant sentiments towards me, and I remain, with high esteem, yours very sincerely,

F. Liszt

Weymar, January 15th, 1860.

231. To Johann von Herbeck.

[Received, according to him, on January 26th, 1860]

Dear Friend,

On getting back from Berlin yesterday evening I find your letter, which has given me especial pleasure by the assurance that the "Prometheus" choruses and, the instrumentation of the "Schubert Marches" fulfill your expectations. You shall very shortly receive two more "Schubert Marches" (the "Funeral March" in E flat minor, and the "Hungarian

March" in C minor out of the "Hungarian Divertissement". [Op. 40, No. 5, and "Marcia" from Op. 54] They could be played one immediately after the other.

The "Prometheus" choruses, together with the "Symphonic Poem" which goes before them (and which has been published by Hartel as No. 5), were composed in July 1850 for the Herder Festival, and were performed in the theater here on the eve of that festival. My pulses were then all beating feverishly, and the thrice- repeated cry of woe of the Oceanides, the Dryads, and the Infernals echoed in my ears from all the trees and lakes of our park.

In my work I strove after an ideal of the antique, which should be represented, not as an ancient skeleton, but as a living and moving form. A beautiful stanza of Andre Chenier,

"Sur des pensers nouveaux faisons des vers antiques," ["On modern thoughts let us fashion verses antique."]

served me for precept, and showed me the way to musical plastic art and symmetry.

The favorable opinion you have formed of the work in reading it through is a token to me that I have not altogether failed—I hope that the performance will not spoil your sympathy for it. I leave the direction, with the utmost confidence, entirely in your hands.—You always hit on the right thing, and navigate satisfactorily with your entire forces the occasional difficulties of the dissonant entries, and of the pathetic delivery which is absolutely essential in several places. It would certainly be a great pleasure to me, dear friend, if I could be present at the performance in Vienna on the 26th February, to enjoy your intelligent and inspired performance, but I am prevented from doing this by various circumstances (an explanation of which would lead me too far).

I beg you therefore not to induce the directors to invite me, because I might not be in a position to make my excuses. So please do you undertake the office of unchaining Prometheus in Vienna; this labour of Hercules will become you well [Footnote below]. There are certainly no powerful eagles to hack and rend in pieces the Titan's liver—but there is a whole host of ravens and creeping vermin ready to do it.—Once more best thanks and greetings from your most highly esteeming and very devoted

F. Liszt

[It took place on the 26th February, 1860. Herbeck notes as follows about it in his diary: "Prometheus, Symphonic Poem, pleased fairly. Chorus of Tritons pleased extremely. The Vintagers' and Reapers' choruses and concluding chorus pleased, but of course there was a formally organized opposition hissing. They had sworn the overthrow of this music, without even knowing a note of it."]

232. To Dr. Franz Brendel.

So then it has happened well that the editor of the Neue Zeitschrift has also become the editor of my "Gesammelte Lieder." Best thanks, dear friend, for the means you have taken to promote this. Kahnt has only to come to an understanding with Schlesinger; I on my side do not wish to place any limitation on his rights. Whether a transcription of this or that song may be made I do not know; if this should be the case I will only beg Kahnt to let me know of any such chance transcriptions before allowing them to appear, mainly because it would not be pleasant to me if any really too stupid arrangements should come out. This is only a matter of artistic consideration—beyond that I have neither restriction nor reservation to make to the proposed edition. As soon as Kahnt is in order with Schlesinger I am satisfied with everything. This or that song may then appear singly, or transcribed for guitar or zither; so much the better if Kahnt can thereby make it pay. N.B.—I should be glad if, in bringing out the songs singly, the same outside cover could be employed as in the complete edition, on account of the index. Probably Kahnt will say nothing against this, as the back of the cover serves as an advertisement of the entire collection of songs.

Yesterday evening Fraulein Berghaus (a daughter of the Potsdam professor) sang two numbers, Freudvoll and leidvoll and Es muss ein Wunderbares sein (out of the sixth part), at a concert given by Singer and Cossmann. I had indeed forbidden it, because this winter I will not have my name put on any concert programme at all—but her exquisite delivery of these songs, which were also received with approbation, reconciled me to it.

At the last Court concert in Berlin Fraulein Genast [A highly gifted singer, afterwards Frau Dr. Merian in Weimar] selected the "Loreley" as her concluding song, and the Frau Princess Victoria expressed herself very favorably about it, remarking that a Schubert spirit breathed in the composition.

One of these days Fraulein Genast is again singing the "Loreley" at the Philharmonic Concert in Hamburg. Otten has specially begged her to do so. The same gentleman wrote about eighteen months ago to Frau von Milde that he must beg to remark "that in regard to the choice of compositions to be performed Robert Schumann is the extreme limit to whom his programme could extend!"

I cannot quite remember whether I sent Gotze a copy of my songs. Please ask him, and if I have not yet done so let me know. Gotze has a special claim to them, for in earlier years he had the courage to sing several of my nonentities—and I will see that he has a copy at once. At the same time ask Fraulein Gotze also whether she has received the copy of the Ballade Leonore. [Liszt had composed this melodrama for Auguste Gotze, and frequently performed it, as well as his later melodramas, with her.] From several places (and quite lately from Carlsruhe and Brunswick) orders for this Ballade have come to me, which—between ourselves—are not convenient to me. My copyist has already had to make at least nine copies of it, which is a pretty good expense. Nevertheless a tenth shall willingly be made, if the one which was intended for Fraulein Gotze did not reach her, of which I am somewhat in doubt, owing to the many demands which the Leonore has brought with it, and which have made me somewhat confused.

It would really be the best for me if Kahnt or Schuberth would save me the trouble of making further copies by publishing the "Leonore". But I should not wish in any way to incommode the publisher, and certainly not to offer anything without knowing that it would be welcome. Under present circumstances a very pronounced reserve has become my rule. My business is simply to continue working unremittingly, and quietly to await the rest.

Accordingly I submit myself without difficulty to your experience as editor in regard to my Munich letter [To Wilkoszewski]— although I could maintain good grounds for publishing it. Certainly it is always the gentlemanly thing entirely to ignore certain things and people. You may therefore be quite right in putting aside all other considerations; and as I am convinced of your most sincere friendship I willingly leave you to decide whether my coming forward in such matters is of use or not. In case you had thought it advisable for my letter to be printed in the "Neue Zeitschrift" (which I left to your judgment), it would have had of necessity to be printed without the slightest alteration, because I have purposely written it thus clearly to Herr W., and any alteration in it might be taken as cowardice (which is far from me). But probably it is better to abandon the matter for a while, and to be somewhat more severe on another occasion. The pack of ragamuffins has richly deserved to be treated as ragamuffins!

This evening is Wagner's first concert in Paris. I expect little good to him from it, and consider such a step on Wagner's part as a mistake. In consequence of this opinion our correspondence is for the time suspended. More about this viva voce—as well as about "Tristan and Isolde." A performance of the Opera was desired—that is to say, commanded for the 8th April (the birthday of the Grand Duchess). But Frau von Milde cannot undertake the chief part —and on that account the parts and score sent to us from Carlsruhe will be sent back again at once!

Has Wagner given his opinion more decidedly about a "Tristan" performance in Leipzig? Can you let me know the contents of his letter?

With heartfelt greetings, your

F. Liszt

Weymar, January 25th, 1860

If you should see Schuberth, tell him that I have something to communicate to him that would perhaps repay him for the trouble of coming to see me here for a couple of hours. I have no intention of coming to Leipzig for the present. Tell him that delays of this kind make me "nervos" [nervous] (He knows what the word "nervos" means with me.)

233. To Friedrich Hebbel

[Communicated by Dr. Felix Bamberg, from the original]

The words which you write to me bear the two-fold eloquence of the praiseworthy man in the fore-rank of Art, and of the friend dearly loved and highly respected by me. Accept my warmest thanks for it, and please excuse me for not having told you sooner what a strengthening and healing effect your letter made on me. Work of all sorts and a long absence from here occasioned this delay. In the interim I was often with you in thought; only the day before yesterday I read to the Princess your two glorious Sonnets an den Kunstler ["To the Artist"], "Ob Du auch bilden magst, was unverganglich"—"Und ob mich diese Zweifel brennen müssen?"["Whether thou canst form what is imperishable": "And whether these doubts must burn me."]—

From Weymar I have nothing interesting nor especially agreeable to tell you. This winter will pass away pretty quietly and insignificantly at the theater, with repertoire works and pieces that will bring in money, and in society with the customary pleasures. A new drama by Rost, "Ludwig der Eiserne," made some sensation, as is peculiar to the very popular productions of this author, who has achieved a public-house notoriety here. The nobles ought to have appeared in it yoked to the plough, but on Dingelstedt's advice Rost toned down that scene!—A translation by Frau Schuselka (who has performed here sometimes) of the "Pere prodigue" of Dumas fils was to have come on the boards; but it appears that there are scruples about making such very ominous demands on the customary powers of digestion of our un-lavish fathers of families! Amongst other inconveniences the piece also contains logarithms, to which the respectable German Philistine cannot attain.

As regards myself, I am quietly waiting for the spring, when I shall in all probability move on further—of course not to renew my occupation of conducting, as it is said I shall do in Munich, Berlin, or elsewhere—an occupation I have gladly given up; —but in order to be able to pursue my work further than I am able to do in Weymar, which to me is a more important matter.

Remember me most kindly to your wife, and be assured that I remain ever in truest devotion yours most faithfully,

F. Liszt

Weymar, February 5th, 1860.

234. To Dr. Franz Brendel

[February 1860]

Dear Friend,

Although as a general rule I consider that it is not the business of the Neue Zeitschrift to go in for polemics, yet it seems to me that the little notice that Hanslick has put in No. 49 of the Vienna Presse, Saturday, the 18th February, is of such a kind that one must not ignore it.

The Presse is a paper with a tremendous circulation in the monarchy, and Hanslick counts among the leaders of our opponents; it would therefore be worth while to make an exception by coming forward on this occasion, unless (which I cannot as yet believe) your Vienna correspondent has been guilty of the mischievous conduct which Hanslick so severely reports. This point must first be made clear—whether in the third (or possibly an earlier) concert of Herr Boskowitz an exchange of a Schumann for a Liszt piece occurred. [Instead of the Liszt piece "Au bord d'une source," which stood on the programme, Boskowitz had played the "Jagdlied" from Schumann's "Waldscenen," which did not prevent a correspondent (namely, the correspondent of the Deutsche Musikzeitung, as the Neue Zeitschrift of 24th February, 1860, gave out) from loudly carping at the supposed Liszt composition.] Possibly also your correspondent made use of the expression "The Vienna Press" in general, and did not refer specially to the paper Die

Presse, [This was actually the case] or was referring to other remarks of Hanslick's...

This is only the second time for many years past, dear friend, that I have drawn your attention to notices in the paper. On the first occasion, when the Augsburger Allgemeine gave that infamous correspondence about the venality of the Neue Zeitschrift, your striking answer gave the most convincing proof of what part the opponents were studying to play!—I hope it will be possible to despatch Hanslick's notice (which I enclose) in a similar fashion. But it is necessary to get at the exact truth before inveighing against them—for Hanslick is no easy opponent, and if one once attacks him it must be with suitable weapons and without giving quarter. The words "denunciation proceedings," "Gessler caps of the party of the future," and especially the concluding sentence, "As long as Herr Brendel," etc., are a challenge, which deserves more than a faint-hearted reproof! I would also advise you to send a duplicate of your reply to the Presse in Vienna, at the same time as it is published in the Zeitschrift. The editors of the Presse will be certain to reject it, according to the usual method of the clique impartiality of those gentlemen. But the scandalous examples of the latter will be thus increased by one more.

It is easy also to see beforehand that Hanslick will not let the matter rest at this first notice, and will continue the discussion.

Hearty greetings.

F.L.P.S.—In case your Vienna correspondent should be quite in the wrong, it would be better simply to be silent and wait for a better opportunity.

235. To Dr. Franz Brendel

[March or April 1860]

Dear Friend,

Do not blame me if this time I follow Pohl's example and keep you waiting for the promised article. I have been working at it pretty continuously during the past week, and the sketch of it is quite ready; but I am not quite satisfied with it, and about Berlioz and Wagner I must say the right thing in the right manner. [No article of the kind by Liszt is contained in the Neue Zeitschrift for the year in question; probably it was unfinished.] This duty requires me to spend more time on it, and unfortunately I have so much on hand this week that it is hardly possible for me to busy myself with polemics. Tomorrow is again a grand Court concert; Bronsart and Fraulein Stark arrived yesterday; Frau von Bulow comes today, and I expect Hans on Saturday. Besides this, there is still more important work for me, which will take up my time entirely till the end of this month.

Well, I will see to it that, if possible, Berlioz and Wagner do not remain forgotten!—

Let me first of all answer your questions.

Whether it would be desirable to hold the second Tonkunstler- Versammlung this year, I already left it to you, at our last meeting, to decide. In my opinion we might wait till next year without injury to the affair. [This was done.] As long as I myself have not made a secure and firm footing in Weymar, I cannot invite you to convene the meeting here. If you hold to the dates of the 17th, 18th, and

19th June, we are bound to Leipzig, where I can then tell you with certainty whether Weymar will suit for the next meeting.

It goes without saying that you, dear friend, must arrange about everything that I can undertake and do for the Tonkunstler- Versammlung. Only my personal help as conductor must be excepted. At our next consultation we shall easily come to an understanding as to the desirability of one conductor or several.

I would indicate and emphasize, as absolutely necessary, the performance of new works by Bulow, Draseke, Bronsart, Singer, Seifriz, etc. I think I understand and can manage the art of programme-making in a masterly manner. When once matters have got so far, I will fix with you the programme of the three performances.

I agree with the choice of the "Prometheus," and at the religious performance, if the latter is not filled up with one single great work, I would suggest perhaps the "Beatitudes," or the 13th Psalm (the former last about ten minutes, the latter twenty-five).

Will you therefore decide definitely where the Tonkunstler- Versammlung shall be held this year and the date of it, about which I have nothing further to say? We will then discuss and settle the rest together.

You will find my remarks as to the statute scheme on the last page of it.

With hearty greetings, your

F. Liszt

A. The revising of the "Leonore" shall be attended to immediately.

B. I shall welcome Fraulein Brauer most cordially.

C. I recommend to you again the manuscripts of Pasque and

 Councillor Muller. Have you replied to Muller?

Herewith is a letter from Weitzmann (14th June, 1859), in which you will find much worthy of consideration and use.

Important! N.B.—When you convene the Tonkunstler-Versammlung, add to it at once the following: "For the foundation of the German Universal Musical Society." This is the principal aim, toward the accomplishment of which we have to work.

[Liszt was, as Princess Wittgenstein distinctly told the editor, the actual founder of the "German Universal Musical Society." He conceived the idea and plan of it, and it was only at his wish that Brendel gave his name to it, and undertook to be president, etc.]

236. To Louis Kohler.

My dear, excellent friend,

You have given me a rare pleasure. Your articles on my "Gesammelte Lieder" are a reproduction, replete with spirit and mind, of what I, alas! must feel and bear much more than I can venture to write down! Reviews such as these are not matters of every-day reviewers—nor must one shame you with such a title.

Accept my warmest thanks for them, and allow me to present to you herewith a couple of little singable things in manuscript. They were jotted down after reading your articles, and, if I mistake not, they spring from the melody of speech. In any case, dear friend, you have a special right to them— as well as to the sincere esteem and faithful attachment with which I remain your

F. Liszt

Weymar, July 5th, 1860

Towards the end of October the two Symphonic Poems, Nos. 10 and 11, which have still to be published—"Hamlet" and the "Hunnenschlacht" [The Battle of the Huns]—will appear at Hartel's; and when these are out all the twelve monsters will have appeared. Shortly afterwards will follow Faust, the choruses to Prometheus, a couple of Psalms, and a new number of songs. I will send you the whole lot. But if possible arrange so that we may soon meet again—at the latest at the next Tonkunstler- Versammlung next year, at which we cannot possibly do without you.

237. To Eduard Liszt

Dearest Eduard,

You remain perpetually in the home of my heart, not at all in countless company, but all the more in picked company. When I think I have done anything pretty good I think of you and rejoice that what I have done will be a pleasure to you—and in the hours when sadness and sorrow take hold of me you are again my comfort and strength by your loving insight into my innermost wishes and yearnings! My thanks, my warmest and truest thanks, to you for all the sustaining and soothing friendship that you show to me. It is to me a special token of Heaven's favor to me, and I pray to God that He may unite us for ever in Himself!—

Cornelius writes me word that you will probably come to Weymar towards the end of the summer. That will be a great pleasure to me; I often feel as if I must have a talk with you out of the depths of my heart—for with writing, as you know, I don't exactly get on. I expect the Princess towards the middle of August. Meanwhile I receive good and satisfactory tidings from Rome. I hope all will turn out for the best.

In these latter weeks I have been completely absorbed in my composing. If I mistake not, my power of production has materially increased, while some things in me are made clear and others are more concentrated. By the end of October the last two of the Symphonic Poems will be out ("Hamlet" and the "Hunnenschlacht"). Then come the Psalms, which you do not yet know, and which I much want you to know-and also a new number of songs which will please you. I shall then work at the Oratorio St. Elizabeth, exclusive of all else, and get it completely finished before the end of the year. May God in His grace accept my endeavors!—

I must express myself not entirely in accord beforehand with your plan for your son, although I consider your way of looking at the present state of things by no means a wrong one. I am also convinced that, when it comes to settling definitely, the talents and capabilities, as well as the bent of mind, of your child will be satisfactory to you. If the young one has a mind for a uniform—well, let it be so. To cut one's way through life with a sabre is indeed for the most part pleasanter than any other mode…The business paper for the Princess I will keep till her return, unless you write to me to forward it to her in Rome.

May I bother you with a commission for provisions? Forgive me for the way in which I am always making use of you, but I do so want to make a little joke for Bulow, and I have no one now in Vienna who could help me in it except just you. It is about sending a pretty considerable amount of Hungarian Paprika [Hungarian, Turkish, or Spanish pepper from Hungary] and a little barrel of Pfefferoni (little green Hungarian pepper-plants preserved in vinegar). Please ask Capellmeister Doppler where these things are to be procured genuine, and send them me as soon as possible to Weymar. I won't hide from you that I intend to go shares with Bulow, as I am particularly fond of Paprika and Pfefferoni. So take care that there is enough sent, and that it arrives in good condition.— And as this will give you occasion to see Doppler, give him my warm thanks for the instrumentation of the Pester Carnaval (in which musical Paprika and Pfefferoni are not wanting). He has again been most successful in it, and I intend to push on in the autumn the publication of the six Rhapsodies for orchestra, for which indeed I shall have to obtain the permission or consent of three separate publishers (Schott, Senff, Haslinger)—a circumstance which may of itself occasion some delay, especially if the gentlemen behave in regard to my wish as Spina did in so unpleasantly surprising a manner in regard to the instrumentation of the Schubert Marches. To tell you this incident briefly: I wrote to Dachs and asked him to request Spina in my name either to publish the three Marches himself in score—without any remuneration for me!—or else to give me permission to bring them out through another publisher. Spina's answer, as Dachs gave me to understand, was that he could not consent to either the one or the other of my proposals (which were certainly reasonable enough)! And thus I must wait until Spina can hit on a better plan! When I have an opportunity, I shall venture to apply to him direct.

For the present, in consideration of the fact that Paprika and Pfefferoni make one very thirsty, a barrel of Gumpoldskirchner (with a slightly sharp, flowery after-taste) would be very welcome to me, if by chance you are able to find a good kind and cheap.—Forgive me for all these Lucullian extravagances!—

I will write soon to Cornelius. Give him my heartfelt greetings. Also please remember me kindly to Dr. Kulke. I will give him my thanks by letter on the first opportunity for his Prometheus articles, as I would have already done through Cornelius, had he not started so suddenly.—

Now farewell, dearest Eduard. Spare yourself and take care of your health. Assure your dear wife of my heartfelt attachment, and kiss your children for your faithful

F. Liszt

Weymar, July 9th, 1860
238. To Ingeborg Stark
[Summer, 1860]

If a sort of idiosyncrasy against letters did not hold me back I should have told you long ago what pleasure your charming letter from Paris gave me, and what a sincere part I have taken in your late successes, dear enchantress. But you must know all that far better than I could succeed in writing it.

So let us talk of something else—for instance, Baron Vietinghoff's [He took the noun de plume Boris Scheel, and in 1885 he performed his opera "Der Daemon" in St. Petersburg, which originated twenty years before that of Rubinstein.] Overture, which you were so kind as to send me, and which I have run through with B[ronsart] during his short stay at Weymar—too short to please me, but doubtless much too long for you!—The Overture in question is not wanting either in imagination or spirit. It is the work of a man musically much gifted, but who has not yet sufficiently handled his subject. When you have an opportunity, will you give my best compliments to the author, and give him also the little scale of chords that I add? It is nothing but a very simple development of the scale, terrifying for all the long and protruding ears, [Figure demonstrating a descending whole-tone scale] that Mr. de Vietinghoff employs in the final presto of his overture (page 66 of the score).

Tausig makes a pretty fair use of it in his Geisterschaff; and in the classes of the Conservatoire, in which the high art of the mad dog is duly taught, the existing elementary exercises of

446

the piano methods, [Figure: Musical example; a five-finger exercise] which are of a sonorousness as disagreeable as they are incomplete, ought to be replaced by this one, which will thus form the unique basis of the method of harmony—all the other chords, in use or not, being unable to be employed except by the arbitrary curtailment of such and such an interval.

In fact it will soon be necessary to complete the system by the admission of quarter and half-quarter tones until something better turns up!—

Behold the abyss of progress into which the abominable "Musicians of the Future" precipitate us!

Take care that you do not let yourself be contaminated by this pest of Art!

For a week past it has done nothing but rain here, and I have been obliged to have fires and stoves lighted in the house. If by chance you are favored with such a temperature at Schwalbach, I invite you to profit by it to make some new Fugues, and to make up, by plenty of work for the pedals, for the pedestrian exercise of which you would be necessarily deprived.

B., to whom I beg you to give my cordial and kind remembrances, led me to hope that you will stay a couple of days at Weymar after your cure. If this could be so arranged I for my part should be delighted, and should pick a quarrel with you (even if it were a German quarrel!) if you were not completely persuaded of it!

Remember me most affectionately to la Sagesse, and do me the kindness to count, under all circumstances, on

Your very sincerely devoted

F. Liszt

239. To Dr. Franz Brendel

Dear Friend,

Your last proposition is the best. Come quite simply to me at Weymar. As I am now quite alone at home we can hold our conference and arrange matters most conveniently at the Altenburg. I am writing at the same time to Bulow at Wiesbaden (where he is giving a concert tomorrow, Friday), to beg him to arrange with you about the day on which the meeting shall be held here. You two have to decide this. Of course you will stay with me. There shall also be a room in readiness for Kahnt.

With regard to Wagner's pardon [Wagner had been exiled from Germany for political reasons.] I am expecting reliable information shortly. It seems strange that the Dresden papers should not have been the first to give the official announcement, and that an act of pardon of H.M. the King of Saxony should be made known through the "Bohemia" (in Prague). Wagner has not yet written to me.

To our speedy meeting. Heartily your

F. Liszt

August 9th, 1860

240. To Princess Caroline Sayn-Wittgenstein.

[Portions of the above were published in the Neue Zeitschrift fur
Musik of 4th May, 1887.]

Weymar, September 14th, 1860

I am writing this down on the 14th September, the day on which the Church celebrates the Festival of the Holy Cross. The denomination of this festival is also that of the glowing and mysterious feeling which has pierced my entire life as with a sacred wound.

Yes, "Jesus Christ on the Cross," a yearning longing after the Cross and the raising of the Cross, —this was ever my true inner calling; I have felt it in my innermost heart ever since my seventeenth year, in which I implored with humility and tears that I might be permitted to enter the Paris Seminary; at that time I hoped it would be granted to me to live the life of the saints and perhaps even to die a martyr's death. This, alas! has not happened—yet, in spite of the transgressions and errors which I have committed, and for which I feel sincere repentance and contrition, the holy light of the Cross has never been entirely withdrawn from me. At times, indeed, the refulgence of this Divine light has overflowed my entire soul.—I thank God for this, and shall die with my soul fixed upon the Cross, our redemption, our highest bliss; and, in acknowledgment of my belief, I wish before my death to receive the holy sacraments of the Catholic, Apostolic, and Romish Church, and thereby to attain the forgiveness and remission of all my sins. Amen.

I thank my mother with reverence and tender love for her continual proofs of goodness and love. In my youth people called me a good son; it was certainly no special merit on my part, for how would it have been possible not to be a good son with so faithfully self-sacrificing a mother?—Should I die before her, her blessing will follow me into the grave.

I owe it to my cousin Eduard Liszt (Dr. and Royal County Councillor of Justice in Vienna) to repeat here my warm and grateful affection for him, and to thank him for his faithfulness and staunch friendship. By his worth, his talents, and his character he does honor to the name I bear, and I pray God for His blessings on him, his wife, and his children.

Among our Art-comrades of the day there is one name which has already become glorious, and which will become so ever more and more—Richard Wagner. His genius has been to me a light which I have followed—and my friendship for Wagner has always been of the character of a noble passion. At a certain period (about ten years ago) I had visions of a new Art-period for Weymar, similar to that of Carl August, in which Wagner and I should have been the leading spirits, as Goethe and Schiller were formerly, —but unfavorable circumstances have brought this dream to nothing.

To my daughter Cosima I bequeath the sketch of Steinle representing St. Francois de Paul, my patron saint; he is walking on the waves, his mantle spread beneath his feet, holding in one hand a red-hot coal, the other raised, either to allay the tempest or to bless the menaced boatmen, his look turned to heaven, where, in a glory, shines the redeeming word "Caritas."— This sketch has always stood on my writing-table. Near it there is an ancient hour-glass in carved wood with four glasses, which is also for my daughter Cosima. Two other things which have belonged to me are to be given as a remembrance to my cousin Eduard Liszt and to my much-loved and brave son-in-law Hans von Bulow.

Some of the members of our Union of the "New German School"—to whom I remain deeply attached—must also receive some remembrance of me; Hans von Bronsart, Peter Cornelius (in Vienna), E. Lassen (in Weymar), Dr. Franz Brendel (in Leipzig), Richard Pohl (in Weymar), Alex. Ritter (in Dresden), Felix Draseke (in Dresden), Professor Weitzmann (in Berlin), Carl Tausig (from Warsaw) — either a ring with my sign-manual, a portrait, or coat-of-arms.— May they continue the work that we have begun—the honor of Art and the inner worth of the artist constrains them to do so. Our cause cannot fail, though it have for the present but few supporters.—

One of my jewels set as a ring is to be sent to Madame Caroline d'Artigaux, nee Countess de St. Cricq (at Pau, France). To the Princess Constantin Hohenlohe (nee Princess Marie Wittgenstein) I bequeath the ivory crucifix (cinque-cento) which was given to me by my kind patron the Prince of Hohenzollern-Hechingen—also a pair of studs with five different stones, which form the five initials of my name.

And now I kneel down once more to pray "Thy kingdom come; Thy will be done on earth as it is in heaven; forgive us our trespasses as we forgive them that trespass against us; and deliver us from evil. Amen."

F. Liszt

Written the 14th September, 1860, on the Festival of the raising of the Holy Cross.

SUPPLEMENT:

To Herr Gross, a member of the Weymar Grand Ducal Royal Orchestra (trombone and double-bass player), who has for a number of years looked after the copying of my works and the arranging of the orchestral and voice parts of them in the library of the Altenburg, I bequeath a present of one hundred thalers for the faithful, devoted service he has rendered me.

To the names of my friends of the New German School is to be added one more, or rather I ought to have mentioned it first; it is that of Mr. Gaetano Belloni (in Paris).—He was my Secretary during the period of my concert tours in Europe, from 1841 to 1847, and was always my faithful and devoted servant and friend. He must not be forgotten. Moreover, whether he will or no, he belongs to the New German School, by his attachment to me, and also by the part he took later on in the Berlioz and Wagner concerts. I wish to be buried simply, without pomp, and if possible at night.—May light everlasting illumine my soul!

241. To Dr. Franz Brendel

September 20th, 1860

Dear Friend,

I send you by my friend Lassen [Born 1830, became Court music- director 1858, and Court conductor in Weimar after Liszt's withdrawal (1861); celebrated as a composer of songs] a little parcel of songs (eight numbers), which I beg you to give to Kahnt. Of several of them I have kept no copy—and

I therefore beg Kahnt not to lose them. As regards the numbering of them (the order of succession), they are to be kept as I noted down some time ago (on a bit of paper which I gave Kahnt when he was here).

I also add a Quartet for men's voices. It is the Verein song "Frisch auf zu neuem Leben," ["Uprouse to newer life."] written for the New Weymar Verein by Hoffmann von Fallersleben. The passage "von Philister Geschrei;" ["Of Philistine cry."] will probably amuse you, and the whole thing is kept rather popular and easy to be performed. If it does not make a bother let it be tried in Leipzig when you have an opportunity.

N.B.—If you think the designation on the title-page "Written and composed for the New Weymar Verein" will give offence, it can be left out, and the title can run simply, "Vereins Lied," by Hoffmann von Fallersleben, composed for male chorus by F. L. In any case I shall be glad if Kahnt can bring the little thing out soon, and will give some sort of illustrated title-page, expressive of the sense of the poem.

The remarks which I have added in pencil are to be engraved with it. I hope the printer will be able to read my bad writing—if not will you be so kind as to make it clear to him?

I am writing to Vienna today. The "Prometheus" parts and score will be sent to you immediately.

I expect Bronsart here at the end of this month..—.

Your statute-sketch is in all essential points as

judicious as it is practical. It offers a sure basis of operations for the next Tonkunstler-Versammlung, where assuredly the great majority of the members will agree with your proposals. Then the point will be to work on vigorously towards the accomplishment, and to put aside the much that is "rotten in the State of Denmark."

Before the Euterpe concerts begin I shall in any case see you.

Next Sunday I go to Sondershausen, where Berlioz' "Harold," a new

Oboe Concerto by Stein, Schumann's "Genoveva" Overture, the

Introduction to "Tristan and Isolde," and my "Mazeppa" will be

given. The latter piece is popular to wit…in Sondershausen!—

Very sonderhauslich, [A play on the words Sondershausen and sonderbar = strange] isn't it?

Hearty greetings to your wife from your

F. Liszt

P.S.—The ninth song by Cornelius is still wanting. [The song "Wieder mocht' ich Dir begegnen" ("Once again I fain would meet thee")] But in the meantime the printing can be going on. The nine numbers form the seventh part of the "Gesammelte Lieder." If Kahnt wishes, each song can be published separately, especially the Zigeuner; Nonnenwerth, etc.

Draseke has been with me a couple of days, and is coming shortly to you. His works captivate me in a special degree, and personally I am very fond of him, which indeed I also was formerly, but this time still more. Capacity and character are there in abundance.

242. To Eduard Liszt

Weymar, September 20th, 1860

The true and loving character of your whole being, as well as of your letter, dearest Eduard, touches me always with joy, and fortifies me; but with your letter of today is mingled also somewhat of sadness. It is conceivable that the ebb of the Milanese and Hungarian Civil Service employes, with its effect on Vienna, has acted as a check upon your very justifiable and well- founded prospects of promotion. This is all the more to be regretted as, years ago, I was assured many times from a trustworthy official source that your suitability and deserts were far above the official position that you hold. Without wanting to preach to you unseasonably, let me assure you of my sincere sympathy in the disappointments you have so undeservedly to bear, and remind you also how things generally go badly in this world with the better and best sort of men. One must not let oneself be embittered by bitter experiences, and one must bear all sorts of mortifications without mortification.

I will also repeat for your amusement a droll saying of General Wrangel's: "A man should never vex himself;—if there must be vexation anywhere, let him rather vex somebody else!"—The best way, in case of extreme necessity to vex others, is to bear imperturbably many an injury and unpleasantness—without prejudice to any defense or help that may offer, when opportunity occurs—for we were not born to sleep our lives away!—

Under the given circumstances one cannot do otherwise than agree with your resolution to let your son go into the Military Academy when he is eleven years old. May this young Franz bring you all the happiness that your older Franziskus wishes you from his innermost heart.—[He did not become a soldier, but the renowned Professor of Law now teaching at the University of Halle.]

In the expectation of this we will comfort ourselves by swallowing Pfefferoni and Paprika together with Gumpoldskirchner. Have I ever told you how excellent the latter, which you had chosen just right, tasted?

It is almost impossible to further B.'s affairs. You think it would be right to let his drama be examined by a "competent authority." Undoubtedly; but that will not help him, so long as this competent authority, who here could be none other than Dingelstedt, is not able to help him any further. As far as I know our Intendant he will NOT condescend to perform King Alphonso; but none the less I will speak to Dingelstedt about it, and will prevail on him first of all to write a few lines to B., as the rules of courtesy demand. I scarcely hope to effect more than this, glad as I should be if it happened so, for you know that I am glad to show myself obliging. It is doubtful also whether B. will have much better chances with other Intendants— for, as it seems, the good man has decidedly bad luck. Please make my excuses to him if I do not answer his letter other than by a silent condolence (in German Beleidsbezeugung!).—It has become horribly difficult nowadays to make a footing on the boards —"which signify the world"—especially for writers of classic tragic-plays, whose lot is far more a tragic than a playing one!—Things certainly are not much better with most of the Opera composers, although that genre is the most thankful one of all. Without a strong dose of obstinacy and resignation there is no doing anything. In spite of the comforting proverb "Geduldige Schafe gehen viele in den Stall," [The English equivalent seems to be "Patience and application will carry us through."] there is for the greater number and most patient of the sheep no more room in the fold, to say nothing of food!— Thus the problem of the literary and artistic proletariat becomes from year to year more clamorous.

Your orchestral concert plan has surprised me very much, and I thank you from my heart for this fresh proof of your energy and goodwill. Yet for this year I think it would be more judicious to pause, for several reasons which it would lead me rather too far to explain, and which, therefore, I prefer to reserve for a viva voce talk. They relate to (A) my personal position and something connected with it socially; (B) the position of musical matters among artists and in the Press, which not only influence but intimidate the public, disconcert it, and palm off upon it ears, with which it cannot hear. This temporary very bad state of things I think I have, alas! at all times quite rightly acknowledged, and, if I do not greatly mistake, it must surely soon perceptibly modify in our favor. Our opponents "triumph far more than they conquer us," as Tacitus says. They will not be able to hold their narrow, malicious, negative, and unproductive thesis much longer against our quiet, assured, positive progress in Art-works. A consoling and significant symptom of this is that they are no longer able to support their adherents among living and working composers, but devour them critically while the public is so indifferent. The resume of the whole criticism of the opposition may be summed up in the following words: "All the heroes of Art in past times find, alas! no worthy successors in our day." But our time will not give up its rights—and the rightful successors will prove themselves such!

More of this when we have an opportunity. You have doubtless heard that a similar plan to yours is in progress in Leipzig. My friend Bronsart undertakes the direction of the Euterpe concerts for this winter, and there will be some rows about it. We will await the result; if it should not be satisfactory, yet the matter is so arranged that it cannot do us any great harm. As regards Vienna I think it would be wisest to let this winter pass by without troubling ourselves about it. Messrs. B., V.B., and their associates may peacefully have Symphonies and other works performed there and mutually blow each other's trumpets.

I have still a request to make to you today, dearest Eduard. Persuade Herbeck to send the score and the chorus and orchestral part of my "Prometheus" at once to C.F. Kahnt, the music publisher in Leipzig. The work is fixed for performance at one of the Euterpe concerts, which will take place before Christmas of this year; so it is necessary that the choruses should be studied in time. Kahnt has already written to Herbeck and also to Spina— but as yet he has received neither an answer nor the parts and score of Prometheus that he wants.

Take the same opportunity of telling Herbeck that I should like once to hear the four Schubert Marches which I instrumented for him, and I beg him to send the score of them to me at Weymar.

Forgive me that I always trouble you with all sorts of commissions—but my Vienna acquaintances are so lazy and unreliable that I have no other alternative but to set you on everywhere..—.

Heartfelt greetings to your wife and children from your faithful and grateful

F. Liszt

P.S.—I have written something to Cornelius about my latest compositions, which he will tell you.

I expect the Princess here in October only. I will tell you, later on, much about her stay in Rome, some of which is agreeable.

243. To Hoffman von Fallersleben

My dear, honored Friend,

The melancholy tidings were reported to me by Grafe on Monday evening (in the New Weymar Verein). [Hoffmann, after he had obtained in May, 1860 the position of librarian to the Duke of Ratibor at Schloss Corvey, near Hoxter-on-the-Weser, lost his wife.] It came upon us all with a most mournful shock, and truly it needs no further words to assure you of my heartfelt sympathy in your grief!—Thank you for having thought of me. The Princess, who was always so attached to your dear good wife, has not yet returned from Rome—and I do not expect her till towards the end of November. Unfortunately I must remain here entirely until then—otherwise I should assuredly come at once to you…Forgive me, therefore, that only from afar can I tell you how sincerely and truly I remain your faithfully attached friend,

F. Liszt

October 30th, 1860

I have sent your charming birthday gift for October 22nd (text and music) to the Princess.

244. To Professor Franz Gotze in Leipzig

Dear, honored Friend,

Do not think me indiscreet if I say something to you about which you yourself must know best. The artistic gifts of your daughter are as rare as they are pronounced. I have heard her sing and declaim several times in the last few days, and each time with increasing interest. Will you not give her carte blanche, and grant your consent to the artistic career which is hers by nature and which can hardly be put aside? [Liszt, like others, was laboring under the mistake (for reasons which cannot be discussed here) that Gotze did not intend his daughter to pursue the career of an artiste, though he had had her educated both as a singer and dramatically.] I know that this may not be a very easy decision for you,—but, much as I usually refrain from giving advice of this kind, yet I cannot do otherwise than make an exception in this case, and intercede with you to let your daughter come out in public—because I am convinced that you will not regret having supported her with fatherly compliance in this.

Dr. Gille much wishes to gain your daughter

for the next concert in Jena. I think that a debut there would in any case do her no harm. Later on I shall ask you whether you will allow Auguste shortly to appear here at a Court concert.

Excuse my interference in so delicate a matter by reason of the sincere interest I take in your daughter, and the faithful friendship with which I remain Your unalterably sincerely attached

F. Liszt

Weymar, November 4, 1860

Send a telegram to Gille in reply—if possible, "Yes," as the concert takes place next Sunday.

245. To Dr. Franz Brendel

Dear Friend,

.—. I take a sincere interest in the progress of the Euterpe concerts—a progress which up to now has been favorable on the whole; you have the chief merit in this, just because it rests with you to neutralize difficult and opposing elements.

I rejoice much that Bronsart so thoroughly fulfills my expectations. He is a director-gentleman ["Gentleman" put in English by Liszt]. I shall hear more about the concerts through Weissheimer [A composer; was for some time second director of the Euterpe concerts], who is advertised here for the day after tomorrow; until now I have only heard something about them from Fraulein Hundt [A composer, at that time in Weimar; has since died] yesterday.

With best greetings, yours in all friendship,

F. Liszt

Weymar, November 16th, 1860

Will you be so kind as to send me at once a

couple of copies of
Muller's new brochure?

.—. If it is possible to hurry the bringing out of my seventh book of songs I shall be glad. Also the "Vereins-Lied."

Give my most friendly greetings to Gotze—and at the same time tell him that his daughter (of whose great artistic powers there is no doubt) sang and declaimed last Sunday in Jena with the greatest success. The vocal numbers were "two songs by Schumann," one of which was encored—and at the end of the concert she declaimed the Ballade Leonore (with my melodramatic pianoforte accompaniment).

Have you heard anything of Wagner? Rienzi is being studied here, and I have undertaken to conduct the rehearsals. With regard to the performance I have at once mentioned decidedly that nothing will induce me to make an exception and conduct it—consequently Musik-director Stor will conduct it.

246. To Dr. Franz Brendel

Dear Friend,

Since I have again had a conference with respect to the Tonkunstler-Versammlung in Weymar next August, I am happy to be able to tell you that not only will there be no obstacle to it, but that we may expect that much will be done to further the matter here. In your next announcement in the Neue Zeitschrift about the Tonkunstler-Versammlung you are therefore fully authorized to intimate the readiness of the artists, both vocal and instrumental, here and in the neighborhood (Jena, Eisenach,

Sondershausen, etc.), as also the favorable disposition of H.R.H. the Grand Duke, for the matter. This latter point must be mentioned with some formality, so that I can submit your article to my gracious master.

According to my opinion it would be well if, in this connection, you were to touch upon the musical antecedents of Weymar (performances of Wagner, Berlioz, Schumann), also the founding of the Academy of Painting by the Grand Duke which took place lately, and also the protectorate which H.R.H. has undertaken of the Allegemeine deutsche Schiller-Stiftung [The Universal German Schiller Scholarship] (the first place of which is to be Weymar next year).

Yours in all friendship,

F. Liszt

December 2nd, 1860

P.S.—With the next Tonkunstler-Versammlung I join three principal things:—

(1) The founding and establishing of the Tonkunstler-Vierein.

(2) That the States should take part (according to your idea) in the principal musical interests to be supported.

(3) The introduction and proposal of the projected music school. [Liszt was endeavoring at that time to found a music school in Weimar.]

247. To C.F. Kahnt, Music Publisher in Leipzig

[Kahnt was the publisher of the Neue Zeitschrift fur Musik for more than thirty years (ever since 1855); also the publisher of several of Liszt's compositions, co-founder and for many years cashier of the Allgemeine deutsche Musikvereins, and, after 1873, Councillor of Commission in Weimar.]

Dear Sir,

I send you herewith the proof-sheets of the seventh book of my songs, and of the "Vereins-Lied" for the chorus of men's voices. I quite concur in the new title-page, which can also be employed for each single song. It is better than the former one, only I shall be glad if there are no other advertisements on the back side, and it is left bare.

On the 17th of this month the Neu-Weymar-Verein intends to give a little Beethoven-Festival, and the "Vereins-Lied" is included in the programme. I beg, therefore, that you will send me some proof-copies by the 12th December—if it is not possible to get the edition ready so soon.—.

The three Chansons and arrangement of the three Quartets for men's voices (published in Basle) are all completed in my head; you shall have them as a new manuscript at the end of the week. There is no hurry about the publishing of the Chansons and Quartets (probably I shall entitle them "Aus dem Zelt," or "Aus dem Lager," three songs, etc.). ["From the Tent," or "From the Camp." They were eventually entitled "Geharnischte Lieder" ("Songs in Armour").] But as you are kind enough to place some reliance on my songs, I should like to commit to you next a little wish of mine—namely, that my Schiller Song (which appeared in the Illustrated in November last) may soon be published, and also a somewhat repaying (rather sweet!) Quartet for men's voices, with a tenor solo—"Huttelein, still and klein." It has been already sung with success by the Vienna Manner-Gesangverein, and by some Liedertafeln. I add the two manuscripts to the parcel of proofs—perhaps you will take an opportunity of trying both the little things in a small circle. If Herr Professor Gotze would have the kindness to undertake the solo-part in the "Huttelein" I should be very much obliged to him. Herr Wallenreiter might make a good thing of the baritone solo-part in the "Schiller Song."

In case you should be disposed to acquiesce in my wish, and to undertake the publishing of the two or three men's choruses, I would propose to you to bring them out as the opening numbers of a short succession of "Compositions for Male Voices," and also, as with the Songs, to give them a title page (with a statement of the different numbers—to which the Basle Quartets might also be added; thus six numbers up to now). Do not fear, dear sir, an over-productiveness in this genre on my part! But if by chance one or other number of these Quartets should have some spread, I should not dislike to write a couple more, either secular or sacred. Among the latter I hope that the Psalm "The Heavens declare," which will be performed next summer at a great Festival of Song, will produce a good effect.

Pray pardon my verbosity—it is not usually my way to indulge in unnecessary words; and accept, dear Sir, the assurance of the well-known sentiments with which I remain,

Yours most truly,

F. Liszt

Weymar, December 2nd, 1860

The first performance of "Rienzi" is announced for the second day of the Christmas holidays. I have engaged to conduct the rehearsals, but at the same time have positively refused to conduct the performances. Herr Musik-director Stor undertakes that. [After the opposition of a coterie that was inimical to Liszt, to which, as is well known, Cornelius's "Barber of Baghdad" fell a sacrifice, Liszt had finally resigned his post as conductor of the theater.]

248. To the Music Publisher C.F. Kahnt

.—. With regard to the publishing of my Songs for men's voices I do not wish in the least to hurry you, dear sir—yet I should be glad if you could advertise the things soon—and possibly on the back of the title-page of my songs (?), if that does not seem impracticable to you. The two collections (the songs and the men's songs) have a certain connection, and that is why I make this suggestion, about which you must decide. A couple of months ago Louis Kohler wrote to me in his witty, friendly manner, "You really owed us some Quartets for men's voices, which Bierbruder ["Beer-drinkers," "brothers of the glass"] metamorphosed into demi-gods!" and when the songs were published, I was already intending to let the men's songs follow shortly after. As most of these latter are tolerably short, I think that the score of the twelve will not require more than forty, or at the most fifty, plates (small size). Economy might be employed in publishing the parts by having them well copied. Of course engraving is always the best, but I do not want to precipitate you into a too ruinous outlay—

and if the copying is done by an experienced copyist it looks very well, and is quite easy to read.

I am writing to Schuberth by the next post to tell him (what he might know without that) how unwillingly and how seldom I meddle with dedications—especially dedications to people and societies that I don't at all know, as he would like me to do! In the somewhat numerous works of mine that have appeared of late years you will find very few dedications. The twelve Symphonic Poems have none. The Gran Mass is also without one—and in the Songs I have left out the earlier dedications. Therefore, before I try in America a method which I have almost given up in Europe, some time may yet elapse. Schuberth means thoroughly well by me, for which I am obliged to him—but he means well in his own way, which cannot always be mine.

May I beg another little favor of you? At the Court concert on the 1st January I should like to let the Reiter-Marsch of F. Schubert (not Julius!), which I instrumented, be performed, and I have no longer either the score or the parts. You would lay me under an obligation if you could quickly send them to me. I have never heard the piece; and as it has already been given with success in Vienna and Leipzig I may almost venture to expect that the company here may be bold enough to go half-way in the same direction!

—

Possibly I shall also attempt the Mephisto Waltz the same evening, as well as a couple of my orchestrated songs. (I may mention, by the way, that I have orchestrated six songs of Schubert's—"the Erlkonig, Gretchen, the junge Nonne, the

Doppelganger, Mignon, and Abschied"—and three of my own— "Loreley, Mignon, and the three Zigeuner." Later on, if a weak moment should come over you, I should be glad to impose these three latter upon you in score—but you shall hear them first.)

A thousand apologies for all this random talk about compositions, and best greetings from yours in all friendliness,

F. Liszt

Weymar, December 19th, 1860

249. To Dr. Franz Brendel

Dear Friend,

Your article "For the New Year" is most capital and worthy of you. In three places I would merely venture to propose some slight alterations for your consideration. You will find them marked + and with the letters A, B, C.

At + A it would suit things better to say as follows: "Concert- rooms and theaters, the scene of the most palpable speculation, personal passion, and severing struggles." Or, if you think the word "most palpable" too strong, let us put another, such as "the commonest" or "the most mercantile speculation," etc.

+ B, instead of opinion, "the most affected assumption" Here there is more question of assumption than of opinion. If angenommen [affected] sounds too much like Anmassung [assumption], let us put "the widespread assumption."

+ C, instead of "outward forces," I would rather have another word, such as "powers," "factors," "levers," or any one that is better. I do not know why the "Machle" [forces] do not seem to me quite right here.

Finally, + D, I think it would be advisable ruthlessly to strike out the following short sentence: "Indeed it would not be saying too much if it were to be asserted that in many circles it takes the place of religion,"—apart from the consideration of whether it is accurate or not, because for the most part the men of the State are sure to take offence at it. "How," they will say, "you wish us to support a movement that aims at nothing less than the doing away with religion?"—and, behold, there is a new bugbear ready, and the most healthy and just endeavors are checked for many a year!—

I am in perfect agreement with all the rest, with the exception of the parenthesis marked * —"without thereby, as has often been the case hitherto, falling into the unpractical mistake of conceding to the public things which they do not want, and diminishing the revenues." For, by the way, let me also say parenthetically that, if I had not done this with most resolute intention for many years, Wagner could not truly have said in his letter to Villot (page 40 of the French edition of his translation of the four Operas): "Tout a coup mes relations avec le public prirent un autre tour, sur lequel je n'avais pas compte le moins du monde: mes operas se repandaient." ["All at once my relations with the public took a fresh turn, on which I had not calculated the least bit in the world: my operas were becoming known."

Both on this account and for other reasons I

think this parenthesis dangerous, and can in no wise subscribe to it!

With friendliest greetings, your sincere

F. Liszt

December 19th, 1860

I have written a long letter to Kahnt today. In case he cannot read my writing, will you be so good as to help him with it?

250. To Felix Draseke

You have again encouraged and rejoiced me, my excellent friend, by your affectionate comprehension of my meaning and endeavors in the "Dante" Symphony.

Once more my heartfelt thanks for it. Later on, when "Hamlet" and the "Hunnenschlacht" are published, please do not refuse me the special satisfaction of publishing the whole of your articles on the Symphonic Poems in the form of a pamphlet. We will speak further of this by word of mouth, and possibly a few musical examples could be added to the earlier ones.

How far have you got with the "Loreley"?— Only take hold of the witch with tender force.— Geibel has lately brought out his opera-text to the "Loreley," and several composers are already setting to work on it (or under it). In the present state of things there is not much to be expected from effusions and feeble attempts of that kind. On the other hand I am expecting something great, beautiful, and magical from the Symphonic form into which you will shape this story—a story which just as easily becomes dry and tedious as, on the other hand, it can be melting. Take care that we bring your work to a hearing at the next Tonkunstler-Versammlung (in July-August) here.

O. Singer's "Entschwandenes Ideal" ["Vanished Ideal"] is full of music; noble in conception and powerfully worked out. I shall write to him shortly about it, and send him my seventh book of songs, as you told me that he rather liked the earlier ones.—

An excellent little work by our friend Weitzmann lies before us again: "The New Science of Harmony at Variance with the Old." The "Album Leaves for the Emancipation of Fifths" as a supplement are stirring; and the "Anthology of Classical Following Fifths," with quotations from Hiller and Hauptmann,. is especially instructive. In Harmony, as in other things, it is no longer a question of reforming what has been laid aside, but rather of the fulfilling of the law.————

On any day, my dear friend, you will be heartily welcome to

Yours very gratefully,

F. Liszt

December 30th, 1860

Towards the middle of January I am going to Paris or a couple of weeks to see my mother (who is still constantly ill).

251. To Dr. Franz Brendel.

[Beginning of January, 1861]

Dear Friend,

A thousand thanks for your letter, and still more excuses that I have delayed so long with my answer. On New Year's Day we had a grand Court-concert—on the top of which there was a banquet at the Erbprinz, which lasted till four o'clock in the morning; on the other days perpetual dinners and suppers, at which I was also obliged to be present. Besides all this, the final revision of my second concerto (and a couple of smaller piano pieces) occupied me much. Schott had undertaken the publication of them, and I did not wish to annoy him by letting the somewhat numerous alterations which had to be made in them wait to be corrected until the proofs were printed, etc., etc.

From all the transitions and connection of the movements (which I am now most carefully working out in the Concerto), I pass at once without transition to the answering of your questions.

1. I think Bronsart's engagement for next year at four hundred thalers is advisable.

2. If Weissheimer has really made himself impossible, Damrosch should be the next one to be thought of, as a colleague of Bronsart. There is no hurry about this affair, and we will talk over it again viva voce.

3. The remaining four hundred thalers for X. I will send you at the end of this month. If you should require them sooner write me a couple of lines.

4. The question of leave of absence is not easy to decide, so long as no definite date is fixed for the concert. Frau Pohl, for instance, had had leave once already—but then the date of the concert was altered, and in consequence of her absence it was of no use. For the rest I don't doubt that Frau Pohl can get leave of absence once more—I only beg you to let me know definitely the day, so that I may inform Dingelstedt of it.

5. With regard to the co-operation of Messrs. v. Milde and Singer, it has its difficulties. They are both not without scruples in regard to the Euterpe, which, though they do not say so in so many words, might be summed up as follows: "If we co- operate in the Euterpe, we shut the golden doors of the Gewandhaus in our faces, and injure ourselves also in other towns, in which the rule of the Gewandhaus prevails. Ergo, it is more desirable, prudent(!), for us to act..." The rest you can add for yourself. Milde complains of the thanklessness of the part in the "Sangers Fluch," ["The Singer's Curse," by Schumann] the awful cold of the winter season, all the disagreeables in connection with obtaining leave, etc. Singer does not know what piece to choose, and also the E string of his violin is not quite safe, and more of that kind.

6. Fraulein Genast is in a still worse position, for she is not quite independent of the intimidation (on classical grounds) of her father, and is, moreover, engaged for the next Gewandhaus concert (for the part of the Rose in Schumann's "Rose's Pilgrimage"). None the less she said to me from the beginning that she was perfectly ready to do whatever I thought advisable. In view of this surmise I must naturally be all the more cautious. She sings on the 22nd in Zwickau, on the 24th (probably) at the Gewandhaus, and on the 31st in Aix-la-Chapelle. I have therefore advised her to come to an understanding with you herself personally in Leipzig on the 23rd, and to co-operate with you by preference as a singer of Lieder (with pianoforte accompaniment) at the soiree of the Euterpe on the

29th. Yesterday evening I marked the following three songs for her, as the most suitable for the purpose:—

A. "The Pilgrimage to Kevlaar" (composed for E. Genast lately by
Hiller, and still in manuscript).

B. A song of Rubinstein's: for instance, "Ah! could it remain so for ever!" (Tender allusion to the Gewandhaus!)

C. The three Zigeuner (by me).

The three songs would make up two numbers of the programme.—

I especially beg of you, dear friend, not to make any protest against the song of Hiller. The plainly fair and just thing, which has nothing in common with the "elevated right" which is bestowed exclusively on Capellmeister Rietz and his associates (as the Leipzig University expressed it), consists simply in not shutting the door to publicity in anybody's face, or maliciously and slyly casting stones and mud at him. Regardless of the fact that we must not expect that they on their side will deal thus with us, we must consistently and faithfully carry out and fulfill this simple justice and fairness, and thus show the gentlemen how people of a nobler mind and more proper cultivation behave. You perhaps remember the opinion which I have many times given and proved by actions—especially at the Versammlung- Versammlung, when Frau Dr. Reclam sang Hiller's (somewhat mediocre) Psalm, and…etc. After that I vote especially for the performance of one of Rubinstein's larger works, such as the proposed Symphony, and beg you to appoint

Bronsart for it.—It would lead me too far to explain my views in detail; that I have no concessions or favoritisms in view in this matter goes without saying.

7. The co-operation of the violinist recommended by Schuberth must be considered, and even qualified, according to his talent.

8. "Tasso" can quite well be performed without the harp. A pianino will do quite well, and I beg you most earnestly not to put yourself to any inconvenience for my things. In my orchestral works I have taken the larger measure of instrumentation (Paris, Vienna, Berlin, Dresden—or, if you prefer personal names, Meyerbeer, Mendelssohn, Wagner, Berlioz); but in spite of this most of them can be performed in smaller proportions, as has been most strikingly shown, for instance, in Sondershausen. The chief thing before all else is the conductor; if he be a good and reliable musician things may then be well managed in a variety of ways—and in "Tasso" especially the harp is hardly wanted. So don't bother yourself any more about it, and soothe Bronsart.

If I am not mistaken, I think I have now answered all the principal questions in your letter. As to what concerns personal matters we will talk about that shortly. I shall write one of these next days to Schuberth (as soon as I have finished my revisions for Schott). He has made me a proposal to which I am inclined to agree. [The rest of the letter is missing.]

252. To Dr. Franz Brendel

Dear friend,

I expressly wish that Weissheimer should

accompany the songs which Fraulein Genast will sing at the Euterpe soiree. I have especially commissioned him to make the motive of this wish of mine, if necessary, still clearer to you. With regard to the choice of songs you will easily come to an understanding with the amiable singer. But I, for my part, hold to the opinion that Hiller's "Wallfahrt nach Kevlaar" is well suited to the programme.

The "Faust" Symphony must be written out quite fresh once more before I send it to Schuberth. By the 15th February he will receive the manuscript, together with a couple of lines for Dorffel, who is almost indispensable to me as the corrector of this work. I shall be over head and ears in work the next few weeks, in order to do all that is necessary before I start on my journey to Paris, which I shall probably do on the 20th February.

Best thanks for all the information in your last letter. Some things, indeed most things, are still going very badly—upon which we cannot and must not make ourselves any illusions;—but if we are proof against these things we shall come out of them.

Before and after Lowenberg (in the middle of February) I shall come and see you in Leipzig.

Meanwhile hearty greetings and thanks from your

F. L.

January 20th, 1861
You shall have the small sum for X. in the

course of the week.

253. To Dr. Franz Brendel

Dear friend.

By yesterday's post I sent you—

A. The score of the second act of the "Flying Dutchman"—and two orchestral parts of the duet (these latter in order that the copyist, in writing it out, may guide himself by these, and may not add the terzet-ending, as it stands in the score—Weissheimer will give Thumler the exact speed). Beg Thumler to send me the score back soon, as it may possibly be wanted at Easter in the theater.

B. The last part (Mephistopheles and final chorus) of the "Faust"

Symphony in score—and the complete arrangement of this same

Symphony for two pianofortes.

Will you be so good as to give these manuscripts to Schuberth? I hope he will keep his promise and not delay the publication of the work. At the end of this week I will send Schuberth the score and the four-hand piano arrangement of the two Faust-episodes ("Der nachtliche Zug" "The Nocturnal Procession")—and the "Mephisto-Waltz"). I should be glad if these two things could come out in the course of this year.

C. For Kahnt, the small score of the chorus "Die Seligkeiten" ["The Beatitudes"], which I also hope may soon be published. It has been given here a couple of times in the Schloss orchestra and the parish church, and, as I have been told many times, has been spoken of in an exceptionally favorable manner. I have written few things that have so welled up from my innermost soul.

I think I shall be ready with the revision of the "Prometheus" score by next Saturday. I have already made two arrangements (for two and four hands, not two pianofortes) of the Reapers' Chorus, which I give Kahnt gratis. He shall get the whole packet early next Monday at the latest. Weissheimer tells me that the edition of the score shall be ready by the middle of July. If Kahnt prefers to let the Prometheus be copied, I have nothing to say against it; I only beg that in this case he will employ a very clever and exact copyist-and, as I have already told him, that he will preserve the size of the other Symphonic Poems.

N.B.—The division and distribution of the score—so that there may be as few unnecessary rests as possible, and that, where it can be done (as, for instance, at the beginning of the Tritons' Chorus, the Reapers' Chorus, etc), two sets of staves should be printed on one page—I beg that this may be entrusted to Herr Dorffel. I also do not wish the work to look like a conductor's score on the outside! —and, before it is given into the hands of the engraver or copyist, it is necessary that the parts where two sets of staves come on to one page should be clearly indicated. My copyist here has made a very careless scrawl of the "Prometheus" score, and I have therefore taken other work out of his hands, and have given him a good scolding. But there is no time to have a new score written, and therefore Dorffel must largely help out with the matter.

N.B.—The piano arrangement must be put

below the score, as it is in the manuscript.

Kahnt can publish the arrangement of the Reapers' Chorus sooner or later, as he likes. The date of the Tonkunstler-Versammlung can remain fixed for the 15th August. I think it would be advisable for you to come soon to Weymar (perhaps at Easter), and to come to a direct understanding with Dingelstedt, M[usic] D[irector] Montag, and some others among those who are principally concerned in the matter.

I would propose to you Dr. Gille, in Jena, as a lawyer, and a zealous co-operator in this affair. He is very ready to help, and reliable.—

Are you really thinking of still giving the "Prometheus" at the Tonkunstler-Versammlung? It certainly would not be incompatible with the "Faust" Symphony (which I wish for in any case)—but I fear that it will bring in its train too much vexation and annoyance.

We will speak further about this.

Weissheimer will tell you some things with regard to the programmes.

Riedel ought to conduct Beethoven's Mass.

With heartfelt greetings, your

F.L.

Weymar March 4th, 1861

P.S.—Advise Schuberth once more to bring out the book of songs by Lassen immediately—as he promised me.

254. To Peter Cornelius in Vienna

Your letters, dearest friend, are ever a joy to my heart, as also this time on the 2nd April [Liszt's name-day]. Although on that day I felt the absence of the Princess the most keenly, and the Altenburg was for me equally perturbed, yet the loving attachment of a few friends touched and filled me with comfort. Remain ever to me, as I remain to you, faithful and steadfast, trusting in God!—

Unfortunately I have been able to do but very little work this winter. Revisions and proof-correcting took up almost my whole time. The two last Symphonic Poems, "Hamlet" and the "Hunnenschlacht," will come out directly. I will send them to you, together with a dozen Quartets for men's voices which Kahnt is publishing. By the end of July the choruses to "Prometheus" and the "Faust" Symphony will also be out. If we should not see each other sooner, I count on you, for certain, to be here for the Tonkunstler-Versammlung (5th, 6th, 7th August), to which I give you, dearest Cornelius, a special invitation. I hope that Eduard, [Liszt's cousin] Tausig, Porges, Laurencin, [Count Laurencin, a writer on music in Vienna] Kulke, Doppler, [Franz Doppler (1821-83), a flute virtuoso; music-conductor at the Royal Opera in Vienna. He arranged with Liszt some of the latter's "Hungarian Rhapsodies" for orchestra.] are coming—and I beg you to give them a preliminary intimation of my invitation. The next number of Brendel's paper will give the programme—with the exception of the third day, which cannot be fixed until later. Perhaps you will give us a fragment of your "Cid." In any case I wish your name not to be wanting; and, if you should not have anything else ready, a couple of numbers from the "Barber Abul Hassan Ali Eber" shall be given. The charming canon at the beginning of the second act would be the best.

I am delighted to think that you have been entirely absorbed for a time in "Tristan." In that work and the "Ring des Nibelungen" Wagner has decidedly attained his zenith! I hope you have received the pianoforte arrangement of "Rheingold" which Schott has published. If not I will send it you. You might render a great service by a discussion of this wonderful work. Allow me to stir you up to do this. The summer days allow you now more working hours; realize some of these with "Rheingold." The task for you is neither a. difficult nor a thankless one; as soon as you have seized upon the principal subjects representing the various personages, and their application and restatement, the greater part of the work is done. Let us then sing with Peter Cornelius,—

"O Lust am Rheine, Am heimischen Strande!
In sonnigem Scheine
 Ergluhen die Lande; Es lachen die Haine, Die Felsengesteine Im
 Strahlengewande Am heimischen Strande, Am wogenden Rheine!"

[Free translation,—
"O joy of the Rhine And its homelike shore! Where the bright sunshine Gilds the landscape o'er; Where the woods are greenest, The skies serenest, In that home of mine By the friendly shore Of the billowy Rhine!"]

On the 30th of this month I am going to Paris for a couple of weeks—and towards the end of May I shall meet my daughter Cosima in Reichenhall, where she has to go through the whey-cure. Thank God, she is again on the road to recovery! You can imagine what grief took possession of me when I saw Cosima last winter suffering from a similar complaint to Daniel!—

I have satisfactory tidings from the Princess from Rome. The climate is having a very beneficial effect on her nerves, and she feels herself, in that respect, far more at home than in Germany...

She writes wonders to me about the last cartoons of Cornelius, [The celebrated painter was the uncle of the addressee.] and her personal relations with the great master have proved most friendly.

What will become of me in the latter part of the summer does not yet appear. But let us hold fast to our meeting again here at the beginning of August.

Yours from my heart,

F. Liszt

April l8th, 1861

A thousand hearty greetings to Tausig.

255. To Hoffmann von Fallersleben

Dear, excellent friend,

I have received the enclosed note for you from the Princess. It comes to you with my most heartfelt greetings. Please forgive me for not having this time sent you my good wishes on the 2nd April; [Hoffmann's birthday, and at the same time Liszt's name- day] but as long as the Princess's absence lasts I recognize only sorrowful anniversaries and no festivals of rejoicing. Meanwhile rest assured that I think of you always with faithful friendship, and remain ever truly devoted to you.

F. Liszt

April 18th, 1861

P.S.—I send you herewith the "Vereins-Lied"—and three other of your songs.

256. To Peter Cornelius

[Autograph in the possession of Constance Bache.]

Dearest Cornelius,

Will you quickly sign the accompanying announcement to the Tonkunstler-Versammlung with your good, beautiful name? You must not fail me on this occasion in Weymar!

And yet another request, dearest friend. Will you go and see F. Doppler and tell him that I very much wish he could arrive with you on the 4th August at latest? I hope he will not refuse me this pleasure—and if it is not inconvenient to him will he also bring his flute and undertake the part in Faust?

With regard to the travelling expenses I have already written to my cousin Eduard; he is to put a couple of hundred florins at your disposal; for it goes without saying that neither you nor Doppler will be allowed to spend a groschen out of your own purse for the journey.

You will meet Eduard here—and also Wagner, Hans, Draseke, Damrosch, Tausig, Lassen, and my daughter (Madame Ollivier).

To our speedy meeting then, my best Cornelius!

Bring your "Cid" with you as far as it is done, and kindly dedicate some days to your heartily devoted

F. Liszt

Weymar, July 12th, 1861

P.S.—Shortly after the Tonkunstler-Versammlung I shall be leaving Weymar for a long time.-

256A. To Peter Cornelius

[Autograph in the possession of Constance Bache. This letter was left out by La Mara, but is inserted by the translator.]

Dearest Cornelius,

I have just been told that the score of the "Barber of Baghdad" is not in the theater library here, as I thought, but that you have kept it.

I can therefore no longer keep it a secret from you that I am intending to give the Terzet [Canon] from the beginning of the second act at the third concert (7th August) of the Tonkunstler-Versammlung, and I have not the smallest doubt as to the capital effect that this exquisite piece of music will produce.

But do send me by return of post the score of your "Barber."

The Terzet is a necessary integral part of our programme, which will consist of the "performance of manuscript works of the present day."—

With heartfelt greetings, your

F. Liszt

July 14th, 1861

257. To Alfred Dorffel

My dear Sir,

Whilst giving you my warmest thanks for the great pains you have taken with the "Faust" score [as corrector of the score] I have, in conclusion, one more request to make.

I wish to modify the prosody of the passage in the tenor solo,

[Here, Liszt writes a 4-measure music score excerpt of the treble portion of the piece at the point where the words, "das Ewig Weibliche" are sung.]

each time, just as I have written it on the accompanying note- sheet. If I mistake not, it would in this way be more singable and weiblicher [more womanly]. [Referring to Goethe's words "Das ewig Weibliche" ("The eternal womanly")]

Accept, my dear sir, the assurance of my highest esteem and most friendly gratitude.

F. Liszt

Weyar, July 18th, 1861

P.S.—The "Faust" Symphony is to be given here on the 6th August. Perhaps it would be possible to you to be present at that concert, and to give me the pleasure of a visit from you.

258. To Hofconcertmeister Edmund Singer in Stuttgart

Dear Friend,

The article in the Allgemeine Zeitung on the Tonkunstler- Versammlung (12th August) is an event, and I thank you sincerely for the part you have taken in it. [It was written by Singer.]

Although, as you know, I must on principle keep myself unconcerned as regards criticism, as I cannot allow it the first word in matters of Art, yet it has long been my wish to see the "systematic opposition" to the present incontrovertible tendency (or, better, "development") of music not exclusively represented in the Allgemeine Zeitung. Just because this paper is not a merely local, but an European and intellectually historical one, did the local aversions and the diatribes of the island "Borneo" appear to me far more inadmissible than in other papers. The reporter of the Tonkunstler-Versammlung has taken an important step towards agreement; may he continue to work with us yet further!

The Altenburg has been closed and locked up since last Sunday— and in a few hours I am leaving Weymar for a long time. In the first place I shall spend some weeks with my patron, Prince Hohenzollern (who is musically very well disposed!), at Lowenberg. I intend to take up again there and quietly to carry on my work which has been too long interrupted. My promised contributions to Herr Stark's Pianoforte School must also soon be taken in hand. Meanwhile remember me most kindly to Herr Lebert, [Professors at the Stuttgart Conservatorium. For the great Pianoforte School edited by Lebert and Stark, Liszt wrote the concert-studies "Waldesrauschen" and "Gnomenreigen."] and assure him that I am most anxious to discharge the task allotted to me in a satisfactory manner.

Pohl has promised me that he will soon send you the "Prometheus" and "Faust" notices that you want. For the rest you don't require any further explanation to enable you satisfactorily to instruct the public in these things. As I am pressed for time I must only give you for today once more my best thanks, and remain

Yours in all friendship,

F. Liszt

August 17th, 1861

My best greetings to your wife.

259. To the music publisher, C.F. Kahnt

Don't be alarmed, dear sir! Once more a manuscript of mine is
coming to you. "Ich glaube, die Wellen verschlingen, Am Ende
Schiffer und...Kahnt!" [A quotation from Heine's poem "Die
Loreley," set to music by Liszt:

"I fear me the waters engulfing
Are drawing the boatman beneath,—
'Tis Loreley, with voice enchanting,
Who lures him on to death!

Liszt makes a play on the words Kahn (a boat) and Kahnt (the publisher).]

The pianoforte transcription of the "Loreley" has cost me more trouble than I expected. But I hope therefore that it has not succeeded badly. Let a clean and correct copy be made of it by a reliable musician (Corno perhaps?) [August Horn in Leipzig, whom Liszt held up as being "very exact and reliable."] before you give the little piece into the engraver's hands. N.B.—The words are to be engraved with it, as in the Vienna edition of my transcription of the Schubert Songs.

As regards the publishing of the scores of my three songs— "Loreley," "Mignon," and the "Zigeuner"—I leave them entirely to your pleasure or the reverse, as also the size of the edition (whether larger or smaller—but in any case, not quite full size)..—.

I shall be staying at Lowenberg up to the 8th September.

I beg that you will send the final proof of "Loreley" to Herr von Bulow—and also the second edition of "Mignon" in time, which is to be engraved from the score left behind by Brendel—for voice and pianoforte accompaniment (without instrumentation) in the first place—as you were kind enough to promise me.

With best greetings, your obliged

F. Liszt

Lowenberg, August 27th, 1861

260. To Dr. Franz Brendel

Dear Friend,

A musical scribble that I had promised, and which I wished to finish here, and various little excursions in the neighborhood, have prevented me from answering your letter sooner.

The Prince [Of Hohenzollern-Hechingen] continues to show me the same amiable friendship as ever, so that it is hard to me to leave Lowenberg. Seifriz will write you word a couple of weeks beforehand to which concert your coming here would be most advantageous. The concert season does not begin till November, and, with the exception of the winter months, when the musical performances take place, a great proportion of the members of the orchestra is absent. His Highness adheres always firmly and faithfully to the endeavors of the "New German School," and is desirous of supporting it still further. On this account I think it would be desirable to elect Seifriz as a member of the Committee of the Allgemeane Deutsche Musikverein. I also vote especially for Stein (of Sondershausen), Eduard Liszt, Herbeck, Ambros, David—without a word against the rest of the names which you have proposed.

As regards the other points of your letter I write as follows:—

1. I believe that N.'s reliability and extensive influence in the affairs of the Mozart Society are a bit hypothetical. You find out more exactly what he is likely to accomplish.

2. I will undertake with pleasure the examination of the manuscripts and the decision as to what works shall be performed at the general assembly—but please do not give me the title of President, but simply the name of Reporter or Head of the musical section.

3. I entirely agree with the intention of distributing Pohl's ["On the Tonkunstler-Versammlung in Leipzig in 1859."] pamphlet gratis to the members of the Society.

Of course the two speeches by yourself and Draseke must be included in it. Should it be necessary, I will gladly contribute a few thalers towards the publication.

4. According to my opinion the Society should not be placed under the protection of the Grand Duke "until everything is ready." According to what

he has said to me there is no doubt about his acceptance of it, but still it is indispensable that you should write to H.R.H. about it. Pohl and Gille will be the best to help you in composing the letter to the Grand Duke, and perhaps they will sign their names to it also. Later on we shall have to discuss in what form and fashion other German Princes are to be invited to give their countenance to the Society-or not.

5. Wagner's photograph has unfortunately been locked up in the Altenburg against my wish. I cannot therefore be of any help with it—and can only advise you to write to Wagner himself, in order to learn which of his likenesses would be the most suitable for publication in the Modenzeitung.

.-.I shall be in Berlin by the evening of the day after tomorrow, and shall probably stay there till the 24th-26th of this month. May I also beg you to remind Pohl of his promise to send me my arrangement of the Dance of Sylphs (from Berlioz' "Faust")? I am now wanting this little piece, of which I did not keep any copy. It is the same with my arrangement of the "Tannhauser" Overture, which I left behind with Pflughaupt. Get Pohl to send me the Dance of Sylphs and the "Tannhauser" Overture as soon as possible to Bulow's address in Berlin. I will then send him my thanks in writing, and will quietly wait for the catalogue of music in his possession out of my library (which he wanted to send me some days after my departure!).

How is it with regard to Damrosch's leadership of the orchestra at Weymar? Pohl must tell me all about it.

Has Bronsart's marriage taken place yet?

If it is not giving you too much trouble, I should be glad to receive the pamphlets, marked with red pencil, by Bronsart, Laurencin, Wagner, and Ambros, while I am in Berlin. The publication of Zellner's brochure on "Faust" shall meanwhile be left to the geniality and munificence of Schuberth. A propos of Lassen's songs (which Schuberth boasted that he should bring out so quickly that last evening he was with you!), the first book only—say three songs!—and not the second, has come out, although Schuberth presented me with two books, relying on my being absent-minded and preoccupied! But he has such an extraordinary talent for tricks of that kind that it would be almost a pity if he did not exercise it here and there!.-.

With friendliest greetings to your wife,

Most faithfully,

F. Liszt

Lowenberg, September 16th, 1861

[Shortly after this Liszt departed from Lowenberg. He took the road which the Princess Wittgenstein had gone before him, and went, by way of Paris, to Rome.]

END OF LETTERS OF FRANZ LISZT, VOL. I.

INFO ABOUT THIS E-TEXT EDITION

This volume of "Letters of Franz Liszt" is the

first volume of a 2-volume set. The letters were selected by La Mara, and translated into English by Constance Bache. The edition used was an original 1893 Charles Scribner edition, printed in America. Each page was cut out of it and fed into an Automatic Document Scanner to make this e-text; hence, the original book was fragmented in order to save it.

Some adaptations from the original text were made while formatting it for an e-text. Italics in the original book were ignored in making this e-text, unless they referred to proper nouns, in which case they are put in quotes in the e-text. Italics are not easily rendered in ASCII text, and in the original book they generally do not seem to add much to Liszt's expression.

Also, special German characters like U with an umlaut, and French characters like a's and e's with various markings above them were ignored, replaced with their closet single-letter equivalents. U with an umlaut is U, A with a caret above it is A, and so on. Words altered include Gotze, Tonkunstler, Gluck, Handel and Bulow, among others.

In addition, the English spellings of words like "honour," "colour," "humour" and "theatre" were changed into American equivalents like "honor," "color," "humor" and "theater."

This electronic text was prepared by John Mamoun with help from numerous other proofreaders, including those associated with Charles Franks' Distributed Proofreaders website. Special thanks to S. Morrison, R. Zimmerman, K. McGuire, A. Montague, M. Fong and N. Harris for proof-reading, and also thanks to B. Schak, D. Maddock, C. Weyant, M. Taylor, K. Rieff, J. Roberts, K. Peterson and others.

THE END of Volume I